THE GIFT OF BEAUTY

THE GIFT OF BEAUTY

THE GOOD AS ART

STEPHEN DAVID ROSS

STATE UNIVERSITY OF NEW YORK PRESS

Published by
State University of New York Press, Albany

For information, address State University of New York Press, State University Plaza, Albany, N.Y., 12246

Production by Diane Ganeles
Marketing by Dana Yanulavich

Library of Congress Cataloging-in-Publication Data

Ross, Stephen David.
    The gift of beauty : the good as art / Stephen David Ross.
        p.   cm.
    Includes bibliographical references and index.
    ISBN 0-7914-3007-3 (alk. paper)
        1. Aesthetics.   2. Art—Philosophy.   3. Art—Moral and ethical
    aspects.   4. Good and evil.   I. Title.
    BH39.R674   1996
    111'.85—dc20   95-41531
                                                                    CIP

10 9 8 7 6 5 4 3 2 1

Contents

The good, gifts, all human works as gifts. The good in Plato. Not a thing, beyond binary relations, beyond measure. The good as cherishment, the preciousness of things. Cherishment, sacrifice, plenishment. General, restricted economy. Socrates' suggestion that the good is cause of knowledge and truth, charges them with authority. Anaximander, injustice. Ideality, the sacred, the divine. List of volumes in the project. Why begin with art? Truth, beauty, have no proper places, ek-static. Art neglected in the Western ethical tradition. Nietzsche's interruption of the authority of the good. We know the interruption of the good in our experience of art, exposed to our surroundings. Gift of the good immeasurable.

Gift of the good everywhere. Things touch each other in their heterogeneity. Neither instrumental nor teleological. The good interrupts the domination of identity, the hold of categories. In art. Judgment as work in response to call of the good. Relation to heterogeneity. Levinas, the good beyond measure, otherwise than being. The debt increases as paid. Levinas and Kierkegaard reject art in relation to the good. Aristotle on slavery and animals. Spinoza on animals. Wittig, exaltation of the "I." The mark of gender. Universality. Man and woman as concepts of opposition, domination. Perhaps all categories are dominating, excluding. The gift of the good as resistance against exclusion. Two gifts. One the gift of the hand, language, *es gibt*, excluding paws, fangs, claws. *Geschlecht*, Derrida, *G1, G2*. Sexual difference/animal difference. An abyss of essence. Spirituality, materiality. The flesh of the hand. Irigaray and the sexual indifference of objectivity. Levinas and spirituality of the breath.

Hyde and gift economy; the gift of art, always moving. Derrida and the impossibility of the gift, in relation to restricted economy.

Plato, *Ion*. Divine inspiration. Question of choice as *technē*. Choosing injustice or divinity. Pharmakeia. Intermediary figures of the good. *Phaedrus, Philebus*. *Diaphora* between *technē* and *poiēsis*. Eros, madness, magic, the Muses. *Mimēsis*. Painting as imitation; lyric poetry excluded from the *polis* and its return. Collingwood and craft. Heidegger and equipmentality. Limit and unlimit, intermediate numbers. Language and music. Knowledge as *technē* and *poiēsis*. Apollo, Dionysus. Choosing good and bad. Water as figure of reflection and fluidity, in Irigaray. Myth of Er. Göttner-Abendroth and matriarchal aesthetics. Addelson, anarchistic ethics. Rorty, Fuller, Harding. Lyotard, politics is no genre, witness is a traitor, inhuman. Whitehead, evil. Kant, genius. Irigaray, question of sexual difference, ethics of sexual difference. Threshold, mucus. *Oedipus at Colonus. Antigone.*

Plato, *Republic*. Imitation, *mimēsis*. Truth of the gods. Poetic truth. Justice, advantage, injustice. *Technē*'s authority. *Poiēsis, technē. Mimēsis, diēgesis.* Derrida, iterability, wandering. Irigaray, Clément, woman as displaced (mimetic) figure: witch, sorceress, hysteric. Kristeva, foreigner, stranger, among us. *Mimēsis* as strange, displaced. Kant, Levinas, heterogeneity. Art for art's sake. Bullough and art as taste, art as distance, distance as *mimēsis*. Lacoue-Labarthe, philosophy and literature, *mimēsis*. Abscission as sensuous, woman, sexual difference. Kierkegaard, aesthetic/ethical. Rejection of art as sensuous, as unethical, as closest proximity to ethical. Levinas also, art as sensual. Neutrality of *Dasein*. Kierkegaard, choosing good and evil, knight of faith. Oblivion to the gift of the good. Lacoue-Labarthe, the veiling of sensuousness, woman. Materiality of desire. Irigaray, heterogeneity, love, sexual difference. Merleau-Ponty, the painter's body. Foucault, materiality. Wittig, *The Lesbian Body*, lesbianization, exaltation. Danto, Goodman, Bakhtin. Art as interruption. Conceptual art. Popular art.

Aristotle's *Poetics* read as ethics. Imitation, *mimēsis*. *Eudaimonia*, virtue. *Poiēsis, technē, phronēsis*. Tragedy, comedy. Dark and terrible things in art as mark of sacred, divine, otherwise. And joy. Domination, subordination, disrupted by strange categories, knowledge, truth, language. Metaphor. Disgusting, ugly, in art. Nature, divided hierarchically into kinds. Nature, moved from itself. Heidegger's reading of *phusis*. Diotima's speech on love as intermediary, leading to a nature of wondrous beauty beyond categories and oppositions. Why that speech is given by a woman (who does not join the party). Women and animals. Spinoza's *conatus*; yearning for eternity throughout nature. Ecofeminism. African philosophy, relation to nature. Relation of art to slavery and oppression.

Art as that whose very apprehension pleases. Divinity and the good. The gift of the good as God. Enlightenment, rationality, and taste. Grounding judgment. Hume's standard of taste. Judgment as praise and blame, rendering verdicts. Hierarchy. Skepticism and heterogeneity. Lyotard, judgment without criteria. Witness to the *différend*. Extended reading of Kant: judgment as middle term without middle, without measure. Beauty as symbol of the good, in relation to the sublime. Territorial images of limits of understanding and reason. Exclusion. The supersensible and binary distinctions. Four moments of taste. Pleasure and gratification, delight in beauty. Possibility of freedom. Free play of imagination. Purpose and purposiveness. Teleological judgment and nature's design. Man as the measure. Moral theology. The sublime and war; the sublime and enthusiasm. Beauty includes ugly and displeasing but not disgusting. Why this exclusion? Productive imagination. The end of art, the endless advancement of science. Heidegger's reversal, the originariness of art. Perfection, teleology, art, and science. Blake's sublime.

End of art. Nietzsche, art as the truly metaphysical activity. The world justified only as aesthetic phenomenon. Lyotard and the modern, postmodern. Postmodernism, iterability. Kant and the sign of history. Hegel and the end of art. Heidegger's posing of Hegel's question of the end of art. Art superseded by thinking in Hegel. Nature, sacrifice, Spirit. All exclusions. Hierarchies of Spirit, subordinating art; hierarchies of art, in art. Nietzsche and the revaluation of all values. Postmodernism as endless wandering. Pluralism and culture. First and Third World cultures. Owens, Trinh, Lugones. Ambiguity of the end. Nihilism and culture. Nietzsche. Philosophizing with a hammer. Apollo and Dionysus. Music as Dionysian. Diotima and Dionysus. Art and sci-

ity. Eroticism. Things. Sovereignty. Miraculous moment. Intimacy. Touch, embrace. Animals. Gifts. Gift economies. Hyde: movement of the gift. Circulation of women. Gift economy as general economy. Art. Nothing: sovereignty is nothing. Art collection, collecting tribal and non-Western artifacts. Other times and places. Collecting gains nothing.

Levinas, *exposition* as exposure/revelation. The gift of abundance as exposure. Exposure precedes truth. Exposure everywhere, in every thing, as touch, not the inspiration or responsibility of subjects. Art as exposure through *mimēsis* and *poiēsis*, as *diaphora*. Exposure as and in the frame. Usefulness and the abundance of reliability. Letting-be and the frame. Western and tribal art. Materiality and wandering in art as abundance and the abundance of abundance. Exposure as cherishment. Exposure as delight, emotion, desire. Delight, fetishism, and *jouissance*. Representation as exposure/exposition. Intimacy and proximity. Identities and kinds. Art and beauty as exposure.

General Preface to the Project: The Gift of the Good

This volume is the first of several devoted to the good, understanding human and natural worlds to be filled with gifts, calling us and others to respond in turn with endless movements in every place, exposing us everywhere to others. The works we know—art, science, philosophy, ethics, and politics—and their most treasured ingredients—beauty, truth, and law—are instilled with reason and emotion, connected through bodies and materiality, extended by technology and teleology. All these and more, all human works and natural kinds, come as precious gifts in the name of something other than themselves, something different from any thing, touching the limits of places and things, circulating beyond measure, on the threshold of something other. I speak of these gifts beyond price as given in the name of the good, responding to the good everywhere in nature, understanding nature as the general economy of the good, the circulation of goods beyond price, the earth's abundance, interrupting measure.[1]

I speak of the good in memory of Plato, but where the good provides no measure. I speak of the good beyond measure rather than instrumentality and teleology, good and bad. I speak of the good remembering desire, think of excesses of love and care recalling privation. I speak of the good rather than power, think of moving toward and way, of touching, rather than force or causation. I speak of the good rather than freedom, think of the call to work, to build, to touch, rather than to unlimit. I speak of the good rather than being, think of natural things showing, touching, caring, as exposure, rather than truth, whether of adequation or unveiling. I speak of the good rather than of God, think of circulating in a general, excessive economy, loving, caring, without ground or law. All these renunciations belong to work, to judgment, as we strive to build and control. But something in this striving summons us to know that building requires work, that judgment's limits can be judged. I

1

think of this something as the good, something that makes work and judgment possible. I speak of the good in memory of disasters.

I speak of the good in memory of Plato, in remembrance of something we may have lost. For Plato remembered Socrates' death as a disaster. And I read every word he wrote in memory of that and other disasters, in memory of the good. Yet we do not find it congenial today to speak of the good. We find the idea of the good foreign. We prefer to speak of value, or virtue, or the good life; and God. We pursue truth as if it bore no ethical exposure. I hope to rehabilitate the thought of the good in relation to each of these and more, as what calls us to them and what disturbs our relation to them, what impels them in circulation. But the good is not any of them, is not a thing, or event, or being; does not belong to us, to human beings; and is not God—though many have spoken of the good in terms of the divine. It is neither in this world nor out, inhabits no immanent or transcendent place, but is the unlimiting of every identity and displacement of every place, exposes each creature and thing to others, moves them to respond. The good of which I speak is not a category, does not oppose the bad or beautiful, does not war with evil, but interrupts the authority of choice and judgment, giving us responsibility for making and unmaking categories, opposing evil, struggling to make things better. The good is not good opposed to bad, right opposed to wrong, justice opposed to injustice.[2] It expresses what is precious, irreplaceable, in things, worth cherishing, in human beings and their works, and other creatures, throughout nature, born in immeasurable exposure to others, imposing a charge to foster them and to pursue the ideal. It haunts the limits of individual things in their relations and of the kinds and collectives of the earth, belongs to nature everywhere, composing the circulation of goods beyond price, beyond measure.

My project is a study in judgment, understanding decisions and choices throughout experience and the world as responding to an exposure that is not judgment, not a choice, yet not some other thing. We do not choose to be exposed to others, do not choose to judge, but in practice, in judgment, we choose, divide and exclude, build and destroy. This task, this call, born of exposure, I speak of here as the good, in memory of something lost in Plato. It has been spoken of in many ways. It can be spoken of in endless ways. None tells its entire story.

To speak of the good is to speak of an exposure given as a gift that comes from no place or thing. The gift is given by no one or thing, circulates everywhere, in every place, a giving without a giver, without a receiver, given everywhere. In this sense, it is impossible to speak of the good, impossible to fix its limits. This is not because the good is something we cannot know, but because speaking of it is endless interruption. My efforts here are endeavors in an ongoing struggle to understand and to participate in working to make things better where every such effort is a betrayal. The struggle is to interrupt the flow of continuities and interruptions that do the work of the good in nature. It is a struggle to keep the gifts moving, not to let them stop in a better that denies its own betrayal.

I call exposure to the good everywhere *cherishment*; I call the impossibility of fulfilling conflicting demands everywhere *sacrifice*; I call work in response to the good, the marriage of cherishment and sacrifice, *plenishment*, inexhaustible responsiveness to the good. These make it possible to undertake and to resist binary divisions between good and bad, true and false, high and low, make it possible to place goods in circulation, unlimiting every limit, dwelling in and crossing every threshold, in the endless responsiveness in which we do ethical work, calling us to work for justice and to resist injustice by struggling against the authority of every category and identity.

This thought pursues Socrates' suggestion that the good bequeaths authority to knowledge and truth, perhaps grants the possibility of being to all things and kinds: "This reality, then, that gives their truth to the objects of knowledge and the power of knowing to the knower, you must say is the idea of the good, and you must conceive it as being the cause *[aitian]* of knowledge, and of truth in so far as known" (Plato, *Republic*, 508e),[3] described by Glaucon as "[a]n inconceivable beauty" (Plato, *Republic*, 509a). This beautiful idea of the good, giving knowledge and truth, and more, meets and surpasses the idea of the sacred: nature's sonance, radiance, glory.[4] Plato speaks of it in Diotima's voice as a "nature of wondrous beauty *[kalon]*" (Plato, *Symposium*, 211). The sacred here touches the mundane with beauty, disturbs the hold of categories and distinctions, bears little echo of the profane, or God. The good touches the sacred with an unending call to resist injustice, including endless injustices perpetrated in the name of God. For the good resists every authority, including the rule of the gods. In the institution of authority, it resists authority.

Socrates' words evoke Anaximander, who understands all things together to bear the mark of the good, demanding restitution for endless injustices.[5] All things. The idea of the good is the *cause (aitian)* of knowledge and truth, and perhaps thereby of the being of all things, imposing a burden on them, accusing them of injustice. All things are *charged* by the good with their truth and being, charged, accused, and blamed, the most prominent meanings of *aitia* and *aitios*: responsible for who and what they are, in the extreme, guilty of injustice no matter what and who they are. The sense of *cause* here is *for the sake of*, exposed to heterogeneity, where knowledge and truth are for the sake of, demanded by, the good, called to unlimited responsiveness everywhere and always. The gift of the good is that which within each thing, everywhere, for the sake of which it is and for which it moves, gives it ideality.

This ideality, as I understand it in Plato, does not measure up the goal for which things strive, but undercuts the inescapable wound of measure, reaches to measure's limits. The interpretation guiding my project follows Levinas's thought that the good does not rule over being, does not reassemble being in its place together with the authority of identity and difference, but interrupts the order of being, disrupts the totality of identities and truths, displaces every place, in immeasurable exposure. The gift of the good interrupts the rule of identity, undermines the domination of being and law, challenges the authority of every rule, brings us face to face with heterogeneity, with other beings and other kinds, touches everywhere with strangeness. The good is less an encounter with the face of the other, something that only humans may know, than touching another, exposed to others in the skin and flesh, reaching beyond one's limits to others, something known to every thing, in every place. The good does not rule over knowledge and truth, does not govern them with its authority, but undermines every authority, including its own, following Anaximander's thought of injustice. For all things, he says, including knowledge and truth, "make reparation to one another for their injustice according to the ordinance of time."[6] This debt incurred by being is a remembrance of the good, lacking forever any possibility of an instituted justice, of inaugurating the good without injustice. Everything is done for the sake of the good, bearing endless responsiveness toward injustice.

I believe that the forms of thought around which philosophy has traditionally coalesced, even understood as Western, Greek, have been sites of interruption, not of work, where the good displaces the hold of work upon us, interposes ideality. The work of human life, the promulgation of rules, the coercion of political powers, all institute excessive authorities against which we struggle to recapture a freedom we never had. This mobilization against the claims of authority, legitimate and otherwise, fills the world of disciplines, including philosophy, themselves filled with clashes of authority, filled with coercion and exclusion. The possibility that an authority might claim legitimacy, or that it might be resisted, both draw sustenance from the good, not a good with overarching authority, preempting this clash of power and resistance, but a good that questions authority, that takes authority always to be something questionable, to be resisted, and yet a good that demands authority to do its work. The space of this ceaseless struggle with authority presupposes the call of the good, demands from us endless responsiveness to the injustices of every authority.

Any project of this magnitude will undergo transformations in its realization. At the time of this first volume, *The Gift of Beauty*, the other volumes projected in this series, with the order of their production, are *The Gift of Truth, The Gift of Touch, The Gift of Nature, The Gift of Work, The Gift of Place, The Gift of Law, The Gift of Authority, The Gift of Property, The Gift of Community, The Gift of History, The Gift of Self, The Gift of Desire, The Gift of Love, The Gift of Sacredness, The Gift of Earth, The Gift of Air, the Gift of Fire, The Gift of Water, The Gift of Peace, The Gift of Life: The Good as Death,* and finally, perhaps, in retrospection, *The Gift of the Good.* There may be others. More likely, more than one of these gifts will be examined together, to avoid repetition. And I may not find myself with time enough to fulfill the promise posed at the beginning.

Why do I begin with beauty and art, planning to follow with truth and work? Why not speak at once, in general, of the gift of the good, throughout nature, specifying beauty and truth in their places? That will take at least one volume to answer, perhaps the entire project, in relation to the good. But I must say at once that truth and beauty have no proper places, but come from the good, as gifts, displaced, unplaced, in Heidegger's words, *ek-static*: out of place. The good places things outside themselves, interrupts the hold of being on all things, not just us, everywhere in nature, everywhere in every kind. The forms of displacement are inexhaustible.

I begin with art because it has been neglected in the Western ethical tradition, because Nietzsche's challenge to the authority of the good was undertaken in the name of art, because I believe that only by taking Nietzsche's challenge seriously, to the limits of Western authority, by interrupting that authority within and without, can we begin to experience the gift of the good. For the gift of the good is never experienced in one place or as a possession. It is neither beauty, nor sublimity, nor truth, nor any other; it is all of them and more. It is the inexhaustible and excessive circulation of things and goods beyond measure and rule, beyond any accounting I or anyone else might hope to give, interrupting every enumeration, which human beings frequently know best in what they experience as art. What we call art, in its multiplicity and variety, is one of the deepest ways in which we are exposed to the plenitude of our surroundings, in their heterogeneity and immeasurability, one of the miraculous joys we know in responding to the call of the good. What we call beauty, in its abundance, is one of the miraculous gifts of the good. Nietzsche speaks of it as power: " 'Beauty' is for the artist something outside all orders of rank, because in beauty opposites are tamed; the highest sign of power" (Nietzsche, *WP*, 422). Beauty is abundance beyond opposition.

I begin with Plato and other Western philosophers to interrupt the hold of their authority and that of the tradition that has fixed their reading, to open them and others to abundance. I understand the call of the good, our responsiveness, to release the authority of every category, including the categories of tradition, by reading traditional works in different ways, and by reading nontraditional works, both interrupting authority.

With this immeasurability before us, I undertake the impossible project of working toward the good without impeding its circulation.

Introduction: The Gift as Art

The gift of which I speak is given from the good, granted to those who live in and upon the earth. The good belongs to every kind of creature and thing, in every place, calling upon them to respond in unknown ways, calling upon others to respond to them, a responsiveness we know for ourselves as responsibility toward them, toward others, toward ourselves. It comes together with being, everywhere. Nothing can be, can exist, nothing can belong to nature, to the earth, without a good for itself and without caring for the good for others, touching others, reaching beyond their limits. Some creatures and things may not, perhaps cannot, know their own good and may not know the good for others, not because they have not been granted the gift of the good, for themselves or others, but because they may lack the gift of knowledge, or knowledge as we understand it, may not bear all gifts. Even so, they touch each other and respond, give birth to new alliances, add to and cherish the heterogeneous things of the earth, disturb every limit, evoke the sacred.

And they may know the good in unknown ways, for where the good is given, it is given to be felt and known, surpassing any anterior categories and kinds, known as strange. As for human beings, who can speak and dream of their good and may hope to know the good for others, we find that we never know enough, that the good pushes us beyond any saying, any knowledge of good and evil, to the limits of our being in the world, touching other creatures and things. For the good resists privilege, including the privilege of language, refuses The Human as its frame. The good circulates everywhere, exceeds every limit, displaces every place, brings us face to face with others, with heterogeneity.

Such a good is neither normative nor instrumental nor teleological, though norms and ends and plans may come before creatures who can consider them, who can calculate benefits and measure opportunities. It belongs to no categories and classifications, though it circulates everywhere, in every kind. It interrupts the hold of categories and rules, the domination of identity, reminding us of the terrible anarchy of the sacred, and of how easily we may forget, how we betray the good in every work and institution. It may be thought of as the burden evoked within an endless sense of injustice that calls upon us to calculate and measure, and makes it possible to criticize calculation and measurement wherever these fail to approach the good. Criticism exposes this burden, unearths something deeper than the hold of any authority upon us, deeper than the judgment of good and evil. In order that we may judge right and wrong, good and evil, in order that we may hold up some as superior to others, some higher than others, in order that we may calculate good and bad, cut off some, excluding them from ethical consideration, we must be able to judge, called to judgment by our exposure to the heterogeneous things around us, by our vulnerability to them through our deepest experiences of them, by their exposure to us, by the touch they bestow upon us. We must be exposed, must be vulnerable, must respond to others in their abundance if we can judge them, know them, responsive toward them. We must be exposed and vulnerable to them face to face as heterogeneous, other, foreign, strange. This exposure is the call of the good. This exposure at the heart of being is the gift of the good. It gives birth to judgment, which presupposes such exposure. It gives birth to the authority of truth, to all authorities, which presuppose that exposure. And it gives birth to resistance to authority. The presence of authority everywhere in our experiences bears witness to the demands of the good, to the possibility of interrupting the hold of authority everywhere upon our judgments and responsibilities.

We may think of all our judgments as responding to the call of the good, answering to endless and unfillable responsibilities to resist injustice, to seek goodness over evil, to criticize the injustices of every judgment. In this way, we may distinguish the sacredness of the good as that which gives birth to the possibility of distinguishing good and bad, right and wrong, justice and injustice, from the goods which inhabit categories and distinctions. The idea of the good of which I speak is not good distinguished from bad, not right distinguished from wrong, justice from injustice. Nor does it belong to humans. The good and the endless responsiveness it calls forth to resist injustice do not belong to binary oppositions, nor do they overcome such oppositions into unity, are not epistemic or ethical categories, to be known, to be inscribed as truth, but resist every inscription, every distinction. For we know that categories exclude, cut and wound, and we know this without other categories to put in their place. The good given everywhere upon the earth is not a category, but gives birth in heterogeneity to the possibility of disturbing every category, undermining every kind. It bears the burden of cherishing heterogeneous kinds against the authority of their classification. In this way, the good gives rise to ethics and to the corresponding possibility of criticizing every ethics, every value, to the endless possibility of and responsiveness toward transvaluation and revaluation. It is spoken of by Anaximander as the injustice of all things to one another, composing the ordinance of time: all things that make restitution to one another for their injustice to each other.[1] It gives birth to unbounded exposure toward others as other, as foreign, belonging to strange and heterogeneous kinds, nature's abundance.

I speak of responding to this unending exposure as plenishment in the earth.[2] It gives birth to art, echoes in art. For us. And others. I speak of bestowing and receiving the gift of the good as beauty in art, but not in art alone, and not as beauty alone. I speak of the gift of the good given elsewhere, received everywhere, as plenishment, speaking of the gift in art, of art, of the good in art as beauty, and the sublime, and art's truth, and more, to retrace the flow of art as an ethical movement, interrupting the hold of categories and identities.[3]

I hope to follow a line of thought I take to move in the West through Plato, Aristotle, and Kant especially to Nietzsche, where the possibility that art bears a precious relation to the good reaches a point of extreme urgency, expressed as revaluation, transvaluation, as something beyond the ethical, beyond good and evil, profoundly critical of every ethical distinction. I associate this thought beyond the ethical, in Western thought and art, and elsewhere, touching everything everywhere, with the gift of the good, a call beyond, exceeding every limit, resounding with a certain poignancy and force in art. This is to say that art moves within itself with a responsiveness toward the good, a responsiveness beyond all responsibility, a good beyond the ethical, found in art. It is not to say that art gives us the truth of good and evil, tells us what to do, but that it bears unlimited responsibility to the good to interrupt the authority of truth and law. Art does its work for the sake of the good.

Levinas speaks of the responsibility to the good as beyond measure, incalculable, otherwise than being *(autrement qu'être)*, a debt increasing with compensation: "in the measure that responsibilities are taken on they multiply. . . . The debt increases in the measures that it is paid" (Levinas, *OB*, 12). This responsibility, this debt, acknowledges the good, responds to its call. The call of the good is heard everywhere. The gift of the good is bequeathed in every place. Including art. Especially, perhaps, given in art, with a sensitivity, a responsiveness, beyond all sensibility and responsibility.

Yet Levinas, perhaps with Kierkegaard in mind, perhaps in resistance to Nietzsche, retains an implacable opposition between beauty and the good, aesthetics and ethics.[4] He and Kierkegaard choose sides in the quarrel between poetry and philosophy, perhaps ironically because the quarrel traditionally in the West represents the triumph of reason over sensibility, of universality over particularity, defines art in opposition to reason. Levinas and Kierkegaard are both suspicious of the authority of reason. Kierkegaard especially, but also Levinas, is suspicious of the contamination of the good by universality. Subjectivity, which bears the burden of the good, is betrayed by universality. Ethics gives up universality within the infinite burden of responsibility toward the Other, of responsiveness toward others. It is no wonder that for both, ethics touches God, that the good demands the touch of God. The ethical matters infinitely, immeasurably. Responsiveness toward the other is beyond limits. Art mimics this limitlessness, especially in relation to the sublime, but it is a mimicry without responsiveness toward the good.

The good for which I speak here, plenishment in the earth, also shares the limitlessness of the good, the alterity associated with God, interrupts the authority of reason and truth, but it does not war with art, does not hallow subjectivity or God. Instead it understands the gift of art, its irony and beauty, to come from the good, to mark its sacredness, to interrupt the plenitude of being with inexhaustible plenitude. This is not to deny a difference between beauty and truth, beauty and the good, any more than to deny a difference between good and evil, right and wrong. But it is to say that the good that gives birth to that difference does not bear that difference within itself, does not exclude. It interrupts the force of the authority with which we impose that difference on others, with which we exclude them from the good and say that it is right to do so. In these ways it resists the absoluteness of differences. Only with a love beyond all love, a cherishment beyond all care, a limitless exposure and vulnerability toward the sacredness of things around us can we take up the ethical responsibility toward them called forth from the good. It is a love, responsiveness, and vulnerability present everywhere in art. It is a love, responsiveness, and vulnerability present as art. The good calls not from a place *other than* being, as if there were another place, but from other places *in* being, places of interruption, disturbing the solidification of being. Touch disassembles being, along with art.

The possibility that the good calls forth in art, as art, the possibility that works of art work in response to cares beyond measure, reminds me of Plato and Kant, but most of all Nietzsche. I mean to reexamine here the history of Western philosophy from the standpoint emphatically called forth by Nietzsche, a standpoint some, including Kierkegaard and Levinas, associate with the aestheticization of the good, with the an-ethicization of the good, with de-sacralization. Others speak of the politicization of art as another betrayal. The ancient *diaphora* of which Plato speaks in his *Republic* between philosophy and poetry is a quarrel between the good and the good for art, as if these were at war, the war Nietzsche describes between Apollo and Dionysus. Yet the quarrel of which Plato speaks may not be a quarrel in which Plato joins, and the opposition of which Nietzsche speaks may not be one in which Nietzsche participates. Apollo and Dionysus both are sacred.

The history of Western philosophy is a history of categories and distinctions, if not only such a story. The distinctions I have marked between philosophy and poetry, ethics and art, all work at once to name and reveal and to control: to dominate and subordinate. This is the crucial thought that gives forth the gift of the good, a gift that does not exclude, a gift that withholds authority in giving forth the possibility of its possession. Of possessions, we may say, some are owners, others are owned. Of human beings, we may say, some are masters, by nature, others are slaves. At least, that is what Aristotle says:

> Hence we see that is the nature and office of a slave; he who is by nature not his own but another's man, is by nature a slave; and he may be said to be another's man who, being a human being, is also a possession. (Aristotle, *Politics*, 1254a)

> Where then there is such a difference as that between soul and body, or between men and animals . . . the lower sort are by nature slaves, and it is better for them as for all inferiors that they should be under the rule of a master. (Aristotle, *Politics*, 1254b)

> In like manner we may infer that, after the birth of animals, plants exist for their sake, and that the other animals exist for the sake of man, the tame for use and food, the wild, if not all, at least the greater part of them, for food, and for the provision of clothing and various instruments. Now if nature makes nothing incomplete, and nothing in vain, the inference must be that she has made all animals for the sake of man. (Aristotle, *Politics*, 1256b)

Leading to the extreme, in Spinoza:

> Except man, we know no individual thing in Nature in whose mind we can take pleasure, nor anything which we can unite with ourselves by friendship or any kind of intercourse, and therefore regard to our own profit does not demand that we should preserve anything which exists in nature except men, but teaches us to preserve it or destroy it in accordance with its varied uses, or to adapt it to our own service in any way whatever. (Spinoza, *E*, Part IV, Appendix, XXVI)

We may use animals, or things, anything whatever that differs from us, to our profit, in any way whatever. This *any way whatever* expresses an ethics without the slightest memory of the good, bearing no gift of exaltation, of sacralization.

I interrupt this historical consideration to recall that Wittig speaks of this exaltation as excess, bearing upon the "I," the subject, speaks of the bar in "the *j/e* of *The Lesbian Body*": "[a] sign that helps to imagine an excess of 'I,' and 'I' exalted" (Wittig, *MG*, 87). It is an exaltation sought by women in the face of the law of gender, a requisite for a woman to bear the gift of the good. "I mean that in spite of the harsh law of gender and its enforcement upon women, no woman can say 'I' without being for herself a total subject—that is, ungendered, universal, whole" (Wittig, *MG*, 80).

Whatever we may wish to say about the ungendered, universal, whole—and I take nature to be gendered everywhere, divided by kind, in the name of the good, resisting universality—the good calls upon us to know and strive toward exaltation, not just in ourselves, but everywhere, in others, in every kind. This everywhere replaces universality and totality for me: an exalted, not a total subject. But these are quibbles in the context of the mark of gender, the sign of exclusion. " 'Man' and 'woman' are political concepts of opposition, and the copula which dialectically unites them is, at the same time, the one which abolishes them. . . . The concept of difference has nothing ontological about it. It is only the way that the masters interpret a historical situation of domination" (Wittig, *SM*, 29).

The categories of man and woman are categories of domination. Perhaps all categories are dominating, excluding. Here we can receive the gift of the good as exaltation against the violence, the domination, of exclusion. This gift and this good resist the hold of that other good, the ethical good, the good we know, that always bears the mark of evil, always pairs off in opposition, always resists the strange and heterogeneous other; divides into good and evil, sacred and profane: the ethics we Westerners know is an ethics of mastery and subjection. Good and evil are political concepts of opposition, represent domination.

I interrupt this interruption before returning from it to add that I understand one of the marks of the good in our time, perhaps its most telling mark, to be the question of sexual difference,[5] interrupting the hold of every category and identity with questions of gender and sexual identity. I will interrupt my discussions repeatedly with questions of gender, from feminist philosophy, expressions of the good. Man and woman, good and evil, are political concepts of opposition, represent domination.

Here we can receive the sacred gift of art. I return from my brief interruption to pursue the possibility, in relation to Nietzsche, that art resists this ethics of good and evil, though perhaps not quite as Nietzsche said. Could the gift of the good touch art against the hold of domination and violence, resisting the categories of domination? And if we imagine that this might be so, how are we to read the works that institute those categories, that emerge from systems of rule? As masterful, dominating, oppressive works, or as works whose reading resists this mastery, domination, and oppression?

I know that the history of the West bears a memory of art touched by the ancient quarrel of which Plato speaks, so ancient that we cannot think of art except in resistance to the good. And yet, if we are to receive the gift of art, to receive it in memory of the good, we must resist this resistance, must hope to let ourselves think of art in closest proximity to the good, think of art as the gift of the good, bearing the deepest mark of that gift. Kant speaks of beauty as a symbol, *hypotyposis*, a sketch or sensible illustration, of the good at a point in the *Critique of Judgment* where that claim wears a supreme mark of paradox. For he denies throughout that beauty is related to teleology. Yet his discussion of beauty as the symbol of the good immediately precedes his discussion of the teleology of nature, at a point where nature cannot be known to possess an end. So this end, this *telos*, of nature cannot be known. Yet the ultimate purpose of nature is man.

Similarly, perhaps, the way in which beauty is a symbol of the good is not as something known, even in sensible and illustrative garb, but as something beyond, beside that knowledge, something foreign, otherwise: other than interest, teleology, good and evil, but not their opposition or exclusion. Beauty is the symbol of a good that knows nothing of interests, plans, empirical goals. Beauty is the symbol of a good beyond calculation, a good that interrupts the march of truth and the conflict of good and evil, a good whose memory makes it possible to pursue the good over evil, an exalted, sacred good.

The history of the West is not the universal history of the good, is but a single strand in the giving and reception of the good. In this reception, the good is given to the West in relation to art and philosophy in a singularly historical way. Which is to say that this gift is given and received in the West differently from the way it is given and received in other places, and that it might have been (in a way yet to be described) given and received differently in the West. All this within a certain historical necessity, yet to be described. And all within a refusal of the category of the good, a refusal given in memory of the good.

If we are to receive this gift, we must consider it in and for the West, if the West is unitary enough to be thought in such terms, and must consider the gift, the good, elsewhere, in other, non-Western and other times and places, when I, and perhaps you, do not live in such other times and places. So we must think of a gift that belongs to us where we are, and moves us to other times and places, but may not belong to us elsewhere—whoever and wherever we may be. This "we" is another gift of the good, a gift that appears in art as a gesture toward a community that cannot be sustained by any movement toward and from the good. The good exalts us, in art and life, exalts us as "Us," beyond our times and places, toward a community which, in its heart, bears no mark of this gift, an exaltation presupposed by every community.

And so we bear a responsibility toward this gift, a responsiveness that exceeds any responsibility we might choose, any debt we might find imposed upon us, any mark of exclusion, exceeds all time and space, all restitution, yet demands restitution in every particular time and place for endless disasters. All this, we may say, with utmost urgency, with the fate of the world upon us. How can art bear up under this debt? How, I ask in return, can art be good without it? How can art be good by turning us away from devastation and oppression except in memory of the debt we bear toward their injustices?

I call your attention to two gifts that bear upon my thought of the gift of the good in art, plenishment in the earth, in different ways. One is the *es gibt*, the gift of Being, language, thought, spoken of repeatedly by Heidegger, but especially in relation to the hand, to flesh. I restrict myself to selective passages:

> In the common view, the hand is part of our bodily organism. But the hand's essence can never be determined, or explained, by its being an organ which can grasp. Apes, too, have organs that can grasp, but they do not have hands. The hand is infinitely different from all the grasping organs—paws, claws, or fangs—different by an abyss of essence. Only a being who can speak, that is, think can have hands and can handily achieve works of handicraft. . . .
>   . . . The hand holds. The hand carries. The hand designs and signs, presumably because man is a sign. . . . All the work of the hand is rooted in thinking. . . .
>   . . . To be capable we must before all else incline toward what addresses itself to thought—and that is that which of itself gives food for thought. What gives us this gift, the gift of what must properly be thought about, is what we call most thought-provoking. (Heidegger, *WCT*, 357)

To this—he calls it "monstrous"—claim Derrida responds (a reply that demands the German):

> Here in effect occurs a sentence that at bottom seems to me Heidegger's most significant, symptomatic, and seriously dogmatic. . . . This sentence in sum comes down to distinguishing the human *Geschlecht*, our *Geschlecht*, and the animal *Geschlecht*, called "animal." (Derrida, *G2*, 173)

> Man's hand then will be a thing apart not as separable organ but because it is different, dissimilar *(verschieden)* from all prehensile organs (paws, claws, talons); man's hand is far from these in an infinite way *(unendlich)* though the abyss of its being *(durch einen Abgrund des Wesens)*. This abyss is speech and thought. (Derrida, *G2*, 174)

Most important, in Derrida's reading of the gifting of the gift, in the handing of the hand: "This passage from the transitive gift, if such can be said, to the gift of what gives *itself*, which gives itself as being-able-to-give, which gives the gift, this passage from the hand that gives something to the hand that gives *itself* is evidently decisive" (Derrida, *G2*, 175).

I have spoken elsewhere of *Geschlecht*, and especially of the sexual difference, gender, it embodies, so that this gift, given to us, separating humanity from animals, also divides men from women, explicitly repeating the logic of sexual domination.[6] Heidegger distinguishes human beings from animals in a gesture that repeats the distinction between men and women. In Derrida's reading, the distinction at the heart of *Geschlecht*, between men and women, the distinction of gender, is in the very same movement a distinction between humans and animals. I have spoken of these themes elsewhere, so I will not repeat them here, but will instead traverse these texts along a different trajectory, arriving at an adjacent place. Yet I would add that the good of which I speak recalls the binary oppositions of man and woman, and human and animal, as modes of being and as categories of domination and exclusion, recalls them to displace them. The gift of language, which seems to know nothing of sexual and animal difference, in *Dasein*'s neutrality, knows them to exclude them. Sexual and animal difference express the gift of the good, from the beginning.

1. This gift, of thought and language, divides human beings from animals by *an abyss of essence*, excludes animals from the good by an infinite difference. Can this or any gift divide those who possess it from those who do not by an absolute difference? Or do we learn from Heidegger himself to resist the call of the absolute in the name of Being, for Levinas in the name of the good? Do we think of this or any such gift, of language, truth, or the good, as a possession, as property, as something to be bought and sold? Or does the gift of the good give itself freely, never exchanged, never owned?

If the gift of language belonged to humanity, if the gift of the good, or art, belonged to human beings, would that, could that divide humans from animals, some creatures from others, by an abyss of essence that could never be crossed? The good, as I understand it, makes that division impossible, refuses to belong to any exclusion, throws us with our exclusions down into the abyss, which never divides by essence, into essence, never divides absolutely, always asks us to resist exclusion, authority, domination. The good, the gift of the good, the gift of language and the hand, in its uttermost spirituality—and we must suspect this endless repetition of spirit—works infinitely against exclusion.

But more extremely, that the gift belongs to some does not mean that it does not belong to others. The gift of the good is not a possession, something that in belonging to some cannot belong to others, that divides the world into us and others. The gift of the good, of art, may belong to all, or may, in its circulation as art, belong to none but be granted to all. For art circulates as a gift that cannot exclude. In its circulation, art retains its strangeness.

The holding of the hand, its handiwork, the hand that gives itself, does not mark it apart from other works and signs, other gifts, but gives other gifts along with its own, the gift of abundance. The giving-of-the-hand itself, the hand giving itself, is not something that divides human from animals, some natural creatures from others. Paws, fangs, and claws, perhaps, clutch something other than themselves, give themselves to others. The hand holds and gives itself. Perhaps. I would say that animals hold and give themselves, by paws, claws, and fangs, by mouth and nose, by touch, in countless embodied ways. To other animals. To children. To us. And elsewhere. This countlessness, extremity, of giving belongs to the gift, to its embodiment, belongs to the good, resisting any classification, any dichotomy, any category. The hand of which Heidegger speaks is not a category, and can give rise to none. That is its monstrosity, the monstrosity of animality, of corporeality.

2. This hand thinks, holds and signs, shows its gift of thought. Is it a fleshy, embodied hand? Is it—Derrida's question—two hands, a pair of hands, material hands? Is the thinking, signing hand a corporeal hand, or is it a spiritualized, airy hand that occupies a doubled space of neutrality and universality? Derrida speaks of the neutrality of *Dasein* as betraying its own lack of neutrality. For in the context of the truth that "Being-there, being *there*, the *there* of being as such, bears no sexual mark" (Derrida, *G1*, 67), Derrida suggests that in this denial lies a suspicion: "What if 'sexuality' already marked the most originary *Selbstheit*? If it were an ontological structure of ipseity? If the *Da* of *Dasein* were already 'sexual'?" (Derrida, *G1*, 74). Perhaps when Spirit wears no animal body, it embodies an animal soul. Perhaps it is not the body's airiness and spirituality that grants it to be called to the good, but flesh and blood, everywhere, divided by sexual difference. But here, sexual difference does not exclude, but demands that the other sex, the other gender, in its corporeal difference be included within the good.

This is to pursue Irigaray's critique of *"the sexual indifference that underlies the truth of any science, the logic of every discourse"* (Irigaray, *PDSF*, 69). Sexual difference, as neutrality, objectivity, sexual indifference, still, as Derrida and Irigaray suggest, reverberates everywhere in Western philosophy. The absence of sexual difference is sexual difference. We cannot escape sexual difference by abolishing exclusion. Nor can we escape corporeality by crossing the abyss to spirituality. Materiality is abyssal. Without embodied difference, neutrality is instrumentality. "For man needs an instrument to touch himself with: a hand, a woman, or some substitute" (Irigaray, *VF*, 232). If we do not already touch the world, touch ourselves and things, in our bodies, we invent instruments replacing touch, undercutting touch's abundance.

The question of the embodied hand is three questions:

a. Is the hand given to us, The Hand, a signing hand without a pair or place, neutral and universal in its essence?

b. Is the hand given to us a hand in flesh, a hand that joins the arm, touches the skin, touches the skin of the other, or a hand that shows its gift?

Leading to a third question, concerning the gift:

c. Is the intransitivity of the gift, the gift that gives itself, is that the gift of the good, or is the good given everywhere and in every place, nothing at all, neither essence nor presence, nowhere and in no place, but still everywhere?

Heidegger speaks of the intransitivity of the giving against the naming of the gift, which I would read against naming the receiver of the gift as well. "Being is thought, but not the 'It gives' as such. The latter withdraws in favor of the gift which It gives" (Heidegger, *TB*, 8).[7] Perhaps this withdrawal betrays the giving, the good in giving, when given only to us, we humans.

I offer an example of the intransitivity of the gift working against its touch, from Levinas, who speaks repeatedly of our endless and immeasurable responsibility toward the good: "Is man not the living being capable of the longest breath in inspiration, without a stopping point, and in expiration, without return?" (Levinas, *OB*, 181–82). Heidegger and Levinas both know, at least suggest that they know, where the gift resides, the kinds from where it comes and to where it goes. In the name of the good, I deny that such a knowledge can be owned, can be claimed. Above all, the gift does not belong to men over women, or to human beings over animals, or to living creatures over the unliving. We bear endless witness to the dead.

The good resists every claim, every ownership, imposes a responsiveness beyond responsibility, a passivity beyond passivity, resisting mastery. The good resists every exclusion, includes everything in the earth. This resistance is plenishment, with the condition that such an inclusion gives rise to exclusion, selection, sacrifice, that inclusion gives no totality. For all things cannot together be included in the earth without conflict, without danger. The sacred preciousness of all things together, in their cherishment, demands sacrifice, but may never justly name those who deserve sacrifice more than others.

Even in art, which we may say in general does not exclude, which is able to include within itself countless works of countless forms, that inclusion excludes. Art includes whatever draws upon our powers of imagination and envisagement. But in this inclusion, in time, art excludes. Not everything can be included within the inclusion of art, within its work. Time is never long enough. There is not enough museum space, or wall space, or artist's time. Even inclusion must exclude in order to be. In time.

3. Finally, what is human (or Human) about the gift, about the good? And what is good? I cannot answer this question without exclusion.

The gift of thought and language excludes. The gift of the good, in art or elsewhere, includes, grants and includes. The gift of thought and language gives itself in memory of the good, excludes in proximity to the inclusiveness of the good. The gift of the good gives the good in the earth, everywhere and elsewhere, sometimes and somehow through art. The gift of the hand excludes paws, claws, and fangs. The gift of the good includes them, includes them in their grasping and seizing, in their corporeality. The gift of the good includes them in the abyss of their differences. The gift of the good belongs to heterogeneity. And here we find the place of art. And the body, joining the sensuousness of art. For the organs that grasp belong to bodies, are embodied, fleshy, material organs, and their materiality pertains to the good within them, bears upon their gift. As Merleau-Ponty says, "we cannot imagine how a *mind* could paint" (Merleau-Ponty, *EM*, 283; *PrP*, 162), but we can imagine a paw, or fang, or claw, or elephant's trunk painting. (They do paint. And touch.) But not upon the gift of thought and language, disembodied. I speak not of food for thought but of food for the body, the soul, the breath, all materially embodied. In flesh and art.

I turn to another gift that bears upon the good, given in Marcel Mauss and Lewis Hyde and spoken of by Bataille.[8] Hyde speaks of gift economies, distinguishing them from market or exchange economies:

> A gift is a thing we do not get by our own efforts. We cannot buy it; we cannot acquire it through an act of will. It is bestowed upon us. (Hyde, *G*, ix)

> The only essential is this: *the gift must always move*. There are other forms of property that stand still, that mark a boundary or resist momentum, but the gift keeps going. (Hyde, *G*, 4)

Hyde's concern is to understand that art is a gift, though in no way given by its maker or anyone else. Art is a gift in virtue of its economy, its movement and circulation, not as a possession.

> It is the assumption of this book that a work of art is a gift, not a commodity. Or, to state the modern case with more precision, that works of art exist simultaneously in two "economies," a market economy and a gift econ-

omy. Only one of these is essential, however: a work of art can survive without the market, but where there is no gift there is no art. (Hyde, *G*, ix)

I do not share Hyde's distinctions between a gift and a commodity, or between a market and a gift economy. I especially doubt that art is more of a gift than a machine or tool. Such a distinction repeats the exclusions I understand to violate the gift of the good. Yet the idea of a gift economy seems to me important, the idea of an economy in which things move, continue to move, circulate in their excesses and heterogeneities, contrasted with economies in which wealth, money, and time are stored up, producing commodities for possession and exchange. The gift of the good, the economy of the good, is an excessive economy, a general, gift economy in which priceless goods circulate and move rather than a restricted or exchange economy. What if the economies we know, which we think of as exchange economies, what if they were all gift economies, but we did not know that? What if they included all things, placed them in circulation, moved them against every rule? I am speaking of a capitalist economy, of the movement of goods from place to place within a market that seems to measure them by its exchanges, yet constantly finds new movements, displaces old movements.

Could a capitalist economy include all circulations? And if it did, what would mark its limits? Would it remain capitalist under general circulation? Exclusions name and restrict. Inclusions, gifts, refuse to measure and name, and exceed. Hyde speaks of property that marks a boundary, that inhabits limits. I would speak instead of restricted, exchange economies that do so. Gift economies, general economies, exceed limits, transgress boundaries. I am speaking of Bataille.[9] For Bataille speaks of restricted economies as bearing limits, and of general economies as transgressing limits, circulating wildly and excessively.

Hyde understands a work of art as a gift, not as a commodity, as something that keeps moving, that does not stop at national or disciplinary borders, while museums and collectors and state officials seek to halt the circulation of works to increase their value and control their work. And this may tell us something about the circulation of goods and works, that their monetary value, their measure of economic worth, increases as the circulation slows, but nothing can stop the circulation. Nothing can reduce the abundance. The gift of art does not stop circulating with museums or thieves, not even with private collectors who take precious works out of public circulation. For the gift continues to circulate in private, and even behind the vault door nothing remains private forever. The stolen or purchased work of art does not cease to be a gift when the storage door is locked. The good keeps going. The gift keeps giving, circulating and moving, regardless of the giver or owner. The gift of good, and of art, is anarchic, chaotic, ek-static, foreign.

This is the paradox behind the standing-reserve of modern technology, as Heidegger tells it, that we demand that things be held in our interest, held for us in thrall, by means that spin the circulation ever faster. Exchange economies hope to slow the circulation by demanding equality of exchange, marketing substitutability. No equivalence, no exchange. Yet no equivalence can be found for works of art, or the good, or anything else. The technological means for reserving things against their disappearance moves them faster, makes them vanish faster. The gift of the good disrupts every equivalence, displaces every place. The ek-static bares the furthest mark of the good.

Nietzsche speaks of this disruption in relation to Dionysus, as if Apollo were the god who knew his place. Yet Apollo's divinity is as excessive as Dionysus's, given to madness and frenzy. Nietzsche reminds us that the passion for order is as mad and anarchic as the passion for disorder, that disruption repeats its overwhelming presence again and again. The good, here, touches us with its madness: Plato calls it divine in *Phaedrus*, associates it with Eros, the god of love, without which nothing can be sacred, can be good. The goodness of things rests in a certain madness, given by the gods, from the good, interrupting the orderly movement of things, as if that movement were not mad.

Plato repeatedly calls the gift of art divinely mad, as if he imagined we might be sane. Yet what if he never thought we could be sane, if sanity were too far from the good, from divine madness, from the sacred? That question takes me to my first chapter, where the gift of beauty presents itself as the madness of *poiēsis*, as the sacredness of language, without exclusion, in the name of the good. In that chapter, and every chapter following, something mad, disruptive, heterogeneous interrupts the authority of our discussion of the good, including Western philosophy's authority over that good in the name of rationality. The discourse of the good is a discourse of interruption.

I think of the surpassing interruption portrayed on the ceiling of the Sistine Chapel, in which the gift of life is given to Adam, in a moment, a vision, that stands out from everything before and after. I believe it is a vision of interruption as well as creation. It is just after creation, so that we can dwell upon its interruption without supposing that it represents endless repetition, either of creation, God, or humanity. Hyde insists that the gift must continue to move. In a timeless moment, Michelangelo shows us the giving of the gift of life, and more. The image rests, unmoving on the ceiling of the chapel, representing God's creation interrupting nothing, darkness on the face of the deep, repeating the gift of light.

All these gifts interrupt. And if we take them solemnly, they stand uninterrupted and uninterrupting forever after: representing God, Creation, Life, Humanity. Each of these interruptions demands its interruptions: the death of god, the artistic imagination creating another nature, life everywhere, not given only to humanity, the good everywhere, not given to humanity alone.

To give in art is to interrupt by giving; here the timelessness of art is interruption, not preservation, constancy, or repetition. Or if we are repeatedly moved by Adam's gift of life, it is by having the familiarity of our lives repeatedly interrupted by something foreign, unfamiliar. Not the unfamiliarity of great art or Michelangelo's genius, but the very image of the gift, given as the enigma of the good. For of course the gift given to Adam is good, we remember, and see its power and glory, remembering that it too will be interrupted by expulsion, by one disaster after another.

I interrupt the play of these gifts, one given as Being, the other as art, to interpose an intermediary figure, a movement between them that does not link them. I take the gift of the good to circulate in intermediary figures that move without halting the circulation, interrupting the hold of categories and identities. I interrupt these gifts of Being and art, perhaps from philosophy and anthropology, to interpose an intermediary movement, for just a moment.

With the *es gibt* of Being in mind, Derrida speaks of the impossibility of the gift, in the extreme. "Not impossible but *the* impossible. The very figure of the impossible. It announces itself, gives itself to be thought as the impossible" (Derrida, *GT*, 7). The giving of Being is the impossible, the impossibility that Being might be given as a present, given to presence. "[A] gift is called a present . . . in French as well as in English" (Derrida, *GT*, 10). The gift gives time. "The gift is not a gift, the gift only gives to the extent it *gives time*. The difference between a gift and every other operation or pure and simple exchange is that the gift gives time. *There where there is gift, there is time*" (Derrida, *GT*, 41). But Being cannot be present in time. The gift cannot be exchanged, cannot be returned. "It must not circulate, it must not be exchanged, it must not in any case be exhausted, as a gift, by the process of exchange, by the movement of circulation of the circle in the form of return to the point of departure" (Derrida, *GT*, 7).

I read this impossibility of an economic gift to deny an anthropology of giving. All such giving is impossible in the name of the gift. I take Derrida to suggest that gifts circulate intermediarily between two different impossibilities: the gift of Being and human gifts, given by someone to another. "There is no gift without the intention of giving" (Derrida, *GT*, 123). "For this is the impossible that seems to give itself to be thought here: These conditions of possibility of the gift (that some "one" gives some "thing" to some "one other") designate simultaneously the conditions of the impossibility of the gift. And already we could translate this into other terms: these conditions of possibility define or produce the annulment, the annihilation, the destruction of the gift" (Derrida, *GT*, 11). A gift "cannot take place between two subjects exchanging objects, things, or symbols. . . . One would even be tempted to say that a subject as such never gives or receives a gift" (Derrida, *GT*, 24).

The giving of which I speak comes from no subject and returns to no subject, is not present and does not come to presence. "We" human beings do not give or receive gifts of the good, though we circulate among such gifts and they circulate among us. Derrida appears to equate circulation with exchange economy. The gifts of which I speak, which always move, belong to general economy, circulate as intermediary figures, from one place to another. I speak of gifts in abundance overwhelming the identity of subjects, things, and kinds, all given from the good. I explore the possibility that in human life we meet this abundance in art.

CHAPTER 1

Diaphoros[1]

Plato suggests that poetry, at least the art of the rhapsode, is a gift of the gods. "This gift you have of speaking well on Homer is not an art; it is a power divine, impelling you like the power in the stone Euripides called the magnet, which most call 'stone of Heraclea'" (Plato, *Ion*, 533d). Art is divine. Socrates says this directly: why should we not believe him, believe he speaks for Plato and that we should believe it too? Perhaps because we are disturbed, unsettled, by the protean images Socrates calls to our attention:

> No, you are just like Proteus; you twist and turn, this way and that, assuming every shape. . . . So if you are an artist *[technikos]*, and, as I said just now, if you only promised me a display on Homer in order to deceive me, then you are at fault. But if you are not an artist, if by lot divine you are possessed by Homer, and so, knowing nothing, speak many things and fine, about the poet, just as I said you did, then you do no wrong. Choose, therefore, how you will be called by us, whether we shall take you for a man unjust, or for a man divine. (Plato, *Ion*, 542a)

If these are our choices, to be unjust or divine, let us choose the gods. If we must choose between knowledge and ignorance, reason and madness, which of us would choose the latter? Yet in *Phaedrus* Socrates chooses madness, at least madness given by the gods. Perhaps he does so elsewhere, in *Ion* and *Republic*. Perhaps everywhere.

But must we choose? And can we choose the gods, or do we exceed choice in choosing the divine? Do the gods choose as gods? Socrates asks Ion to choose, and Western philosophers typically read Plato, who shows the madness of choosing between justice and the divine, as making choices, as paying allegiance to the Ideas, and with the Ideas, to rationality, *technē*. We read him as choosing *technē* twice, first insisting on a choice, demanded by *technē* more than by the gods, then choosing *technē*'s rationality over the

23

gods, over divine, erotic madness. Over *poiēsis*. Yet how can we think that Plato chooses to join the divine and erotic madness of the Ideas with reason's sanity, as if they were alike, or that he chooses one over the other? To the contrary, in *Phaedrus, psuchē* travels incessantly between heaven and earth, a protean, "intermediary figure."[2] Perhaps the gods do not choose, but in their divinity know that what is sacred cannot cut off the good from the bad, that what is sacred is not cut away from the mundane, as if it were profane, but haunts intermediary figures. Eros and angels, sacred intermediary figures, move without choosing between like and unlike, where we mortals find ourselves called upon to choose, as if we knew better than the gods. Intermediary figures, Eros, divine madness, all speak of a good that does not cut, that includes, in whose memory we are called upon to choose, to cut, to exclude.

But this choosing, this cutting off and excluding the one from the other, the bad from the good, the sacred from the mortal, madness from rationality, all this belongs to what descends from the good, where the good in its glory resists every choice, resists the exclusions of work. We cannot choose the good that includes over goods that exclude, cannot choose the sacred over the mundane. The good, the gods, the sacred are not beings, things, to choose, but intermediary figures disturbing the hold of judgments, choices, exclusions, retaining a sense of strangeness in the other. I speak of the good as resistance to, interrupting authority, including divine authority. All this is expressed in the idea of intermediary figures, where the good is the circulation of intermediary figures, where intermediaries do not go to stay in one place or another, heaven and earth, as if these were different places, but circulate excessively, disturbing every place, foreign in every state. But I choose to defer this resistance to choosing for the moment, as if we might insist that Plato choose. I will recall the injustice and impossibility of such choices later.

So for the moment, let us accept Socrates' demand that Ion, that we, choose between injustice and the divine. I do not think injustice and divinity are our only choices, though in this context that truth is immaterial. I find it more important that where we Westerners, we philosophical readers of Plato, think that we must choose reason and truth over irrationality and falsity, thinking that we thereby choose good over evil, Socrates understands the choice in reverse, if we demand a choice. Ion must choose between injustice or divine madness; and of course, he cannot, must not, choose injustice; and besides, "it is far lovelier to be deemed divine" (Plato, *Ion*, 542b). And just.

For the gift of the gods is both lovely and just, beautiful and good. Socrates says this explicitly here, and says it elsewhere, in every dialogue that takes up the gift of beauty, contrasting art as *technē*, frequently called knowledge, *epistēmē* or *sophia*, with something divine, something mad. Repeatedly, madness is a gift from the gods, a certain kind of madness, linked with *erōs* and *poiēsis*, always more divine than "mere" knowledge, "mere" *technē*, where this *technē*, this kind of art, bears nothing of a gift from the gods. Another example, a brief interruption, before returning to *Ion*. In *Phaedrus*, near the beginning, Phaedrus asks whether he and Socrates are close to where Boreas seized Orithyia from the river Ilissus, and whether Socrates believes the story. Socrates replies:

> I might proceed to give a scientific account of how the maiden, while at play with Pharmacia *[Pharmakeia]*, was blown by a gust of Boreas down from the rocks hard by, and having thus met her death was said to have been seized by Boreas, though it may have happened on the Areopagus, according to another version of the occurrence. For my part, Phaedrus, I regard such theories as no doubt attractive, but as the invention of clever, industrious people who are not exactly to be envied. . . . If our skeptic, with his somewhat crude science *[sophia]*, means to reduce every one of them to the standard of probability, he'll need a deal of time for it. I myself have certainly no time for the business. (Plato, *Phaedrus*, 229de)

Socrates associates *sophia* (frequently translated as *wisdom*) here with cleverness and industry, measure and probability, with *technē*. He has no time for the business: "and I'll tell you why, my friend. I can't as yet 'know myself'; as the inscription at Delphi enjoins, and so long as that ignorance remains it seems to me ridiculous to inquire into extraneous matters" (Plato, *Phaedrus*, 230). This represents a famous Socratic rule, that one's first business is to know oneself *(gnōnai hemautōn)*. But to know oneself is an endless pursuit, more like madness than *epistēmē*, more prophetic, divine:

> in reality, the greatest blessings come by way of madness *[manian]* indeed of madness that is heaven sent. . . . No, it was because they held madness *[manias]* to be a valuable gift, when due to divine dispensation, that they named that art as they did, though the men of today, having no sense of values, have put in an extra letter, making it not *manic* but *mantic [mantikēn]*. (Plato, *Phaedrus*, 244ac)[3]

More sacred than mundane.

Pharmakeia appears in *Phaedrus* to warn us that we must be suspicious of a *sophia* and an *epistēmē* that lack gifts of love and madness, gifts called by many different names, but in *Phaedrus* represented by *pharmakeia* as medicine, drug, madness, remedy, poison, potion, agent, dye, pigment, color; *pharmakos* as sacrifice, scapegoat; *pharmakeus* as wizard. These gifts, in their madness, bring confusion as well as passion, bring a knowledge that never solidifies into security, never brings us to safety, that recalls the injustices of choice. For in *Phaedrus*, the knowledge that calls us, bearing relation to the good, remains forever contested. "But what about the words 'just' and 'good'? Don't we diverge, and dispute not only with one another but with our own selves?" (Plato, *Phaedrus*, 263). Love, justice, goodness—*erōs, dikē, agathon*—all appear as terms that we dispute about not only with one another but endlessly within ourselves.

Ion speaks of these concerns in a different way. For Socrates asks Ion if he *knows* of what he speaks when he interprets, when he performs, scenes from Homer. Does he know the art of war when he proclaims Homer's words on war? This art, this knowledge, is *technē*, where *epistēmē* and *sophia* are *technē*s. Does the rhapsodist, does the artist, possess *technē* or something else, some other gift, closer to divine madness? The answer approaches the gift of art. Or rather, the question of art approaches the gift of the good. The choice demanded of us is between *technē* and *poiēsis*, between art and divine madness. "[I]t is plain to everyone that not from art and knowledge comes your power to speak concerning Homer. If it were art *[technē]* that gave you power, then you could speak about all the other poets as well" (Plato, *Ion*, 532c). Ion agrees, and describes Socrates as a wise man *(sophōn)*. The Ion who cannot choose by rule is prepared to choose by rule, desiring the art of rule. Yet Socrates responds to being called "wise" by saying: "I only wish you were right in saying that, Ion. But 'wise men'! That means you, the rhapsodists and actors, and the men whose poems you chant, while I have nothing else to tell besides the truth, after the fashion of the ordinary man" (Plato, *Ion*, 532d). Rhapsodes and poets are wise without *technē*.

Socrates plainly says that he is not wise, that others like Ion are wise lacking *technē*, suggests that perhaps wisdom and self-knowledge are not *technē*s, arts by rule, but divine and poetic madnesses, filled with disputed terms like justice, beauty, and the good. The divine and sacred, perhaps, remain disputed, without rules for exclusion. Art remains sacred and divine:

> this gift you have of speaking well on Homer is not an art; it is a power divine, impelling you like the power in the stone Euripides called the magnet, which most call "stone of Heraclea." This stone does not simply attract the iron rings, just by themselves; it also imparts to the rings a force enabling them to do the same thing as the stone itself, that is, to attract another ring, so that sometimes a chain is formed, quite a long one, of iron rings, suspended from one another. For all of them, however, their power depends upon that loadstone. Just so the Muse. She first makes men inspired, and then through these inspired ones others share in the enthusiasm, and a chain is formed, for the epic poets, all the good ones, have their excellence, not from art, but are inspired, possessed, and thus they utter all these admirable poems. So is it also with the good lyric poets. (Plato, *Ion*, 533d–534)

The Muses retain their divinity, their divine and sacred fount of inspiration, and by an infinite and indeterminate movement, the poets are possessed by divine madness, by a gift from the gods, as Muses. Or perhaps as Hercules, facing endless trials.

Or perhaps as cicadas, or bees, throughout nature:

> The story is that once upon a time these creatures were men—men of an age before there were any Muses—and that when the latter came into the world, and music made its appearance, some of the people of those days were so thrilled with pleasure that they went on singing, and quite forgot to eat and drink until they actually died without noticing. From them in due course sprang the race of cicadas, to which the Muses have granted the boon of needing no sustenance right from their birth, but of singing from the very first, without food or drink, until the day of their death, after which they go and report to the Muses how they severally are paid honor among mankind, and by whom. (Plato, *Phaedrus*, 259c)

> For the poets tell us, don't they, that the melodies they bring us are gathered from rills that run with honey, out of glens and gardens of the Muses, and they bring them as the bees do honey, flying like the bees? And what they say is true, for a poet is a light and winged thing, and holy, and never able to compose until he has become inspired, and is beside himself, and reason *[nous]* is no longer in him. So long as he has this in his possession, no man is able to make poetry or to chant in prophecy. (Plato, *Ion*, 534b)

Where Heidegger takes the gift of language to exclude mammals and birds, everything inhuman, Plato includes cicadas and bees in the sacred gift of art, includes all inanimate things under *psuchē*'s care,[4] gifts from the Muses. Where the gift of *nous*, including the art of reason, excludes, divides, and cuts, demanding that we choose, the gift of *poiēsis*, in its madness, knows nothing of exclusion, cuts nothing off from the gift of the good. Yet even so, rhapsodes and poets "speak many things and fine," participate in the good.

Certainly we wish to escape injustice, to avoid evil, to tell good from bad, to choose beauty rather than ugliness. Yet in art's *poiēsis*, beauty resists exclusion, resists being cut off from ugliness, evil, repulsiveness, or what disgusts us. Aristotle's famous words on how repulsiveness becomes transformed by art into beauty remain a challenge to our acceptance of the gift of art: "though the objects themselves may be painful to see, we delight to view the most realistic representations of them in art, the forms for example of the lowest animals and of dead bodies" (Aristotle, *Poetics*, 1448b). Freud and Nietzsche understand this delight as a dark truth about dark experience: we take joy in pain and suffering. And that may be. I would add that Aristotle's insight goes deeper, that art does not exclude the ugly, painful, or bad. Art includes everything in nature, under the good. In art we take joy in everything around us, given as the gift of beauty from the good, in art.

Yet if we hope to escape from evil, and art will not help us do so, then we may conclude that art is either evil or without ethical value. We reinstate the quarrel between philosophy and poetry, ethics and art: art will not choose the good over the bad even where ethics demands it. Yet we have neglected another possibility, that the quarrel is not between poetry and philosophy, art and ethics, as if we must choose the one over the other, or in refusing the choice, refuse the good. The alternative is that the choice belongs to ethics and to philosophy, to arts under *technē*, but that in order for us to make such a choice, we must be in touch with something divine, something mad, something beyond all choice, all exclusion, something that retains, includes, all parties in its care, animate and inanimate, good and bad, right and wrong, beautiful and ugly. Here the gift of art refuses choice, not against ethics but in the name of the good. Repeatedly, we find ourselves understanding the quarrel as given by a demand to choose where we cannot, must not, choose, even where we cannot avoid choice. A refusal we find in art, under *poiēsis*.

Even here, Plato's account of the choice is expressed in enigmatic form. For he speaks of the quarrel between poets and philosophers in an extraordinary setting and in extraordinary words. First, this quarrel arises under reason's constraints:

> Let us, then, conclude our return to the topic of poetry and our apology, and affirm that we really had good grounds then for dismissing her from our city, since such was her character. For reason *[logos]* constrained us. And let us further say to her, lest she condemn us for harshness and rusticity, that there is from old a quarrel *[diaphora]* between philosophy and poetry. (Plato, *Republic*, 607b).

We may ask, is this *diaphora* a war, a strife, or something else, something stranger? For although Socrates speaks of *henantiōseōs* a few lines later, and *henantios* is opposition, conflict, *diaphora* is unlikeness, difference, closer to heterogeneity than to *polemos*. Poetry and philosophy are unlike, but do they quarrel, and must we choose between them? Moreover, if and when we choose, our choice may not be between them, as if they existed independent of our choice, but our choosing may define each. If so, then in the *diaphora* of which Socrates speaks, art and philosophy are born together as separate disciplines in a *polemos* emerging from something that is not either of them, from which we may derive their difference.

We may also ask, who engages in this war, the philosopher or the poet? Who imposes its authority? One answer is, Socrates himself, from the beginning, in Book II of *Republic*. Poetry knows nothing of this *diaphora*, knows nothing of quarrels with philosophy, does not bother with such distinctions. The quarrel between philosophy and poetry does not belong to each, though it may define them, but belongs to one, to philosophy's reason. Why should the poet accept the quarrel? And what may philosophy learn from poetry?

Socrates speaks of this quarrel as from old, *palaia*; and we may recall that what comes from old, ancient wisdoms in Plato recalled by Socrates is always strange, touched by the gods. In *Philebus* he speaks of another tale of "men of old," "a gift of the gods," that "[a]ll things, so it ran, that are ever said to be consist of a one and a many, and have in their nature a conjunction of limit and unlimitedness" (Plato, *Philebus*, 16d). We are to discern the number of forms intermediate between the one and unlimited many. "It is only then, when we have done that, that we may let each one of all these intermediate forms pass away into the unlimited and cease bothering about them" (Plato, *Philebus*, 16e). We must know the intermediate numbers and must then let them pass away to unlimit without bothering about them. How, in any sense of *logos* and *epistēmē*, are we to let our knowledge pass away unless it responds to another call? How let anything pass away to unlimit? All said of old to be given from the gods.

Socrates suggests that poetry may return from reason's exile on its own terms, yet still under the rule of reason, within an acknowledgment of poetic madness (Plato, *Republic*, 607d). The quarrel is repeatedly carried out on reason's terms, demanding that poetry demonstrate her benefit to human beings, her goodness over her evil. And repeatedly, the quarrel is undermined by poetry's gifts, for it is not poetry's responsibility or its gift to defend the good over the bad, but to portray the magical touch of the good against exclusion.

This magical force of *poiēsis* falls between two famous moments in Book X, one the contamination of work, falling away from the Idea, especially in painting, the other the myth of Er. Leaving aside the considerable distance between painting and poetry expressed by Plato and many others, which may bear upon the quarrel, we may read Socrates' argument opening Book X as an event in that quarrel, as we may read the entire *Republic* as framed by that quarrel as well as the quarrel over which is more profitable, justice or injustice.[5] What does painting profit us if we seek useful things? If we think of painting as a craft, if we think of producing by craft, by *technē*, according to an Idea, then the painted bed, produced by the painter, is twice removed from that Idea, and useless, where the artisan, who builds a bed, and builds according to the Idea, makes something useful. Painting is likened to a mirror, which can easily produce and imitate all things, with no knowledge whatever of their truth and of no use whatever to our possession of objects. "You could do it most quickly if you should choose to take a mirror and carry it about everywhere. You will speedily produce the sun and all the things in the sky, and speedily the earth and yourself and the other animals and implements and plants and all the objects of which we just now spoke" (Plato, *Republic*, 596e).

Socrates does not hesitate to extend this critique to poetry, including tragedy, among the least plausible examples of productive imitation according to *technē*, exceeded, perhaps, only by music:

> The producer of the product three removes from nature you call the imitator?
> By all means, he said.
> This, then, will apply to the maker of tragedies also, if he is an imitator and is in his nature three removes from the king and the truth, as are all other imitators. (Plato, *Republic*, 597e)

Countless commentators have acknowledged that where the representational painter represents a bed, a couch, an object that otherwise would be presented by craft, the poet does not do so, because no object in a text is present to hand. The poet does not make a bed, does not make an object; the poem, a work, is not an object, not a material thing. Here the difference between plastic and literary art is one of sensibility, and we might refuse to take sides with poetry over plastic art in virtue of its immateriality. To the contrary.

Countless other commentators have also acknowledged that Socrates sets aside with the briefest comment another possibility attractive to the Romantics. Art does not remove us further from the Idea, but brings us closer, works in proximity to the Idea, and can do so in virtue of their shared spirituality. Socrates' dismissal of this possibility is brief: "For surely no craftsman makes the idea itself. How could he?" (Plato, *Republic*, 596c). No craftsman indeed, for *technē* presupposes the Idea, and perhaps not even the gods can make Ideas. But if art cannot make Ideas, perhaps art by *technē* is subservient to the Idea, according to its use—that is what Socrates says—while art by *poiēsis* brings nonbeing into being touching the Idea in its glory. We remember the sun, which gives no light directly to any of the shadows on the wall of the cave, but in some inexplicable way gives light itself, disrupting the fetters upon the bodies and souls of those in the cave. The good charges all things with responsibility for their being.

As his account accelerates, Socrates says that "It quite necessarily follows, then, that the user of anything is the one who knows most of it by experience, and that he reports to the maker of the good or bad effects in use of the thing he uses" (Plato, *Republic*, 601de). Everything in the argument, the quarrel, depends on this premise, that the user, the *technēn*, of the bed, the implement, knows its good and bad. And perhaps that may be true of beds, but it seems untrue about goodness, beauty, and truth, all disputed terms. What remains at stake repeatedly is the subservience of the craft to the Idea, as if the Ideas exist to distinguish the good from the bad, right from wrong, to set the norm, to normalize the craft, though repeatedly as well, we are told that no one, including Socrates, possesses that knowledge.

Famously, Socrates' argument is read as a denigration of the art of painting. Yet it pertains much less to any art of painting than to an analogous craft of mechanical drawing, picturing objects for use. And indeed, drawing and words, if not the arts of painting and tragedy, are used (the repeated word becomes essential) as aids to use, aids to practice (but perhaps not *praxis*, neither ethics nor politics). Some say a picture is worth a thousand words. Perhaps Socrates disagrees. But I am not speaking of the painting we call art. I am speaking of what Collingwood calls craft (Collingwood, *PA*, chap. 2; Ross, *AIS*, 191–201), of what in a more extended sense I have called *technē*, the production of objects and works to an end, under an idea, shaping materials to a goal, however laudatory.

In this light, the art of painting is not useful, does not give us objects for or in use, but—especially in modernism and postmodernism—displays objects away from their use, distorted, twisted, so that their usefulness is either held in abeyance or displayed as usefulness, which is quite different from objects in use.

Socrates speaks of those who "tell us that these poets know all the arts and all things human pertaining to virtue and vice, and all things divine" (Plato, *Republic*, 598e). He suggests at times that others than the poets know these things, though virtue and vice and all things divine are very different from couches and beds. And he suggests at other times that no one can know these things, including the poets, so that the crucial movement of critique must be to show how things divine may be known through *technē*, *sophia*, or *epistēmē*.

And here we find another role for art, closely related to the Greeks. For they repeatedly deny that virtue and vice and things divine are known by human beings, by mortals, or by anyone, including the gods. Our lives are buffeted by the winds of a fate, a divine, beyond understanding. Greek tragedy touches the limits of our world, natural and otherwise, in their vulnerability and fragility, in their horror, and makes us aware of our own vulnerability and the terrible side of the gods' demands upon us from beyond *technē*.

If we take art as *technē*, then we may expect that knowledge of good and bad, right and wrong, virtue and vice, and of the gods, all given by poetry, music, painting, and dance, will make them ready to hand, objects like good hammers and plump sheep. I must say immediately, against such a technical idea of use, that hammers and sheep are no more ready to hand than virtue and vice. That is because all things are touched by *psuchē*, by things erotic and divine, interrupted in their usefulness, even as we must use them and must order them according to our uses, with memories of familiar things become unfamiliar, of the sacred and the good, given to us deeply and profoundly in art.

The Romantics, who read and deeply cared for Plato, took music and poetry to touch the divine. Plato grants that possibility. But within the *diaphora* between philosophy and poetry, between reason and madness, poetry and art fail to give us reason, *technē*'s reason. Perhaps. But then reason does not give us *technē*'s reason either, but must, as in *Phaedrus* and *Philebus*, grant the impossibility of reaching the divine, of bringing it ready to hand, of cutting it down to size. Rather, reason and divine madness exist in a quarrel that belongs entirely to reason, where we live in their juncture, surrounded by intermediary figures constantly moving between heaven and earth, between *poiēsis* and *technē*, without strife. The quarrel represents the demand, within *technē*, that we choose one over the other—for it is not supported by *poiēsis* that we must choose between them, nor by the gods. The divinity of the Idea, the madness of the gods, interrupts every choice. Art seems to give us this choice, but it all the more tells us—as Socrates says repeatedly about himself—that we do not know the good as if it were an object ready to hand, but know it as the divine madness that displaces every object, every thing, that we may hope to make ready to hand under *technē*.

Socrates names the quarrel of old, between *poiēsis* and *technē*, after he has chosen sides, after he has defended *technē*'s relation to the Ideas, to the divine, at a point at which, on my reading, he reinstates lyric poetry, the most useless form of *poiēsis*, to give a defense in its own terms. Yet also, on my reading, the entire account of the quarrel, of defense and attack, of choosing at all, of choosing between *poiēsis* and *technē*, belongs to *technē*, not *poiēsis*. And more extremely, the entire *Republic* is framed within a view of justice that belongs to *technē*, not *poiēsis*. *Poiēsis* does not defend, does not argue, does not distinguish, does not quarrel, does not choose, does not exclude, but includes too much. How are we to think of this excessive inclusion? If we think of it as *technē*, it is useless and dangerous. Inclusion is dangerous in two different ways: it fails to cut off evil; it passes itself off as judgmental, as the result of choice.

We may describe the quarrel in a different way. Let us suppose that *poiēsis* and *technē* represent two modes of judgment. One contains at its heart a sense that the divine includes all things, a sense of cherishment, identified with the good, the sacred, and the gods, where *psuchē* stands on the back of the world and cares for everything, in beauty. The other, *technē*, judges the good from the bad, passes judgment dividing the world on the right and left. On the Day of Judgment God will judge everything, divide the world of human beings, and more, on right and left; but God is undivided. I am naming the Manichean offense; these matters are not new. To divide God into good and bad is to deny divinity; to divide God among the good and bad, as if divine goodness were matched by Satanic evil, as if God belonged to the world, is to deny divinity. The sacredness of God is before, alongside, away from, interrupts the domination of identities and the hierarchy of judgments. If there be God. This is what Nietzsche in part asks us to recognize in the relation between Apollo and Dionysus: Apollo orders the world from high to low, but does not belong to that hierarchy; rather, he coexists with Dionysus as his twin, not his opposite. No quarrel is possible between Apollo and Dionysus, but neither are they One.

Socrates describes the quarrel of old between *poiēsis* and *technē* at a point at which he begins to pass from *technē*'s view of this quarrel, on my reading a quarrel that belongs exclusively to *technē*, never to *poiēsis*, begins to pass from *technē* to the divine, or if we resist the divine, to heterogeneity, passing through *poiēsis*. So we may read Book X as presenting *technē*'s view of painting and tragedy, where it is mistaken to think of them as *technēs*— that is, providing useful knowledge of the essences and identities of things— and also mistaken to think of them as opposing useful knowledge of essences and identities. Painting and tragedy, as *poiēsis,* are *otherwise* to the domain of use. Imitation, as Socrates describes it at the beginning of Book X, belongs to the sphere of use, either as a repetition or an opposition, by contradiction. But *poiēsis* neither belongs to use nor opposes it; nor does it bear no relation to it. This enigmatic relation is the thought of the good. It is a thought Plato repeatedly traverses whenever he deeply and profoundly seeks the thought of Ideas, which are neither the essences of things, as if given over to technical use, nor entirely Other, oppositional. On my reading here, only for *technē* does the Idea define the norm. Only under *technē* are there norms. Ideas as such are not norms, though under *technē* they are useful as norms. But the Plato of the allegories of the sun and cave, for whom the good is cause of and care for the authority of knowledge and truth, for whom all soul has care of all inanimate things, this Plato cannot understand the Idea of the Good as a norm, a model, a rule. Instead, the idea of the good charges norms, models, and rules with their authority.

In this light, we may consider two famous passages in *Philebus,* more than any other dialogue, perhaps, on the rule of the good. One passage I have already touched on briefly presents a different tale of "men of old," "a gift of the gods," who "passed on this gift in the form of a saying," "through Prometheus, or one like him":

> All things, so it ran, that are ever said to be consist of a one and a many, and have in their nature a conjunction of limit and unlimitedness. This then being the ordering of things we ought, they said, whatever it be that we are

dealing with, to assume a single form and search for it, for we shall find it
there contained; then, if we have laid hold of that, we must go on from one
form to look for two, if the case admits of there being two, otherwise for
three or some other number of forms. And we must do the same again with
each of the "ones" thus reached, until we come to see not merely that the
one that we started with is a one and an unlimited many, but also just how
many it is. But we are not to apply the character of unlimitedness to our plu-
rality until we have discerned the total number of forms the thing in question has intermediate between its one and its unlimited number. It is only
then, when we have done that, that we may let each one of all these intermediate forms pass away into the unlimited and cease bothering about
them. (Plato, *Philebus*, 16de)

   This account, up to a certain point, belongs to *technē*, with two extraordinary qualifications. One is that the tale, a gift of the gods, is brought to
us by Prometheus, who brought the gift of fire, where Prometheus, and fire,
and perhaps this gift as well, all circulate as intermediary figures—that is, figures of divine unrest interrupting mundane things. Prometheus is so explicit
an intermediary figure, preserving divinity in human terms, that I would add
only that he is forced to remember his act through unending torment. And
so, perhaps, the divine endlessly and painfully disturbs the flow of human life
and practice by endless disasters. Or perhaps the intermediation of the
strange and other is met in life by the coercive powers of the State. The other
qualification is that the intermediate numbers, representing *technē*, pass
away to unlimit, opening themselves from fixed and normative intermediate
limits to intermediary figures of the divine.
   The most striking feature of this enigmatic passage, alluding to the indefinite dyad, is that we are not to remain in the intermediate numbers, are
not to remain content with knowing the total number of intermediate forms,
but when we know that are to let all of these intermediates *pass away into
the unlimited and cease bothering about them*. But we are not to let these
intermediates pass away to unlimit too quickly, but must pass through and
attend to the intermediates before we cease bothering about them. In other
words, to limit and unlimit Plato adds intermediate numbers, but these do
not replace or exclude unlimit, nor does unlimit exclude definite numbers.
Both belong in a relation that belongs neither to the one or the other, neither
to limit or to unlimit or to number, but . . . I would say, to the good.
   Socrates gives several examples. One is language, letters and sounds. Alluding to Theuth as he does in *Phaedrus*, Socrates suggests that Theuth (or
someone else) put order into language by combining many different vowels
and intermediate sounds into letters, where each letter represents a kind of
bond among disparate sounds. This is an immensely contemporary view of
linguistics, but it leads Philebus to remark that "I still feel the same dissatis-

faction about what has been said as I did a while ago" (Plato, *Philebus*, 18d). And indeed, the bond of unity established among disparate sounds, essential on Saussure's view for *langue*, is an untamed intermediary figure in which identity and difference continue to divide each other endlessly.

Socrates repeats that our responsibility—some would say, in the name of truth, I say in the name of the good: "is just this, to show how each of them is both one and many, and how—mind you, we are not to take the unlimited variety straightaway—each possesses a certain number before the unlimited variety is reached" (Plato, *Philebus*, 18e). Mind you, we are to take the unlimited number, if not straightaway. The unlimited nature of language, thought, and truth calls to us in our examination of the elements of language. If we do not listen to the unlimit, we will turn language and thought into mechanical, technical instruments. If we ignore the elements, we wallow in the miasma of meaningless thought.

Another example, following shortly, is hot and cold, the example read by many commentators as alluding explicitly to the indefinite dyad. "Take 'hotter' and 'colder' to begin with, and ask yourself whether you can ever observe any sort of limit attaching to them, or whether these kinds of thing have 'more' and 'less' actually resident in them, so that for the period of that residence there can be no question of suffering any bounds to be set" (Plato, *Philebus*, 24b). This example suggests that *unlimit* means *more or less*. "When we find things becoming 'more' or 'less' so-and-so, or admitting of terms like 'strongly,' 'slightly,' 'very,' and so forth, we ought to reckon them all as belonging to a single kind, namely that of the unlimited" (Plato, *Philebus*, 25). I consider the possibility that the One and the unlimited are not kinds, that to think of them as kinds is to think of them as belonging to *technē*, that we must distinguish hot and cold from good and bad, beauty and truth, where the latter are disputed terms, intermediary figures.

For Socrates alludes to a third example repeatedly, that of music, which on the one hand possesses intermediate numbers, intervals between high and low pitch, but is also filled with more and less, this *technical* unlimited kind (Plato, *Philebus*, 17d). We must grasp the intervals, the scales, systems of notes, and so on. And even within these intervals, notes, and scales are unlimits and infinites. But we may also ask our technicist, our musical gymnast, do you know music when you know the intervals, notes, and scales? And do you know music when you don't? By analogy, do we know language without knowing letters and rules of grammar? And do we know language when we do know letters and rules of grammar? Contemporary linguistics, especially transformational generative grammar, struggles with this *diaphora*, that those who speak may not know the parts and rules of language, while those who do know, may not speak and write well or truthfully or beautifully. When Socrates returns to music, it is to contrast its imprecision with the building of ships and houses (Plato, *Philebus*, 56a). Whatever the good of music may be, it does not reside in measures and instruments (Plato, *Philebus*, 56bc). The unlimit of more and less pertains to such measure and instruments, to carpentry and woodworking. Music touches another unlimit. Music dwells in beauty (Plato, *Republic*, 402).

This is our quarrel repeated, if it is a quarrel. About it Socrates says two things in *Philebus*, one that he wanted to discover "not which art or which form of knowledge is superior to all others in respect of being the greatest or the best or the most serviceable, but which devotes its attention to precision, exactness, and the fullest truth, though it may be small and of small profit" (Plato, *Philebus*, 58b). The good, the greatest, is not the most precise or exact, possibly not even the fullest truth. Socrates is exploring the precise or exact, the technical: carpentry and woodworking; grammar; what we call musical theory. Philosophy, music, poetry, art are something else, even something incomparable with this exact precision, which in its realm includes the comparable, but not separable from it.

The other thing Socrates says, shortly afterward, the second passage I alluded to some time ago, arises in speaking of justice, divine and human. "Will such a man be adequately possessed of knowledge, if he can give his account of the divine circle and the divine sphere themselves, but knows nothing of these human spheres and circles of ours, so that, when he is building a house, the rules that he uses, no less than the circles, are of the other sort?" (Plato, *Philebus*, 62ab). After a brief reference to music once more, situated we may suppose in the same difficult place as justice, we find the following exchange:

> SOCRATES: Do you want me, may I ask, to give way like a porter jostled and knocked about by the crowd, to fling open the doors and allow every sort of knowledge to stream in, the inferior mingling with the pure?
>
> PROTARCHUS: I don't really see, Socrates, what harm one would suffer by taking all those other sorts of knowledge, providing one had the first sort.
>
> SOCRATES: Then I am to allow the whole company to stream in and be gathered together in a splendid Homeric mingling of the waters? (Plato, *Philebus*, 62de)

Another, different, far-reaching image of unlimit. I call attention to the mingling of the waters, postponing its discussion for a moment.

The passage at 62ab seems as clear as anything Socrates says that the philosopher or poet who would claim knowledge of divine justice and divine being, of the sacred good, who stands on the back of the world and knows nothing of mundane justice and goodness, knows nothing worth claiming as knowledge. Knowledge of the good demands knowledge of *technē*. That is the truth that Socrates claims to be the gift of the gods. But Socrates says equally explicitly that *technē*'s knowledge alone, human knowledge, untouched by the divine, by madness and love, is dead. That is what Socrates says in *Phaedrus*, and he says it in *Philebus*. The knowledge gained by *technē* cuts off the very knowledge that we must let burst in, inspired, mad, disorderly, cuts it off as if the mundane could be divine—for knowledge, truth, and the good are divine. That is the enigmatic, oracular truth of the self-knowledge that Socrates endlessly seeks: it is mad, disorderly, divine.

Philosophy is love of wisdom, touched by the light of the sun, called from the good. Such a wisdom and such an *erōs* comes by way of the gods, retains its memory of the divine, which touches it with madness. Knowledge of being, the good, justice, and beauty all resonate endlessly with what *technē* can never know, pass away in their movements to unlimit, but without *technē* are nothing at all.

Why does Plato not say as directly as possible what Nietzsche says of tragedy: that tragedy falls between Apollo and Dionysus, that all things that come from the good are brought by *poiēsis* and *technē* together? Well, Nietzsche didn't say it that explicitly either, and we may easily read him to repeat the quarrel between Apollo and Dionysus. Or put another way, if tragedy bears the mark of the two different gods, memories of the divine in its different places, it is not without conflict between them, even as we know without a doubt that only together do the gods give us tragedy. Something impossible is touched by tragedy, between Apollo and Dionysus. Something impossible is touched by justice, beauty, by judgments of good and bad. The impossibility is that finite and infinite, limit and unlimit, meet at every such point, demand mobility, intermediary movements, but every such point is experienced by the finite as a quarrel over strangeness. It is the impossibility of *diaphora*.

Recall that the *diaphora* of old, between poetry and philosophy, madness and reason, is unknown as *polemos* to poetry and madness, to the divine. The gods give their gifts without understanding them to conflict with humans, but human works bear the mark of conflict, of sacrifice. Reason's nature is to quarrel, to divide the good from the bad, the one from the other, even if this means destroying the gods. Reason, *technē*, would obey the gods, would understand itself to be a gift of the gods, containing madness and inspiration. But in itself, it takes on all authority, cuts poetry off not because poetry is bad poetry, bad art, bad for the gods, but because it is bad *technē*, not useful enough, not useful in the most apparent ways. Moreover, poetry is frequently taken by its readers to be useful, truthful, where it is anything but, where it is divine. Music even more is holy, expressed in the mad singing of the cicadas, who do nothing but make music no matter what the cost. This is crazy under *technē*; crazy under any impulse than that of art, which reaches to the stars, driven by the same unlimited desire for truth and the good that inspires philosophy.

Of course, tragedy is Apollo joined with Dionysus. Except that under Dionysus, this crossing is masked, enigmatic. Under Apollo it is a quarrel. This is the impossible place where tragedy emerges. And of course justice falls between a good without measure, a gift of the gods, repeatedly surpassing every measure given by *technē*, and *technē*'s measures, where *technē* wars with everything that would undermine its measure.

The good demands that after we have reached and counted the intermediates, we must let them pass away to unlimit and cease bothering about them. But we must not go directly to unlimit, as if we did not inhabit intermediates. The good, the divine, the sacred, haunts the human, mundane world with memories of injustice, disaster, given by the intermediates. But there is no escape.

Yet we remember the divine and sacred. And we experience them in art, if not art alone. Still, if anything is certain in human experience, it is that counting the intervals and scales is not music, that counting the vowels and consonants is not poetry, that something in art surpasses any *technē*, reaches for the divine. The question for us at this moment is whether this divine beauty is the good. I take it to be the good that Plato says gives birth to knowledge and truth, all coming from the gods, all that we know in some way or another comes as a gift.

That is what he says in *Ion*:

> Herein lies the reason why the deity has bereft them of their senses, and uses them as ministers, along with soothsayers and godly seers; it is in order that we listeners may know that it is not they who utter these precious revelations while their mind is not within them, but that it is the god himself who speaks, and through them becomes articulate to us. (Plato, *Ion*, 534d)

> these lovely poems are not of man or human workmanship, but are divine and from the gods, and . . . the poets are nothing but interpreters of the gods, each one possessed by the divinity to whom he is in bondage. (Plato, *Ion*, 534e)

This gift is not just the gift of inspiration, from the Muses, not just the inexplicable soul of poetry, the light and holy madness of the poet. The god speaks in the poem; the sacred shows itself; the good calls from within the poem to us. Art is not *technē* but from the gods, possessed by the gift of the good.

Ion tells its tale within the *diaphora* between philosophy and poetry, *technē* and *poiēsis*. Ion is asked to choose whether he would be unjust or divine, and chooses the divine. Who would choose otherwise—except, perhaps, two millennia of Western rationality? Homer is not to be praised as *technōn*, but as artist, divine. Plato writes within the *diaphora* of a choice that is no choice, a judgment that cannot judge, because we cannot give up *technē*, cannot choose the divine over *technē*. *Technē* owns the right of choice. This is the aporia at the heart of judgment in relation to the good, repeated endlessly through time, but returning with a certain force after the crimes of our century with the understanding that we do not know how to judge any better now than then. Human beings must choose but cannot choose with assurance between the good and bad. Both the demand to judge and its impossibility come as gifts from the good.

I left the *diaphora* suspended between the duplicity and poverty of the painting regarded as belonging to *technē*'s reason and the unintelligibility of the madness that made it art. The poets who must, on all ethical and political grounds, be banished from the state will return on lyric poetry's terms. The defense will be pleaded in lyric measure, which will touch the soul without an understanding of benefit or harm. And those who love poetry who are not poets may defend poetry in prose. Those who love. Yet the question remains of poetry's benefit; good and bad give us an account of art against which art measures up very badly. Yet as we come to understand this truth, we pass away from measure to the divine. We understand the intermediates as intermediary figures, retaining within themselves the sacredness of the good.

The "chief accusation" (Plato, *Republic*, 605c) to which the poets and their defenders must reply is not poetry's imitativeness and lies or its relation to truth, but poetry's "power to corrupt" (Plato, *Republic*, 605c), to stir the emotions, making us unhappy, ruling us rather than being ruled. "For it waters and fosters these feelings when what we ought to do is to dry them up, and it establishes them as our rulers when they ought to be ruled, to the end that we may be better and happier men instead of worse and more miserable" (Plato, *Republic*, 605d). I again postpone the waters for a moment.

But I think of Tolstoy's thought of beauty as disease, of art as infection of feelings: *"The stronger the infection the better is the art,* as art" (Tolstoy, *WA*; Ross, *AIS*, 178). This truth that art transmits feelings, that beauty moves us to tears, this goodness of beauty is for a moment said by Socrates to be art's disadvantage. This harm that *poiēsis* does is told entirely in the voice of advantage. What profit do we receive from art? Socrates replies in terms of the injuries we receive, claiming that art harms our souls, governs our emotions, in virtue of its extreme materiality. A natural reply is that art benefits us by releasing the darker side of our emotions, releases them to the gift of the good, that the delight that art brings improves us, benefits us, does us good.

Both voices exercise authority and rule, and indeed, *poiēsis* is not a good of rule and does not establish authority in or out of the soul, but works as love. That is how I have asked that we think of the good in Plato, origin of the

work we do that does not occupy the space of work. Socrates speaks of the
work that art does, the work of *poiēsis*, which must be governed by *technē*
because *technē* is the voice of authority. But something other, heterogeneous, must displace the authority of authority if it is to respond to the good,
something closer to immortality, that knows nothing of profit and advantage,
something erotic, filled with divine madness, with intermediary figures moving between the sacred and mundane, disturbing and arousing (but not ruling) our emotions, filling us with joy.

And indeed that is how Socrates continues, for he follows his accusation
with the possibility that lyric poetry may return from exile, may be able to defend herself in lyric voice, now ignoring her illusion and deceit. And he goes
on to speak of immortality, first in terms of advantage and profit, but concluding, on my reading, with the story of Er, where advantages and benefits
disappear in memories of immortality. For the story of Er returns us to the
question of choice in an entirely different way, where choice knows nothing
of *technē*, nothing of profit. Adeimantus and Glaucon ask Socrates in Book
II to show that justice is more profitable to the just person than injustice,
given the possibility that a just person, like Job, might suffer endless oppro-
brium and misfortune, while the unjust person may profit in countless ways.
Perhaps Socrates answers that request in arguing that the well-run soul is
governed by reason, and the order of such a soul is named justice. But now,
in Book X, an entirely different level of discussion opens up, in relation to
the gods.

For lyric poetry's defense will not be that poetry is profitable, but that it
is inspired, ecstatic, contains a sacred joy. The account of profit and benefit
presupposes a certain view of good and bad, governed by *technē*. Socrates follows the suggestion that poetry must demonstrate its profitability in this
mundane world by speaking of eternity, of "all time" (Plato, *Republic*, 608d).
In a single life, injustice might be more profitable, but an immortal soul must
be concerned for all time. Read as an account of benefit, good and bad,
Socrates' suggestion here runs directly counter to his suggestion in *Philebus*,
discussed above, that the divine does not give us knowledge of the mundane.

I read *Phaedrus* and *Philebus* as instituting the quarrel between *poiēsis*
and *technē* in order to disrupt the possibility of any quarrel in relation to
poiēsis. Poetry knows nothing of justifying a choice between poetry over philosophy, one poem over another. Poetry has nothing to do with justification,
with reason's exclusions, and everything to do with choice, but not in relation to limits. Art comes from the sacred and divine as inclusive, not exclusive, even where we understand that every work excludes. This care for what
may be included where we cannot live except by exclusion marks a certain
sense of art, a sense incompatible with the sense of art both as giving us a wisdom comparable to benefit and loss, and as irrelevant to the good.

I briefly interrupt this reading of the sacred gift of art in Plato to turn toward a more mundane figure of the good, water, waves of water, appearing recurrently throughout our discussions. For mirroring Socrates' account of *technē* and *mimēsis* is his account of water, in two figures. One is the figure of reflection, dominating Book X but recurrent throughout Socrates' discussions, beginning with music, an extraordinary place to find a figure of visible images and reflections, a hard, adamantine figure, whose mobility would destroy any likeness. "And is it not also true that if there are any likenesses of letters reflected in water or mirrors, we shall never know them until we know the originals, but such knowledge belongs to the same art and discipline?" (Plato, *Republic*, 402b). Continuing in discussions of the divided line and beyond, contrasting the rigidity of reflections and the mobility of the changing world:

> By images I mean, first, shadows, and then reflections in water and on surfaces of dense, smooth, and bright texture, and everything of that kind, if you apprehend. (Plato, *Republic*, 510a)

> And at first he would most easily discern the shadows and, after that, the likenesses or reflections in water of men and other things, and later, the things themselves, and from these he would go on to contemplate the appearances in the heavens and heaven itself, . . . (Plato, *Republic*, 516ab)[6]

This repetition of the figure of mirror reflections in water reflects a contrast with unchanging being and truth. Mirror reflections do not give truth, do not give us the Idea itself, but an easy, mindless simulacrum, something we could not plausibly say of art or poetry, even less of music, but might say of draftsmanship to those who took the drawing for the thing. But we might say something similar to the *sophoi* who took their knowledge for the thing itself, for the truth, without divine inspiration.

The second figure of water is its fluidity and mobility, adding the impossibility of holding truth fast within its reflections. If reflections are illusory, watery reflections are inconstant as well. Socrates repeats this image of water's mobility to enforce, not the unreliability of truth but the power of growth and movement. Imitation "waters and fosters these feelings when what we ought to do is to dry them up" (606d). Perhaps, if any Greek would wish to dry up human passions under the eyes of the watchful gods. But this movement moves on to the story of Er, where waters recall the forgetfulness of being, drinking of oblivion before returning to life, the River of Lethe.[7] This oblivion in waters seems to me quite different from the watery illusions and unreliabilities that surround human life, closer to the heart of truth and being, in oblivion, of which Heidegger speaks, much closer to *poiēsis* than *technē*. For we must cross the River of Lethe to live, to be, must enter upon and drink the waters, cross the ocean, throw ourselves into the sea, embark on nature's journeys, always with mobility, fluidity, and forgetfulness, an oblivion we cannot overcome.

I have passed over other figures of water. They lead to another interruption in the name of the good. For when Socrates interrupts his own account of justice in the *polis*, abstracted from most everyday considerations except for relishes, meat, and war (Plato, *Republic*, 372–373),[8] to consider mundane matters of utmost importance for the *polis*, women and children, interrupts the account of guardians as if they might all be male to consider women guardians and family affairs, he does so in repeated figures of water, if somewhat obliquely, waves of aporia.[9] Socrates associates women with water in an aporia so distant from the rigid reflections of watery mirrors that we cannot reasonably follow the movement from the one to the other. Water gives us useful reflections, too mobile to be of much use or truth. But water flows on to the very heart of being, in forgetfulness, in waves of mobility and fluidity, where we find women and children. Without women, what possibility of *technē* can there be? Without water's mobility and fluidity. No state can be built without *technē*, but also without mobility and fluidity, without women, and children, without sexual difference, all exceeding any *technē*.

Leading me to another interruption, interrupting my interruption of an interruption, where Irigaray speaks of water, fluidity and mobility, against the cutting edges of volume. Yet before I turn to Irigaray, procrastinating for just a moment, I recall that what is interrupted by Socrates' account of women, in waves of aporia, is his most demanding account of justice in the *polis*, again given in the figure of water. Where he speaks of justice in the individual and in the city as the same, he speaks of waters: "Through these waters, then, said I, we have with difficulty made our way and we are fairly agreed that the same kinds equal in number are to be found in the state and in the soul of each one of us" (Plato, *Republic*, 441c). These are the waters through which we hope to make our way. But perhaps they are the way, these waters, in their fluidity and mobility. Perhaps the fluidity of waters opens the way.

Returning to women and our interruption. For I believe no thought is possible of law and world, of the mundane or divine, without sexual difference, women, something heterogeneous, something intermediary. Nor of art:

> Woman is neither open nor closed. She is indefinite, infinite, *form is never complete in her*. (Irigaray, *VF*, 229)

> *Fluid* has to remain that secret *remainder*, of the one. Blood, but also milk, sperm, lymph, saliva, spit, tears, humors, gas, waves, airs, fire . . . light. All threaten to deform, propagate, evaporate, consume him, to flow out of him and into another who cannot be easily held on to. (Irigaray, *VF*, 237)

The/a woman never closes up into a volume. (Irigaray, *VF*, 239)

Yes, I am coming back from far, far away. . . .
. . . You had fashioned me into a mirror but I have dipped that mirror in the waters of oblivion—that you call life. (Irigaray, *ML*, 4 ["Speaking of Immemorial Waters"])

Woman, in granting the heterogeneity of sexual difference, appears in a figure of fluidity, mobility, indeterminacy, resisting the specular rigidity of mirrors, a different figure of production and reproduction. Water flows from *technē* to *poiēsis*,[10] across the *diaphora*, intermediary figure of mobility, unclosure, disclosure, a different, incomplete truth, always wrapped in forgetfulness, others', men's forgetfulness.

Water, women, fluidity all cross without joining *poiēsis* and *technē*, cross the waters of Lethe without demanding a bridge, leaving life and truth moving fluently in the hands of the gods, where we always find them. Water in Plato moves us across and in the *diaphora* opened between art and philosophy, *poiēsis* and *technē*, and more, between men and women and more, humans and gods, humans and animals, humanity and nature, spaces crossed by diaphoric figures, washed by waters which never turn to ice except for moments in which we demand rigidity—sometimes moments longer than millennia; sometimes in disciplinary places in which we turn the waves to stone. I think of the waters as gifts of life, from the good, nature's abundance.

I return from these interruptions inside interruptions to the myth of Er. I read the close of Book X of Plato's *Republic* as returning us to this space of mobility, less in relation to art than beauty and the divine, though we have just finished with painting and poetry, finished them off, first banishing them in the name of *technē*, then recognizing that poetry bears a dangerous magic that perhaps we cannot exclude in the name of the good. Socrates closes his discussion of poetry repeating his insistence that unless it can be shown to be both magical and beneficial, we should guard against its charms. Immediately following, and before the story of Er, he considers the profit to an immortal soul of justice for all time, purified of the mundane:

> we must view it not marred by communion with the body and other miseries as we now contemplate it, but consider adequately in the light of reason *[logismē]* what it is when it is purified, and then you will find it to be a far more beautiful thing and will more clearly distinguish justice and injustice and all the matters that we have now discussed. (Plato, *Republic*, 611c)

Yet the passage above from *Philebus* presents what we may take to be a conclusive reason for rejecting every account of profitability in relation to the gods and immortality, to a purified soul. Only what is profitable in relation to mundane experience can be accepted as knowledge of good and bad. Only what is like building a house.

Perhaps justice and injustice, good and evil, are not like building a house. Perhaps they bear a touch of madness, ecstasy, like art, inspired by the Muses, disturbed in their materiality and sensuality, in their fluidity. Perhaps they come as gifts from the gods. Perhaps they move fluidly, circulate mobilely, crossing the *diaphora*, moving intermediarily.[11]

The story of Er is another such crossing, passing between heaven and earth and returning, given to Socrates again from elsewhere, told to Alcinous by unknown narrators, perhaps by Er upon his return, speaks directly to this question of choosing justice over injustice ecstatically. Er is slain in battle and passes to a place of judgment, between heaven and earth, where the just pass to the right and the unjust to the left, coming to a meadow where returning souls tell of their punishments for their wrongdoings and blessings for their good deeds (Plato, *Republic*, 614d–616b). Here we find the famous repeated image of a divine judgment that punishes evil and rewards good, tenfold or any multiple desired. Here justice is better than injustice because it profits the immortal soul more.

But only seven days (Plato, *Republic*, 616b) in a much longer and more complex narrative of the divine is given to this account of punishments and rewards. The souls then pass by the spindle of necessity to a light linking heaven and earth where the Fates, daughters of necessity, insist that they choose another mortal life. Moreover, "No divinity shall cast lots for you, but you shall choose your own deity"; "The blame is his who chooses. God is blameless" (Plato, *Republic*, 617e). Here, between repeated images linking heaven and earth, every soul shall choose between good and bad, justice and injustice. I wonder if they do so by *technē*.

Socrates tells us what it means to choose; "But all other considerations he will dismiss, for we have seen that this is the best choice, both for life and death. And a man must take with him to the house of death an adamantine faith in this, . . . " (Plato, *Republic*, 619). Yet the souls he describes choose impetuously or in memory of their other lives: "a strange, pitiful, and ridiculous spectacle, as the choice was determined for the most part by the habits of their former lives" (Plato, *Republic*, 620a); but not entirely. We must reconsider the "adamantine faith" [*doxan hexonta*: a belief but also a dream, cared for deeply in the soul], reconsider its glittering hardness surrounded by the waters of Lethe. If we understand the choices of souls in such close proximity to the gods to be governed by reason, but also because such souls are not divine, are subject to weaknesses of desire, then good and evil are determined by rational choice, however difficult. What Socrates describes, however, is a choice given by habits and memories of former lives, requiring but lacking an adamantine faith in, a dream of, justice and the good. Against this sovereignty of reason, described as largely irrelevant, we may understand the divine and sacred place where justice and injustice have their origin as adamantine but not rational; as ethical but not technical; as closer to the gods and art than to governance and profit; as enduring but fluid and mobile, watering the earth that things may grow.

If the gods know and care for the difference between good and evil, justice and injustice, they do not reason concerning it. And perhaps, though Socrates never quite says this, reason belongs to the mundane more than to the divine. Reason's cuts and exclusions are essential to *praxis*, but do not give us the good. Perhaps, we may say after Lyotard, without criteria: judgment and choice without criteria, in the name of the good. But that will not quite do, because there are criteria here if not rules. Justice and injustice are criteria, along with good and bad. They are the criteria, that we abhor injustice and seek justice; that we forgo the bad to achieve the good, that we dream of something beyond good and evil. Here Plato's principle that everyone strives for the good, read as an account of *technē*, suggests that everyone who knows what is good will pursue it. Instead, read in relation to the divine, in relation to the mobile waters, no one knows what is good but everyone pursues it, yearns for it, because it is the origin, the call, the demand, the touch of judgment, choice, because we and all things are touched by it as we touch each other. This is as true for the souls that choose tyranny and miserable lives as for souls that prosper. They choose in the name of the good, reaching out toward justice.

Socrates reminds us that this possibility of choice presupposes a distinction between justice and injustice, but a distinction without any criteria other than its own. The story of Er tells us of a choice between justice and injustice that cannot be avoided and cannot be rationalized, but is presupposed by every rational consideration, watered by the River of Lethe. "And it will save us if we believe it" (Plato, *Republic*, 621c). Lethe marks the *diaphora*, an intermediary figure of crossing.

This choice, between good and evil, justice and injustice, given in the name of the good, is divine and sacred, immortal, without reference to mundane temporality, oblivious to *technē*. This escape from temporality on my reading evokes the dream of an escape from profit even as we cannot live without considerations of profit and loss. Put another way, we live within restricted, exchange economies of profit and loss, good and bad, which presuppose the general economy given from the good, the earth's abundance. Together with works of art, we live in our bodies, sensual, material, gendered bodies, live within the limits of our embodiment, displaced in all embodied places by divine inspiration, circulating in the general economy of the good.

Holding this thought of general economy in abeyance for a while, I conclude this chapter with several interruptions, returning to the gift of art, ringing a different note, interrupting my reading of Plato.

Göttner-Abendroth speaks of a *matriarchal aesthetics* in terms of nine principles, suggesting a binary opposition between patriarchal and matriarchal art, men's and women's production and response to art (Göttner-Abendroth, *MA;* Ross, *AIS,* 566; Ecker, *FA,* 81). She suggests, that is, a choice between one aesthetics and another, as if to suggest to women that they choose a women's rather than a man's art. We may think of this as a double binary: feminine versus masculine aesthetics; and a situated aesthetics, masculine or feminine, versus a neutered aesthetics. All the choices here are oppositional. And this question of oppositionality is what is in question. For I understand such oppositions and conflicts to belong to *technē* while I have questioned whether the gift of art bears an oppositional structure within itself.

What then of art and aesthetics? Does it divide into men's and women's art, men's and women's aesthetics, Western and non-Western art and aesthetics? Or, if we refuse the opposition, do we replay the masculine as the neuter, effectively excluding women and non-Westerners from the highest art? For this question of the neuter is the central question of feminism, as I understand it: what Irigaray calls *"the sexual indifference that underlies the truth of any science, the logic of every discourse"* (Irigaray, *PDSF,* 69). Sexual difference suggests an essential and inexpugnable divide between masculine and feminine, men and women. Sexual indifference, in the name of neutrality, passes off the masculine in the name of objectivity and universality. We are, in Wittig's words, in a logic of domination and oppression either way. We are caught in the coils of *technē,* insisting that we choose, exclude, in the name of reason, or that we exclude by not choosing, still in the name of reason.

I have understood the gift of the good, given in and as art, as opening another possibility of choice—or, perhaps more truthfully, opening another understanding of choice. It consists in interrupting the irresistible claims of *technē* upon the nature of judgment. I have traced the movement of the divine and sacred, in Plato, as an expression of another relation to the good. Here I wish to consider the possibility that within the polarity of men and women, patriarchy and matriarchy, we may find an analogous displacement, figured earlier as fluidity, intimately related to art. For alongside the binary structure of matriarchy and patriarchy, the binarity of the requirement that women change the world dominated by men in order to empower themselves, there can be found another vision of empowerment interrupting the domination of Western reason, another diaphoric figure.

A matriarchal aesthetics has nine principles:

First: Matriarchal art is located beyond the fictional, both in the past and in the present. Beyond the fictional art becomes magic. . . .
Second: Matriarchal art has an enduring and predetermined framework: the structure of matriarchal mythology. . . .
Third: Matriarchal art transcends the traditional mode of communication which consists of: author-text (art-product)-reader. Matriarchal art is not "text," it is not limited to manufacturing art products. . . .
Fourth: Matriarchal art demands the total commitment of all participants. . . . In matriarchal art there is no division between emotion and thought. . . .
Fifth: Matriarchal art does not correspond to an extended model of communication with the elements: author-text-dealer-agent-audience. . . .
Sixth: Matriarchal art cannot be subdivided into genres because it cannot be objectified. . . .
Seventh: As matriarchal art derives from the structure of matriarchal mythology which has a complete different value system . . . from that of patriarchy, it too shares this different system of values. . . .
Eighth: The social changes which matriarchal art brings about override the divisions in the aesthetic sphere. . . .
Ninth: Matriarchal art is not "art." For "art" is necessarily defined in terms of the fictional; . . .
Matriarchal art is independent of the fictional . . . (Göttner-Abendroth, *MA; Ross, AIS*, 566–69; Ecker, *FA*, 81–84)

Of these principles, the first through sixth do not explicitly inhabit a binary opposition. Matriarchal art is magical, mythological, diaphoric, not text or work, undivided by genre, participants, or mode of communication, but something different, intermediary. In every case, we may read this difference as an opposition to traditional, patriarchal art, but also as naming something more enigmatic, otherwise. With the seventh through ninth principle, matriarchal art becomes explicitly oppositional, bearing a different value system, overriding traditional oppositions, including fictional and real.

If we took the magical or mythical as our point of departure, we could understand all nine principles as resistance to an oppositional structure in patriarchal aesthetics and rational thought in which binary oppositions are assumed to be fundamental at women's and others' expense. It is by no means obvious that matriarchal art generates a "different system of values" that work in the same spaces as traditional systems of value. Put another way, matriarchal art suggests an art that gives up the necessity of work, the sites of *technē*, to extend the realm of art to what I have called the sacred, but called here mythological and magical, beyond work. Matriarchal art gives up the elements that define the place and work of artifacts in traditional societies. We may take for granted that such an art bears the mark of the good and does not compete with works of art.

Yet Göttner-Abendroth also speaks of developing a "matriarchal art utopia" (Göttner-Abendroth, *MA;* Ross, *AIS*, 566; Ecker, *FA*, 81). Such an art would be provocative, resistant to traditional art and thought. "It demonstrates nature's unity with human beings as opposed to nature's exploitation and utilisation by men" (Göttner-Abendroth, *MA;* Ross, *AIS*, 576; Ecker, *FA*, 93). Yet perhaps such a demonstration is impossible. For "after all, isn't the process of matriarchal art in its assumptions and the course it takes essentially esoteric? Who knows what the structure of matriarchal mythology is? Who can reach true ecstasy?" (Göttner-Abendroth, *MA;* Ross, *AIS*, 575; Ecker, *FA*, 92). And here, I suggest, matriarchal art may touch the good. For to insist that it demonstrates anything, even nature's unity with human beings and within itself, the goodness of things, is to insist that it do the work of traditional art and aesthetics, work that has always excluded, dominated, and oppressed. Why should we assume that matriarchal art, as work, could work any better, without exclusion?

The matriarchal art that evokes infinite possibilities of ecstasy and exalted experience can do so, must do so, without exclusion or oppression. But I am making a more radical point. I am suggesting that what Göttner-Abendroth describes as ecstasy, magic, and mythology, as breaking down the divisions and barriers to human experience, are already known in the name of the good, by men as well as women, are experienced recurrently in art, too frequently by exclusion. The very possibility of art or any other work depends on being touched by the ecstasy given by the good. Matriarchal art brings forth an ecstasy granted to us in all our work, including the most oppositional, dominating, and oppressive. For we know injustice when we encounter it, and art has always contained within itself resistance to its own oppressions. These have not been successful, nor can they be expected to be successful in the world of work. The same would be true of matriarchal art.

I think matriarchal art brings before us the thought of the good, of the sacred, magical, and mythological as intermediary figures without which we could not think of art at all, the possibilities in art foreclosed in the world of its appropriation and manipulation, of its work. Only those excluded from the oppressions of this world of work can speak in a certain voice about its alternative possibilities. Let me put this in another way. I do not believe that women's art is or would be better than men's art, though it might be better in certain ways, might care for different things in different ways. I do think that both men and women should and do produce works of art, and that the structure of thought that has excluded women is to the detriment of art, and men, and women. And we know this, all of us, and in a certain way know, or sense, what we sacrifice to live in the mundane. We always know, granted to us in the name of the good, the sacrifices demanded of us. That is the greatest gift of the good. And it is expressed and realized most forcefully in art, something beyond any work of art.

The gift of the good is anarchistic, unstable, diaphoric, resistant to criteria.[12] When Lyotard says that politics is no genre (Lyotard, *D*, 139), that judgment is without criteria (Lyotard, *P*, 27), that we must bear witness to the *différend* (Lyotard, *D*, xiii), and that the witness is a traitor (Lyotard, *I*, 204), he may be read as speaking of a political judgment that works without criteria, that imposes no genre, resists every genre, bears witness to the impossibility of deducing, legitimating authority (Lyotard, *D*, 142). In other words, his claims may be read as pointing to a more truthful and responsive ethics|politics that confronts the impossibility of establishing epistemic and normative authority, as improving model for all other ethics, politics, and science. The goal of feminist philosophy of science, Harding argues elsewhere, is to produce a better science, a better *technē* (Harding, *SQF*). But in *IACFP*, she suggests that the instability is not "better," but inherent. The instability, anarchy, of judgment is inherent, beyond "better."

Lyotard speaks of this *diaphora*, perhaps differently, in memory of Levinas, as two sorts of inhuman: "It is indispensable to keep them dissociated. The inhumanity of the system which is currently being consolidated under the name of development (among others) must not be confused with the infinitely secret one of which the soul is hostage" (Lyotard, *I*, 2). I am by no means sure that it is possible, much less indispensable, to keep them dissociated. But the one, the inhumanity of development and technology, calls for resistance to its inhumanity, its evil, bears the burden of responsibility for improving technology and bettering the human and natural worlds. The other, to which the soul is hostage, called by many different names by Lyotard himself: "work, figural, heterogeneity, dissensus, event, thing" (Lyotard, *I*, 4); to which I add for him, *le différend*, and the Forgotten, the Other, the Law (Lyotard, *HJ*, 89); and I add for us, here, the gift of the good: these improve nothing.

What is indispensable is not, perhaps, to keep these dissociated, separate, from evil. That may not be possible. What is indispensable is to think of them as forgotten, other, otherwise, diaphoric, interrupting work. The inhumanity, the evil, of things belongs to work, even in Whitehead's understanding of evil:

> The ultimate evil in the temporal world is deeper than any specific evil. It lies in the fact that the past fades, that time is a "perpetual perishing." . . . The nature of evil is that the characters of things are mutually obstructive. Thus the depths of life require a process of selection. . . . Selection is at once the measure of evil, and the process of its evasion. (Whitehead, *PR*, 340)

This is what I mean by sacrifice, but presupposes an ideality beyond evil, an ideality impossible to produce or imagine, but nevertheless relevant to every thing and place. Whitehead speaks of it as "an ideal peculiar to each particular actual entity," each individual event and process, for "[t]here is not just one ideal 'order' which all actual entities should attain and fail to attain" (Whitehead, *PR*, 84). I call the sense of this ideality *cherishment*, and understand it in relation to inexhaustibility. Every thing and every kind is inexhaustible, beyond any limit, inciting other things and kinds to respond, to question, the limit of every thing and work. What is indispensable is to know that cherishment does no work, but that all work depends upon it. This is the gift of the good, to work where the good does no work, can do no work, where we cannot even imagine the possibility of work according to the ideal, without injustice, but from which the gift of work, of practice, of what we call ethics and politics emerges.

An anarchist ethics|politics may be better than a rule-governed ethics|politics. Judgment without criteria may be better, more responsive, than judgments according to rules. But this better and worse belong to a judgment without criteria, always in question. Here the idea of art— painting, sculpture, music, poetry—without criteria but within work appears to follow Kant's view of genius, exceeding rules,[13] plausibly read as an account of the work that genius does, leading to the critique that such Romanticism is elitist. Lyotard, following Kant, may also be read as suggesting that judgment without criteria does the work of the good. But if we recall that Kant's account of genius is given in the Analytic of the Sublime, where what belongs to work evokes something beyond work, a memory of the good, then the absence of a rule is not a work without rules or criteria, nor does it give rules which are not rules, examples, for example, but, like nature, is touched by a beauty unknown to work, unsuitable for work, but without which no work can be done, at least no beautiful work that recalls the good.

Even so, examples exercise undue authority, instituting rules. Genius's example sets the stage for others, demands that they conform, even where other geniuses need not do so. Such an authoritarian model escapes from the coerciveness of law, but it does not resist coerciveness.

All this is to say that an anarchist view of ethics may not be more responsive to the gift of the good, but suggests another ethics more or less responsive to the conditions of life. The alternative is that the anarchist demand belongs to something forgotten that calls us to the good, whether its implementation be by criterion or rule. The gift of the good gives itself to work, works of art and works of practice, working as *diaphora*. But the politics that is no genre, the judgment without criteria, are not works but traces of something otherwise, forgotten, the good without which judgment would be impossible, senseless, unintelligible.

We may read Kant to ask us to take very seriously the possibility that the place where the Forgotten appears, the gift of the good, is art. The quarrel between *poiēsis* and *technē* is a quarrel about the very goodness of art, given to us by the gods, beyond the gods. If we can grant this, perhaps we can also grant that feminist writings also speak of the gift of the good, but in a different voice, that of gender and sexual difference. That is where I would hope to take their writings, the instability and anarchy of their insights, not into *technē*, where a better science, or craft, or practice, would be better for women, or men, or human beings, or others; but touching something about men and women, in nature and the world, public and private, touched by sexual difference and gender, by love, given as gifts without which we cannot judge or reach for better and worse.

At least, this is the thought I would pursue along the line of Irigaray's *An Ethic of Sexual Difference*, another interruption, where she speaks of the saving thought of our age: "Sexual difference represents one of the questions or the question that is to be thought in our age. According to Heidegger, each age has one thought to think. One only. Sexual difference is probably the thought of our time. The thing of our time that, thought, will bring us 'salvation'?" [my translation].[14] The thing that will bring us to "salvation" is what I call the gift of the good. The thought to which Irigaray leads us, and which I have discussed elsewhere in detail,[15] is that the thought of the good is a thought of sexual difference, away from a etherealized, spiritualized divine to a palpable touch of heterogeneity:

> A new morning of and for the world? A remaking of immanence and transcendence, notably through this *threshold* which has never been examined as such: the female sex. The threshold that gives access to the *mucous*. Beyond classical oppositions of love and hate, liquid and ice—a threshold that is always *half-open*. The threshold of the *lips*, which are strangers to dichotomy and oppositions. (Irigaray, *ESD*, 18)[16]

Irigaray evokes Heidegger's reading of Trakl's poem, *A Winter Evening*, containing the line: "[p]ain has turned the threshold to stone" (Heidegger, *L*, 203). "The intimacy of world and thing is not a fusion. Intimacy obtains only where the intimate—world and thing—divides itself cleanly and remains separated. In the midst of the two, in the between of world and thing, in their *inter*, division prevails: a *dif-ference*" (Heidegger, *L*, 202). This "dif-ference," pain in Heidegger, becomes mucus, lips that touch, and move, a threshold between heaven and earth, diaphoric, touched by sexual difference, resistant to *technē*'s sexual in-difference.

This is the striking quality of *technē*'s indifference, called to our attention repeatedly by Irigaray. The domain of *technē*'s work is that of making differences, distinctions, always oppositional, always hierarchical, between good and bad, high and low, including sexual difference. *Technē* does its work of distinguishing good from bad, the work of ethics, in the name of reason's objectivity at the expense of women, in the name of a sexual indifference that is anything but indifferent. Sexual indifference is not indifferent, not neutral, but passes off the masculine as the universal.

This truth belongs to the good. The good, in its madness, otherwise, touches *technē* against the injustices of its oppositions, subordinating women to men in the name of neutrality. The good bears sexual difference within itself, in part for historical reasons, *technē*'s contaminations, in part because sexual difference touches a heterogeneity masked in *technē*, masked in the very heart of reason. Another name for the Forgotten is sexual difference. Another name for the inhuman to which our soul is hostage is sexual difference. Another endless betrayal is named by sexual difference. All of this can be said only in memory of the good, against the incessant injustices of men against women.

Revealed in art. Repeated in art. Interliminal. Crossing thresholds, limens, touching heterogeneous, gendered, sexual bodies.

That is why I find myself led repeatedly from Plato to contemporary feminist writing, where the good finds its expression as the burning question of our age, that of sexual difference. Perhaps. In a new poetics or art, perhaps. But I will defer this question for a while longer, turning away from sexual difference to address the quarrel between reason and poetic madness in a different way, still in Plato.

But first I interpose another interruption, another Greek *diaphora*. I am led to think of Sophocles' Oedipus trilogy (or pseudotrilogy) diaphorically, filled with intermediary figures. I mean to pursue *Oedipus at Colonus*, itself intermediary in multiple ways, between *Oedipus the King* and *Antigone*, between them in dramatic time but composed later, recrossing the diaphoric lines of the Oedipus story, already multiply diaphoric.

For the Oedipus trilogy is filled with diaphoric moments, almost as if Sophocles had crossings in mind, intermediary movements. The list of such figures is long; I offer a partial list, touching a bit more upon some than others. *Oedipus the King* opens with the plague sent by the gods to Thebes within diaphoric figures of mortals and immortals, *polis* and *theos*, justice and injustice, rulers and ruled, surrounded by blood, blood as death, blood as kinship, blood as blight, deranged kinship.

One of the most extraordinary figures of the trilogy is its dwelling between, diaphoric crossing, spaces of sexual difference, public and private, between mother and son, wife and husband, sister and brother, father and daughter, all gender crossings, crossings of kind, exemplified especially by Teiresias, who appears in *Oedipus the King* and *Oedipus at Colonus*, the seer famed for his own gender crossings, and by Oedipus's story, where mother becomes wife, daughter becomes sister, son becomes brother. Sophocles adds domestic spaces to public events, something largely unavailable at the time in stories of Teiresias. In these domestic spaces, other domestic crossings emerge, between sister and sister, brother and brother, father and son, kinship crossings, related to and given by sexual differences, but not their repetition. Pervading all of them is the most famous crossing of the trilogy, the relationship between mother and son.

Another striking and repeated figure is the curse, joined with prayer in the crossing between human beings and gods. Oedipus and his parents are cursed, he curses his sons and Creon, the entire trilogy works in the space of a curse, leavened by prayer, Oedipus's prayers to save Thebes, his prayers at Colonus to ward off his contamination of the site sacred to the Erinyes. Curse and prayer join contamination as figures of crossing between humans and gods, crossings of time and memory but also, in Greece, of family and kinship, crossings of fate and chance.

But most of all, perhaps, in Greece and the Oedipus trilogy, these are diaphoric crossings of justice and injustice, life and death, to the point where the intermediary figures of justice and injustice, life and death, honor and dishonor, mortal and immortal, all open onto other intermediary figures between the pairs. Oedipus accepts the horror of his life in *Oedipus the King* but repeatedly denies his injustice in *Oedipus at Colonus*. He did the best he could, could not have known the stranger who attacked him was his father, could not have known Jocasta was his mother. Justice and injustice are both absolutely different, in the eyes of the gods, and impossible to separate, in human life, diaphoric.[17] We live surrounded by injustice, pursuing justice, living in justice.

Oedipus prays for justice, speaking of a hidden guilt, a guilt we have seen in Anaximander, but given diaphoric irony here. "I pray solemnly that the slayer, whoso he be, whether his hidden guilt is lonely or hath partners, evilly, as he is evil, may wear out his unblest life. And for myself I pray that if, with my privity, he should become an inmate of my house, I may suffer the same things which even now I called down upon others" (Sophocles, *OK*, 375). Adding another diaphoric crossing between public and private, nature's and human reproduction. "And for those who obey me not, I pray that the gods send them neither harvest of the earth nor fruit of the womb, but that they be wasted by their lot that now is, or by none yet more dire" (Sophocles, *OK*, 375).

Oedipus turns truth into *diaphora*, hovering between heaven and earth, justice and injustice, exemplified in Teiresias's blindness, repeated in Oedipus's blinding, double and triple blindness to the hidden truth, self-blinded by horror at the truth. In relation to the gods, to the passing of time, no human is secure, no truth is free from blindness. In the Oedipus trilogy reason and truth show themselves as diaphoric, filled with light, with the firmness of proof, undermined repeatedly by fate and hidden injustices.[18]

The ruler, the higher, is a traitor. The relation between high and low is diaphoric. Oedipus brings down forever the possibility of a relation between high and low that does not bear within itself the *diaphora* of endless injustice. Every high is sometimes low; every greatness is false. Yet Oedipus is great, not free from lowliness or falsity, but in demanding the truth at the cost of his own destruction, blindness repeating blindness, greatness repeating lowness, justice repeating injustice, all diaphoric crossings of truth with injustice, reason with *hubris*. Oedipus would be master, for which he is admonished by Creon upon his fall, a Creon who later insists on being master. "Crave not to be master in all things: for the mastery which thou didst win hath not followed thee through life" (Sophocles, *OK*, 416). Perhaps mastery cannot be sustained in mortal life. Perhaps mastery rules in diaphoric crossings, over diaphoric crossings, refuses *diaphora*.

This last passage repeats in the language of lineage the diaphoric themes of kinship and blood, bringing us back to the curse around the crossing of kin and gods, the curse of light, of truth. "Thou light, may I now look my last on thee—I who have been found accursed in birth, accursed in wedlock, accursed in the shedding of blood!" (Sophocles, *OK*, 408). Blood joins injustice and the gods in the figure of the curse. Torture and blood. But blood joins family and kinship as the movement of human time, the mark of human history. Around human and other families, in kin and kind, circulate the diaphoric crossings of the world. We might wish to remember that Oedipus killed his father where three roads meet, that Oedipus solves the riddle of the Sphinx in another crossing, a riddle repeating the figure of human time and life and kin, a riddle set by a creature crossing diaphorically from humanity to animals and nature, from humans to gods, and that Teiresias tells Oedipus that he does not know his kin, crossing repeatedly around kinship and kind (Sophocles, *OK*, 380–81). The place where injustice works, in the story of Oedipus, is in marriage and family, in kin (Sophocles, *OK*, 415), another crossing of earth, womb, and kin; another plague crossing between humans and gods. The plagues of time, of death, of memory, of injustice, all diaphoric crossings, crossing everywhere, crossed in memories of death, in burials and mournings, in women's oppression, and in their refusal.

Oedipus ensures that all those touched by disaster within his proximity are to be buried, touched as much as possible still by the good, crossed by journeys to and before the gods. But Creon refuses to bury Polyneices in the name of goodness, puts his own city's goodness above the gods, refusing a crossing that reinstitutes crossings. All my examples of *diaphora* in the trilogy, to this point, have come from *Oedipus the King*. I add a few from *Antigone* on my way to *Oedipus at Colonus*.

Many are repetitions, burials passing from humans to gods, life to death, earth to heaven (Sophocles, *A*, 423–24). Family and kinship crossings pass from sister to brother, brother to brother, father to son. Creon's rule is said to be given by kinship (Sophocles, *A*, 428). The language of kinship is blood, kindred blood, crossing from kinship to death, bloodshed, injustice, from love to destruction. Throughout the trilogy, and elsewhere in Greek tragedy, justice crosses with injustice, Dionysus crosses with Apollo (Sophocles, *A*, 427; *OC*, 638), life with death, in Sophocles' famous words. "Wonders are many, and none is more wonderful than man; . . . / . . . only against Death shall he call for aid in vain" (Sophocles, *A*, 432).

Several extreme diaphoric crossings belong especially powerfully to *Antigone*. One is that of divine law crossed with human law, Antigone's burial of Polyneices with Creon's refusal. Only those who would insist on the primacy of one over the other can deny the impossible *diaphora* in justice's law, those who cannot read the drama as a conflict. For example, those who would agree with Antigone that divine law takes absolute precedence over human law must refuse the entire dramatic movement. The other is that of kin, sister bonded to brother beyond any other bondings, that of marriage or even mother-child. Against all likelihood of women's testimony, I believe, Antigone insists on the primacy of her kinship bond over any other bond. She could find another husband, have other children, but can never replace her brother:

> Never, had I been a mother of children, or if a husband had been mouldering in death, would I have taken this task upon me in the city's despite. What law, ye ask, is my warrant for that word? The husband lost, another might have been found, and child from another, to replace the first-born; but, father and mother hidden with Hades, no brother's life could every bloom for me again. (Sophocles, *A*, 447–48)

In these thoughts, in her defiance, she is both a woman, a Greek woman, and something else, opens up possibilities for women beyond any thought in Greece, perhaps elsewhere. Ismene represents women, represents them well, typically and lovingly. First, their weakness:

> think how we shall perish, more miserably than all the rest, if, in defiance of the law, we brave a king's decree or his powers. Nay, we must remember, first, that we were born women, as who should not strive with men; next, that we are ruled of the stronger, so that we must obey in these things, and in things yet sorer. (Sophocles, *A*, 424–25)

I do them no dishonour; but to defy the State,—I have no strength for that. (Sophocles, *A*, 425*)*

Then their wisdom: "A hopeless quest should not be made at all" (Sophocles, *A*, 426). Returned by Antigone with venomous scorn and hatred, repeating the vilification everywhere directed against them. And repeating it even where Ismene hopes to share her fate, caring for her sister more than for herself—"But, now that ills beset thee, I am not ashamed to sail the sea of trouble at thy side" (Sophocles, *A*, 437), rejected by Antigone with venom: "a friend in words is not the friend that I love" (Sophocles, *A*, 437). Ismene asks, "And what life is dear to me, bereft of thee?," to which Antigone responds, quite hatefully, "Ask Creon; all thy care is for him" (Sophocles, *A*, 437); "Thy choice was to live; mine, to die" (Sophocles, *A*, 438). And finally, a supreme rejection of diaphoric crossings, perhaps the mark of Antigone's *hubris* beyond the impossible crossings between humans and gods: "One world approved thy wisdom; another, mine" (Sophocles, *A*, 438), a repetition of Creon's arrogance, a complete refusal of intermediary figures.

Creon insists on Haemon's obedience to his father's will, cautions him not to "dethrone thy reason for a woman's sake" (Sophocles, *A*, 441), crossing kinship and justice once more, speaks of "the majesty of kindred blood" (Sophocles, *A*, 441). Antigone and Creon share the absoluteness of moral conviction, an arrogance known in Greece as *hubris*, punishable by death. We may remember Oedipus's *hubris*, but also remember his claims to reason, dethroned, we might say, by a woman, his mother. Perhaps none of Creon's advice can be good where we divide the good from bad, justice from injustice, forgetting *diaphora*. Haemon's words in response to Creon's lecture are: "if any man thinks that he alone is wise,—that in speech, or in mind, he hath no peer,—such a soul, when laid open, is ever found empty" (Sophocles, *A*, 442). Except for power and authority, such a rebuke falls equally on Antigone.

Ismene responds to Antigone's scorn with love, mentioned in passing in *Oedipus the King*, now permeating *Antigone* and *Oedipus at Colonus*. Love is an extreme diaphoric crossing, a supreme intermediary figure, a messenger from humans to gods, as Diotima tells us.[19] And perhaps we should think of hope, closely related to love, another intermediary figure that crosses us diaphorically from past to future, from injustice to justice. Perhaps we should remember Teiresias and the other messengers in Greece who travel, together with the oracles, between one city and another, one system of authority to another, from humanity to the divine, and back.

Antigone is no paragon. But she is loved, by Haemon, though her love is directed elsewhere. And she speaks of love. " 'Tis not my nature to join in hating, but in loving" (Sophocles, *A*, 437). Love is diaphoric, frequently destructive, disturbing the hold of Creon's authority over Antigone, destroying his authority through intermediation of his son. Haemon loves Antigone; Creon loves Haemon. These loves reinforce the diaphoric nature of the relation between gods and humans, destructively and constructively.

Love is madness, reminding us of *Phaedrus*, but including the gods (Sophocles, *A*, 445). Love's madness continues at Colonus. I pause diaphorically to touch on suicide, the final diaphoric figure in *Antigone*. For Jocasta kills herself, but Oedipus does not; and Antigone and Haemon both kill themselves, wreaking Creon's destruction. Within the madness of love, perhaps only there, suicide is devastating violence against others as well as oneself. So much philosophic discussion has been devoted to death, the finality and terror of death, that suicide has fallen beneath it, obscured by its finality and terror. Sophocles, I believe, knows that suicide is something other, more than death, something more deeply diaphoric. Not just in choosing what the entire discourse of death chooses to avoid, choosing what cannot be chosen. Instead, facing us in reverse with the impossibility of joining the gods, pursuing the sacred. The reversal is that we can kill ourselves quite easily if that is the thing to do, if as the Chorus says in *Oedipus at Colonus* it were better not to be born, and if born, better to die quickly. "Not to be born is, past all prizing, best; but, when a man hath seen the light, this is next best by far, that with all speed he should go thither, whence he hath come" (Sophocles, *OC*, 654). This is a mostly nondiaphoric reading of the impossible *diaphora* of life and death in the figure of suicide, a chosen death, choosing the impossible as if it were a choice.

Of course, suicide is easy to choose. But is that to choose the impossible, the sacred? It is all too easy. And for Haemon and Antigone, some of that easiness shows. Not for Creon. Their suicide is his disaster. In this diaphoric place, between life and death, suicide is an intermediary figure, not of choosing death over life, but of the possibility of the impossible. From which the Chorus recoils, returning to absolute obedience, the last thing Creon needs to learn. "Wisdom is the supreme part of happiness; and reverence towards the gods must be inviolate. Great words of prideful men are every punished with great blows, and, in old age, teach the chastened to be wise" (Sophocles, *A*, 459). Words of chastened old age bring us to Colonus.

I mentioned that *Oedipus at Colonus* is itself an intermediary figure, between Oedipus's life and his death, between *Oedipus the King* and *Antigone*, coming to pass after the fact. It does not simply lie between the two earlier dramas, but moves onto other realms, yet occupies the space, the time and memory, between them. Between Oedipus's *hubris*, destroying himself and what he holds dear, and Antigone's *hubris*, destroying herself, Creon, and Haemon, perhaps those she does not hold dear, is Oedipus's death, or ascendance, a striking figure of *diaphora*, between mortals and immortals. At Colonus, Oedipus enters an extreme and diaphoric place, close to the gods.

But I am ahead of myself. For Oedipus enters such a diaphoric place at the very beginning, in the sacred place of the Erinyes, belonging to "awful Poseidon" (Sophocles, *OC*, 615). And perhaps we have been waiting for the Furies from the first word of Oedipus's story, waiting for the goddesses of vengeance to tear him limb to limb for a crime far worse than Orestes', not matricide but too great a mother love accompanied by patricide. Another gender crossing, crossed by mother and son and by father and daughter, fulfilled for Antigone finally in suicide, facing the impossibility of the good. And another, from Herodotus, where Oedipus speaks of "the ways of Egypt" where "the men sit weaving in the house, but the wives go forth to win the daily bread" (Sophocles, *OC*, 625). Oedipus knows as deeply as anyone save Teiresias of diaphoric gender crossings.

But for the moment, Oedipus seeks the close of his life, treading on forbidden ground, entering forbidden spaces, seeking to placate the dreaded goddesses, returning to nature and nature's gods. He has forgotten the horror of his crimes, remembers only that he did his best, investing that best with innocence. "And yet in *nature* how was I evil? I, who was but requiting a wrong, so that, had I been acting with knowledge, even then I could not be accounted wicked; but, as it was, all unknowing went I—whither I went—while they who wronged me knowingly sought my ruin" (Sophocles, *OC*, 622).[20] Oedipus must need innocence beyond all accounts. Yet in Greece, innocence does not belong to human beings, who may commit injustice in the best, doing the best. Oedipus does the best he can, the best possible, committing horrifying crimes in his own name and the name of the gods.

I have spoken of curses and plagues as diaphoric figures. Here another, related figure appears, that of supplication. Oedipus and his son, Polyneices, are supplicants before the gods, something neither Oedipus nor Antigone have been before (Sophocles, *OC*, 630, 636, 652). And in supplication, Oedipus offers himself, his body, his corpse as a gift (Sophocles, *OC*, 634). Creon and Polyneices come to gain; Oedipus comes to give, comes to this sacred place of vengeance and justice to give supplication to the gods and the good to Athens. Surrounded by curses and violence, pollution and contamination, by bloodshed, Oedipus comes to give. The story of Oedipus ends in gifts.

He comes to give prosperity to Athens; he gives curses to Creon and Polyneices. But to Ismene and Antigone he brings the gift of love:

> My children, this day ends your father's life. For now all hath perished that was mine, and no more shall ye bear the burden of tending me,—no light one, well I know, my children; yet one little word makes all those toils as nought; *love* had ye from me, as from one beside; and now ye shall have me with you no more, through all your days to come. (Sophocles, *OC*, 664)

But love remains, that one little diaphoric word that makes all the difference between humans and gods. Before curses, bloodshed, and death, love moves without destruction, even before the gods.[21]

Love in kin and kind, beyond kin and kind, care for others, others of our kin and strangers beside, cherishment in the earth, all intermediary figures, all moving, circulating between the one and the other, in the earth. If we do not think that love is the diaphoric figure in which Oedipus passes beyond, we must think either that he passes in his guilt or that the gods come to know his innocence. He did not know; he could not help himself. I take Oedipus to be fully guilty of heinous crimes, but that other crimes do not follow from his own, broken by the diaphoric figures circulating around him, especially figures of his daughters, his kin, and love. Justice and injustice, punishment and reward, all resist diaphoric movements, locking them into praise and blame, requiring mourning.

Mourning is a figure of loss without *diaphora*, or else it is itself diaphoric. With death, and mourning, perhaps without mourning, we confront the great *diaphora* of the impossibility of knowing *diaphora*, holding it firmly in place. No one can mourn for Oedipus without praise and blame, where his life is beyond blame and praise, finally beyond justice and injustice. He is not innocent but guilty. But his guilt touches another good, not the goodness of guilt and innocence.

And with this impossibility of judgment, I bring my discussion of Oedipus to a close, without mourning but filled with *diaphora*, and with love. Returning to art, filled with *diaphora*, and love, and more.

CHAPTER 2

Mimēsis

When Socrates speaks of imitation by art in Books II and III of Plato's *Republic*, he insists that art's responsibility is to tell the truth, while poetry's stories tell one lie after another about the gods, and human beings, and good and bad. The greatest poetry of "Hesiod and Homer and the other poets related to us" (Plato, *Republic*, 377d) tells lies about the gods, but "[t]he true quality of God we must always surely attribute to him whether we compose in epic, melic, or tragic verse" (Plato, *Republic*, 379a).

At the very moment at which we consider poetry for the first time in Socrates' imagined city, we confront the quarrel between *poiēsis* and *technē* in the guise of divine truth, truth about the gods. Do we imagine, in poetry or philosophy, or anywhere else, that the truth of the gods is a truth to be told in *technē*, a truth to be told, to be possessed? Yet that is what Socrates suggests, that a craft exists—we Westerners call it "theology"—that gives us divine truth. Yet we know that divine truth is mad, erotic, otherwise, enigmatic. The truth of the gods is not to be told. The idea of *mimēsis*, imitation by art, is divided under the sign of the quarrel between *poiēsis* and *technē*, and belonging to *technē* lacks all signs of madness and love, lacks every mark of soul, which has care of all things, everywhere and in every place, under the good.

We may choose to recall that Socrates speaks of the lies told by the poets, rejects *mimēsis*, in relation to what he calls a "fevered state," not "the healthy state" described by Glaucon as not even fit for "a city of pigs" (Plato, *Republic*, 372de).[1] For even pigs deserve a city filled with luxuries, with couches and "tables and other furniture, yes, and relishes and myrrh and incense and girls and cakes—all sorts of them" (Plato, *Republic*, 373). And meat. A life fit for human beings must be complex, with the temptations of complexity; a life filled with art.

I pause for a moment to note that this "luxurious state" (Plato, *Republic*, 372e) requires "cattle in large numbers if they are to be eaten" (Plato,

Republic, 373c), demands large territories to feed them, leading to war (Plato, *Republic*, 373de). The city from which art is excluded because of its deceits and disadvantages is a city of war, of injustice, including injustices to animals, herded and eaten, against Socrates' repeated suggestion that the responsibility of shepherds is to the sheep as that of governors to their people. Plato links the uselessness of art to war and the use of animals as food, all under the rule of *technē*.

I say that we may *choose* to recall this setting in thinking of art, because we may choose not to. But if we do so, we will choose at the same time to read Plato "mimetically," not "diegetically," paying attention to form and figure and misdirection rather than to simple narrative (Plato, *Republic*, 393–94). The form of discourse of which Socrates speaks is bound inseparably to the form of the state. Perhaps we may imagine a human life without couches or relishes, without luxuries, without using other creatures to human purposes. In the same way, we may imagine a human life without art, without *mimēsis*, may imagine philosophy without *mimēsis*, without writing. Perhaps we could imagine such a life as human, as good. Perhaps we could not.

What if the demand Socrates imposes, that poetry tell the truth, belonged to this "fevered" rather than "healthy" state, tied inseparably to war? I do not mean that within a sick and luxurious state we must worry about poets' lies. I mean that the demand for truth may belong to a social contract, instituted in a political state, under political requirements, dividing Us from Them, citizens from foreigners, where the call of the good calls us to our own foreignness. In the "healthy" state without poetry, the question of poetic truth does not arise. The suggestion is that truth is subordinate to something political, under the aegis of the good; not that political considerations should lead us to prefer one truth over another, even untruth to truth, but that the question of truth arises in an established ethical and political domain together with the value of art. In the extreme, truth is derivative from the work of the good.

Questions of *poiēsis* and *mimēsis* antedate (in some remarkable way) questions of knowledge and truth. This is a reading of Socrates' claim that knowledge and truth emerge from the idea of the good. The quarrel between poetry and philosophy, between *mimēsis* and *diēgesis*, presupposes the idea of the good, not the superiority of truth. For Socrates is perfectly willing that lies be told, in the service of the state. His words on the subject are incredible, read in any way other than I am reading them, subservient to the good. For it is because "we must surely prize truth most highly" (Plato, *Republic*, 389b) that "the rulers then of the city may, if anybody, fitly lie on account of enemies or citizens for the benefit of the state; no others may have anything to do with it" (Plato, *Republic*, 389c). Truth is a high value under the governance of the good, but not superior to the good of the state. *Mimēsis* appears in this space between the truth and the good, closer to the latter than the former.

We may choose to retreat further in our reading of Book II, recalling two moments of Book I. One is expressed by Thrasymachus, accusing Socrates of force: "you won't get the better of me by stealth and, failing stealth, you are not of the force to beat me in the debate" (Plato, *Republic*, 341b), followed by the complaint, "And how am I to persuade you? he said. If you are not convinced by what I just now was saying, what more can I do for you? Shall I take the argument and ram it into your head?" (Plato, *Republic*, 345bc). I read this as suggesting that the reason Socrates employs against Thrasymachus is to be understood as force, that Socrates does beat Thrasymachus, beats him up, triumphs in the quarrel, in an act of violence. Reason's truth is not outside violence, but exists in violent quarrel, turns *diaphora* into *polemos*. Moreover, it imposes its will on others, demanding as Socrates does of Thrasymachus, that they fight on reason's terms.[2] Finally, Thrasymachus withdraws, not because reason's truth is better, but not to give offense. "Revel in your discourse, he said, without fear, for I shall not oppose you, so as not to offend your partisans here" (Plato, *Republic*, 352b). I add that Thrasymachus was regarded as a much less threatening figure to Athens than Socrates himself.

The second point in Book I to which we may return frames the central project of the dialogue concerning what justice *(dikē)* is and what good it serves. For Thrasymachus speaks of justice as the "advantage of the stronger" (Plato, *Republic*, 338c). Adeimantus and Glaucon ask Socrates to show that justice is more advantageous, more profitable, than injustice (Plato, *Republic*, 362bd) *in itself*, imagining a social contract in which the state imposes punishments on those who commit acts of injustice, thereby making it unprofitable (Plato, *Republic*, 359ab). I suggest the possibility that the entire *Republic* is framed around the question of the advantage and profitability of justice, understanding these to belong to *technē*. In this light, when Socrates proposes creating a city (Plato, *Republic*, 369c), he is reinstating a social contract based on advantage and profit. And that is how he defines the fundamental principle of his state, the principle that he later equates with justice: "more things are produced, and better and more easily when one man performs one task according to his nature, at the right moment, and at leisure from other occupations" (Plato, *Republic*, 370c). This is an argument exclusively from *technē*.

I would recall that *Symposium* ends with Socrates arguing that the same person may write comedy and tragedy (Plato, *Symposium*, 223d), although he argues in Book III, based on this principle of *technē*, that no one can succeed in both tragedy and comedy (Plato, *Republic*, 395a). I would recall that in *Phaedrus*, Lysias's speech and Socrates' first speech both defend the advantage to the beloved of accepting a nonlover as a lover. Socrates replies that such a view is blasphemy. Love is not something sought for advantage and profit, not pursued as *technē*, but something between humans and gods. And so must justice be. And art. But the good and truth of which Socrates speaks in Books II and III of *Republic* belong to *technē*.

In this light, the entire argument of *Republic* is to be read as an argument from *technē*, all the way through to Book X, when the lyric poets are allowed to return, and we encounter the myth of Er, where we see profit and advantage still at work, but framed by something other, the beauty of the good. The state Socrates describes, built on a single virtue, is framed from beginning to end by advantage, profit. Eating meat can be justified solely under the heading of human profit. Perhaps. But not, perhaps, in relation to the good. Justice is what profits the state and profits the soul. Yet the good that gives birth to truth and knowledge cannot be their profit, must be the life of the soul that stands on the back of the world with the gods and beholds their beauty. We are responsible for justice not because it is profitable but called by something different, something beautiful, that allows us to judge profit and loss where they are absent or obscure, something touched by *erōs* and *poiēsis*.

The city Socrates describes is a state under a social contract, built on advantage, within a restricted economy, suggesting that the truth and justice he describes and their privileges are given their force by that contract. The privilege of truth is granted by the state under a social contract. We begin with the state to establish its rule over justice and truth, and especially over art and poetry, *technē*'s rule over *poiēsis*. But that rule presupposes something other, touched by *poiēsis*, something spoken of only where the good rules over knowledge and truth, rules as the sun casts its light on mundane things.

From the beginning, the critique of *mimēsis* represents the authority of a good that belongs to *technē*, does the work of the state, within repeated memories of something—Socrates speaks of the good—that gives rise to *technē*'s authority. The critique of art arises in memory of an immemorial *poiēsis* that can never be ruled by *technē*, yet repeats itself endlessly as *mimēsis*. The possibility of a truth of *mimēsis* and the good that knows nothing of *technē*, of work, a truth that belongs to the gods and the good, echoes unsaid, unspoken, everywhere within this account. For what comes from the gods is erotic, mad, heterogeneous; and so with it must be its truth and its imitations. Truth and representation are mad, erotic, burdened by impossible responsibilities under the good to resist injustice, where every work under *technē* institutes injustice.

Socrates suggests that poetic *mimēsis* fails to give us the truth of the gods, divine truth, as if philosophy, or politics, or theology gave us that truth. Yet no one more than Plato expresses the failure of such a view of philosophy, without *erōs*, a politics without divine madness, or a theology that would seize the gods under the hold of *technē*. No one more than Plato and, at least somewhat, at times, the Aristotle who is more typically read as entirely subservient to *technē*, to the mundane, except in touches of something otherwise, the unmoved mover or active *nous*.

Socrates' account begins with the truth of the gods, the truth we seek to tell about the gods, their virtues, their truths and lies. Are we to forget Dionysus, with his masks, the god who lies? To forget the other Greek gods, who lie, and cheat, and deceive each other and human beings, and who in their masks and deceptions and madnesses reveal something of the good unknown to *technē?* Socrates says that it is untrue that gods war with gods (Plato, *Republic*, 378bc); untrue that the good is cause of all things, beneficent and ill (Plato, *Republic*, 379c); untrue that the gods disguise themselves as mortals (Plato, *Republic*, 381d); untrue that unjust human beings may be happy, just humans wretched (Plato, *Republic*, 392b). Rather, "God is altogether simple and true in deed and word, and neither changes himself nor deceives others by visions or words or the sending of signs in waking or in dreams" (Plato, *Republic*, 382e). Divine care for all things, animate and inanimate, erotic madness, divine *poiēsis*, all intermediary figures are set aside. Shall we suppose that this vision of the gods wars with the visions of *Symposium* and *Phaedrus?* On my reading, such a war belongs to *technē*, for conflict and opposition, categories and distinctions, domination and rule, all bear upon *technē*. The simplicity and truth of the divine are its madness and heterogeneity. Divine madness, of the bees and cicadas, is something else, something otherwise. The gods always appear to us in madness, in our madness, and as mad, erotic, otherwise. The appearance of the gods, and the good, is a madness. That is what Socrates says:

> If a man, then, it seems, who was capable by his cunning of assuming every kind of shape and imitating all things should arrive in our city, bringing with himself the poems which he wished to exhibit, we should fall down and worship him as a holy and wondrous and delightful creature, but should say to him that there is no man of that kind among us in our city, nor is it lawful for such a man to arise among us, and we should send him away to another city, after pouring myrrh down over his head and crowning him with fillets of wood, but we ourselves, for our souls' good, should continue to employ the more austere and less delightful poet and taleteller, who would imitate the diction of the good man and would tell his tale in the patterns which we prescribed in the beginning, when we set out to educate our soldiers. (Plato, *Republic*, 398ab)

Socrates chooses to restrict his politics for the moment to *technē*, leaving aside the gods, leaving aside all holy and wondrous and delightful creatures who deserve to be crowned with myrrh and wood. Socrates abandons the gods at this moment in his discussion, as if we might choose to build a city without divine inspiration, alienating the gods. Can we doubt for a moment that when we exile the poets we exile the gods, and with them the good, the beautiful, the true, that the norms that insist that we choose *techne*'s truth over lies give up every relation to the good, to the sacred, and the divine? It is no coincidence that in this discussion in Books II and III, Socrates speaks of the poets speaking of the gods as lies, but offers no other truth, does not himself speak of the gods in simple narration, but employs simple narration to speak of human beings.[3] What greater sin than thinking that we could bring the gods before us without masks, overcoming their obscurity, making them available to our use?[4]

And here we find *mimēsis*, divided between *poiēsis* and *technē*. *Mimēsis* circulates everywhere, joined with *poiēsis*, separated from *diēgesis* in the diaphoric movement instituting philosophy, separating philosophy from art. Speaking, knowing, being are mimetic, masked, obscured, forgotten, diaphoric. Art knows this as beauty, given in the name of the good. Philosophy seems not to know it, though I insist that it knows it obliquely in relation to the good or the divine. We must avoid instituting another opposition between gods and human beings, sacred and mundane, where *mimēsis* breaks off from its other within an opposition belonging to *technē*. Instead, *mimēsis* and *poiēsis* are intermediary figures, constantly in motion between heaven and earth, sacred and mundane, constantly disturbing us and our work with madness and heterogeneity. And so with *technē*. The call of the good bears upon the idea of imitation, in *technē*, keeping them madly in motion, circulating against the authority of any categorial opposition.

The truth of the gods, under *technē*, is a truth that opposes falsehood, belonging to theology, the science of the divine. The truth of the gods under the good is erotic, mad, disturbed, displaced, otherwise, as the gods are otherwise, where this otherwise does not inhabit another opposition, but haunts every opposition, interrupting its authority. The truth of narrative, of diction, repeats this nonoppositional pairing of work and unwork in relation to *mimēsis*. For Socrates distinguishes simple narration, *diēgesis*, from narration by imitation as if the person named were speaking, alternating speeches as if the protagonists were speaking, and names this diction *mimēsis* (Plato, *Republic*, 393c).

We know that such an account of *mimēsis* names a sin that poetry, that writing, cannot avoid—though lyric poetry comes closest to eluding it, written in the poet's voice, and dramatic poetry is most guilty of it. We know that Plato never composed a work in other than a mimetic narrative voice, speakers alternating in dramatic form, heightened in poetic extremity by references to stories told of old, heard elsewhere, repeated in mimetic voice. If this *mimēsis* is a crime, then Plato composed nothing free from offense. We continually repeat, in the voice of opposition, the opposition between *poiēsis* and *technē*, where opposition belongs to *technē*, leaving the divinity of the gods aside, forgetting everything otherwise. I am struggling to resist this opposition without instituting another.

The simple narrative voice, as Socrates describes it—and Plato offers many descriptions of narrative in the dialogues, many following oral histories, many recalling the transition from oral narrative to writing—is the sober, somber voice of *technē*, doing good work, but in that voice lacks all memory of divine inspiration, erotic madness, in that voice lacks life. The narrative voice described by Socrates does the work of *technē*, as good philosophy should do, but throughout Plato's writings works in memory of that which gives life to that work, something otherwise, unlike, diaphoric but not oppositional. In this sense, *mimēsis* bears in its voice something close to Ion's madness, divine inspiration, something of a divine truth, erotic madness, the terrors and glories of Dionysus and Pharmakeia, which simple *diēgesis* has forgotten, but without which it tells no truth, knows nothing of the good. Poetic *mimēsis* does not imitate in the name of a truth that might be presented without *mimēsis*, a missing object whose lack we would hope to overcome. We do not in poetry imitate to make the absent present, but to present something in the object that is absent, otherwise, that could not be otherwise made present. I think of it as the good.

Something of this understanding can be heard in Derrida. For imitation is repetition joined with representation, both brought by him under the sign of iterability. In art, we do not imitate to bring the original before us again as it might be without imitation. We do not seek to restore the origin. But we seek, instead, as Derrida argues repeatedly (but always differently) to imitate such that the imitation exists as imitation, in art, to retain its truth as representation, keeping a memory of both the origin and its impossibility. All of this under the call of the good. For he speaks of it in the context of justice and violence:

> Iterability requires the origin to repeat itself originarily, to alter itself so as to have the value of origin, that is, to conserve itself. Right away there are police and the police legislate, not content to enforce a law that would have had no force before the police. This iterability inscribes conservation in the essential structure of foundation. (Derrida, *FL*, 43)

Mimēsis links with iterability, always original, always originary, as imitation, founding and conserving. The other—that is, the original—shows itself as imitation, in both *mimēsis* and *diēgesis*. And the imitation shows itself, as well, as if it were original.

Mimēsis, here, bears no opposition to *diēgesis*, any more than the origin opposes the repetition in iteration, but reminds us of the impossibility of imitation without origination. Iterability implies that the imitation repeats the originating, as if original, in that sense conserving, as imitation. In this sense, simple narrative, *diēgesis*, is as mimetic as any *mimēsis*, as heterogeneous, and all imitations in their repetitions originate and repeat the originating movement. Perhaps this is what Socrates opposes, but at most on one side, the side in which *mimēsis* passes itself off as the original. The other side, in which the origin imitates, in which the origin dissolves, entails that the truest philosophy, the truest truth, is mimetic—that is, in Plato's language, divine, mad, erotic, diaphoric: the truth of the gods; the heterogeneous truth of the good. The nonoriginary disturbs the origin; the origin disturbs the imitation. The good madly disturbs, circulates, every thought, truth, representation.

And that is the point of the ruler's lies. For although the ruler as ruler presumes to rule out all other lies, the ruler can rule only by lying. The masks of truth come to it as gifts from the good, dwelling in beauty (Plato, *Republic*, 402). The gift of the good calls us to beauty, even within the rule of the state. I suggest that our response to this call is what we call *mimēsis*.

This opens the door to Pandora's box of mimetic figures, all madly circulating, exceeding any attempt at control. For the story of Pandora is a story of mad energies and circulations, an account of general economy in which all rules of restricted economy collapse. Here *mimēsis* represents not the lies against which truth is marshaled, but the untruths, strangenesses, masks, deceptions, madnesses, within every truth, including Plato's and the ruler's. This is the Pandora's box mentioned in *Philebus*: "flinging open the doors and allow[ing] every sort of knowledge to stream in, the inferior mingling with the pure?" (Plato, *Philebus*, 62de), all intermediary figures. The door opens onto endless intermediary figures that circulate madly and erotically without a home or place, always displaced, always moving, like women, who Irigaray tells us, have no place, but are place for men, but who in this role displace every place for men. It is no coincidence that Pandora is a woman, opening multiple interruptions toward the good in the remainder of this chapter:

> If, traditionally, and as a mother, woman represents *place* for man, such a limit means that she becomes *a thing*, with some possibility of change from one historical period to another. She finds herself delineated as a thing. Moreover, the maternal-feminine also serves as an *envelope*, a *container*, the starting point from which man limits his things. . . .
>
> The maternal-feminine remains the *place separated from "its" own place*, deprived of "its" place. (Irigaray, *ESD*, 10)

Clément says something similar, if more devastating, about the ambiguity of women's place:

> This feminine role, the role of sorceress, of hysteric, is ambiguous, antiestablishment, and conservative at the same time. Antiestablishment because the symptoms—the attacks—revolt and shake up the public, the group, the men, the others to whom they are exhibited. The sorceress heals, against the Church's canon; she performs abortions, favors nonconjugal love, converts the unlivable space of a stifling Christianity. The hysteric unties familiar bonds, introduces disorder into the well-regulated unfolding of everyday life, gives rise to magic in ostensible reason. These roles are *conservative* because every sorceress ends up being destroyed, and nothing is registered of her but mythical traces. Every hysteric ends up inuring others to her symptoms, and the family closes around her again, whether she is curable or incurable. (Clément, *GO*, 5)

Woman, as sorceress or hysteric, as woman, is an ambiguous, intermediary figure, heterogeneous and alien, a figure of radical displacement and of destruction. The injustice that Irigaray and Clément protest is the endless destruction of women. If intermediary figures touch the mad, erotic, dark side of life, endlessly repeated injustices are imposed on women as women, have historically been and continue to be imposed on Jews, and others, aftermaths of slavery and colonization. Intermediary figures occupy multiply ambiguous places, displacing the hold of the limits, boundaries, identities of places, resisting being situated as a mundane thing, disturbing restricted and exchange economies of identity and place with displacements, disturbances, gifts of the good. Intermediary figures work under the hold of domination and oppression, within the mundane, to the point of the destruction of one kind of human being after another, foreigners within us and surrounding us: Jews, women, Africans, Muslims, indigenous peoples, one kind of creature after another, animals, plants, forests, plains.

And so with art, and with *mimēsis*, intermediary figures of disturbance, given from the good, in mundane experience repeatedly held in the grip of one political power after another that would destroy it for conflicting reasons, one because it is held in that grip, art under control of the state, another because it moves too quickly, reminds us of the good, disturbs the authority of the state. Art does not alone nor more powerfully disturb the place of reason's authority, but in the name of *mimēsis* is the recurrent symbol, figure, of intermediary movements given from the good, resistant to authority, resistant to the institution of identities and places that would exclude the strange and foreign in the name of the good.

Art resists identity's exclusion in response to the call of the good because art remains strange, alien and foreign, reminds us of heterogeneity and others even when under the domination of the state. Indeed, art always remains strange in the institution of public policies, remains face to face with strangeness. This is as true of familiar village and tribal art as of strange, erotic, and expressive art in institutionally regulated societies. Public officials hope to regulate the production of art as they would regulate the flow of foreigners in their midst, with their strange words, customs, and values. Yet the highest borders in the contemporary state do not keep out strangers, the most coercive measures do not silence artists, and the most familiar movements do not abolish the strangeness of art. Strangeness, foreignness, alterity circulate among us, exceeding every restricted economy:

> the Other falls out of the starry sky. . . . (Irigaray, *SOW*, 136)

> the foreigner lives within us; he is the hidden face of our identity, the space that wrecks our abode, the time in which understanding and affinity founder. By recognizing him in ourselves, we are spared detesting him in himself. (Kristeva, *SO*, 1)

Perhaps. Or perhaps we detest both ourselves and others. But such a hatred, like it or not, belongs to the good, comes from the good, circulates as the gift of the other within us that resists the Same.

I speak of this gift as art. Art and *mimēsis* haunt the world of the familiar state, of *technē* and work, with memories and insistences of others. I think of paintings from Picasso's *Guernica* to Magritte's *The Human Condition*, writings from Kafka to Borges. The stranger within us reminds us of the other. The stranger around us insists on being the other, from Antigone to Rabbit. The other is the gift brought to us from the good, bearing upon us endless responsibility to the good, to the other, witness to heterogeneity, to the *différend*, to the inhuman. The other, witnessed in art, and elsewhere, witnesses its own betrayal, inhumanity, heterogeneity, strangeness.

Mimēsis is the strangeness, first in narrative, in *diēgesis*—that is, in language—then as art in all human work, in *technē* everywhere in human life and every limit and boundary, in every restricted economy of identities and kinds throughout nature, circulating everywhere as the good. This strangeness, marked for us, as Kristeva says, by the foreigner who lives beside us, is within us. The strangeness of *diēgesis* is revealed within by *mimēsis* besides, wherever we are, everywhere in nature, in language and everywhere as art. The strangeness of thought, life, and representation is revealed within by art besides, otherwise. The familiarity of *mimēsis*, in metaphor and other figuration, reveals the alienness of the nonmetaphorical, its impossibility and its strangeness. The familiarity of art is the work of strangeness within every judgment and in every place.

Here we may wish to come to terms with the relics in our contemporary world of what passed in Kant, and before and after, as "art for art's sake," as if the sake of art were art alone—some say it is; as if the sake of art were independent of the good; and as if the sake of art were not strange. My exploration here is the pursuit of a thought of the good for whose sake we bear responsibilities, enacted in judgment.

We respond to gifts from the good where every work is performed for the sake of something, but not always something known, familiar, or given antecedently, but something disclosed in the performance, unknown from beginning to end, excessive, mad, strange. If art were for art's sake, and we took that sake as seriously as it deserves to be taken—that is, as a gift imposing endless responsibilities upon us, calling upon us to respond—then art might be for art's sake because art bore the endless burden of heterogeneity. I do not say this, do not pursue this line of thought, because I wish to understand art in service to the good, where that good sets no norms, but calls, silently or aloud, to our obsessions. And what has been more obsessive for us than art?

These questions lead to Kant and his predecessors and successors, lead to a later chapter. I wish to sidestep Kant for a chapter or two to examine the force of the sake of art, in memory of the good, but also in memory of the strangeness and madness of *mimēsis*, in every place. I put my concern forthrightly: Why might we think that art could have nothing to do with the demands of heterogeneity when nothing is more heterogeneous than art?

I have Kierkegaard and Levinas in mind, both of whom reject art and the aesthetic in the name of the good. And in reverse, I have Whitehead in mind for whom the intrinsic reality of things is their value: each precious beyond price. In the reality of things is ideality (Whitehead, *PR*, 83–84); things exist for the sake of intensity of feeling (Whitehead, *PR*, 27); intensity of feeling responds to contrasts, and contrasts of contrasts, endlessly, to the play of synthesis and heterogeneity, realized as beauty, expressed in art, the joy we know in responding to the good, through art.[5] It is the ecstasy I understand as given by *mimēsis*. The good in things, their intrinsic reality, is their heterogeneity within the synthesis we think of as *mimēsis*. Heterogeneity demands mimetic displacement. Heterogeneity brings upon us a heterogeneous joy, the ecstasy of the other, called in French *jouissance*.

I am concerned at the moment with the critique of art as mimetic displacement, taking us away from the good we must choose over evil. First, let us consider an account of the aesthetic that claims to lead us away from the good, away from the ethical, in the name of heterogeneity. I have in mind Bullough's account of art, a famous account of the distance that separates art from life, an account of "the aesthetic," which I understand as the conception of art that refuses its relation to the good while at the same time it exhibits that relation. Kant is the major figure in this refusal; Bullough is among its most persuasive exemplars.

In Kant's words, expressed in the first moment of the beautiful: *"Taste is the faculty of judging of an object or a method of representing it by an entirely disinterested satisfaction or dissatisfaction.* The object of such satisfaction is called *beautiful"* (Kant, *CJ*, § 45, 45; Ross, *AIS*, 103). In Bullough's words:

> As a rule, experience constantly turns the same side towards us, namely, that which has the strongest practical force of appeal. We are not ordinarily aware of those aspects of things which do not touch us immediately and practically, nor are we generally conscious of impressions apart from our own self which is impressed. The sudden view of things from their reverse, usually unnoticed, side, comes upon us as a revelation, and such revelations are precisely those of Art. In this most general sense, Distance is a factor in all Art. (Bullough, *PD;* Ross, *AIS*, 460)

Psychic or aesthetic distance disengages the practical side of our experience, distances us from things which touch us immediately and practically, disengages us from feeling, suffering or joy. If we identify, as Bullough does, the ethical with the practical, then the aesthetic disengages the ethical and sets it at a distance. My entire discussion has been based on returning to a thought and relation to the good that bears no distance from the ethical, does not, cannot, "disengage" it, yet which is not the practical, binary side of ethical life, but challenges, displaces, and disrupts the hold of the binaries of practical experience. Here art touches the good, not with distance or opposition, but with something excessive, strange, in the practical, interested side of experience. What Kant calls *disinterested* is ethical, understood as given from the good. The idea of "art for art's sake" is an ambiguous interpretation of art's difference. I have understood "art's sake" as ethical, diaphoric, as interrupting the movement of practical goods in memory of something immeasurable, of the good.

Bullough's appeal is to define the unmistakable *diaphora* between art and practical judgment in terms of the almost tangible and vivid figure of distance, albeit entirely mimetic. And perhaps we may understand the mimetic nature of the spatial figure that expresses the *diaphora* that defines art as repeating the strangeness of *mimēsis*. Art is strange; art touches the strangeness of practical, ethical life with a difference I have associated with the good, but in any case one that bears the burden of sacred, immemorial, immeasurable gifts. The difference of art, its strangeness, appears in Plato as *mimēsis*, disturbing the even flow of every narrative, interrupting *diēgesis* with its difference. And so I have pursued the thought into Bullough of the mimetic, metaphorical site where art's *diaphora* shows itself.

Bullough speaks of the paradox of art, "the antinomy of Distance" (Bullough, *PD;* Ross, *AIS*, 462): "What is therefore, both in appreciation and production, most desirable is the *utmost decrease of Distance without its disappearance*" (Bullough, *PD*; Ross, *AIS*, 463). The difference—"Distance"—of art from practical experience, from *diēgesis*, must become as small as possible without disappearing. I read Bullough as saying, almost explicitly, if without the language to do so, that aesthetic or psychic distance has no measure, that the difference between art and the good is immeasurable, but is nevertheless a difference beyond all differences. The difference between the good and the binary oppositions of good and evil is immeasurable, unlimited, beyond the very large and very small, but is displacement, disturbance nevertheless. The good interrupts the practical; art interrupts the practical in memory of the good; *mimēsis* interrupts the narrative flow of *diēgesis*; immeasure interrupts the calculations of measure. Again, this is close to what Bullough explicitly says. "To say that Art is anti-realistic simply insists upon the fact that Art is not nature, never pretends to nature and strongly resists any confusion with nature" (Bullough, *PD*; Ross, *AIS*, 467).

Writing in 1912, Bullough had little sense of the impact of modernism, where art would pretend to be nature, would insist on being taken for nature, all at the same time claiming to be art. I take him to be saying that art is mimetic even when naturalistic, that art must call attention to itself as *mimēsis* to be art, call attention to its interruptive, disorderly, masked, and excessive side, no matter how realistic it is, must interrupt nature with *mimēsis*. And in doing so, in interrupting nature with representation, art reveals that nature and representation were always interrupted, diaphoric. The possibility of this interruption, imposing obligations and responsibilities, is given from the good. Art does not interrupt the flow of judgment to be art. That is what Bullough says, but it is too restrictive. Art shows the flow of nature and judgment to be interrupted by something excessive, shows the general economy whose gifts displace every restricted economy. The reason for this is that art can do its work anywhere and everywhere, bears responsibility in every place to interrupt and displace that place. Art gives the good in every place, and is given from the good to every place.

With this understanding that the displacement of art from practice is a displacement of the hold of *technē*, within *technē* from the start, given as the circulation of gifts whose movement *technē* hopes to hold up, to stop, but whose unrestricted movement *technē* presupposes, art reveals something in practice that practice strives to halt, but which practice needs for its work. In this sense, for *technē* to secure the binary oppositions of good and evil, that which many people claim is the good toward which they hope to work, would be to end ethical judgment and to give up ethical responsibility. This is Nietzsche's message, that the responsibility we bear toward the good is a responsibility to revalue, transvalue, to exceed every value. To work within the hold of instituted values is to give up responsibility for the good. That is why the traditional Western understanding of Socrates and Christ, perhaps of every world-historical religious figure, in the name of God institutes an event of cosmic ethical proportions founding an ethical order beyond all prior ethical orders, bound by a responsibility beyond measure. Within the instituted order, such a responsibility appears to abandon ethical responsibility. Dostoevsky touches on this in *The Brothers Karamazov* in the name of the Grand Inquisitor: the freedom from which the Grand Inquisitor would save his people is the responsibility toward the good without which they cannot be ethical, cannot be free. No one can be ethical for another, can take responsibility for another. The place where we encounter this truth most fully is in art—for example, in *The Brothers Karamazov*. It is a truth that insists on *mimēsis* for its expression.

With this understanding, we may now turn to other extraordinary struggles against *mimēsis*, extraordinary, like Plato's, because within the critique of *mimēsis* in the name of the good, Kierkegaard and Levinas both recognize that the good can appear only mimetically—that is, disruptively—as if mad, insane. They write madly, figuratively, interrupting the flow of philosophical discourse; yet they resist the disruptiveness of art, perhaps because they find it too smooth, resisting interruption. This, more than anything Bullough says, is the paradox of art. For he understands art to interrupt the circulation of practical experience. The paradox of art is that somehow, within its interruptions and displacements, it smooths out the interruptions it imposes in memory of the good. Perhaps, in Nietzsche's terms, Apollo triumphs in art. Perhaps, instead, nothing in or out of art can remove the Dionysian side of *mimēsis*. The strangeness of art is its *mimēsis*; the interruptions of *mimēsis* are gifts from the good.

Kierkegaard speaks of the aesthetic in two ways, one related to the sensuous, the genius and spirituality of music:

> The genius of sensuousness is hence the absolute subject of music. In its very essence sensuousness is absolutely lyrical, and in music it breaks forth in all its lyrical impatience. It is, namely, spiritually determined, and is, therefore, force, life, movement, constant unrest, perpetual succession; but this unrest, this succession, does not enrich it, it remains always the same, it does not unfold itself, but it storms uninterruptedly forward as if in a single breath. (Kierkegaard, *E/O* I, 70)

This panegyric to music must be heard in its fullness. Music is absolutely lyrical, absolute genius, spiritually determined and in perpetual movement. But it does not unfold, interrupts nothing, keeps moving as if in a single breath. The aesthetic presents itself as spirit itself, but not as interruption, not as the movement of individual spirituality. And this is an absolute difference. At least, that is what Kierkegaard says repeatedly: "It is incumbent upon me to examine dialectically the part played by concealment in aesthetics and ethics, for the point is to show the absolute difference between the aesthetic concealment and the paradox [of Abraham, beyond the ethical]" (Kierkegaard, *FT*, 94).[6] This difference is absolute, not diaphoric.

Kierkegaard links the ethical to the aesthetic, finds Abraham's faith beyond the ethical within an absolute difference with the aesthetic. Before I examine this absolute difference, replaying the *diaphora* between art and philosophy, I will pursue the understanding of this conflict in spiritual and sensual terms. For in the glowing account he gives of music, Kierkegaard rejects the possibility that the sensuality of music might be ethical, and does so by denying that the sensuality—the mimetic side—of music might interrupt the relation of the individual to itself. The interruption is spiritual.

We find something similar in Levinas:

> Art is the pre-eminent exhibition in which the said is reduced to a pure theme, to absolute exposition, even to shamelessness capable of holding all looks for which it is exclusively destined. The said is reduced to the Beautiful, which supports Western ontology . . .
>
> In the inexhaustible diversity of works, that is, in the *essential renewal* of art, colors, forms, sounds, words, buildings—already on the verge of being identified as entities, already disclosing their nature and their qualities in the substantives that bear adjectives—recommence being. (Levinas, *OB*, 40).

In art, the interruption of the good is reduced to theme, to pure presentation, to being without interruption. Levinas does not speak of the sensuousness of art, but of its appearance, its presentation: exposition, looks, colors, forms, sounds and tone, of the beautiful. But he does speak of sensuousness in a profoundly contaminated form:

> But is not the diachrony of the inspiration and expiration separated by the instant that belongs to an animality? Would animality be the openness upon the beyond essence? But perhaps animality is only the soul's still being too short of breath. . . . Is man not the living being capable of the longest breath in inspiration, without a stopping point, and in expiration, without return? (Levinas, *OB*, 181–82)

The diachrony of the good, the interruption of being, is the breath of spirit, said to be impossible for animals and even for human animality. The sensuousness of art belongs to the assembling of being. The materiality of human and animal bodies belongs to the assembling of being. Art does not interrupt the flow of being, nor does embodiment. The face of the other is never an embodied face, as the gift of the hand is never two embodied hands.[7]

All this is to enforce the link between *mimēsis* and embodiment as the basis of the absolute difference between the aesthetic and ethical. The sensuousness of bodies disqualifies them from the good. The sensuousness of *mimēsis* disqualifies it from ethics. The striking mark of this disqualification is that it has traditionally excluded women and animals from ethical consideration. I have replied that the interruption of the good bears the burden of responsibility toward others, of different kinds, including women and minorities, and animals, and other creatures, throughout nature. The ethical contamination of *mimēsis* constantly repeats acts of exclusion and domination, even in Kierkegaard and Levinas, who come as close to the good as any Western philosopher.

The good appears as interruption and exposure. These are Levinas's terms, and I take them seriously. The good interrupts the hold of categories of domination and exclusion by an infinite exposure to the heterogeneity of others, which I associate with different kinds, not with individuals alone. This marks a major departure from Kierkegaard and Levinas, for whom the individual subject is the exclusive site of the good. And perhaps this individual subject is a repetition of the abyss between mind and body, spirit and embodiment: the absolute, individual subject who is like others when embodied, who disappears in animals and other "lower" creatures. I respond that materiality, animality, and sexual difference interrupt the hold of spirituality with heterogeneity. In other words, heterogeneity, alterity, relations to others, belong to kinds, not to singular individuals.

This topic requires detailed exploration, in relation to Kierkegaard especially, but also Levinas. I will return to it momentarily. But I have passed over a side of Kierkegaard's treatment of art and the aesthetic closely related to this topic. And I have passed over with but casual mention Kierkegaard's devotion to the absolute difference between art and ethics. It is, I believe, closely related to the idea of the absolute difference said to be ethics, represented in the choice he describes as *either/or*: not between good and evil, but between ethics and nonethics. "My either/or does not in the first instance denote the choice between good and evil; it denotes the choice whereby one chooses good *and* evil/or excludes them" (Kierkegaard, *E/O*, II, 173). He goes on to say that "the man who chooses good and evil chooses the good" (Kierkegaard, *E/O*, II, 173); and understands this in a Hegelian movement despite his differences with Hegel: "He who chooses the ethical chooses the good, but here the good is entirely abstract, only its being is posited, and hence it does not follow by any means that the chooser cannot in turn choose the evil" (Kierkegaard, *E/O*, II, 173).

This account is close to my understanding of the good, shows a striking awareness that the ethical is beyond good and evil at the same time that it enables judgment of good and evil. Kierkegaard forcefully reaches toward the good. And yet his understanding betrays it in one way after another, betrays it while it displays it. And perhaps that is all we can expect of any understanding of the good: to reach for it, to respond to its call, by betrayal. For the witness is a traitor.

In the first instance, Kierkegaard continues to work in Hegel's shadow, continues the spiritual line of thought brought to fruition in Hegel, pursues the dialectic of universal and particular, if at least one step beyond Hegel. In this dialectic of spirit, materiality is ethical only spiritualized, and spirit is ethical only universalized, even where the individual is higher than the universal. Art's sensuousness betrays it, drags it down to a lower stage of the dialectic, prevents it from passing through the universal. More of that in a moment.

In the second instance, Kierkegaard marks an absolute difference between the aesthetic and ethical, more accurately, reveals the ethical only in a movement in which the aesthetic and ethical are in closest proximity within what he calls an absolute difference. In all his writing on the ethical, the aesthetic haunts every stage, every moment, passes for the ethical, passes by the ethical in a proximity so close that every measure must be taken, every precaution, to mark an absolute difference between them. Here, the aesthetic is as close as possible to the good but absolutely different.

How are we to understand this closest proximity except diaphorically? How are we to understand the successive moments of a dialectic that would mark an absolute difference but finds that it must continue to re-mark this difference endlessly? I would recall that Heidegger marks another absolute difference, a difference "by an abyss of essence" between the human hand and animal paws, claws, and fangs.[8] In this infinite difference between the Human and the Animal, we find a closest proximity, between humanity and animality, between the gift of language and the gift of embodiment. I read these as given from the good. And similarly, where Heidegger marks an infinite space between *Dasein*'s neutrality and sexual difference,[9] Derrida finds another closest proximity.

Kierkegaard finds that the ethical—our relation to the good and God—demands that we pass through a gap that is infinitely wide and at the same time so small that it requires marking and re-marking again and again. The aesthetic is infinitely close to the ethical and infinitely far. Art is as close as possible to the good and different by an abyss. Why, I ask, not understand that art is given by the good as difference, interruption, *diaphora*, and that a good without art, an ethics uninterrupted by art, cannot bear the mark of the good? Art is given by the good, a gift of and from the good, in its difference with the good, as interruption. Difference, interruption, heterogeneity, all are the gifts of the good.

Kierkegaard understands the ethical, the gift of the good, in an infinitely close proximity to art, and resists that proximity by an act of exclusion, excluding the aesthetic from the good. Heidegger understands The Human as bearing the gift of language, given from Being, in an infinitely close proximity to the body, The Human Body, and resists that proximity by an act of exclusion, excluding animals from the gift of Being. He also understands *Dasein*'s neutrality as opening onto Being, bearing the gift of thought and care, in so close a proximity to sexual difference, to love, and to *Geschlecht*, to humankind, that he must exclude that sexual difference from *Dasein*'s fundamental essence. To all these exclusions I respond that the call of the good is inclusion, that the differences marked by exclusion belong to the good as differences, heterogeneity, marked by the madness and *erōs* of art. Here art and the aesthetic bear the gift of the good as a call to beauty, and beyond. The infinitely close proximity of beauty to the good marks them both with their difference, but not with exclusion.

I have said that Kierkegaard repeatedly, almost endlessly, traces the infinite proximity between the aesthetical and the ethical, beauty and the good, as if this proximity required unending vigilance toward a difference that might vanish were we to falter. In *Fear and Trembling*, of the three problemata of the paradox of faith, one is devoted entirely to the proximity of aesthetics and ethics.

> Aesthetics permitted, yea, required of the individual silence, when he knew that by keeping silent he could save another. This is already sufficient proof that Abraham does not lie within the circumference of aesthetics. His silence has by no means the intention of saving Isaac, and in general his whole task of sacrificing Isaac for his own sake and for God's sake is an offense to aesthetics, for aesthetics can well understand that I sacrifice myself, but not that I sacrifice another for my own sake. (Kierkegaard, *FT*, 121–22)

I respond that the aesthetic has no such limits, perhaps no limits at all, or of this kind. Art takes upon itself, especially in our century but at all times and everywhere as well, the task of expressing the inexpressible, at least what is inexpressible in any other way. Perhaps aesthetics cannot *understand* the paradox; perhaps ethics cannot also; perhaps it is not understandable. But the form in which paradoxes are made accessible, rather than obdurate, belongs to *mimēsis*.

Kierkegaard pauses in the paradox of faith to tell us that the ethical is not present in aesthetics, so that what art seems to tell us of faith cannot be reached through art. And he tells us this again and again, suggesting—this is my thesis—that the infinite, the paradox, lies between aesthetics and ethics, in their proximity, where they touch each other face to face. And further, because the aesthetic responds to the multifariousness of things and differences, this is a mad, wild proximity, circulating and recirculating beauties and goods, interrupting each other endlessly. "Either the individual as the individual is able to stand in an absolute relation to the absolute (and then the ethical is not the highest)/or Abraham is lost—he is neither a tragic hero, nor an aesthetic hero" (Kierkegaard, *FT*, 122). Perhaps Abraham is no hero, neither tragic nor aesthetic. Perhaps heroism belongs to tragedy and art, while what Abraham does appears heroic but is something different. I understand these differences, possibly including heroism, to belong to *technē*. The hero belongs to *technē*, but Abraham belongs to God, to the good, to *poiēsis*. But more, the highest also belongs to *technē*. There is no high and low under *poiēsis*. What if no high and low were given by the good, but every such distinction were interrupted by its gifts? The idea that the good is highest is a betrayal. But it is the betrayal of and by the witness to the good.

In this spirit, may we imagine that Abraham sacrificed Isaac, and that the biblical story covered it up, covered up God's injustice?

The distinction between good and evil, in Kierkegaard's terms, belongs to ethics, but something is higher, other, than ethics that gives it meaning, something absolute. Perhaps the other to the ethical is the unethical, but faith is not *unethical* but the other that makes the ethical ethical, that fulfills it. And here we see the problem of the aesthetic, that it comes as close as possible to this other beyond the ethical that makes it ethical, yet Kierkegaard insists that it is close to the unethical. Perhaps the difficulty is that he retains the binary opposition—named as choice—between good and evil, ethics and its other, in a sphere of relations to the good where binaries and choices no longer apply.

An example from *Either/Or*, where he repeatedly speaks of choosing:

> My either/or does not in the first instance denote the choice between good and evil; it denotes the choice whereby one chooses good *and* evil/or excludes them. . . . He who chooses the ethical chooses the good, but here the good is entirely abstract, only its being is posited, and hence it does not follow by any means that the chooser cannot in turn choose the evil. (Kierkegaard, *E/O*, II, 173)

We may consider the possibility that Kierkegaard chooses too many times, certainly twice: choosing good over evil, and choosing ethics—good over evil—over aesthetics. I speak of the one *over* the other; Kierkegaard, more openly, speaks of exclusion. The ethical person chooses good and excludes evil, and chooses this choice, of good over evil, over neutrality.

I have suggested that choice and judgment belong to *technē*, with nothing to resist it. Aesthetics here is equated with unethics, with ethical neutrality, not with art, beauty, or the good. Kierkegaard has no idea of a nonethics which is not unethical, no idea of a good which resists the injustice of choosing good and excluding evil. The ethical person chooses the good and excludes the bad. And what, we may ask, would allow any person, ethical or not, to wonder if what we exclude is bad, if it might be good in another place, if we have excluded it? With what good do we *include* evil as perhaps not evil, injustice as sometimes justice? With what good do we resist justice as injustice?

I consider it a scandal that Kierkegaard equates aesthetics with unethics, a scandal justified by nothing in his writing, by nothing in his world, or ours, carried to an extreme.[10] Ethics emerges in endless choices within the distinctions between authentic and inauthentic, good and bad, essential and accidental. For ethics, everything in every choice is essential. "Every aesthetical life view is despair, it was said. This was attributed to the fact that it was built upon what may be and may not be. Such is not the case with the ethical life view, for it builds life upon what essentially belongs to being" (Kierkegaard, *E/O*, 229).

Against this view (but not excluding it) that everything matters essentially to ethics while everything matters accidentally to aesthetics we may consider two alternatives: (1) What if ethics were entirely contingent? What if the good insisted that the responsibility we bear, necessarily and seriously, was to contingency everywhere, against necessity? What if judgment were always without criteria in the name of the good? And (2) what if both ethics and aesthetics faced contingency with utmost seriousness, to such an extent that our ethical task seemed to require us to separate them? What if that belied the seriousness of the task? What if, in virtue of *mimēsis*, every such separation were impossible, in the name of the good? That would mean that we could divide the good from the bad only in light of a responsibility and a gravity in which no such division could be sustained.

And indeed, this proximity of aesthetics and ethics expresses Kierkegaard's much more serious side, with far greater gravity and care than his exclusion of aesthetics. In the extreme, he repudiates aesthetics.

> The aesthetical, it was said, is that in a man whereby he immediately is the man he is; the ethical is that whereby a man becomes what he becomes. By this I do not intend to say that the man who lives aesthetically does not de-

velop, but he develops by necessity not by freedom, no metamorphosis takes
place in him, no infinite movement whereby he reaches the point from
whence he becomes what he becomes. (Kierkegaard, *E/O*, 229)

And excludes art from the highest good, even beauty (Kierkegaard, *E/O*,
276–77). Yet the striking thing remains that within this exclusion of art and
beauty from ethics, Kierkegaard must constantly return to find them in
ethics. "When I regard life ethically I regard it with a view to its beauty; life
then to me becomes rich in beauty, not poor in beauty as it really is for you.
I do not need to travel all over the land to discover beauties, nor to follow
them up in the streets. *I do not need to appraise and reject*" (Kierkegaard,
E/O, 280). Repeatedly and inexorably, ethics circles around beauty, demands
beauty in the name of the good. Beauty can neither be denied nor excluded.
The most ethical life is the most beautiful. The danger of art for Kierkegaard
is that it interrupts the universality of the good over the bad. I have repeatedly replied that this interruption interrupts the dominance of good over bad,
of appraisal and rejection. Art is a site where we may openly reject the demand
to appraise and exclude. Except that it has been handed down to us as a domination of the highest over the lower, the most spiritual over the sensuous,
the male over the female, and so forth.

On my reading, Kierkegaard is struggling with an ethics of inclusion, resisting valuation and exclusion. He struggles in the name of choosing good
over evil, at least ethics over aesthetics, where every over is domination. And,
though everything in his thought repeats it, he fails to consider that art's inclusion reveals something he ascribes to the knight of faith. From the standpoint of faith, and the good as I understand it, all is included. There is no
choice of faith or of the good, no either/or. Perhaps even worse, Kierkegaard
understands the ethical to resist and to destroy the aesthetic, but never considers that art shows something of the way faith interrupts the universality
of reason. Perhaps he does not understand the divinity of art, its godly madness. Perhaps he gives too much to the universal as Hegel's universal, rather
than some other universality, some other exaltation:

> The ethical is the universal, and as such it is again the divine. One has
> therefore a right to say that fundamentally every duty is a duty toward God;
> but if one cannot say more, then one affirms at the same time that properly
> I have no duty toward God. Duty becomes duty by being referred to God, but
> in duty itself I do not come into relation with God. Thus it is a duty to love
> one's neighbor, but in performing this duty I do not come into relation with
> God but with the neighbor whom I love. (Kierkegaard, *FT*, 78)

I understand this to speak of the good. By choosing, excluding, I reach toward
the good, but the good is not exclusion.

What is given in the name of the good? What but interruption in endless profusion, under one name after another, never held fast? What but . . . ? I return to art's sensuous materiality, within another interruption given from the good, everywhere but especially in art as *mimēsis*, and more, as ecstasy, and everywhere as materiality. *Mimēsis* is materiality. What of this materiality? How do we know its interruptions? I return to link romantic art with *mimēsis*, where Lacoue-Labarthe joins them to art's sensuality and women's sexuality.

"What if, after all," Lacoue-Labarthe asks, "philosophy were nothing but literature?" (Lacoue-Labarthe, *SP*, 1). What if, after all, women were nothing but men?" Why can't a woman be more like a man? *Viva la différence*. What if the difference between philosophy and art, named *mimēsis*, were nothing? Does that remind you of sexual difference? Might that too be nothing, yet gave birth to the world? We have seen that sexual difference may be the question of our age, the one question that might transform all our relations to ourselves and nature. Lacoue-Labarthe suggests that that question, the very question of sexual difference, might be the question of *mimēsis*, as strange as that thought may be. We are to keep in mind that sexual difference imposes issues of domination and oppression, issues we may not associate with *mimēsis*. I think of animals, who circulate within sexual difference and *mimēsis*, repeating every domination and subordination.

Lacoue-Labarthe links *mimēsis* to sexual difference through the sensual side of representation. "That the 'sensuous' figure may give itself as an 'end in itself' is, from the point of view of the speculative, something intolerable. That is to say, *unbearable*. The speculative cannot bear that anything non-spiritual be considered an 'end in itself'—be, if you will, *cut-off* from the spiritual. The *abscission* is intolerable" (Lacoue-Labarthe, *SP*, 157). This unbearableness of the sensuous, re-marking sexual difference (to which I will repeatedly return) and erotic ecstasy, marks the absolute difference between art and philosophy, the aesthetical and ethical, where such an absolute difference is marked, in philosophers of whom we would not expect it, who would resist Hegel:

> If woman alone needs to be veiled, it is because she alone expresses—and arouses?—*sensual* desire. In accordance with what the whole philosophical tradition has always said or implied, there is, properly speaking, no *pudendum* other than female *pudendum*; or, what amounts to exactly the same thing, male homosexual desire (we should write: *hommosexual* desire) is spiritual desire: the phallus is the "organ" of the spirit. (Lacoue-Labarthe, *SP*, 141)

I respond with several questions:

1. This veil that woman alone needs, "woman" a category of domination, is that veil another category demarcating the limits of truth, discourse, language, philosophy? In other words, is truth still a woman, under the category of veils? Does the veil—for Derrida, the *parergon*[11]—fall into language and truth as another metaphysical category, another binary opposition, veiled|unveiled, resisting the good, still excluding women and *mimēsis* together? Here we understand the conflicted and dangerous possibility that veils veil women only, at least European veils, and European women, and similarly, that masks mask only European men from within the very gesture that would resist both Eurocentrism and phallogocentrism, a gesture with the name of philosophy, against *mimēsis*.

2. The question then becomes, in Lacoue-Labarthe's words, what do veils veil, in mine, what do masks mask? To what are we exposed within the hidden call of the good? Foucault speaks directly on this subject: "we are difference . . . our reason is the difference of discourses, our history the difference of times, our selves the difference of masks" (Foucault, *AK*, 131). "We," our selves *(notre moi)* are the difference of masks, where difference and masks mark dispersion, discontinuity, and rupture, expose the groundlessness of our identity, break open the hold of reason on discourse. And philosophy. Masks mask nothing (or everything). But veils veil women's *pudendum*—coveted, owned, we may say, by men.

3. Is this *pudendum* flesh, this erotic sexuality that attaches to women as men's desire, that must be veiled? Or rather, is the sensuality, the desire, of which Lacoue-Labarthe speaks here and elsewhere, in relation to *Lucinde* and the threat of romantic art for Hegel, is it flesh, material and bodily sensuality, or is it still spiritual? I think of literature as philosophy's poltergeist, still too spiritual, perhaps not fleshy, not filled with mucus, oozing, spilling, fragrant with embodied life, with natural juices. I wonder if the women born from the domination of the categories of man and woman are their remainder, if they remain dominated and dominating, not because we cannot escape from domination, in language or whatever. I am not at all sure we can. But because language, writing, philosophy, literature, and art continue to contribute profoundly to domination without knowing anything in themselves of oppression, of pain and suffering, of materiality, of *jouissances*.

4. All this spiritualization comes to a head in the name, the gender, of the sensuous in art, the body, with its pudenda, which remains, I fear, no body at all, knows no ecstasy, without a gender. The name of the sensuous remains female, Venus. The despiritualization of homosexual spirituality retains its name, not Venus but *homosexuality*. We should write, Lacoue-Labarthe says, *hommosexual* desire. My final question, gathering up the others, is what it might mean to write "homosexuality" as "hommosexual desire," for us, for

men. Do we silence women, silence lesbian women, once more, another exclusion imposed on desire?

I do not mean to abandon the subject of philosophy, certainly not to abandon art together with literature, which seem to be the subject of philosophy, at least intimate with the subject of philosophy, and art, in tracing the economy of the feminine in Lacoue-Labarthe and romanticism. I am tempted to imagine that art relates to philosophy as what within the subject that threatens speculation relates to speculation; that is, as madness places reason at risk, as Dionysus threatens Apollo, art and literature threaten philosophy with being mad, Dionysian, unphilosophical at its very core, because they are sensuous, material, because of their pudenda, marked as *mimēsis*. I am tracing the gender of the subject of philosophy along two intersecting lines, following four questions, one line that the subject that risks philosophy is named and gendered, woman, the other that the living people who suffer the dominations and oppressions of gender, the mark of gender, have no voice, no place, in this discourse of the literariness, the sensuous form, of philosophy. It is as if women get it both ways, coming and going, up and down, get it no matter what steps are taken to liberate them, no matter who takes the steps. And with them, men.

For I have not done with my four questions, have not traversed them to the point where the mark of gender appears and disappears at the heart of philosophy, marking the inescapability of *mimēsis*.

1. The first question concerns the veiling of truth in relation to Dionysian masks and unveiling, concerns the possibility that philosophy's truth, historically, an adequation that knows nothing of unveiling, of *mimēsis*, at least in its metaphysical and categorial representations, replays the domination of women even in its resistance to metaphysics, given as unveiling, still *mimēsis*. Historically, from the standpoint of unveiling, we may resist the classifications in which, it seems, we desire to know the world through categories in order to dominate it, and them. The structure of binary pairs is master-slave, dominant-subordinate. The lower exist for the sake of the higher; every pair of categories orders from higher to lower. A taxonomic, representational, correspondence truth belongs to a system of categories of domination. And this is true even, or especially, where we distinguish facts from values, where we suppose that scientific knowledge might be free from domination. The ideas of objectivity, neutrality, and universality at the heart of valuelessness belong to systems of domination, are driven by a will to power and a will to truth.

Against this image of domination through truth, of subjection through categorization, Heidegger reminds us of *alētheia*, of an unveiling that owes a debt both to the forgetting of Being and to the systems of domination that compose modern thought. He does not, perhaps, consider that the thought of *alētheia* may be another domination. In this way, perhaps, he fails to hear what I think of as Nietzsche's secret and telling thought, that the thought of masks is masked, that masks proceed from domination to domination, that *mimēsis* is diaphoric. Nietzsche is not excepted. Nor is Heidegger. Nor are we, or Lacoue-Labarthe. The veiling and the unveiling occupy systems of domination, occupy them in relation to the binary oppositions to which they relate—as veiling and unveiling, in the very thought of oblivion—and as another binary pair resistant to opposition.

And women get it both ways, coming and going. Women's *pudendum* remains the *parergon* for men, for philosophy, pervading writing. If truth is veiled, she wears female clothing. And cosmetics. All simulations. All *mimēsis*.

Women get it both ways because the responsibility of which Levinas speaks, called from the good, an infinite exposure toward the Other as other, as heterogeneous, refuses heterogeneity except within the force of domination. Levinas himself is not excepted. When Irigaray asks Levinas, "is there otherness outside of sexual difference?" (Irigaray, *QEL*, 178), she answers:

> The function of the other sex as an alterity irreducible to myself eludes Levinas for at least two reasons:
> He knows nothing of communion in pleasure . . .
> . . . he substitutes the son for the feminine. (Irigaray, *QEL*, 180–81)

He knows nothing of a communion in pleasure between the one and the other, nothing of the erotic, reduces the heterogeneity, the dangerous, ecstatic heterogeneity of the other gender|sex, to a neuter other.

Women get it both ways because they vanish, obliterated, in the neuter, but are named only in categories of domination, situated as the one and only *pudendum*.

2. What do veils veil, what do masks mask, except sexual difference, violence and domination, *mimēsis*? When Lacoue-Labarthe asks, in reading Hegel, "what exactly does the veil veil?," he answers for Hegel that clothing covers human shame, refusing animality, signifying Man's spirituality. I respond that we cannot say what veils veil, what masks mask, cannot give it a name without domination, and cannot refuse it a name without another domination. Getting women both ways, coming and going. And others. For I must remind you that animals get it every way, get it in virtue of their kind and blood. As do all the others who differ from us by blood. All in the name of neutrality. Against *mimēsis*.

3. Is the (one and only) (female) *pudendum* flesh? Or rather, because this question divides in three, is the seat of (man's) desire, which must be veiled in order for man to speculate, first, woman, second, flesh, and, third, does she in her one *pudendum* replay the duality of mind and body, where the only body present belongs to the mind, to the masculine subject, in art? Does the seating of desire between the legs, under the law, fall upon women in spiritualized form, in the form of writing, language, thought, and spirit, but never inscribed on the body in flesh? Is the sensuality of art its embodiment, our fleshiness, or another aestheticization, another oblivion?

I pause at the sensuousness of art, which remains spiritual in Lacoue-Labarthe and Kant, and especially Cassirer, who makes this point of Kant repeatedly: the sensuousness of art, which in Hegel makes it fallen, still belongs to spirit. To reinstate the sensuousness of art and writing, thereby of philosophy, continues to circle around spirit and spirituality. I describe this circling as our falling repeatedly into the mind|body abyss so deeply that even as we might hope to rehabilitate the body against the spiritualization of mind, of thought, of humanism, we think of a spiritualized body, a masculinized, *hommosexual* body. We remain in the mind's grip upon the body. We refuse the possibility of ecstasy.

I do not offer this as a question. I am convinced we Europeans, humans, are far beyond this question, unable to set spirit aside when we press the flesh of the body. If we ever do so. I cite three passages circling around the body to enforce this point. First, I think of threshold as an intermediary figure, between earth and sky, without sexuality, materiality, embodiment, linking sky and earth, mortals and divinities, under the call of language, without sexual difference. I speak again of Heidegger's reading of Trakl's poem, *A Winter Evening*.[12] Against this spiritualization of difference at the expense of women, animals, and art, Merleau-Ponty asks us to remember the corporeality of both paint and painter, still denying the living body:

> The painter "takes his body with him," says Valéry. Indeed we cannot imagine how a *mind* could paint. It is by lending his body to the world that the artist changes the world into paintings. To understand these transubstantiations we must go back to the working, actual body—not the body as a chunk of space or a bundle of functions but that body which is an intertwining of vision and movement. (Merleau-Ponty, *EM*, 162; Ross, *AIS*, 283)

We must go back to the living body, to bodies in the world, nature's bodies, filled with work, illuminated by vision, movement, displaced by *mimēsis*. The painter responds to the glory of the good in every body.

In greater contrast, Irigaray gives us in her place a material, embodied threshold, an intermediary region that is as far from the sensuous in art as that sensuousness is from the spiritual. "The threshold that gives access to the *mucous*" (Irigaray, *ESD*, 18).[13] We find an unmistakably engendered, sexual figure, a place of woman, add to the redeployment of space, threshold, mucosity, lips, all (perhaps?) vaginal. To the sexlessness of the fourfold we add an undeniably material and sexual figure. Here the pudenda are female in a way no longer, perhaps, owned by men. Here the limens are engendered.

A different possibility, second, can be found in Foucault, as far as possible from spirit. For Foucault speaks of bodies and their doubling, one the represented, disciplined body, the body as object and target of power, the emergence of the art of the body, the other the always-present body to which descent attaches and around which genealogy circles:

> The body is the inscribed surface of events (traced by language and dissolved by ideas), the locus of a dissociated Self (adopting the illusion of a substantial unity), and a volume in perpetual disintegration. Genealogy, as an analysis of descent *[Herkunft]*, is thus situated within the articulation of the body and history. Its task is to expose a body totally imprinted by history and the process of history's destruction of the body. (Foucault, *NGH*, 148)

Here the body exposed by genealogy is both totally imprinted by history and representation, and a fleshy, material site where bodies suffer and are destroyed. I remind you of natural juices, of mucus, of bodily membranes, where sexual desire does its work, and where we experience pain and death.

I remind you, third, of Wittig, who speaks of lesbianization, this time in a different voice, another interruption.

> not one will be able to bear seeing you with eyes turned up lids cut off your yellow smoking intestines spread in the hollow of your hands your tongue spat from your mouth long green strings of your bile flowing over your breasts, not one will be able to bear your low frenetic insistent laughter. . . . The gleam of your teeth your joy your sorrow the hidden life your viscera your blood your arteries your veins your hollow habitations your organs your nerves their rupture their spurting forth death slow decomposition stench being devoured by worms your open skull, all will be equally unbearable to her. (Wittig, *LB*, 15)

This is at the very beginning, the very first paragraph of *The Lesbian Body*. It opens in several directions.

(a) The unnamed narrator, the *J/e* (who cannot appear in English, who cannot be heard in French, who disappears in English into the undivided *I*, while in French reflexives divides again and again, profusely, for example, in "*j//arrive; j//atteins; j//arrache*" [Wittig, *CL*, 9]), this *J/e* repeatedly names the parts of her unnamed lover's body,[14] opens the erotic body in its profusion and plenitude, by naming, by *mimēsis*. Flesh, and tissues, and blood, excrement, rotting, vomit, all the moving impulses of living bodies, living in proximity to death and age and rot. This mimetic profusion of bodily parts, French and English parts, inwards, organs, materials, tissues, shares a heterogenous space between languages and the immateriality of embodiment,[15] an erotic, fleshy, ecstatic space. Anatomical science is one of the forms by which nature's profusion may be known erotically. Nature's plenitude opens to us through the opening of language and work, of *mimēsis*.

(b) The profusion and plenitude of nature enter the flesh, the body, enter its crevices, organs, tissues, and materiality, in the form of love. We love each other, we know (if we are lesbians, lesbianized) a love incarnate, embodied, that does not impose a transcendental signifier, that does not glorify a single organ or site, but pervades, permeates, suffuses, sometimes in terrible, awful ways, the lover's body, everywhere in nature, refusing to stop at the skin. Penetration takes on another meaning, not the entering of one privileged organ into another, one organ, one act, repeated endlessly, but a profusion of penetrations and permeations, along every fold of flesh, including folds we cannot know, do not know, may never know, including lines of biology and anatomy that romantic love, romantic male lovers, disdain. All in virtue of *mimēsis*.

(c) The inward fleshiness of the lover that the unnamed narrator portrays, describes, inhabits is a space, many spaces, that lovers cannot inhabit without language and without violence. This is not men's violence against women, but it is no less shocking, intimidating.[16] The permeation everywhere in the body is described in destructive, violent terms, resolved into intimacy, proximity, love.[17]

Wittig asks us to recognize that heterosexual categories permeate our lives and experiences. Catharine MacKinnon asks us to recognize that under conditions of gender inequality, acts and events touch men and women differently, unequally, foster inequality and oppression (MacKinnon, *FU* and *TFTS*). Perhaps under conditions of gender inequality, only lesbians, only women together, can cherish every morsel of the other's body, beyond any considerations of domination and oppression. For the beloved remains beloved, and always comes back together. Perhaps, in a somewhat Nietzschean way, a celebration of every facet of life and body, including suffering, grief, and mourning, is closed to men in relation to women because of gender inequality. Perhaps the Dionysian that Nietzsche describes cannot be celebrated between men and women, cannot enter the spaces between men and women, because of women's historical subjection. Perhaps men and women cannot be exposed to each other in the name of the good under conditions of gender inequality. Perhaps nature's abundance hides from us under conditions of systematic inequality.

(d) The language of *The Lesbian Body* is violent, but it is especially and repeatedly violent in animal form. In the materiality of embodiment, in the lesbianization of humanity, Wittig bridges a close affinity with animal flesh and animal soul:

> You stand upright on your paws *(pattes dressées)* [raised paws] one of them intermittently scratching the ground. Your head weighs on the nape of m/y neck, your canines gash m/y flesh where it is most sensitive, you hold m/e between your paws, you constrain m/e to lean on m/y elbows . . . you rip off m/y skin with the claws of your four paws, a great sweat comes over m/e hot then soon cold, a white foam spreads the length of your black chops *(babines noirs)* . . . (Wittig, *LB*, 22)

I add a partial list of animals and other corporeal places in nature that materialize in *The Lesbian Body*: worms, amoebas, spores, butterflies, monkeys, turtledoves, swans, flowers, bitches, water, wings, bats, birds, spiders, fish, mares, sharks, vegetables, snakes, finches, felines, Gorgons.

The profusion of embodiment and materiality in *The Lesbian Body* opposes the hegemony of the Form of the Human, the Perfection of Mankind, under whose dominion women and animals have been subjected. The *elles*, which opens the space for women together, without men, as if there were no men (at least in language), that opening moves with immense speed from the *entres*, the diaphoric spaces, of women together to nature's and women's *antres*, the animality of women not understood as subjection to the rationality of men, but as exposure to nature's plenitude. I understand this plenitude to inhabit the heart of ethics, not singularity but profusion, multiplicity, impurity, heterogeneity, pervading every pore of the body, every body and every kind. We can reach it, reach knowledge of the knowledge of the other through words, even as we cannot know that knowledge.

(e) Wittig speaks, in *The Lesbian Body*, of something that has no existence, cannot even be forbidden. "*Le Corps Lesbien* has lesbianism as its theme, that is, a theme which cannot even be described as taboo, for it has no real existence in the history of literature" (Wittig, *LB*, 9). We may wonder at the forgetting of women who love women, who live together with women, who have done so throughout Western history and throughout other places in the history and world. If they did not write, if they did not say "I am lesbian," did they exist? Homosexuality, Wittig claims, was named and written, but lesbians had no name. And still, in many countries of the world, women still live alone or together, but do not practice something called (in any language) "lesbianism." The kind asks for a name, demands *mimēsis*.

4. The final question, the question I have suggested includes the others, is that of *hommosexuality*, a word that cannot appear in English. And perhaps we must ask what it means for it to appear in Lacoue-Labarthe. Does he resist a heterosexual economy with what Wittig calls "lesbianization"? Or does he repeat that economy in the figure of Aphrodite, who remains man's desire even when unveiled?

Put another way, does philosophy remain within the economy described as the ancient quarrel even when it becomes literature?

But first, lesbianization:

> The bar in the *j/e* of *The Lesbian Body* [actually, *Le corps lesbien*] is a sign of excess. A sign that helps to imagine an excess of "I," an "I" exalted. "I" has become so powerful in *The Lesbian Body* that it can attack the order of heterosexuality in texts and assault the so-called love, the heroes of love, and lesbianize them, lesbianize the symbols, lesbianize the gods and the goddesses, lesbianize the men and the women. (Wittig, *MG*, 87)

I read the bar in *j/e* as *mimēsis*, read the entire corpus of *The Lesbian Body* as *mimēsis*, saying something that can only be said in writing, mimetically, naming all the parts of the body, lovingly, tearing the body apart in words. I read the link between *mimēsis* and embodiment, reaching toward exaltation, as something Wittig explores, something possible only in *mimēsis*. What Wittig says of exaltation I suggest calls for *mimēsis* in the name of the good. I link ecstasy and exaltation.

The good includes everything (and nothing) in an ethical movement without domination, a movement Wittig calls "lesbianization," a movement perhaps impossible in a heterosexual economy, impossible for men and for women, a movement impossible in an ethical|political economy, impossible for men and women, and others, who would be ethical by pursuing the good rather than the bad, the philosophical rather than the literary, but impossible also for those who would pursue the good together with the bad, philosophy together with literature, masculinity joined with femininity. All these junctures replay binary exclusion, under inversion.

Wittig speaks of an exalted "I," exalted by the bar in *j/e*, exalted by and as *mimēsis*, the "I" that does not impose masculine gender on the *elles*, on the woman who can be woman only by passing through masculine gender, or who may escape from masculine gender only as what Wittig calls "an escapee, a fugitive slave, a lesbian" (Wittig, *SME*, xiii). Lesbians are fugitive slaves, better off no doubt than slaves, but not in an exalted state. What then is the exaltation of the subject to which we might be brought by lesbianization, an exaltation of the subject in philosophy? This subject bears what Levinas calls a responsibility to the good, an exaltation of the "I" that might be powerful enough to accept a responsibility that Wittig and MacKinnon tell us, rightly, no one can accept under conditions of gender inequality.

We are all fugitives, differing profoundly in our fugitiveness, escapees from gender and other inequalities, wounded in our bodies and souls, unable to be ethical, forced by life and experience and within ourselves to be nothing but ethical, responsible to and for the good, to and for the other, where that other as other is thrown down into our subjection. Even those who rule, who occupy the center of the state, are wounded by the wounding of others, subjected by their subjection. Even so, the wounds are incomparable, not equal, some kinds suffer the burdens of injustice, others reap their privileges.

But in the fugitiveness of lesbians, in their resistance, perhaps including others lesbianized, the possibility of another "I" emerges, an exalted "I." And as Wittig suggests, with Irigaray, this "I" is not the subject of philosophy, not a neutral and universal "I" that knows nothing of exaltation because it passes itself off as everything. The exalted "I" is never total. The exalted "I" is never neutral. Here, in our time, exaltation may be denied to men, denied to humanity as Human. If women are human, they may be human otherwise, opening the human *aentre* to exaltation. And perhaps this exaltation belongs to those kinds who can occupy other sites in memory of the good. This exaltation, pertaining to the good, collapses the distinction between philosophy and literature, collapses every categorial measure, into univocity but not identity, comes from *mimēsis*.

I interrupt this long interruption dwelling upon the relation of *mimēsis* to the good as exposure to consider other interruptions, still exposure, responding to the good. I pursue the idea of endless interruptions, bearing responsibility in the name of the good. Here endless interruptions bear the mark of *mimēsis*.

Following Arthur Danto's lead, let us imagine some paintings, largely identical in all respects, uniform red rectangles with largely uniform brushwork smoothly spreading the red throughout. One is called *Escape from Egypt*; another is called *Rage*; a third is called *The Beginning*; another is called *Composition 32*; a fifth is *Untitled*. These are not Danto's examples, but are similar. The first is explained as the Red Sea after it has parted and returned to its normal state, swallowing the Egyptian soldiers. The second is said to be the intense inner mood of anger. The third is described as the universe right after the Big Bang. And so forth. Danto explains this phenomenon as follows:

> There may be a question whether this difference makes the difference we want it to make. But it is a difference beyond visual congruity and identity of content. And the principle by which the example was generated may be extended and generalized. Any representation not an artwork can be

> matched by one that is one, the difference lying in the fact that the artwork
> uses the way the nonartwork presents its content to make a point about how
> that content is presented. . . .
>   The thesis is that works of art, in categorical contrast with mere rep-
> resentations, use the means of representation in a way that is not exhaus-
> tively specified when one has exhaustively specified what is being
> represented. (Danto, *TC*, 146–48)

I identify this thesis with my theory of contrast, which includes it: theses of
inexhaustibility, not restricted to works of art, but expressed in *mimēsis*.
Works of art, and other things, exceed any limits or identities established in
things, natural or otherwise. Identity is inexhaustibility.

Danto tells us that the paintings are identical. Nelson Goodman, speaking of forgery, but in a remark directly relevant to the examples, suggests that
confronted with an original and a known copy, however much alike:

> *notice now that no one can ever ascertain by merely looking at the pictures*
> *that no one ever has been or will be able to tell them apart by merely look-*
> *ing at them.* (Goodman, *LA*, 101–102)

> My knowledge of the difference between the two pictures, just because it af-
> fects the relationship of the present to future lookings, informs the very
> character of my present looking. This knowledge instructs me to look at the
> two pictures differently now, even if what I see is the same. (Goodman, *LA*,
> 104).

Merleau-Ponty speaks of this as making the invisible visible. Goodman suggests that the invisible is or may become visible, related diaphorically, that
we cannot say that the paintings are identical and will be seen as identical forever. Insignificant, irrelevant differences, however tiny, may be understood to
belong to the one rather than the other, to the original or copy, to the different though apparently similar red paintings described above.

The inexhaustible differences in paintings, between paintings, and in
and between things and kinds of things, unknown, unrecognized, unvalued
differences, belong to the good. In relation to literature and art, they belong
to *mimēsis*. Goodman speaks of them in relation to the world and worldmaking, and in relation to art as symptoms of the aesthetic (Goodman, *WW*,
67–68; Ross, *AIS*, 244–45). He does not recognize them as belonging to the
good. But he does recognize that they are not restricted to art, but are found
in all forms of knowledge and truth. The inexhaustibility of representation,
expressed in these symptoms of art, with their interruptions and displacements, is what Plato calls *mimēsis*, found everywhere together with truth,
truth's concealments, *alētheia*.

I expand this inexhaustible sense of *mimēsis* with two concluding thoughts:

> For the writer of artistic prose, on the contrary [as against the poetic image], the object reveals first of all precisely the socially heteroglot multiplicity of its names, definitions and value judgments. Instead of the virginal fullness and inexhaustibility of the object itself, the prose writer confronts a multitude of routes, roads and paths that have been laid down in the object by social consciousness. Along with the internal contradictions inside the object itself, the prose writer witnesses as well the unfolding of social heteroglossia *surrounding* the object, the Tower-of-Babel mixing of languages that goes on around any object; the dialectics of the object are interwoven with the social dialogue surrounding it. (Bakhtin, *DN*, 486; Ross, *AIS*, 278)

This inexhaustibility, exceeding all limits of the object, language, or social world, is touched by, expressed in, *mimēsis*. It is representation itself, bound to no antecedent set of expectations.[18] It is touched more closely by art, in art, than any other site of representation, though it belongs to representation, to truth, themselves. And as these authors may perhaps not have said as clearly, it responds to the good, bears a responsibility given as the gift of art.

In closing, I return to the opening words of this chapter where Socrates speaks of "greater stories" telling lies. This entire chapter has explored diaphoric spaces between *mimēsis* and truth. I should say something here of greatness, foreshadowing later discussions. For what we have learned of the inexhaustibility of art is frequently restricted to works of "greatness." I wish to consider the extreme possibility that the distinction between great art and other art, high and low art, whatever and wherever that distinction may be, betrays the responsibility in art, expressed by *mimēsis*, to take every difference seriously. Following Goodman's thought, with a twist, I think that we will never be able to tell at any time whether a work we consider poor, or weak, or broken, may not be found to be wonderful at some time in the future, because of changes in the nature of art, and the world. And second, more extreme, the distinction between good and bad, high and low, betrays art and the good.

One of the lessons of our century, expressed in Danto's examples perhaps more than others mentioned, is that strange, weird works of art tell us strange, weird things about art and other things, express the inexpressible, reveal differences beyond differences, exceeding every measure, including measures of high and low in art, greatness and mediocrity. In its different works, popular, folk, kitsch art reveals the gift of the good because it opens, reveals, interrupts, touches heterogeneity, differences among individuals and kinds, everywhere in nature. Even familiar works hung on motel walls interrupt the blankness of empty space, ask us if we notice them at all why they are there, what they reveal, and what might illuminate that space instead. The possibility of art, high, low, mediocre, whatever—all distinctions that do not bear on *poiēsis* or *mimēsis*—bears the touch of the good in relation to the "finest differences," differences beyond differences, toward heterogeneity. This bearing, expressing, of heterogeneity belongs to art as *mimēsis*, is the gift of beauty. But it does not belong to art alone, to literature and language. It belongs to us everywhere, circulates everywhere as the gift of beauty, given from the good. Among the goods that circulate wildly, beyond measure, is beauty, and wherever goods circulate without measure we find beautiful things. Where beauty is associated with measure, it is at the very limit of the possibility of order, the very limit of limit. It passes on from that limit to unlimit, as Socrates says in *Philebus*. It circulates as *mimēsis*.

CHAPTER 3

Nature

When we read Aristotle's *Poetics*, after Nietzsche, could we find ourselves reading an ethics, responding to the call of the good, a good given without domination or violence? We know the received opinion, in the West, that *Poetics* is not a work of ethics, from the good, but a work on art, on poetry, that it falls within the *diaphora* between *poiēsis* and *technē*, divided by Aristotle into making and doing. Poetry is a making; ethics is a doing. The question I hope to ask is what reading *Poetics* in memory of the good might tell us of the gift of art as the good, refusing the quarrel or, perhaps more deeply, understanding the *diaphora* in a different way.

"Our subject being Poetry" (Aristotle, *Poetics*, 1447a), Aristotle begins, and proposes to speak of the art in general and its species. This general and its species suggest the categories of art, and even of the good, perhaps, in memory of the categories of metaphysics, of being qua being. Except that being is no category, no genus. There are metaphysical categories and causes, but being is no genus. And perhaps art and poetry are not categories, represent no genera, not at least in the sense in which they belong to a binary opposition. Perhaps. And with them, perhaps, we may find the good, again no genus, a good resistant to binary opposition.

For epic poetry, tragedy, comedy, and flute- and lyre-playing, the examples of which Aristotle speaks (Aristotle, *Poetics*, 1447a), are modes of *mimēsis*, an imitation, which, again, may belong to no binary opposition. If at any moment we must choose between poetry and music, tragedy and comedy, within the constraints of the mundane, we know despite every effort of philosophers to rank the different arts from high to low, we do not choose superior over inferior. Music and poetry as such know nothing of the superiority of one art over the others.

I suggest, again resisting the Western philosophic tradition, that within an art the ranking of works and artists over others does not belong to art, but to a contaminated activity called *criticism*, under *technē*, that would rank what is not ranked as art. Critics insist that we rank, gain reputations by high and low. *Mimēsis* knows nothing of rank, of high and low, superior and inferior, but gives us the gift of art as the goodness of things and works with no memory of their hierarchy. Socrates' complaint may be that music and poetry do not divide the good from bad, do not tell us what to do, do not judge, but are taken to do so. I have suggested that it is *technē*'s task to judge, to help us choose, but that perhaps it is the task of *mimēsis* to know something unknown to *technē*. I read Aristotle as expressing that responsibility.

In his *Republic*, Plato distinguishes *mimēsis* from *diēgesis*, speaks disparagingly of imitation in relation to *technē*, and we have seen how far we may go with that. At least, we have seen how far we can go with *mimēsis* regarded as the presentation and representation of objects, evoking something beyond such objects and representations, reminiscent of the good. If painting presents a bed once more, recalling the bedmaker's craft, presents a bed belonging to *technē*, it must fail in its aim, fail in its imitation. The painter's bed gives no rest. Nor perhaps does it give something else, better or worse than rest, but gives unrest, something supplementary in rest, beyond the place of rest, touching the gods. The quarrel between *technē* and *poiēsis* divides *mimēsis* accordingly into two, an imitation or representation of things, absent or present, in the place of and for the sake of the things presented, and an imitation without representation, taking us back to the things themselves, perhaps, called by their good, imbued with endless possibility. The idea of art as *technē* presupposes something beyond *technē*, *poiēsis* or beyond, a gift of the gods.

I wonder if *mimēsis* in *Poetics* echoes this gift of the gods, not an imitation setting a norm, under *technē*, and not an imitation mirroring an object ready to hand, of use, again under *technē*, but a madness, inspiration, exposing us to the good, to the dangers we have seen in Plato of Eros and Pharmakeia, and to Nietzsche's memories of Dionysus. *Mimēsis*, here, is associated with *poiēsis* where neither is a making according to *technē*, bringing things ready to hand from one place to another, but bringing being forth from nonbeing, repeating divine creation. *Mimēsis*, here, diaphorically divides in two, under *technē* and under *poiēsis*, the one a bringing to hand, where the art of *technē* bears responsibility for the bringing, the other a bringing forth from nonbeing, after the gods, where *poiēsis* expresses the sacred responsibility borne by the mundane to the divine.

The subject is *mimēsis*. The question I have asked in reading Aristotle is whether *mimēsis*, and the subject of *mimēsis* or any other subject, human or otherwise, can be a category. Can *mimēsis*, *technē*, and *poiēsis* be categories, and under what sign can we find an answer? Stretching further, if *technē* is the art of classifying, taxonomy, knowledge of dividing this from that, good from bad, what Plato at times calls *dialectic*, does *technē* itself belong to classification, to *technē?* And what of *poiēsis?* I have read Plato as confronting this question deeply, with the answer, Heidegger's answer, that the thought of *technē* cannot itself belong to *technē*, any more than reason can belong to reason, as if from itself (modernity's claim) it would give itself supreme authority.

By what mark, we may ask, can thought and language disturb the hold of *technē* upon the everyday, as if our entire experience, the entire world of nature, *phusis*, were mundane, controlled by *technē*, ready to hand? What could represent the sacred within the hold of categorial thought, the otherwise? What could respond to the call of the good, undermine the domination of identities and categories? I have read Plato as suggesting that the mark of *poiēsis*, of divine madness, is *mimēsis*, a writing or thought that marks its own madness, thereby its divine and anarchic origins. I now read Aristotle as saying something similar: "the poet's function is to describe, not the thing that has happened [as if without representation], but a kind of thing that might happen, i. e. what is possible as being probable or necessary [as it were, another nature, a nature whose possibility, whose imitation, remains within it]" (Aristotle, *Poetics*, 1451). The poem retains the sense of its *mimēsis*, its representativity, expressed as a possibility, however probable or necessary, but not an actuality or reality, where the historian, the *technēn*, passes off categories as if without representation, as if bare truth, as if truth might be bare. In other words, if both poem and work of craft are productions, one tells the impossible truth about its genesis, the other lies, pretends that it had no genesis in representation or *mimēsis*, denies its heterogeneity.

This inversion of the argument in Plato's *Republic* may be read to enforce the opposite position from Socrates', that imitation is superior to simple narration. Or it may be read instead as expressing something of the good that *mimēsis* knows, and says, without opposition, something of the diaphoric truth of representation. And art. Poetic representation, *mimēsis*, is good because in showing that it is mimetic, it undercuts the possibility of its own authority. Poetry shows itself, even in its supremacy, to lack authority, a response to the call of the good. Poetry shows itself never to lie about the truthfulness of its representativity. The truthfulness of *poiēsis* is its *mimēsis*. The truthfulness of *mimēsis* is its resistance to its own authority.

What, I have asked, if reading Aristotle's *Poetics* after Nietzsche, we read it as an ethics, pertaining to the good? What would that do to our understanding of ethics, including the *Nicomachean Ethics?* In perhaps the most famous line on ethics in the history of the West, the line that defines both ethics as we know it and Aristotle's understanding of ethics, he tells us that "[e]very art and every inquiry, and similarly every action and pursuit, is thought to aim at some good; and for this reason the good has rightly been declared to be that at which all things aim" (Aristotle, *Nicomachean Ethics*, 1094a). Something about this remarkable claim has fallen into disrepute, disregarded in modernity, that *every* action, inquiry, pursuit, including science and the quest for truth, aims at some good, aims at the good. For read in a certain way, Aristotle's claim repeats Plato's, that the good rules over knowledge and truth, over inquiry and practice, as the end for which all things do their work.

Yet where, on my reading, Plato speaks of the idea of the good as coming from the gods, working through intermediary figures of divine love and madness, disrupting the places of mundane work, Aristotle is typically read within the realm of work. On this reading, he names the good toward which all things aim, the good that attracts all activities and pursuits, names the end of ends, at least for human beings. For human beings, at least, the end of all pursuits is happiness, *eudaimonia*. "[B]oth the general run of men and people of superior refinement say that it is happiness, and identify living well and doing well with being happy; but with regard to what happiness is they differ" (Aristotle, *Nicomachean Ethics*, 1095a).

How far do Plato and Aristotle differ, and how? And is their difference diaphoric? Do they differ on the things and activities to be regarded as producing happiness—pleasure, profit, joy, knowledge, virtue—and on the idea of *eudaimonia*, reinstituting the quarrel between *poiēsis* and *technē?* Is *eudaimonia* something for which we act, some thing or state or possession for which we strive, some *thing* we seek in the name of desire, under the good? Or is it perhaps not a thing, not a state or possession, but that for the sake of which we act that is not something we can hold, something that keeps circulating, something enigmatic?

I leave aside the question of whether this good for the sake of which all things are pursued is one good, universal, one for all. I leave it aside for a while because it seems to me that this immensely important question of whether the good, called *eudaimonia*, is the same for all or heterogeneous, different at every moment, in every place, requires prior consideration of the question I have posed, whether the good is a thing to be possessed, the same for all or different everywhere, or no thing at all, but something heterogeneous at its core, expressed as a divine madness. If divine, and mad, what would we care if *eudaimonia* or the good were the same for all, everywhere? What same would we name?

In *Nicomachean Ethics*, Aristotle's answer is that *eudaimonia*, the good for human beings, is not pleasure, that those who think so are *slavish* (Aristotle, *Nicomachean Ethics*, 1095b), echoing a memory of what we may take to be the most heinous side of his work, dividing the world into high and low, master and slave, where the latter may be used by the former. In the name of use, the world divides into those who use and those who are used. But what divides this world, what prior claim of good or evil, justice or injustice, in this way? And is happiness the good, the end of ends, for all, including those Aristotle calls *slavish*?

On this reading, opening *Nicomachean Ethics*, we find ourselves before the claims of use, the categories and distinctions of *technē*, with far-reaching implications and ramifications. Our crucial question of ethics, before we can undertake any thoughts of the good, is whether this ethics belongs to *technē* so profoundly that it knows nothing of the good in any other way, nothing of the good otherwise than *technē*? That is the question I bring to Aristotle's *Poetics*, marking something otherwise in ethics, brought from the good, the question almost impossible to produce from within a reading of *Nicomachean Ethics*. Almost, but not altogether. At least within the Western tradition.

For setting aside the high and low in relation to which Aristotle sets aside pleasure and wealth, and with them suggests setting aside all possessions as well, he tells us that this good of goods, *eudaimonia*, is not pleasure, joy, or wealth, though it bears relation to fortune, perhaps in memory of fortune's gifts more than any other possession. Fortune, *tuchē*, expresses the good that comes from the gods without the will of human beings. The good, *eudaimonia*, is that which might be chosen as the most final end, for which all things aim, within a complete life reflecting *tuchē*, revealing divine gifts at which we cannot aim. And Aristotle repeats this giftedness twice, for if "human good turns out to be activity of soul in accordance with virtue" (Aristotle, *Nicomachean Ethics*, 1098a), "in a complete life" (*NE*, 1098a), then both virtue and blessedness are gifts, the one from human beings to other human beings, the other from the gods.

Moreover, he repeats this sense of the good as gift in his concluding chapter. For "if happiness is activity in accordance with virtue, it is reasonable that it should be in accordance with the highest virtue; and this will be that of the best thing in us" (Aristotle, *Nicomachean Ethics*, 1188a). But this best thing in us, contemplative activity, is reason; and "is not in so far as he is man that he will live so, but in so far as something divine is present in him" (Aristotle, *Nicomachean Ethics*, 1177b). *Nous* and reason are present in human beings as divine gifts. And here Aristotle marks something only obliquely present in my earlier discussions of Plato, where Socrates seems to contrast reason's truth with divine madness, as if only the latter were gifts from the gods, as if only *poiēsis* were divine, and not *technē*, neither *epistēmē* nor *sophia*. All of these, as works, come as gifts. If there is a good for human beings, a good of virtue, that virtue belongs to the divine, comes from the good, bears the gifts of the gods as truly and completely as divine, poetic madness. This is the truth that the poets know and that philosophers seem to have forgotten. For the Greeks, reason is not rational.

We may recall that in *Meno*, Socrates expresses deep and endless doubts that virtue can be taught, that parents can inculcate virtue in their children, suggests that virtue comes as a gift, from the gods. "On our present reasoning then, whoever has virtue gets it by divine dispensation" (Plato, *Meno*, 100b). On my reading here, Aristotle says something similar about virtue, happiness, and reason, that these come as gifts, not by rule.

Yet he also says that virtue belongs to *technē* as *eudaimonia* does not, first because virtue can be praised, belongs to the kinds of things we praise, while happiness does not (Aristotle, *Nicomachean Ethics*, 1101b); second because virtue appears to be something we can acquire by habit and repetition; and third because virtue is calculable, according to the mean. Yet his words do not support the possibility of acquiring virtue by rule, but suggest something intermediary between gift and maxim. "Neither by nature, then, nor contrary to nature do the virtues arise in us; rather we are adapted by nature to receive them, and are made perfect by habit" (Aristotle, *Nicomachean Ethics*, 1103a). Would we not say exactly the same of Ion, under divine dispensation, that the rhapsode whose gifts come from the gods is neither gifted by nature, nor contrary to nature, both understood here as mundane, but sublimely gifted by divine gift, perfected by repetition?

The idea of perfection belongs at first glance to *technē*: calculable perfection, determined by a norm. And such a norm seems to follow from the mean, determined according to reason. "Virtue, then, is a state of character concerned with choice, lying in a mean, i.e. the mean relative to us, this being determined by a rational principle, and by that principle by which the man of practical wisdom would determine it" (Aristotle, *Nicomachean Ethics*, 1107a). Yet Aristotle explicitly denies that we can calculate according to this principle, but rather must emulate the person of practical wisdom according to character. The virtuous person sets a norm as a model, an exemplar, but in language reminiscent of Kant's view of genius, Aristotle describes *phronēsis* as not according to a rule but giving a norm by example, as according to character. "Actions, then, are called just and temperate when they are such as the just or the temperate man would do; but it is not the man who does these that is just and temperate, but the man who also does them *as* just and temperate men do them" (Aristotle, *Nicomachean Ethics*, 1105b). Moreover, practical wisdom is neither scientific or universal nor an art according to *technē*, lacking excellence: "a virtue and not an art" (Aristotle, *Nicomachean Ethics*, 1140b).

Virtue is not art because it produces nothing excellent by art, indeed, produces nothing at all. Action and making are different, and where virtue is action, doing, it makes nothing at all. If we think of *technē* as making rather than doing, as making excellent things according to a separable and distinct idea, then arts like poetry and music produce works, but make nothing excellent, do not make objects, excellent or otherwise. I am reminded of Plato's argument concerning painting, that the painted object, the bed, must be derivative and parasitic upon the bed made by the bedmaker according to the Idea. I replied that it all depends on our understanding of painting and sculpture as making things, beds, according to a knowledge possessed by a craftsman, according to and emulating *technē*. But poetry and music, and perhaps painting and sculpture as well, perhaps all fine arts, of *poiēsis*, if they produce works do not produce objects, excellent or otherwise. Works here are otherwise than objects, things, otherwise than excellent material things. This otherwise is under the call of the good, called by the good otherwise.

I acknowledge the perversity of this suggestion within the traditional reading of Aristotle. For doing and making are distinguished as ethics and politics are distinguished from art, *technē* from *poiēsis*. But Aristotle also classifies *poiēsis* under *technē*, poetic making under making according to *technē*. And here the *diaphora* between *poiēsis* and *technē* changes its form, undermining the distinction between doing and making. If doing is not making, then perhaps *poiēsis*, divine madness and inspiration, is not making either, where making a work, bringing forth art, being from nonbeing, is not making something, making a thing. *Phronēsis*, then, is closer to genius than to science or to *technē*, to genius as following no rule in order to work according to rule. Just like virtue, by character rather than by normative idea. Producing nothing useful, creating nothing ready to hand, owned or possessed.

To express these thoughts in a different way, we may say that Aristotle's distinctions among saying, doing, and making, between *phronēsis* and *epistēmē*, *poiēsis* and *technē*, are made to distinguish different senses of *for the sake of*, diaphoric relations to the good. Making by art, under *technē*, produces according to an idea of what is normative, excellent, for the sake of that art. Something is made according to a plan, for the sake of the excellences of that idea, producing something that can be possessed, at hand. Virtue has no such excellence, but is action for its own sake. Virtue is for the sake of itself, for the sake of a good that cannot be owned: it is the good and the producing. In this sense, virtue is for the sake of *poiēsis* rather than *technē*, for there is no separable idea of the good for virtue: virtue itself is habit, repetition, character. The gift of the good draws from us, in our responses toward it, undertakings and pursuits for the sake of something that is no object, knows no excellence, toward which we bear endless debts, but can never own.

We may now consider the possibility that the *diaphora* in Plato between *poiēsis* and *technē* is reflected in Aristotle in the *diaphora* between ethical rationality, virtue or *phronēsis*, and technical rationality, art by *technē*. The mean is not a point of calculation, an accounting for what is excellent. Perhaps nothing offers such a point of excellence.[1] The reason of which

Aristotle speaks concerns not the universal, demonstrable, but the particular, exemplarily, with a good toward which we strive, a good for desire, which defines no point of excellence, perfection, but presents another sense of perfectibility, without measure. All these distinctions are relevant to art in the *diaphora* between *technē* and *poiēsis*.

What kind of ethics, what relation to the good, might we come to if we explored our relation to the good not with *Nicomachean Ethics* but with *Poetics*? Or rather, what if we brought our understanding of the good in *Poetics* into *Nicomachean Ethics*, where I have suggested that we may find a relation to the good that echoes *technē*, but also bears a memory of gifts little known to *technē*?[2]

Where ethics demands from the start, forgetting the good, that we concern ourselves with ends for which we undertake projects and plans, poetry asks us from the beginning to concern ourselves with works. "Our subject being Poetry, I propose to speak not only of the art in general but also of its species and their respective capacities; of the structure of plot required for a good poem; of the number and nature of the constituent parts of a poem; and likewise of any other matters in the same line of inquiry" (Aristotle, *Poetics*, 1447a). Nothing is said, though it may be inferred, of the idea of excellence that would define a poem or tragedy, of the norm, though Aristotle speaks of species and constituent parts and structures of plot required for a good poem. So we must wonder from the beginning what good he has in mind in relation to the poetic, tragic work: a good of form and idea, setting the norm and rule for the work, or perhaps another good called to us from within the poem, reminiscent of the good that calls us to respond to heterogeneity?

All these kinds of works, "epic poetry and Tragedy, as also Comedy, Dithyrambic poetry, and most flute-playing and lyre-playing, are all, viewed as a whole, modes of imitation *[mimēsis]*" (Aristotle, *Poetics*, 1447a). All these, music and poetry, are imitation, but they are the arts known in Greece and elsewhere in the West to be the least mimetic of objects, things. If imitative, what do they imitate? Aristotle offers two kinds of answer:

> A tragedy, then, is the imitation of an action that is serious and also, as having magnitude, complete in itself; in language with pleasurable accessories, each kind brought in separately in the parts of the work; in a dramatic, not in a narrative form; with incidents arousing pity and fear, wherewith to accomplish its catharsis of such emotions. (Aristotle, *Poetics*, 1449b)

> From what we have said it will be seen that the poet's function is to describe, not the thing that has happened, but a kind of thing that might happen, i.e. what is possible as being probable or necessary. (Aristotle, *Poetics*, 1451)

As Kant says, another nature, filled with probability, necessity, and chance.

Repeatedly we find ourselves recalling the theme of alterity opposing the reading that we are to understand art as *technē* against any theme of otherness. Let us give the categories of poetry as if we might define by such categories the good work that poetry does. Let us give the categories of poetry so that we might define poetic truth and diction. Let us define the objects imitated in tragedy—actions performed by characters—so that we might grasp the objects of poetic art.

In every case, the categories lose their hold, open onto something heterogeneous: divine, erotic, mad, inspired. What is imitated are not actions we have encountered, known and experienced, though many who write of art write as if every thought or dream, every inspiration, were familiar. We can think, and dream, and write, and experience art as if every word and line and form were mundane or an imitation of something mundane. Jung criticizes Freud for that mistake: the greatness of art cannot be found in everyday psychological experiences, however striking or emotional (Jung, *PL*; Ross, *AIS*, 507–20). Art touches something archaic, fully accepted by Freud if neglected in his writings on art in relation to the everyday (Freud, *RPD*; Ross, *AIS*, 500–506), by no means neglected in his writing on Moses or Da Vinci. Yet this archaic is given another categorial form in Jung, as if it required its theology. I am following another track, of the good as otherwise, reminiscent of something so old that nothing can represent it, but which calls us into its service, every day. We know this call as ecstasy, as joy and love, bearing up under the gift of the good.

The "number and nature of the constituent parts of a poem"; the "imitation of an action that is serious and also, as having magnitude, complete in itself"; the description of "a kind of thing that might happen, i.e. what is possible as being probable or necessary"; all these parts, magnitude, probability and necessity, all may be and have repeatedly been interpreted as belonging to *technē*, to the places in human experience where categories work, where we divine the good from bad, justice from injustice. In every case, however, something other continues to circulate in Aristotle's account, especially perhaps in the distinction between "the thing that has happened" and "a kind of thing that might happen," where the latter opens onto another nature, beyond our nature, as the world of gods opens onto the good. Some arts, especially dramatic and poetic arts, do present the thing that has happened, bringing tragedy into an imitation of history. Poetry imitates history, though Aristotle carefully distinguishes them, however diaphorically: "Hence poetry is something more philosophic and of graver import than history, since its statements are of the nature rather of universals, whereas those of history are singulars" (Aristotle, *Poetics*, 1451b). Even here, we may interpret universals to belong to *technē*, "what such or such a kind of man will probably or necessarily say or do" (Aristotle, *Poetics*, 1451b). We may read the *probably* and *necessity* within *technē*.

Aristotle says that poetry imitates history while art presents everyday events under masks. Indeed, that is what art typically does. Perhaps it is precisely this work that art does, or our taking it as the work of art, that Socrates criticizes. Whatever art is for, whatever its end, it is not an imitation of everyday life or knowledge, and cannot pass itself off as these. It bears its masks in the open, carried by its *mimēsis*. Instead, art, poetry, touch something beyond, otherwise, reach for glory. What might happen belongs to the gods in their madness and in its destiny. Jung's criticism of Freud's view is of much wider import than its bearing on psychoanalysis. It is that art can be read entirely as everyday, within *technē*, can be read that way and loved that way. But something glorious, otherwise, archaic, is missed on that reading. The nature opened onto by art, that might happen, is not one set of events that could take place historically rather than another set, but another world, a world beyond this world, filled with madness, inspiration, touched with glory, responding to the good.

And here we may turn to the lines in Aristotle that may represent a crucial juncture in Nietzsche's revaluation of all values and the reaffirmation of the Dionysian. For Aristotle's famous remarks on good and evil in art pertain to his understanding of *mimēsis*:

> Imitation is natural to man from childhood, one of his advantages over the lower animals being this, that he is the most imitative creature in the world, and learns at first by imitation. And it is also natural for all to delight in works of imitation. The truth of this second point is shown by experience; though the objects themselves may be painful to see, we delight to view the most realistic representations of them in art, the forms for example of the lowest animals and of dead bodies. . . . the reason of the delight in seeing the picture is that one is at the same time learning—gathering the meaning of things. (Aristotle, *Poetics*, 1448b)

This passage deserves extended consideration of quite a different nature than it has traditionally been given. I mean something beyond the readings given by philosophers influenced by Nietzsche and Sade. For we may read this passage in multiple ways regarding the delight and pleasure we take in ugly, terrible, painful events. Perhaps ugly and terrible things are made pleasant in sensible form for us to enjoy. Perhaps terrible and destructive events are pleasant to us, reflecting our dark and appalling sides that we can bear to face only masked.

Both of these readings remain mundane. But the second opens another possibility, disclosed by Nietzsche, that something Dionysian carries the memory of this dark and appalling side of things, something demanding the revaluation of all values. I think of this as the call of the good. I wish to examine the possibility that throughout his *Poetics*, Aristotle repeatedly disrupts the mundaneness of the mundane in relation to art, all the while in mundane terms. I wish to consider the possibility that the painful, lowest, and dead, the delight and meaning given by art, come as gifts from the good, otherwise, beyond or away from, other than the mundane, but not by making the divine mundane, which is what theology does, and what art does not do except mistaken for theology. And that mistake is what I take Socrates to criticize in Books II and III of *Republic*.

Let us then consider some aspects of this passage:

1. This passage, concerning the delight we take in imitating dark and terrible events and things, is not restricted to that side of life and experience, as if we must consider such painful matters alongside joys and fulfillments. The passage concerns the nature of imitation, in general, its nature and how it is natural to human beings. Human beings imitate naturally, from childhood, learn by imitation. And the nature of such learning by imitation is that we face the most terrible things, learning from them and of them, by *mimēsis*, in art. Pictures (and words, of which Aristotle does not speak here) tell us, however painfully, of the conditions of life and experience.

Such an imitation cannot be restricted to art any more than to science or ethics, and in art cannot be restricted to *technē*. To the contrary. If Aristotle is telling us that *mimēsis* is both natural to human beings and an instrument—more than an instrument—whereby human beings learn of the world, through pictures and song, words and music, gesture and signs, then it bears the mark of the most varied forms of representation. More deeply still, *mimēsis is* representation, where representation is not restricted to any particular mode or norm. It is natural for human beings to represent—that is, to speak, to sing, to portray, to sign, and more—in order to learn, as learning, and more.[3]

Such an imitation, pertaining to the endless possibilities of representation, exists in no binary opposition, not even that of representation and reality. Rather, to the extent that human beings imitate and represent to learn, everything they do in thought and art is to learn and express, by representation and imitation. We may say that some representations are painful, others pleasant; some ugly, others beautiful. But the ways in which human beings are the most imitative creatures in the world—if that is true, to be considered momentarily—are inexhaustible. Both *poiēsis* and *technē* are imitations, representations, by art under the one and the other, but also by science, *epistēmē*, and by philosophy. Human work is representation, imitation, *mimēsis*, and we take delight—if that is the word—in what we learn by such *mimēsis*. And again, to be considered momentarily, perhaps not just human work, perhaps all things work by representation. In any case, if there is mimetic as well as narrative representation, and if the latter is more useful, true, then that binary opposition falls within *mimēsis*. It does not define a distinction between *mimēsis* and a more truthful exposition.

2. From the first, apparently irresistibly, Aristotle's thought bears the structure of domination and subordination, even within an account of a representation that knows nothing of that structure. For what is natural to humanity is denied to animals in the face of all the evidence. Are humans the most imitative creatures? Kittens and puppies imitate endlessly in their play. Elephants and primates use tools and paint, perhaps use and understand words.

Aristotle believes it is not worth the slightest reference to evidence concerning animals and human beings to claim that the latter imitate and the former do not, or not as much. Human beings are the most imitative creatures, and learn by imitation. We know that animals learn by imitation, but we wish to reiterate human superiority. Analogously, we know that women and slaves are as human as any other human beings, know this beyond a doubt. But even so, some are masters and some are slaves, by nature, also without a doubt, and without the slightest evidence. The link between the domination of human beings and the domination of nature is complete, both by nature.[4]

I noted earlier how easily this understanding of the hierarchy of nature becomes excessive, so that what demands justification by nature passes to infinity and can be claimed with no justification whatever. Spinoza, of all philosophers, the Spinoza for whom everything in nature bears the mark of eternity, of God, understands that anything whatever in nature, at least from the standpoint of human beings, exists for human use in any way whatever.[5]

Whatever the criterion—here *mimēsis*, in other places *logos*—it works against any criteria, passes from criteria and justifications to the extreme, as if the order of nature, from high to low, dominant to subordinate, mirrored God's rule, where that rule fell under the good, bore the mark of injustice. I understand the call of the good in this place, after Anaximander, to demand that we endlessly resist injustice, where every thing in its place imposes injustices on others. Such an understanding of our responsiveness toward the good, toward its heterogeneities, cannot sustain in any place a natural hierarchy of high and low without resistance, without restitution, in the name of the good.

In the name of such a restitution, let us imagine that this criterion, natural to humanity, is not reason or *eudaimonia*, not the good for humanity, but imitation, *mimēsis*, either representation in general or by art. And if it is by art, here in *Poetics*, it is less *technē* than *poiēsis*. What, we may ask, might it mean to think that poetry or music divides human beings from animals, divides the natural world into high and low? I have claimed repeatedly that *poiēsis* knows nothing of such high and low, nothing of such distinctions, that the hierarchy of domination and subordination cannot belong to art by *poiēsis*, to music, poetry, dance, painting, or sculpture, but belongs to *technē*, to use. It is *technē*'s task to divide good from bad, high from low, to make distinctions and to impose categories.

In what voice, then, do we understand Aristotle to speak of *poiēsis*, if that is what *Poetics* is about, as if poetry were the mark of the highest humanity? Let us leave aside the disparity between this mark of high and low and that of *Nicomachean Ethics*, where *eudaimonia* and *nous* express the divine in human terms. They are united, perhaps, under the sign of learning and meaning. We human beings imitate to learn, to mean, to express, to gather, perhaps to assemble in place the identities and essences of things. Except that *poiēsis* disassembles, displaces, disrupts, interrupts the assembling of identities.

Aristotle virtually says this in speaking of metaphor. For "[m]etaphor consists in giving the thing a name that belongs to something else" (Aristotle, *Poetics*, 1457b), while "the greatest thing by far is to be a master of metaphor. It is the one thing that cannot be learnt from others; and it is also a sign of genius, . . . " (Aristotle, *Poetics*, 1459a). His understanding of metaphor bears two marks of domination, one a contrast between the "unfamiliar terms" in metaphor and "ordinary words" (Aristotle, *Poetics*, 1458b), the other that "a good metaphor implies an intuitive perception of the similarity in dissimilars" (Aristotle, *Poetics*, 1459a). We may read Aristotle and nearly all subsequent writers to insist that the strangeness of metaphors and other poetic language be regulated, brought under rational control. But Aristotle without a doubt insists that "the greatest thing by far" is to interrupt the regulation of discourse by "ordinary words" to "save the language from seeming mean and prosaic" (Aristotle, *Poetics*, 1458b).

On this account, the subordination of metaphor to literal discourse is a mark of *technē*, reminiscent of the subordination of women to men and slaves to masters—reminiscent, that is, of the domination and oppression of categories and identities. I have interposed questions of sexual difference, in Wittig and Irigaray among others, to interrupt the hold of such identities, the thought of categories and identities, to bring us to a different relation of individuals and kinds. Under the call of the good, we must reinterpret our relation to kinds, human and otherwise. This interruption belongs to *poiēsis*, to imitation and representation. The possibility of interrupting the hold of identity, under our responsibility toward the good, comes through representation, imitation, by art under *poiēsis*. And under *technē*, where that is understood to be interrupted and displaced by *poiēsis*, by divine madness and by love.

And, perhaps incredibly, by nature, *phusis*, in the name of animals, and women, and slaves. The very dominations and oppositions of men over women, humans over animals, masters over slaves, human nature over inanimate nature, in their interruptions, interrupt the hold of categories of domination and oppression in their own name. This is, as I understand it, the deepest truth of ecological feminism, the thought that the domination of women and the domination of nature are linked. The thought of women, in our Western history, is a thought of domination and oppression. The category of woman is a category of oppression.[6] In the same sense exactly, the categories of animal and nature are categories of oppression and domination. To which I suggest that we should respond that nature is no category; nor is woman; and nor are animals, humans, lesbians, gays, or straights. All are queer and strange, where the good insists that the queer and strange interrupt the straight and narrow by memories of heterogeneity.

Historically speaking, by slavery and other dark considerations, the domination of women parallels other dominations: slavery, colonization, marginalization. And in every place, those dominated, oppressed, have responded with art: African, African-American, Caribbean art. And in every place, those dominated, oppressed, created art before they were placed under domination. Including women. Leading to another domination, subordinating such arts as inferior. On this reading, art enters the hierarchies of domination repeatedly, to open resistance to such domination, responsible to the good, and as a repeated side of hierarchical oppression. Again, women repeatedly have borne the weight of such domination, as women.

This subject of the relation between the domination of women and the domination of nature, and other dominations, in relation to the good, and art, is too important to be passed over so quickly. And even more important, perhaps, for our purposes, is the relation between our resistance to domination, under the good, and the subject of imitation, or art, under *poiēsis* and *technē*. Postponing this topic for just a moment, I will enumerate some additional features of the passage in question.

3. It is natural for human beings, perhaps for other creatures, animate and inanimate, to imitate, to represent. Things represent themselves and others. Things interrupt the hold of identities in response to each other, to heterogeneity. Things work in response to the demands of the good. Interrupting the assembling of being is not restricted to human beings.

But what of the delight—if that is the word—we human beings take in painful, disgusting, terrible things. Aristotle speaks of *delight* and of lowest animals and dead bodies. As Derrida suggests, in speaking of Kant on this subject, even here, in the name of beauty, in the name of the good, if ugliness can be accepted in art, some things cannot: vomit, excrement, disgusting things.[7] The good in art, beauty, imposes a norm, cuts away from things, excludes, at the very point at which Aristotle and Kant consider the possibility that *everything* may give us delight, *everything* may be beautiful, in art, by art.

This subject divides in two, expressed in certain ways by Kant's view of the sublime, expressed in other ways by Nietzsche's view of the Dionysian. On one side of this question of the ugly, painful, disgusting in art, the exclusions borne by the beautiful, the suggestion that the good must exclude to be good, is my claim that exclusion belongs to *technē*, that the good that calls us to respond, in relation to art and beauty and the sublime, does not cut, does not exclude, includes everything in its glory. This question, of the mundane, touches both the delight of which Aristotle speaks and the exclusions of vomit, excrement, disgusting, violent things and events—represented, as we know, in glorious painted works by Bosch and Bruegel, in our day by Francis Bacon, but also in some of the most haunting and terrible poems and tales by Celan and Levi. We say that The Holocaust cannot be represented, in the singularity of its horror. We know that it is represented repeatedly, by terrible works that bear the burden of our ethical responsibility. Not to represent it is to refuse a memory of responsibility, not to respond. It is to perform another cut doing the work of *technē*.

But first, the pleasure we take in pain and horror. In relation to the mundane, following Jung's understanding of this psychological domain, we find that violence and pain, in representation, give us pleasure, fulfill a certain mundane satisfaction. We laugh when someone falls down, scream with joy when the axe murderer carves up his victim on the screen. And still in relation to the mundane, we may consider the possibility that we delight in horror, that pain delights us in art because we delight in pain, in ourselves and others, that within us, still mundane and however masked, covert, covered over, we enjoy suffering, our own and the suffering of others. We bear a dark and terrible understanding, however deeply buried, of evil within ourselves.

I call this mundane because on this reading, however covert, however deeply forgotten, Sade was right about human life and experience. Pain and suffering belong to the joys of human life, and we must know them, must know this truth, to belong to human being, assembled in human experience, covered over. Civilization would like to cover over dark truths of violence and death, but they reemerge in times of struggle, reemerge far too readily, in Bosnia and Rwanda today for example.

We may read Aristotle and Kant to speak in the mundane, to which we reply, perhaps, that Aristotle does not acknowledge the full truth of the violence of the mundane, that he civilizes the pain and violence of human experience in saying that we enjoy violence in art. We enjoy violence everywhere, in ourselves and others, enjoy it and commit it. Art is merely the most acceptable manifestation. Or, if not in art alone, violence and suffering, ugliness and loathsomeness, are enjoyable when we learn from them. And what, still within the mundane, if we learned nothing but enjoyed much? Civilization is a darker and more terrible place, still mundane.

This mundane theme of enjoyment remains commensurate with other forms of delight. And here we face the possibility, on one side, that art gives us the kind of joy we might derive from sexual pursuit and conquest or from competitive sports. On the other side is Jung's claim that the delight we gain from art touches another place entirely, perhaps no place at all, reaches toward something archaic.

4. For Dionysus is a god, however terrible, and the sublime is beyond representation, however painful and disturbing. Dionysus interrupts the flow of orderly life, and the sublime interrupts the order of beautiful representations, with something beyond, excessive. I think of this as given from the good. I mean especially to consider the possibility that the "realistic representations" of painful things, of violent, degrading, disgusting, loathsome, terrible events and things, not only may open certain sides of our mundane experience to us, hidden, masked, and more, but also open and reveal by interruption something otherwise than the mundane, or otherwise in the mundane—I do not call it extramundane; I do not mean to reinstitute the city of God. What we may learn from these terrible representations is not only a dark and terrible side of ourselves, let us say one we might wish to avoid or suppress rather than reveal, but a dark and terrible side of things that is not for us to choose, that makes choice possible, intelligible, however strained.[8]

Here, the meaning of things we gather from this dark and painful place is not of dark and painful things alongside bright and joyous things, but meanings beyond the identities of mundane things, archaic and sacred meanings, otherwise, ecstatic joys. Again, I leave open the question, raised by Levinas, of whether these archaic and sacred meanings are otherwise *than* being or, as I understand them, are otherwise *in* being, interrupting the assembling of beings and meanings together with responsibility toward the good, intermediary and never transcendent. In facing terrible events and things in the name of the sublime or archaic, we face something that interrupts the flow of events and things with a responsibility beyond all responsibilities. And we find that we are exposed in the deepest and far-reaching ways, ambiguous and terrible ways, to such responsibilities and calls.

If we always shuddered at painful events and took pleasure from good ones, if we always reacted to painfulness with pain and to pleasant things with pleasure, we would have unmistakable criteria for the work of the good. The good interrupts the work of such criteria with conflicting and ambiguous responses. We enjoy evil and sometimes find goodness boring. And even worse, experiences are enjoyable when evil and boring when good. And even worse, we must face the ambiguity of such experiences twice, once in being unsure from our experience what is good and what is bad, and worse, that what we "normally" take to be good and bad must be incessantly reexamined from the standpoint of the good. What is bad may be good; what is good may be bad. And worse, what is bad *is good*; what is good *is bad*, always and everywhere, but not in every way. This is in part what it means to understand that responsiveness given from the good is infinite, endless.

We are exposed and vulnerable in our responsibilities toward others, other people and things, beyond any criteria and norms, beyond any work, not a beyond that is "greater than" criteria, norms, and work.[9] Rather, our exposure and vulnerability to the good interrupt all criteria, norms, and work. We can do nothing but appeal to our experience for ethical judgments. There is nothing else. But our experiences are conflicting, ambiguous, in dark and terrible ways, pointing beyond themselves to the impossibility of the good.

On this reading, the *delight* of which Aristotle speaks in relation to monstrous and terrible events and things is not a mundane joy but ecstatic, interruption. There is delight in this interruption, a joy—a *jouissance*—directed toward the good, inseparable from and indistinguishable from pain, lacking all sense of high and low, of categorial distinctions, but still a demand, an exposure, a vulnerability. We take joy in our exposure to the good, a joy in the wounding we feel within ourselves as the burden of injustice, a joy—however terrible—in wounding others from within our responsibility toward the good. For without that joy, we could not bear that responsibility within ourselves. Despite everything I have said of Spinoza's hierarchization of the world from a human standpoint in Book IV of his *Ethics*, this is a joy he knows and expresses beyond any other philosopher's representation.

5. That the delight of which Aristotle speaks may be understood in terms of both sacred and mundane entails that we understand the learning of which he speaks in terms of *technē* and *poiēsis*, mundane and sacred. I have suggested this already in relation to the divinity of Dionysus and learning by *poiēsis*. Here I wish to move from the mundane, from *technē*, learning by art, to consider the central theme of Aristotle's *Poetics*, that we learn in art and poetry by *mimēsis*, learn from them as art—that is, as *poiēsis*—under divine inspiration. What might we learn from the gods if they do not command our obedience under the sign of *technē?* What of these meanings of things, gathered together under the sign of *legein*, given by the gods?

Such a question must be considered in its full gravity, not reduced in scale, somehow, by reference to poetics. Learning is mentioned in this passage as what may seem a modest good. But Aristotle begins his *Metaphysics* with what may be read as so extreme an account of the desire to learn as to rule over all other human desires. "All men by nature desire to know" (Aristotle, *Metaphysics*, 980), and they desire to know beyond all limits, for this

knowledge is related to sight, and "we prefer seeing to everything else" (Aristotle, *Metaphysics*, 980). On the one hand, this excessive desire for knowledge
beyond anything else is related to rule, to masters and slaves, "for the wise
man must not be ordered but must order, and he must not obey another, but
the less wise must obey *him*" (Aristotle, *Metaphysics*, 982a).[10] Things by nature, and the excessive desire for knowledge and truth, lead to mastery and
subordination. On this side, knowledge, truth, and nature are inseparable
from the good, led through desire's excesses.

On the other hand, learning in relation to poetry brings us to strange
places, to metaphor and figuration, to what Plato calls *mimēsis*. It brings us,
that is, to *poiēsis*. And if we pause for just a moment to gather up this thought
and consider it elsewhere, otherwise, then perhaps in *Metaphysics* and even
in *Prior Analytics*, Aristotle recognizes that desire's excesses pertain to knowledge and learning everywhere, to wisdom, so that the desire beyond all other
desires for knowledge, in *Metaphysics*, demands *poiēsis*, insists on *mimēsis*.
Here mimetic narrative does not impede the desire for knowledge, but com-
pletes it. Philosophy's recoil from *mimēsis* has always been accompanied by
recognition that only through *mimēsis*, of geometry if not of poetry,[11] can philosophy fulfill its debts. Here we return to divine madness and inspiration.

And indeed this is what we have seen in Plato, in *Ion* and *Phaedrus* especially, where the rhapsode's inspiration comes from the gods, bears the sacred weight of something beyond the mundane, where souls stand on the
back of the world (Plato, *Phaedrus*, 247c), and writing, thought, knowledge
without erotic madness is lifeless, dead (*Phaedrus*, 264c; 276b). Here I mean
to consider the possibility that something similar can be found in Aristotle,
at least in his *Poetics*, unlike in Plato, who writes poetically even of *technē*,
for Aristotle's writing follows *technē* even when *poiēsis* is in question. Even
so, the learning that obsesses us everywhere in Aristotle belongs to poetry as
much as to science, belongs perhaps to the sacred as well as the mundane.

On this reading, poetry's diction always speaks in a mimetic voice, as
if no narrative can be told except under the sign of *mimēsis*. Moreover, this
poetic diction gives us learning and truth, satisfies our desire for learning
and truth, as much as any *technē*. Here, then, poetry touches the gods, bears
the touch of divine inspiration, madness, as Plato suggests repeatedly. And
Aristotle.

What if the learning of which Aristotle speaks in the passage we are con-
sidering in detail, the learning we have understood as touching something
beyond the mundane, something sacred, what if that learning belonged to
poiēsis? What if learning belonged to *poiēsis* as well as *technē*, not by a technical distinction, repeating *technē*, but by a madness and inspiration given
in *poiēsis*? What, that is, if the burden of Aristotle's *Poetics*, on my reading
here, were to mark the sign of the good, the gift, touched by a divine inspi-

ration known to us as *poiēsis?* We learn the meaning of things—here painful, difficult, terrible things—from art, poetic art, learn some things from art by *poiēsis* we cannot learn from art by *technē*.

We are called here to knowledge and truth by a desire beyond all other desires, a gift that cannot come from truth itself, but comes from the good as desire. The good calls us to a knowledge and truth that exceed art by *technē*, exceed reason, demand the madness and terror of Dionysus. Nature in its enormity, monstrosity, terror, fearfulness, fearsomeness, nature in its plenitude, haunted by Dionysus's revelries, obscured by Dionysian masks, calls to us as endless desire to pursue its truth, a truth hidden to *technē*, demanding the mad resources of *poiēsis*.

Here, animals and bodies are gifts of the sacred as well as the mundane, come to us from the good where truth belongs to the mundane. When we consider this passage from the standpoint of the good, we cannot think that Aristotle is telling us only of mundane truths of painful things. We consider the possibility that he is touching upon excessive truths belonging to the gods. *Poiēsis*, with its truths, is an intermediary figure, between heaven and earth, sacred and mundane. Art by *poiēsis* reveals to us something of the good, and of the gods, that cannot be remembered by *technē*.

6. If *mimēsis* is natural, and belongs to *poiēsis*, then a close and intimate link exists between nature and art that touches in this passage on the dark and fearful side of nature, called from the good. Here we reconsider the possibility, mentioned earlier, that Aristotle's account of the dark and painful truths of art reveal something of the natural world, its interruption by the good. What is interrupted, we have seen repeatedly, is the hierarchization of categories of knowledge, the domination and oppression of identities assembled under the sign of nature. Nature's truths order the world from high to low, good to bad, subordinating women and "lower" creatures, animate and inanimate. In Aristotle, repeatedly, categories of knowledge exist to rule, masters over slaves, higher over lower; and alongside this domination, the ends of human life are higher in the service of domination and oppression.

Yet the idea of *eudaimonia*, unlike that of pleasure, is not a domination. And the idea of the painful and terrible representations brought to our attention by art is not a domination, but perhaps the reverse. The joy given to us by art confronting the "lowest" is not a joy in the hierarchy, the domination, but works against the distinction between high and low. At its heart, perhaps the ethical difficulty with *mimēsis* is that it undermines in its presentation all the distinctions we have produced so painfully in our rational work between good and bad, high and low. But what it presents, in this undermining, undercutting, is not the bad in place of the good, but the good in bad, the good that calls within the good and bad against the authority of the distinction.

On this reading, nature's plenitude imposes on us an endless responsibility, fulfilled more poignantly for us in art than anywhere else in our experience, to understand and care for what we destroy, the sacrifices we must
make, in order to live and choose. Ethics is justified sacrifice. Where do we
look to reconsider the justification, to question sacrifice's authority? Not to
reason or to ethics, not to *techne*, for reason can provide us only with another
authority, this for that. *Techne* never touches the arbitrariness of authority
at its heart, because it requires authority for its work. *Poiesis*, in its response
to the good, gives us nature's plenitude lacking all authority for destruction.
Only facing such a total absence of authority for the authority of judgment
can we respond to the call of the good.

Nature, here, is a plenitude of things and events, under the good, that
does not divide into categories and kinds, under the good, except in response
to gifts from the good that resist the evil in every division. This term, *evil*, is
Whitehead's. He speaks of "the intrinsic reality of an event" as value (Whitehead, *SMW*, 131); each event, each thing, is precious. But things cannot all
coexist without selection, destruction, sacrifice. And sacrifice, the destruction of this for that, the subordination of some that others may thrive, can
never be justified, rationalized, in the name of the good, only in the work of
judgment under *techne*, already sacrificial. The good calls us to know, to care
for, to respond to the low, the painful, the terrible, to what we regard as evil,
to recognize the intrinsic nature of things and kinds beyond any authority we
or anyone else may impose to regulate them.

I call this sense of the good in all things, *cherishment*. It can do work in
time only as sacrifice. The conjunction of cherishment and sacrifice is plenishment. On my reading, Aristotle suggests in relation to art (but not to
ethics) a sensitivity through *poiesis* to the dark, difficult, terrible, forbidding
side of things, of nature. And it is nature, indeed, that is in question. *Poiesis*
works under the good to recall to us what we under the sign of *techne* must
forget, cannot help but forget, the goodness of the most terrible things, their
ideality: an ideality we can never allow ourselves to forget, even as what we
repeatedly forget is that ideality. We could not live except by forgetting. But
the good demands that we remember. And it is a demand so mad, so difficult,
that it requires all the resources of *poiesis* for its expression.

7. Returning now to the understanding that the domination of
women—and others, masters and slaves—is inseparable from the domination of nature, I have explored the possibility that the Aristotle whose writings represent the heart of the Western understanding of the domination of
nature together with women and slaves, for whom domination is legitimated
by hierarchical categories, that very same Aristotle also touches upon the
possibility that the gift of the good shows itself in art, at least art by *poiesis*,

where the categories of high and low collapse under the force of *mimēsis*. I read this collapse as a sign of the good.

But I must now reverse this recognition, from women and the oppression of human beings in the name of high and low, to nature. For the domination of nature, in Aristotle, exists in virtue of hierarchical categories under the sign of desire for truth. In *poiēsis*, however, there exists a resistance to this domination that retains the desire for truth, at least, poetic truth, bearing within itself a divine and erotic madness without which no desire for truth could mark the good. And here we may consider something of Heidegger's reading of *phusis* in Aristotle (Heidegger, *OBCP*). For on his reading, in *Physics* II, Aristotle speaks of that which moves out of itself toward itself, nature, *phusis*, being, contrasted with that which moves according to an end, *technē*. *"Nature is a source or cause of being moved and of being at rest in that to which it belongs primarily*, and not in virtue of a concomitant attribute" (Aristotle, *Physics*, 192b). Nature moves within itself; artificial products do not. Nature circulates beyond limits; artificial products limit themselves in relation to their ends.

Heidegger pursues a line of thought in which, we may say, the nature, *phusis*, that moves within itself is not originarily hierarchical. Hierarchy belongs to *technē* in virtue of the concomitant attribute or end for which artificial things are made. And indeed, all things by nature that dominate do so, even by nature, according to an end or essence. But Heidegger never considers that this line of thought against hierarchy is more than a thought of nature's truth, but of nature's good. Resistance to hierarchy is not by nature in truth alone, but by nature in the call of the good. Or rather, it is responsibility under the good that calls upon us to repudiate hierarchy from the standpoint of the nature that moves within itself.

Or rather, the nature that circulates things against the hold of any authority, any hierarchy, any particular categories and ends, against the hold of *technē*, that nature exceeds any limits possible under *technē*. It is a nature to be understood as general economy, the circulation of goods and gifts beyond any slowing down, any limits given by a restricted economy under *technē*. *Technē* works—and works well—in restricted economies, imposes restricted economies to do its work. The call, the gift, of the good circulates beyond any restricted economy, exceeds any work. Nature, here, is the general economy of goods and gifts, circulating madly, gifted from the gods. Perhaps nature, here, is the good; perhaps nature, here, is the economy of the good, intermediary and excessive, beyond any work under *technē*, still recalling the good.

This nature, under the good, is a nature otherwise, in memory of divine and erotic madness, but in no other place. The otherwise in nature belongs to nature, belongs to the gods in nature. It does not belong to the gods in their places. This is the truth of *poiēsis* beyond all other truths: that in reminding us of the good, responding to its call, circulating the giving of the good, art shows us the good here, where we are, in and as interruption. Aristotle speaks of painful and terrible things in nature that interrupt the order of technical production, the order of the state, teach us of meanings beyond any other meanings—here before us, where we are, in our places. The gift of the good, as read in Aristotle's *Poetics*, given by art under *poiēsis*, is given to us where we are, not in another place. This is what we may say is what art tells us more than anything else: that the gods and their madness are not away from being, in another place, even descending from that place to ours, but belong to nature, given as interruption. In this sense, nature is the circulation of the good. And in this sense as well, art is the gift of the good, circulating itself as a gift in memory of the good, everywhere.

Where I see ecological feminism touching the good in nature is along the lines of hierarchy dividing men from women, humans from animals, good from bad, and other dominations, masters and slaves, all hierarchical dominations said to belong to nature. In response, I understand that the good calls to us from that nature, present to us in our experiences of individuals and kinds, resistant to hierarchy and domination. Every thing and every place in nature is given to us from the good, as are women, animals, and other natural things. Without that gift, we could not resist domination. Without that gift, we could not impose domination. We are, must be, exposed to things in nature, inexhaustibly, endlessly, to respond to them however we do, to be responsive toward them inexhaustibly. It is nature itself, interrupted everywhere, to which we are vulnerable, exposed, in our desires beyond all desires, for truth, order, regulation, all interrupted by endless gifts under the good. It is nature itself, interrupted everywhere by heterogeneous kinds, to which we bring hierarchical categories of domination, and in which we find endless resistance to domination.

All of this can be read in Aristotle's *Poetics*, related to poetic *mimēsis*, interrupting the control of narrative exposition at every point. Here *mimēsis*, in its interruptions, is the gift of the good in art, expresses the possibility of interrupting nature at every point to ask about its beauty, a question of the good.

A much more radical, heterogeneous place, interrupting our reading of Aristotle's *Poetics*, a place where nature touches the good together with sexual difference, is given in Diotima's speech in Plato's *Symposium*. For we cannot read what may be among the most supreme accounts of the good in Plato, where love meets beauty in the light of the good, without wondering why Diotima is the only woman allowed to speak eloquently in Plato, and the significance of what she says, as a woman, though she does not appear. The extraordinary thing about her speech in the present context is its closing, where she speaks of those who have learned the lessons of love:

> when he comes toward the end will suddenly perceive a nature of wondrous beauty *[phusin kalon]* (and this, Socrates, is the final cause of all our former toils)—a nature which in the first place is everlasting, not growing and decaying, or waxing and waning; secondly, not fair in one point of view and foul in another, or at one time or in one relation or at one place fair, at another time or in another relation or in another place foul, as if fair to some and foul to others, or in the likeness of a face or hands or any other part of the bodily frame, or in any form of speech or knowledge, or existing in any other being, as for example in an animal, or in heaven, or in earth, or in any other place; but beauty absolute, separate, simple, and everlasting, which without diminution and without increase, or any change, is imparted to the ever-growing and perishing beauties of all other things. (Plato, *Symposium*, 210–211a)

I read this as a glowing account of the good, in Diotima's voice, given as *phusis*, not a nature to be known, of truth, but of love and beauty, of *poiēsis*, described as nature beautiful.[12] Such a nature is undivided by being and becoming, is undivided and unconditional beauty and love, messengers from the good, giving birth to the nature we know under *technē*, divided by categories and identities, differences of rank and place. We may think of this nature, this good, as absolute, separate, simple, and everlasting, as if it were another place. I think of it as nature still, not *another nature*, another place or world, but nature itself, which, like *phusis* in Aristotle, moves within itself undivided as nature, giving birth to divisions and categories from within itself. Nature bears two souls, diaphorically, related as the good to particular goods, general to restricted economy, perhaps like *poiēsis* and *technē*, giving another meaning to the relation of universality to particularity. Not the one throughout the many, which I understand in terms of families, kinds, but the exaltation of the many given from the good.[13] This is the nature that Spinoza knows, where we may read Part IV to bear the mark of *technē* under the glory of eternity from God.

There is much more to consider in Diotima's speech. For I would return to the questions I asked above about her sex in Plato to wonder if this other nature, heterogeneous, can be spoken of in relation to love and immortality only in the voice of a woman, an otherwise silent woman. I wonder, that is, as a supplement to the critique of Plato that he allows a woman to speak only once, only here, that what he allows her to say is something so astonishing, so remarkable, about heterogeneity, alterity, and temporality that it took a Diotima of Mantineia, touched by divine madness, prophecy *(manteia)*,[14] and ancient, wise, to be able to speak of love at all. I wonder, that is, whether the strangeness of the truth requires recognition of the heterogeneity of which Irigaray speaks, belonging to sexual difference, where she speaks of "the other sex as an alterity irreducible to myself" (Irigaray, *QED*, 180).[15] This thought pursues the possibility that we may find in this place in Plato acknowledgment that just as we can speak of the nature we know, hierarchized into systems of domination, only given from another nature, beautiful in gifts from the good, we can think of something other, truthful, in the ways of the world, only in the voice of the Other, given as love. Women here, under the sign of sexual difference, touch alterity in the intermediary voice of love.

I do not mean to offer a reading here of Plato's *Symposium*, which involves a wealth of other mimetic figures. I mean to think of Diotima's speech by itself as a pinnacle of beauty, framed by different speeches on love, many concerned with its advantages and technicalities, followed by Alcibiades' paean to Socrates as the pinnacle of the good, at least the human good, closing, as I have mentioned, with Socrates still sober, still working, proclaiming the virtues and possibilities of comedy and tragedy. The dialogue as a whole links love and beauty with *poiēsis* under the sign, I would say, of the good. Diotima's speech is a climax in that mimetic progression, spoken by Socrates in the voice of a woman.

The close of that speech presents the good in a surpassing vision of nature, undivided, beautiful, inspiring, giving birth to knowledge and truth, spoken in the voice of a woman, inspired by love, inspired on love, expressing its heterogeneity. I imagine that we may learn something of our thought of ecological feminism, joining nature and women under categories of domination, hoping to free them both, inspired perhaps by Diotima's vision. At least, that is my hope, and I find traces of it in Irigaray, who speaks of intermediary figures, angels, moving between earth and sky, *technē* and *poiēsis*. She speaks of these in memory of Diotima.

For Diotima denies that Eros is a god, says that he is between mortals and immortals (Plato, *Symposium*, 202e), a very powerful *daimon*, where *daimon*s do the diaphoric work of interpreting and mediating between gods and humans (Plato, *Symposium*, 203). We must ask ourselves whether the being and truth of the good might reside in intermediary figures. This would deny the separability of the gods, however blasphemous, and it would deny as well the lack of spirituality and divinity of the earth. We live in intermediary figures; nature moves in intermediary movements; the world is filled with *daimon*s, all diaphoric.

Diotima speaks of movements, denies that love can come to rest, even in death:

> He is by nature neither mortal nor immortal, but alive and flourishing at one moment when he is in plenty, and dead at another moment, and again

alive by reason of his father's nature. But that which is always flowing in is always flowing out, and so he is never in want and never in wealth; and, further, he is in a mean between ignorance and knowledge. (Plato, *Symposium*, 203e–204)

Like Socrates himself, another *daimon*, who is always in a mean between ignorance and knowledge, love is always moving. And perhaps nature, *phusis*, and *poiēsis*, and even, or especially, *technē*, are all intermediaries, moving around, flowing, moving in between, touched by the gods, dead without their inspiration.

Socrates asks Diotima, of what use *(chreian)* is love to human beings (Plato, *Symposium*, 204c), bringing us back to the profit and advantage around which our discussions of the good have moved. At this point we may wonder if we have returned to love as *technē*. But Diotima replies against the possibility of that reading. For she does not answer with the profits brought by love. Love is of beauty. And what does beauty bring? She gives two analogies. Think of love as you think of the good. The good brings happiness *(eudaimonia)* when it brings good things. Yet you and I know that good things do not bring *eudaimonia*. She then compares the parts of love with the parts of *poiēsis*, where *poiēsis* is the "creation or passage of non-being into being" (Plato, *Symposium*, 205c); but only those are poets who are concerned with music and meter. She speaks of love in intimate relation with the good and *poiēsis*, as we cannot think of love without thinking of *poiēsis* and the good. But she concludes that "you may say generally that all desire of good and happiness is only the great and subtle power of love; but they who are drawn towards him by any other path, whether the path of money-making or gymnastics or philosophy, are not called lovers. . . . The simple truth is, that men love the good" (Plato, *Symposium*, 205–206).[16] Nothing could more closely touch the thought I am pursuing here, that we can be happy only in the gift of the good, loving the good, working by *poiēsis*. As nature, and in nature, by *poiēsis* and by love, the good gives birth to knowledge, truth, and happiness, and more, gives poetry and music, and inexhaustibly more. But what it gives as profit and advantage is given as *technē* without love, without love of the good, without life. Without love of the good, without a touch of divine madness and inspiration, earthly things are dead. Good things have nothing to do with happiness without love. We hear this most in human life, frequently dead, forgetting the Muses. For nature is abundant, plenitudinous, beautiful. In Plato. And where we hear this most in return, filled with life, is in art, filled with *mimēsis*.

There is much more in Diotima's speech. For she goes on to interpret love of the good by dissolving binary oppositions between body and soul, and humans and animals. Against virtually all idealistic readings of Plato,

Diotima speaks here of "birth in beauty, whether of body or soul" (Plato, *Symposium,* 206c)—that is, of procreation—in relation to immortality. And beauty is a gift of the gods (Plato, Symposium, 206cd), flowing over with begetting and bringing forth, with what she has called poiēsis.

Perhaps we have another reason here why Diotima's speech on love must be given by an absent woman. The theme of love demands women in the name of procreation, in nature's memory, memory of the good, and with it *poiēsis.* Love reaches for immortality, in time, by *poiēsis,* through the love of men and women, through beauty in body and soul, and cannot reach forward in time without women. Love between men and men or women and women does not bear the weight of desire for immortality, does not reach toward the future. Unlike Socrates' speech in *Phaedrus,* Diotima's speech is procreative, productive. Love in time demands its future; time demands heterogeneity, alterity, fulfilled by men and women together. Including animals.

For Diotima dissolves the limits of humanity as defined by animals as impossible to sustain in relation to body and soul. Animals as well as human beings love immortality (Plato, *Symposium,* 207a). Moreover, while such a love in human beings may be due to reason *(logismon)* (Plato, *Symposium,* 207c), it is due in animals and elsewhere in nature to the love of immortality in mortal things (Plato, *Symposium,* 207d) everywhere in nature, as soul in *Phaedrus* has care of all things in nature. We find something similar in Spinoza, where the essence of each thing is its *conatus,* its effort to persevere in its own being, a finite image of eternity (Spinoza, *Ethics,* Part 3, Prop. 6, 7). Even so, this yearning for immortality in Spinoza is a perseverance, and he concludes from it that all things other than human beings are for the sake of humanity (Spinoza, *Ethics,* Part 4, Appendix, 26). Love for immortality and the good in Plato arouses movement, interrupts familiar things. All natural, mortal things are touched by love of the good, disturbed in their timely places by something untimely, interrupting their pursuit of profit and advantage. All restricted economies exceed their limits, exceed any prices, values, profits, whirl as general economies, given from the good. Including *technē.* Every earthly thing and place and economy is interrupted by something other, related to love of the good and immortality. All this includes animals as well as humans, interrupts the closing of the limits of human nature around human reason. Reason may be uniquely human, but the reason that belongs to *technē,* concerned with profit and advantage, knows nothing of the immortal side of the good, which itself knows nothing of opposition in *diaphora.* The reason that belongs to the gods is filled with love, desire, for the good, for something that knows nothing of the conflicts of time, reaches for immortality, however madly. Such a love for the good does not belong to human beings alone, but includes animals and everything else in nature, includes body and soul, a yearning for generation and becoming Diotima associates with *poiēsis*.

That is why when we understand and respond to the call of the good we encounter a nature of wondrous beauty undivided by distinctions and oppositions, between good and evil, high and low, mine and yours, men's and women's. All are equal gifts of the good, an equality without measure. All is one as given by the good, a one without limit. Love is everywhere, unconditioned and undivided by mortality as love, everywhere, as a call, responsibility, yearning, desire. *Poiēsis* is everywhere, in every place, and places are not divided by love, the gods, immortality, or *poiēsis*. Love makes the world go round, moved and inspired by endless intermediary figures of limit and unlimit. We never dwell in heaven, with the gods, never dwell in immortality, never inhabit a nature of inexhaustible and undivided beauty. But we can live in beauty as an intermediary figure, moved by love, dwelling with justice, goodness, and truth, all themselves intermediary figures.

This is how I read Diotima's speech, on love and the good as calling everywhere in nature, in time, interrupting the hold of time's authority. I read her speech, remembering that she is a woman, linking nature with the good, with sexual difference, remembering that she is excluded from the party. I think that under *technē*, categories and distinctions serve to rule, to dominate and oppress, over women and slaves, and throughout nature. In memory of the good, called by it to a responsibility beyond measure, we encounter a nature of unconditional love, which I call *cherishment,* where we are exposed to things and kinds, exposed and vulnerable everywhere, exposed not masters through reason, exposed not governed or governing by rule, vulnerable to truth by way of the good. Cherishment is an intermediary figure of unconditional love, given to us everywhere in the name of the good, demanding sacrifice, another exposure, where we are vulnerable to our own injustices.

We respond with plenishment, all things respond everywhere with plenishment, where love and beauty and truth are intermediary figures in memory of a good, a nature, that knows and justifies no distinctions, no categories and identities legitimating domination. Diotima tells us that the nature we know, filled with distinctions and dominations, comes from another nature undivided, nature as the good, and that we can partake of the nature we know only through intermediary figures touched by the inspirations of nature undivided under the good. All the work we do is through intermediary figures, saved from injustice and domination by the inspirations and memories it bears of the good through love and beauty and *poiēsis*, all inspirations for the work of *technē*, all interrupting the dominating hold of *technē* over our thoughts of the good.

Even so, we should not forget the ambiguities of nature:

> Naturizing, originary, and productive *phusis*, nature can be *on the one hand* the great, generous, and genial donor to which everything returns, with the result that all of nature's others (art, law *[nomos, thesis]*, freedom, society, mind, and so forth) come back to nature, are still nature *itself in difference:* and, *on the other hand*, let us say after a Cartesian epoch, nature can be the order of so-called necessities—in opposition, precisely, to art, law *[nomos]*, freedom, society, history, mind and so forth. So the natural is once again referred to the gift but this time in the form of the given. (Derrida, *GT*, 127)

In closing, by way of a different interruption, we may consider something said of African philosophy in relation to nature, opening another intermediary figure. "[T]he European man is the only creature who attempts to demonstrate independence from the forces of nature. To be independent is to be just that; not dependent. To be dependent means that one is *somehow* related to the forces of nature. The African man has typically identified this relationship is one of interdependence" (Clark, *SINC*, 117). Within the binary opposition European and African, European thought is binary while African thought is nonoppositional. The structure of this opposition is diaphoric, repeating the *diaphora* between *poiēsis* and *technē*, where one of the pair is oppositional. Europeans here divide the world into causes and effects, humanity and nature, one dependent on the other, one high the other low. Africans do not divide the world, take it as whole, interdependent. European thought is dominating, oppressive, in its categorization. African thought is not. And African art is not. We may think of African thought as superior, thinking in a European way. Or we may think of African thought as interrupting European categories and oppositions, linking African and European thought without demanding a choice between them. Between Europe and Africa opens another intermediary figure, supplemented by countless others, between Europe and Asia, Judeo-Christian and Muslim, Jewish and Christian, and so on and on, all diaphoric, intermediary.

Ecological feminism sees the domination of women as linked inseparably with the domination of nature. Perhaps we may see the domination of Africans, slavery and colonization, as linked inseparably to these other dominations. But in resisting domination, we may hope to think of a better ethics, for women and Africans, free from domination. We think, here, within the work of *technē*. And we may do good work. But in both Western thought and African thought, frequently unnoticed, is another possibility, expressed in the idea of art, associated with magic and the gods, interrupting the hold of *technē* upon us, which insists that we choose one over the other. It is the possibility of cherishment beyond any choice or measure, giving us responsibility to measure and choose, an exposure to things from which we gather the possibility of measure.

But when we do so, we do not gather this possibility of measure as if we owned a measure of good gathering, dividing judgments into high and low, north and south, but pursue a gathering beyond measure that haunts every measure with dangers to its authority, permeated with intermediary movements. We relate to choice in a heterogeneous rather than a technical way, in terms of beauty rather than profit and advantage, where heterogeneity and beauty circulate as intermediaries in every place. And with this thought, we find another way to conclude this discussion of nature. In the West, art haunts the margins of reason with challenges to its authority, but not by instituting another, higher authority. In many African societies, and in ecological feminism, ways of thought and life challenge the margins of reason with gifts of the good not uniquely associated with art, but with nature. The gifts of the good surpass art. Art's beauty is not the only gift of the good. And further, to pursue ways of life that bear the disruptive gifts of the good is not always to do good work, is sometimes to do terrible work. The giving of the good never replaces the good of *technē*, but lies within it intermediarily as alternative possibilities and resistances, as interruptions. That is where art has served human life, as the conscience that will not let its oppressions rest, even where art is subservient to the powers of the state. As women have resisted the authority of men even when entirely subservient to their powers. Eros and *poiēsis* interrupt the powers of reason and the state even where they are dominated. That is how I understand Clément and Irigaray, and ecological feminism, in relation to women, art, and nature.

I conclude with another interruption, opening another intermediary figure between Europe and Africa, one that must not be forgotten:

> Portuguese sailors brought to Europe the first *feitiços*, African objects supposedly having mysterious powers, in the late fifteenth century. . . .
> The black continent was still on the maps a *terra incognita*. . . .
> In this atmosphere of intense and violent exchanges, *feitiços* became symbols of African art. They were viewed as primitive, simple, childish, and nonsensical. Mary H. Kingsley, at the beginning of this century, summed it up with an axiomatic evaluation: "The African has never made an even fourteenth-rate piece of cloth or pottery." (Mudimbe, *IA*; Ross, *AIS*, 604–5)

In a context of violent opposition, domination and subordination, objects neither beautiful nor useful to a European gaze became objects of fascination. The slave trade linked with objects and people regarded as primitive and ugly. Art for art's sake joined the slave trade, presented African people and their works as exotic and deficient. Along with their views of nature, art, and the good.

I add, foreshadowing later discussions in chapters 6 through 8, that perhaps no objects have been more fetishized than works of Western art, that the care we give to works of art joins the fascination we feel toward collected objects. Here another intermediary figure opens onto art and its works, intermediaries, and fetishized objects, saturated with desire and fascination, all gifts from the good.

Still we remember that the idea and practice of art bear memories of violence and destruction. Artistic judgment is historically linked with practices of domination and subordination. The gift of the good is a betrayal. The judgment of beauty is a betrayal. I hope it is also an insurrection. The gift of the good gives itself in intermediary figures of betrayal and insurrection. In the West, the intermediary figure of intermediary figures is judgment.

CHAPTER 4

Judgment

If art was born in the *diaphora* between poetry and philosophy, literature, Foucault tells us, was born with classical representation, born in excess
(*OT*, 44, 299–300).[1] And this excess, of poetry or art, fed philosophy, fed
the birth of a reason that could almost reach God, bearing the insane marks
of its own divinity, in Descartes, and Spinoza, separated from art by an abyss
that bore the weight of art's materiality.[2] In this materiality, the sensuousness of painting and sculpture bore affinities with *mimēsis*, which I have
associated after Plato with art's intermediariness, with gifts from the gods.
With the birth of literature as language's excess, art's materiality entered
another mad *diaphora* face to face with language's spirituality, still the
diaphora of *mimēsis*, still in conflict with philosophy, still a conflict claimed
by philosophy.

If art was born in this struggle with philosophy, born from exclusion,
then philosophy was nurtured by modern science, drawn inexorably into science's orbit, while art struggled for its truth against charges of unreason, passion, sensuousness, and madness, all gifts of the gods, intermediary figures.
But in this struggle, economic forces had their powers, and elites frequently
had their way. If art was born in a struggle for philosophy's supremacy, if art
and philosophy were born together, then as philosophy gained its supremacy
from science, art gained its identity in other exclusions, other binary distinctions, between high and low, great and mediocre, beautiful and trivial art,
halting its intermediary movements. If we could estimate the value of art,
requisite to its marketability, we could demand a standard of taste that repeated the hold of *technē* within the circulations of *poiēsis*. Art was born in
technē, divided by *technē* from philosophy and rationality, separated from
technē as *poiēsis*, only to reinstitute itself as *technē* in the distinctions that
have given weight traditionally to art, halting its movement. I speak of taste
especially, and of the culmination of this development in Kant, who returns

art to the good from within all the movements of separation, returns it to its circulation from every effort to halt its movement, in Aquinas and Spinoza for example, despite Augustine's recognition of the divinity of art and the beauty of God's world.

For beauty is "that whose very apprehension pleases," in Aquinas, marking thereby the work of God (Aquinas, *ST*, Ia, IIae, 27, ad 3), but dividing beauty from the good, at least *technē*'s good. In Augustine, perhaps in contrast, but in words that can be read to lend support, the beauty of the universe, "as it were an exquisite poem set off with antitheses," is "a tale of the circulation of good and wickedness" (Augustine, *CG*, Book XI, chap. 18; *BWA*, 159). This good, Augustine's divine good, bears the mark of wickedness, the mark of Cain. Even God does the work of *technē*, commands the height, brings beauty. And as if to reinstitute God's divinity, which bears an intimate relation to beauty and the good, but does not thereby do *technē*'s work, Aquinas gives beauty over to what pleases in *mere* apprehension. The *mere* breaks off any relation to *technē*, serious or play, reinstitutes, I would say, a deeper relation to the good.

Without any relation to the good, even that relation known as *technē*, beauty knows nothing of estimating judgment. The apprehension pleases in the fullness or drabness of our lives, wherever we find ourselves, pleases anywhere in world or nature. Beauty is in God's universe everywhere, wherever we find apprehension pleasant, gratifying—shall we say good? Beauty belongs to the universe everywhere, in nature and in human work, all God's work, large or small, all beautiful because it is good, in the words of Genesis. When "God saw the light, that it was good"; when God divided the earth from the seas and "saw that *it was* good"; when the earth yielded fruit, and "God saw that *it was* good"; when God set the stars in the firmament and "God saw that it was good"; when God created creatures upon the waters and earth that multiplied according to their kind and "God saw that *it was* good"; and finally, when "God saw every thing that he had made, and, behold, *it was* very good": it is obstinate to think that God's work is better than it might be, that the light is better than the dark, especially when after God saw that the light was good, "God divided the light from the darkness" (Genesis, 1). It is obstinate and worse, even blasphemous, to imagine that light is good because it is better than darkness, or that the way God divided light from darkness is better than some other work, or that creatures that do not multiply according to their kind are bad. This good knows nothing, at this point, of high and low, of estimation. It is not a measure, but a joy, closer to beauty than to appraisal. There is no better, but a good without better and worse. And it is not a neutral good, not neuter, as if without appraisal we have nothing.

The beauty that touches such a good, the good marked by beauty, is wondrous not because it is unified rather than divided, whole rather than fragmented, total rather than incomplete. The world was without form and division before God created heaven and earth. But it was not better before, and not better after. Nor was it world. Better and worse and world do not apply, but demand a thought, an experience, a response, that is not divided, that knows nothing of such divisions, of estimation, magnitude, and evaluation. Something—not a thing at all, not a magnitude, quantity, or quality—gives rise, as God does, to divisions and measures, this God who is not divided yet divided in some places into three, in other places into genders, in still other places endlessly and unboundedly divided.

In order to respond to the demands of the things around us, in their different places, endless and heterogeneous things, in their multifarious variety, we must be touched by a gift of unlimit, unboundedness, abundance, in the form of a summons, a touch, a caress. This is the giving, the embrace, of the good. It is known to Augustine as God, but spoken of still in the language of wickedness. It is known to Aquinas as God, but spoken of as subtraction: *mere* apprehension pleases. Except that in Aquinas and in Kant the apprehension touches the soul of the world. Beauty reveals the touch of God. I say this in memory of the oppressiveness of every worldly religion, of endless dominations and oppressions in the name of reason and truth. I think we can remember because of gifts given in the name of the good. The name does not matter. The gifts are everywhere.

Yet it is a mark of Enlightenment rationality to attempt to divide what cannot be divided, to claim the right of reason to exclude, to impose a law. And perhaps nothing is clearer on that imperative than where Hume imposes laws where he knows there are no laws, insists on standards without standards. And perhaps nothing is more striking in response to this imperative than Kant's restoration of the anarchy, the immeasurability, of the good within the imperative to establish law. Hume grants the endless variety of taste and the impossibility of grounding judgment, only to insist on a standard of taste, of estimation.

For within the very thought of taste's variety, Hume interposes a standard, once, twice, and more, multiple standards, repeating the hold of *technē*. The variety is a multiplicity of estimations:

> As this variety of taste is obvious to the most careless enquirer; so will it be found, on examination, to be still greater in reality than in appearance. The sentiments of men often differ with regard to beauty and deformity of all kinds, even while their general discourse is the same. There are certain terms in every language, which import blame, and others praise; and all

men, who use the same tongue, must agree in their application of them. (Hume, *OST*, 78)

He has noted a greater, more sweeping extreme in this sense of taste: "we are apt to call *barbarous* whatever departs widely from our own taste and apprehension" (Hume, *OST;* Ross, *AIS*, 78). Here taste has four defining characteristics belonging to and repeating *technē*: (1) unlimited variety and heterogeneity; (2) estimation, praise and blame; (3) a demand for agreement; (4) exclusion. Judgment here demands agreement on approbation and condemnations within a heterogeneity beyond any limits. The standard of taste is required by *technē* in a sphere where any standard is impossible.

Hume seeks a standard of judgment where judgment pertains to praise and blame, to approbation and condemnation, divides and excludes. He knows that such terms belong to morality, if also in his terms to art and beauty. "The word *virtue*, with its equivalent in every tongue, implies praise; as that of *vice* does blame" (Hume, *OST;* Ross, *AIS*, 79). At the center of his essay is the claim that "it is natural for us to seek a *Standard of Taste*; a rule, by which the various sentiments of men may be reconciled; at least, a decision, afforded, confirming one sentiment, and condemning another" (Hume, *OST;* Ross, *AIS*, 80). After Augustine and Aquinas, we might suppose that beauty demanded such a standard, a rule of judgment, certainly the hope that humanity might be reconciled under the glory of God. Yet nothing in the glory of God demands that we be reconciled to agreement concerning beauty. We might take the plenitude of God's work to show in inexhaustibly heterogeneous beauties and wonders of the world. We might take God's eye to include the sparrow and all things, to know nothing of exclusion. If we must agree concerning God, and faith, and worship, that very agreement may demand liberation from exclusion and rule in the glory of God's work.

Even so, we might insist that we agree under God's dominion to the beauties of the universe. We might insist on agreement yet deny that what we agree on is estimation. We might condemn and praise those who do not agree, yet not insist that they agree on praise and blame. If they are not pleased by God's work, they are sinful; if they share our pleasure, they are members of God's community. But their pleasure may not in either case be judgmental in the sense of verdicts and appraisals.

In Hume, however, judgments render verdicts. "Strong sense, united to delicate sentiment, improved by practice, perfected by comparison, and cleared of all prejudice, can alone entitle critics to this valuable character; and the joint verdict of such, wherever they are to be found, is the true standard of taste and beauty" (Hume, *OST;* Ross, *AIS*, 87). His language is repeatedly affirmation and condemnation. Art is brought before the tribunal of taste and judged. He speaks from the first of praise and blame, speaks of the multiplicity and heterogeneity of taste as praise of beauty and blame of deformity. Within this din of blame and praise we need agreement, uniformity. What we require of morality is to stop the circulation of judgments under which we are endlessly brought to the tribunal of justice.

Hume speaks of morality in the same language as that of taste. We praise virtue, blame vice (Hume, *OST;* Ross, *AIS*, 79); we find strengths and faults in the poets, however famous (Hume, *OST;* Ross, *AIS*, 81); we seek a standard such that "amidst all the variety and caprice of taste, there are certain general principles of approbation or blame, whose influence a careful eye may trace in all operations of the mind" (Hume, *OST;* Ross, *AIS*, 82): a repeatable standard of reaching verdicts that all careful judges may retrace. "It is impossible to continue in the practice of contemplating any order of beauty, without being frequently obliged to form *comparisons* between the several species and degrees of excellence, and estimating their proportion to each other" (Hume, *OST;* Ross, *AIS*, 85). We may wonder if contemplation allows for such active comparisons as appraisals and verdicts. We may think of a contemplation beyond comparisons of artistic excellence. Must we think that Shakespeare is greater than Milton, *Hamlet* greater than *Lear,* to give ourselves over to either? Must we think that some works and artists are inferior if others are glorious? Is artistic beauty a superiority? Hume does not hesitate for a moment in equating artistic judgment with estimation. And he says so.

He equates artistic *delicacy* of criticism with hierarchical distinctions. "Where the organs are so fine, as to allow nothing to escape them; and at the same time so exact as to perceive every ingredient in the composition: This we call delicacy of taste, whether we employ these terms in the literal or metaphorical sense" (Hume, *OST;* Ross, *AIS*, 83). Yet nothing here demands hierarchies, nothing invidious or superior. We may judge nuances, respond to every detail, every feature, hidden and overt, without praise and blame. Such responsiveness I associate with cherishment, with the good everywhere. Hume, however, insists that within the myriad variety of poetic works and tastes, we must impose government for all, organized from high to low. "But though poetry can never submit to exact truth, it must be confined by rules of art, discovered to the author either by genius or observation" (Hume, *OST;* Ross, *AIS*, 81). Delicacy insists on hierarchies. "But allow him to acquire experience in those objects, his feeling becomes more exact and nice: He not only perceives the beauties and defects of each part, but marks the distinguishing species of each quality, and assigns it suitable praise or blame" (Hume, *OST;* Ross, *AIS*, 85).

Perhaps we should take seriously the possibility that to form a distinction is always invidious, that every distinction, every identity, institutes domination. All this is within *technē*, and the hypothesis is that the work of *technē* is oppositional, hierarchical. The assumption is stated by Hume before Kant makes it law. "Every work of art has also a certain end or purpose, for which it is calculated and is to be deemed more or less perfect, as it is more or less fitted to attain this end" (Hume, *OST;* Ross, *AIS*, 87).

Can we suppose that beauty offers work without hierarchies? Or that beauty does no work but displaces the authoritarian hold of hierarchical categories? The latter is the line of thought I am pursuing, in the name of the good. It does not show itself in Hume at all, at least in the essay I am reading here. It shows itself elsewhere, in his *Treatise*, for example, where his skeptical concerns overpower his respect for reason. And even here, he is more overpowered himself than filled with wonder, overcome and cast into the abyss. "I am first affrighted and confounded with that forlorn solitude, in which I am plac'd in my philosophy, and fancy myself some strange uncouth monster, who not being able to mingle and unite in society, has been expell'd all human commerce, and left utterly abandon'd and disconsolate" (Hume, *T*, 1, 4, 7; 264). Skepticism opens onto heterogeneity, onto the possibility of reason, meaning, and intelligibility from the other side, the anarchic side of *poiēsis*, as if we were on the edge of the abyss. And so with art, at least from the side of *poiēsis*, demanding that we refrain, that we hold fast the necessary and vital distinctions of social life, in terms of which we avoid the monsters in ourselves and others. The standard of taste is a standard of life and thought resisting, excluding monsters.

What makes Hume monstrous is that he does not belong to human society, is not united with others. Human social life is bonded, not fragmented. And worse, he has been banished from all human commerce, the field of restricted, exchange economy where identities and limits hold fast, where things circulate according to expectations and rules. The general economy of heterogeneity, in which we are surrounded by others whose identities are not secure, terrifies us and makes us into monsters. We are monsters surrounded by chaos, filled with insecurity, teetering on the edge of the abyss. Excluded ourselves, we exclude others. Security comes by holding off the abyss, excluding its terrors, halting the circulation of intermediary figures who incessantly disturb the endless movement of identities and limits.

Human commerce demands that we halt the movement, a movement I have described to this point as belonging to *poiēsis* rather than *technē*, where *technē* slows down the excessive movement of intermediary figures by naming, numbering, counting, measuring them. Gifts from the gods continue their endless, inexhaustible circulation while human life imposes and encounters limits. Finiteness means limits. The question for us from the beginning is whether the limits that belong to us as finite require that we forget unlimit, whether the circulations that we must halt to live, for example, to possess property, the gifts we own, can be good if we forget that they came as gifts from nature, beyond measure. In the name of reason and human commerce, Hume resists the skepticism that brings him over the abyss facing madness and chaos, turning to distinctions and valuations at the very point where he has acknowledged that they do not exist, where we are surrounded by heterogeneity.

This movement, this resistance, is more striking in Kant, perhaps as far-reaching there as anywhere in the Western tradition, not least because Kant goes much further than Hume in establishing realms of law to hold unlimit at bay, only to insist on its return, everywhere, to experience its abyssal pull. For Kant reaches toward unlimit in the name of freedom, not disconsolation. The limits of sense, well demarcated, institute the possibility of freedom. This freedom, entirely unlimited and emerging from itself, is a realm of law, reinstituting limits. And yet this law, together with causal law, two realms of legislation, demand something outside law to reconcile them. It is what Kant calls judgment, working in the creative imagination as free conformity to law. So the free and wild imagination is brought to heel again by law, as taste clips the wings of genius. Kant gives judgment over to freedom beyond limits only to demand its return to law, to limit, order, and harmony. The sublime opens onto unlimit only to be returned to order, in the name of reason and the good. Yet something resists this return, also in the name of the good, in Kant. This resistance is what I wish to explore.

Judgment in Hume renders verdicts. Judgment judges, condemns and praises, includes and excludes, settles disputes. In the extreme, judgment imposes verdicts where we have no disputes, where we might hope to share our differences together, shared as multiplicity and heterogeneity, forbidding any standard, demanding that we agree to differ. Even so, the territory of judgment is one of hierarchy, exclusion and inclusion, domination and subordination, praise and blame, even where we give ourselves over to beauty through contemplation, a meditation many would hope to be without praise and blame.

Judgment in Kant does not in the same ways render verdicts. It mediates and links, joins unlike to like, crosses chasms and abysses. Judgment is an intermediary figure, always moving, though Kant never quite allows himself to say so. But he comes close. For "the judgment, which in the order of our cognitive faculties forms a mediating link [*Mittelglied*: middle term] between [*zwischen*] understanding and reason" (Kant, *CJ*, Pref., 4), links two realms of law, two legislations, links the "sensible realm of the concept of nature and supersensible realm of the concept of freedom" (Kant, *CJ*, Int., 12), is the "ground of the *unity* of the supersensible, which lies at the basis of nature, with that which the concept of freedom practically contains" (Kant, *CJ*, Int., 12), is the "middle term [*Mittelglied*] between the understanding and the reason" (Kant, *CJ*, Int., 13); "in general is the faculty of thinking the particular as contained under the universal" (Kant, *CJ*, Int., 15), joins universal and particular. More enigmatically, "a judgment, therefore, is the mediate cognition of an object, consequently the representation of a representation of it" (Kant, *CPR*, 73), where representation itself is an intermediary figure.[3]

I interpose a brief interruption, still under the sign of Kant. Judgment, Lyotard suggests, is linking, without criteria, under the sign of *le différend*, a figure in proximity to the good. Judgment *(jugement)* is everywhere as linking *(enchaîner)*, entwined everywhere with *le différend*, an intermediary figure of the good. We are "to bear witness to the differend *[témoigner du différend]*" (Lyotard, *DPD*, xiii), though "the witness is a traitor" (Lyotard, *I*, 204), every witness. More relevant to our immediate discussion, "the title of this book suggests (through the generic value of the definite article) that a universal rule of judgment between heterogeneous genres is lacking in general" (Lyotard, *DPD*, xi). The definite article, *LE différend*, speaks to the mobility and fluidity of judgment, the impossibility of halting the incessant movement of heterogeneous *régimes*, in general, speaks in the space of judgment as an intermediary figure of heterogeneity, of the good. Where there is judgment, linking, without criteria, there are *différends*, heterogeneous spaces between. Nothing halts the flow of linking in between. Nothing fills the *diaphora*. Nothing halts the betrayal.

I interrupt this interruption to return to Kant, not to halt the movement of thought, of judgment. I will return to Lyotard following Kant, return to witnessing and betrayal. First I return to the *diaphora* between Hume and Kant, repeating the movement of unlikeness and the institution of endless quarrels.

Between Hume and Kant, regarded as unlike, the ancient *diaphora* emerges twice, first between Hume and Kant, second between judgments as intermediary figures, Eros and Pharmakeia, and judgments as decisions, verdicts, dividing high and low. The judgment that links moves between heaven and earth, circulates without exclusion, reaches toward difference and heterogeneity. The judgment that renders verdicts excludes, cuts the one off from the other, resists heterogeneity. Both are to be considered under the call of the good, a good that includes, that fosters care, that bestows a responsibility to care for things everywhere, divided from a good that divides, excludes, cuts off some things from its care because they are bad, imperfect, sinful, unjust.

Joined with this repeated diaphoric movement, given from the good, circulating endlessly everywhere in nature, we find another *diaphora* toward which we are asked to choose, between one good and another, between caring for all things and dividing them from each other. I have called this the *diaphora* between *poiēsis* and *technē*, the first knowing nothing of choice, the second demanding it, everywhere, in the institution of identities and places.

And I have suggested that if we must choose between *poiēsis* and *technē*, now between the good that does not exclude and goods divided from evils and imperfections, that such a demand does not belong to the good, not the one that does not divide, but to goods that insist that one always be chosen over the other.

In other words, in the intermediary movements that haunt the idea of judgment, between the judgment that links and the judgment that divides, between intermediary figures and judgments under law, judgment itself names the *diaphora* between *poiēsis* and *technē*, the intermediary movement at the heart of the good. The good that does not exclude, does not measure or calculate, cannot be divided from the good that excludes, that cuts up the world according to identities and units, discards what it cannot use. I believe this *diaphora* pervades Kant's understanding of judgment.

For judgment is the middle term *(Mittelglied)* where there is no middle term, no golden mean, no measure. Judgment links without a rule, links realms of law without a law. And judgment must do so if there is to be a law. In other words, the territories of law, nature and freedom, understanding and reason, are realms of legislation, which can exist and exercise authority only where we find a linking without legislation, without law, if not without authority. And what if judgment knew no authority, especially the authority of linking by measure? What would that tell us of the good?

Beauty, Kant tells us, is a symbol of morality, a *"hypotyposis* (presentation, *subjectio sub adspectum*), or sensible illustration" (Kant, *CJ*, § 59, p. 197; Ross, *AIS*, 136) of the "morally good" (Kant, *CJ*, § 59, p. 198; Ross, *AIS*, 137). On the one side, this repeats the analytic of the sublime in the voice of ethics, extending from the sublime to beauty. For *"the sublime is that, the mere ability to think which shows a faculty of the mind surpassing every standard of sense"* (Kant, *CJ*, § 25, p. 89; Ross, *AIS*, 117). It is that which exceeds the possibility of both presentation and representation, but which appears nevertheless *in* representation. The sublime is what exceeds presentation in representation. And what exceeds presentation, in measure or might, in the mathematical or dynamical sublime, is the unconditioned, the ground of freedom, the good.

It is not, however, the sublime that Kant tells us is a sensible illustration, an intuitive presentation, of the good, of freedom, but beauty. Moreover, beauty takes precedence over sublimity in importance and richness, at least with respect to nature, in whose abundance we dwell. And this despite the fact that the length of the Analytic of the Sublime is more than twice as long as the Analytic of the Aesthetical:

> we see that the concept of the sublime is not nearly so important or rich in consequences as the concept of the beautiful; and that, in general, it displays

nothing purposive in nature itself, but only in that possible use of our intuitions of it by which there is produced in us a feeling of a purposiveness quite independent of nature. (Kant, *CJ*, § 24, p. 84; Ross, *AIS*, 115)

The argument is from free, independent natural beauty, which "discovers to us a technique of nature which represents it as a system in accordance with laws, the principle of which we do not find in the whole of our faculty of understanding" (Kant, *CJ*, § 24, p. 84; Ross, *AIS*, 115). Beauty discloses nature's purposiveness and lawfulness, while "nature excites the ideas of the sublime in its chaos or in its wildest and most irregular disorder and desolation" (Kant, *CJ*, § 24, p. 84; Ross, *AIS*, 115). And we know that the purposiveness of nature discloses the ultimate and final reason for the world, under the rule of the good,[4] discloses the rule of Man and the order of God. All this despite the chaos and wildness of nature. On the one hand, then, "the sublime is not to be sought in the things of nature" (Kant, *CJ*, § 25, p. 88; Ross, *AIS*, 117), in organized and purposive things, perhaps not in nature altogether; except that "nature is therefore sublime in those of its phenomena whose intuition brings with it the idea of its infinity" (Kant, *CJ*, § 26, p. 94; Ross, *AIS*, 118), where again we understand infinity here in relation to wildness and chaos.

What if nature were the wild and chaotic circulation of organized things, organized according to means and ends, as if according to purposes? What if our intuitions told us of both the chaos and wildness, and the organization? What if we could think of nature as a whole only as chaos, but could think of nature's *organized products* only according to purposes, how would we reconcile these? I take this question and the premises to pertain to the good, to what Kant calls freedom. Freedom institutes itself as law, under legislation, but at its heart it is free, unconstrained, chaotic, and wild. Kant says so, says that nature is under the dominion of both Apollo and Dionysus, though he gives priority to Apollo.

From the beginning I have suggested that the relation between necessity and freedom, order and disorder, Apollo and Dionysus, is not intermediate, a middle term *(Mittelglied)*, a golden mean, a bond, but a mobile intermediary in endless movement. That is how I understand judgment, as intermediary, in incessant motion, diaphoric but not mediated. Between *poiēsis* and *technē*, in endless circulation. And that is how I understand beauty and the sublime.

Beauty is first distinguished from the sublime by form. "The beautiful in nature is connected with the form of the object, which consists in having definite boundaries. The sublime, on the other hand, is to be found in a formless object, so far as in it or by occasion of it *boundlessness* is represented, and yet the totality is also present to thought" (Kant, *CJ*, § 23, p. 82;

Ross, *AIS*, 114). It is tempting to think of beauty as beautiful form and to think of the sublime as formless: beauty as Apollinian, ordered, sublimity as Dionysian, anarchic.

Except that Kant goes on to say that "[t]hus the beautiful seems to be regarded as the presentation of an indefinite concept of understanding, the sublime as that of a like concept of reason" (Kant, *CJ*, § 23, p. 82; Ross, *AIS*, 114). Both are indefinite; both present an indefinite concept rather than something beyond, otherwise than concepts. In this irresistible call of the concept, Kant gives birth to Hegel. For the possibility that the sublime touches something otherwise than being, concepts, presentations, whatever, that freedom knows nothing of any concept, indeed the possibility that beauty, sublimity, art, *poiēsis*, all touch something other, different, unlike concepts is repeatedly presented and rejected by Kant.

But Kant has from the first in the *Critique of Judgment* established a metaphor to which he returns repeatedly in different *Critiques*, a metaphor that bears down upon the thought of the good, imprisons it in a space from which we may hope to free it in the name of freedom. The metaphor is spatial. In its most extreme and paradoxical form, it appears in the Introduction to the *Critique of Judgment*: "Understanding and reason exercise, therefore, two distinct legislations on one and the same territory *[Boden]* of experience, without prejudice to each other" (Kant, *CJ*, Int., p. 11). Understanding and reason meet in a place, one and the same territory, do not interfere with each other, but occupy a space together, perhaps like a domestic scene, perhaps like a national destiny. Understanding and reason are like a happily married couple who have learned to live together without enmity, without interference, without interruption. Perhaps beauty, truth, and the good interrupt each other, disturb each other's work, without participating in that work, because they occupy different territories; or, perhaps, because the good, at least, occupies no territory.

Similarly, two famous images in the *Critique of Pure Reason* are spatial, speaking of what cannot possibly be found in space. He begins his discussion of the distinction between phenomena and noumena with one such image:

> We have now not only traversed the region of the pure understanding, and carefully surveyed every part of it, but we have also measured it, and assigned to everything therein its proper place. But this land is an island, and inclosed by nature herself within unchangeable limits. It is the land of truth (an attractive word), surrounded by a wide and stormy ocean, the region of illusion, where many a fog-bank, many an iceberg, seems to the mariner, on his voyage of discovery, a new country, and while constantly deluding him with vain hopes, engages him in dangerous adventures, from which he can never desist, and which yet he never can bring to termination. (Kant, *CPR*, 156)

He begins Part II of the *Critique of Pure Reason*, the transcendental doctrine of method, with another:

> We have found, indeed, that although we had purposed to build for our-
> selves a tower which should reach to Heaven, the supply of materials suf-
> ficed merely for a habitation, which was spacious enough for all terrestrial
> purposes, and high enough to enable us to survey the level plain of experi-
> ence, but that the bold undertaking designed necessarily failed for want of
> materials—not to mention the confusion of tongues, which gave rise to
> endless disputes among the laborers on the plan of the edifice, and at last
> scattered them over all the world, each to erect a separate building for
> himself, according to his own plans and his own inclinations. (Kant, *CPR*,
> 397)

The first presents the domain, the territory, of understanding, enclosed by limits that threaten its integrity and its truth by illusion, suggesting non-existent farther shores that the seafarer will never reach. But we know that there are no seas upon which seafarers may embark.

The second speaks of the unalterable limits of experience in terms of a paucity of materials, as if we might build a tower to reach the heavens, had we enough time and bricks. The imperative is for architectural works, per-haps other works of art, to rise as high as possible. This passage speaks of het-erogeneity in a compelling image of divided territories and dwellings as if we all shared a single project. Or rather, as if we shared a Grand Design, in mem-ory of the tower of Babel, undermined by heterogeneous and multifarious de-signs. As if we were forced to choose between order and chaos, conditioned and unconditioned, instead of moving endlessly between them in intermedi-ary movement.

It is conventional faced with such passages to speak of the inescapabil-ity of metaphor to suggest that Kant founders on the impossibility of speak-ing about the unconditioned except in metaphorical terms. The territories and spatiality, the materials and impoverishments, all belong to the limita-tions of metaphor, of language, attempting to say what cannot be said. But perhaps may be thought. Or at least, may be, but may not. The figure of metaphor touches Kant's writing at the point at which the impossibility of the project comes to the fore.

But that is not my point here. I am interested instead in the very idea of limits and design conceived in spatial or material, architectural terms, as realm *(Gebiet)*, territory *(Bode)*, dwelling *(Aufenthalt)*, habitation (or dwelling-house) *(Wohnhause)*, material spaces, where space and matter are understood as determinate, but where Kant's distinctions render the forms of material life indeterminate. Kant says that understanding and reason oc-cupy the same territory as if they might occupy other territories, speaks of the domain of pure understanding as if there were other domains, occupied by reason, or noumena, or the sublime, or nature. His language suggests as strongly as possible that the limits of understanding have an inside and an outside. And we may read every spatial metaphor as expressing the same truth, that we establish limits in a domain that might be divided differently, that limits cut into a territory, dividing into yours and mine, or ours and others. We build the edifice of the state whose walls separate us from the barbarians.

The metaphor enforces the sense of limits cutting, dividing, distinguishing. Limits exclude. The territory of understanding and reason excludes some other territory. What of the distinction between understanding and practical reason, which seems to exclude each from the other, yet where they touch at every point without interference? Is this an image of a distinction that is not a distinction, an unlikeness that is not an opposition, a *diaphora* that is not a quarrel? In the same way, could the distinction between phenomena and noumena be no distinction at all, but a difference, an unlikeness, and otherness, otherwise? An interruption? Could the distinctions between beauty and the sublime, understanding and judgment, judgment and reason, be no distinctions at all, but interruptions, intermediary movements? Including distinctions between earth and heaven, noumena and phenomena, limit and unlimit, all intermediary movements otherwise? When Kant claims that his critiques will end the battlefield of endless controversies known as metaphysics (Kant, *CPR* [*NKS*], Pref. to 1st ed., p. 1), shall we understand this peace to be without unlikeness, difference, heterogeneity, or as *diaphora* without *polemos*, heterogeneity without exclusion, *Ungleichartigkeit* without *Kampf?* We consider the possibility that philosophy bears *diaphora* at its heart but struggles against *polemos*.

The question I am asking is whether making distinctions speaks truthfully of what is unconditioned, free, of the good, perhaps of any limit, however mundane, whether truth is something otherwise than making distinctions, setting limits, occupying territories, something responsible in the name of the good, of freedom, something masked. In Kant. I am asking whether in Kant, whose work is filled with the most delicate and nuanced distinctions, carefully worked-out categories, we find that distinctions and categories must be defeated in order that they may say what they are designed to say.

This is to bring before us the question of design in another way, resisting the *diaphora* between the Grand Design and dispersed outhouse designs *(anzubauen)* (Kant, *KRV*, 213) under which we live. For Kant presents us with nature's design, however indeterminate and beyond the powers of our understanding, reaching to the heavens, to freedom, immortality, and God (Kant, *CJ*, 325). In the *Critique of Pure Reason*, these appear in three famous questions: "What can I know? What ought I to do? What may I hope?" (Kant, *CPR*, 451). I may hope for nature's Grand Design. But that design is not grounded in either the understanding or theoretical reason. We are cast upon the ground, dispersed throughout the world, each with our little marginal huts, unfit for dwelling. Here we enter another quarrel, and if we cannot choose definitively between them, because we are not equipped to do so, still we know the meaning of the choice. Yet when Kant disrupts his distinctions and categories, defeats them so that he may speak of the truth they embody, we do not choose, indeed we give up the idea of choosing between making and defeating categories. As we gave up the idea of choosing between *poiēsis* and *technē*, understanding that to choose was to privilege *technē*. We cannot choose under *technē*, and cannot deny a choice under *poiēsis*. We cannot choose nature's Grand Design and cannot deny nature's design.

But still we choose, and refuse to choose. Or, if that is impossible, we choose and hope to resist that choice, but cannot refuse to choose as if there were a realm, a world, so beautiful in which we did not need to choose, to exclude, to estimate, measure, and cut off. We cannot live without exclusion. But we can face up to the injustice, the gravity of choice, of categories and distinctions. We can refuse to let the truth of distinctions, the limits of identities, the boundaries of concepts, however indeterminate, interpose a neutrality that refuses the work of the good. Between *poiēsis* and *technē* is no neutrality, and neutrality belongs to neither. *Technē* is never neutral, and resistance to *technē* cannot be neutral. I mean by neutrality all the terms of Western reason that claim objectivity, freedom from prejudice, fairness, equity, impartiality, and justice as if one might possess them and thereby cease to be partial, unfair, unjust, interested. Judgment is never neutral, never escapes the *différend*, silencing the others. Witnessing the *différend* does not escape betrayal.

Kant says something of this in the very title of the third *Critique*, inaudible in English: *Kritik der Urteilskraft*. The faculty, the power and force *(Kraft)* of judgment, make it ethical, bring it in relation to the good. To claim objectivity is to hope to inhabit no relation to the good. That is impossible. We and others are called to respond. We are responsible, along with others, for the others. Yet still we claim in the name of truth a knowledge that would be beneficial and for which we are responsible without a relation to the good. It is what I have called attention to in Irigaray's critique of neutrality as sexual indifference.[5] The logic of science and of every cognitive discourse claims indifference to all the weights of the world falling upon us from the good.

That is what Kant says of science. But he also says it of art, of beauty, says that beauty has nothing to do with ethics, though it illustrates the good. For he equates ethics with interest, and emphasizes the disinterestedness of art. I am returning to the moments that define the beautiful before Kant opens onto the sublime, the moments that define beauty as if it bore no relation beyond itself. I will return to nature through the sublime and its relation to teleology. All of these, I believe, are relations to the good.

I offered a reading of Aristotle's *Poetics* as ethical, responding to the call of the good. I now suggest that we read Kant's *Critique of Judgment* as ethical, pursuing intermediary movements in which judgment links the understanding and practical reason, necessity and freedom. Kant traces the boundaries of the ethical in his account of beauty before returning to the good. I have noted his view of the structure of judgment as intermediary and of beauty as symbol of the good. I now wish to trace the movement from the intermediation of aesthetic judgment through beauty and the sublime to the good, then to nature and God. I wish to trace beauty's intermediary movements.

Beauty is defined in the critique of the aesthetical judgment through four moments of taste: according to quality, quantity, purpose, and satisfaction. First moment: beauty pleases disinterestedly (Kant, *CJ*, § 5, p. 45; Ross, *AIS*, 103); second moment: beauty pleases universally without a concept (Kant, *CJ*, § 9, p. 54; Ross, *AIS*, 106); third moment: beauty represents purposiveness without purpose (Kant, *CJ*, § 17, p. 73; Ross, *AIS*, 111); fourth moment: beauty pleases necessarily without a concept (Kant, *CJ*, § 22, p. 77; Ross, *AIS*, 113). All are related by negation to morality understood as a realm of legislation: freedom as self-legislation under universal and categorical law, in relation to desire and will. The good without qualification under freedom is the good will, the will to universal law, grounded subjectively on respect for law. In contrast, beauty is disinterested rather than interested in actualities; like morality, beauty is universal, shared by all rational creatures, without concept or law; beauty is delight in purposiveness, in design, while morality presupposes purposes and ends; beauty pleases necessarily, while in morality necessity comes from law.

Despite the overarching importance in the structure of Kant's system of freedom of an indeterminate relation to something beyond sense, beyond ethical practice, these four moments belong to moral practice, to ethics as *technē*, to a restricted, measured, calculable economy. The will here is a practical will, moved by interest, seeking happiness, calculating outcomes, establishing boundaries, all within the rule of concepts, universality, law, and necessity. The paradox of freedom in Kant is its necessity. That is where the two realms meet in one territory, diaphorically but without opposition. The paradox of beauty in Kant is its universality, the universality of a design without law, expressed in the distinction between purposiveness, design, and purposes, ends.

We may state this paradoxicality in relation to beauty more gener-
ically, expressed by Susanne Langer as follows: "We have Significant Form
that must not, at any price, be permitted to signify anything—illusion that
is the highest truth—disciplined spontaneity—concrete ideal structures—impersonal feeling, 'pleasure objectified'—and public dreaming"
(Langer, *FF*, 15). In Kant, we have disinterested interest, subjective universality, purposiveness without purpose, free necessity. The aesthetic
imagination is *free conformity to law*. All these paradoxes represent
the linking of the two realms of freedom and necessity, understanding
and reason, in a single territory without conflict. But not without paradox.
Or at least, not without the appearance of paradox and antinomy, resolved by distinguishing between sensible and supersensible, phenomena
and noumena.

Kant never considers the possibility that the antinomies and paradoxes
that demand resolution can do so only under rational imperatives that
are themselves cast in question by the supersensible, under whose rule all
the demands of reason may be undermined. This is another way of saying
that the reason that demands that the paradoxes be resolved, dialectically or otherwise, cannot reach the supersensible, has no claim upon it. A
more pervasive paradox lies at the heart of Kant's system than any of those
enunciated above, the shared territory of two realms of law, where truthfulness to freedom demands that we recognize that we have no legal claim
upon it. Morality may be a realm of law, but the good, the unqualified good,
is unqualified by law. Law belongs to *technē*, to restricted, exchange
economies, to economies of measure and calculation, of concepts, identities,
and limits.

That is why beauty is repeatedly defined negatively, to be read as disentanglement from law under the possibility of freedom. In the economy of interest and the will, qualified or unqualified, universality is possible only by
concept and rule. Yet beauty touches something free from rule, opening upon
something shared and glorious. The pleasure, the delight, in beauty, the terror and fear in the sublime, are not pleasures of the subjective, particular will,
gratifications, nor are they what fulfills our interests, according to which we
calculate benefits and estimate values, good and bad:

> The pleasant, the beautiful, and the good designate then three differ-
> ent relations of representations to the feeling of pleasure and pain, in refer-
> ence to which we distinguish from one another objects or methods of
> representing them. . . . That which *gratifies* a man is called *pleasant*; that
> which merely *pleases* him is *beautiful*; that which is *esteemed* [or *approved*
> (2nd ed.)] by him, i.e. that to which he accords an objective worth, is *good*.
> (Kant, *CJ*, § 6, p. 44; Ross, *AIS*, 102)

This good is defined by estimation and approval, by good and bad, high and low, superior and inferior. This good belongs to *technē*, to restricted economies of measure and exclusion. Pleasure is distinguished from estimation by a subjective, variable measure, expressed by one pole of the antinomy of taste: there is no quarrel over taste, over what pleases us, however much unlike our pleasures may be. We are gratified by different things. In morality, however, we demand a standard, a measure, according to which we can evaluate what is good and separate it from what is bad. And while beauty does not provide a measurable standard, it demands something beyond the immeasurability of pleasures, demands universality without a measure.

From the beginning I have associated universality and necessity with measure, so that without measurable concepts with determinate limits, beauty can give rise to no necessity and no universality. In this light, *poiēsis* is immeasurable, exceeds *technē*, where measure, calculation, quantity, and quality all express determinate concepts with determinate limits. Yet in relation to judgment, Kant gives up the determinateness of concepts, and at the same time seeks to establish the universality of taste as if it were a measure. And perhaps the idea of something indeterminate that works as if it were a concept, a universality without measure that works as if it were a measure, is paradoxical. But if it is paradoxical, it is so within the rule of concepts and limits, where paradoxes exercise their force. The alternative is to read Kant's distinctions as diaphoric, avoiding oppositions between beauty and morality. The difficulty for this reading is that he distinguishes the supersensible from sense, what is beyond presentation from presentation, within the rule of concepts with limits and boundaries.

We have seen that the very act of distinguishing *poiēsis* from *technē*, general from restricted economy, does not belong to *poiēsis* and general economy. Distinctions belong to *technē*, to restricted economy. That is how I understand the rule of concepts, distinctions, exclusions, binary judgments. Kant denies that all judgments estimate; perhaps we should deny that all judgments separate. Rather, they link, join, as intermediary movements countering estimations, appraisals, hierarchies, identities, but not by establishing alternative identities of what has no identity, or the rule of unlimit as if it belonged to a territory with boundaries and limits. General economy is not different from restricted economies, but their mobile circulation. The supersensible is not other to the domain of sense, separated by a wall, but the sites of heterogeneity and excess belonging to the domain of sense, loosening the determinateness of its limits. All limits are limited, and because of this are excessive, unlimited. Limits limit and those limits are limited, opening onto unlimit. Restricted economies have limited powers to restrict, contain, define, delimit. At the borders of these limits, everywhere in every restricted economy, things move excessively, given from the good.

Art, beauty, whatever expresses the possibility of representing these movements, intermediary and excessive, gives delight, and fear, and all other emotions at the mobility of limits moving wildly against and away from themselves. This movement is given by and as the good, given nowhere and everywhere, supersensible and sensible, given as a call, a responsiveness, touch, caress, everywhere and in relation to all things. The call to beauty, the delight that moves us to art, to glory in the beauty and sublimity of the world and natural things, is a call from the good, given as beauty. In art, and nature.

I believe that Kant comes so close to saying this that differences can be neglected. But he says other things as well, driven by his demand for law and rule. The moment of taste according to quality defines beauty as without interest, accepts will's demand to own the good, insists on beauty's neutrality rather than its passion toward the good. In Plato, beauty beckons, leads us in intermediary movements away from our mundane selves. Also in Kant, but not in this moment. The moment of taste according to quantity defines beauty as pleasing universally, without a concept, where the quantity of universality demands a measure, demands a concept. Beauty pleases indefinitely, not just for me, or mine, but anywhere, elsewhere as well as here. Beauty touches down anywhere, but not with assurance, countably, everywhere. We can count everywhere only under a concept of measure, estimating by counting, accountable by measure.

Universality as a quantity belongs to judgment as estimation. The alternative is an indeterminate universality belonging to an indeterminate concept, both immeasurable. The *universal capability of communication* of which Kant speaks, the *sensus communis*, is either objective, indifferent to difference, total, and measured, or it exceeds any limit immeasurably. The *sensus communis* is not a quantity but unlimit; universality breaks the hold of limit without imposing another limit. Even so, Kant claims both universal agreement and rightness, under law: "Thus the agreement of a representation with these conditions of judgment must be capable of being assumed as valid *a priori* for everyone. That is, we may rightly impute to everyone the pleasure or the subjective purposiveness of the representation" (Kant, *CJ*, § 38, p. 132; Ross, *AIS*, 126). He speaks of right and law in relation to that which knows no right.

We might speak here of the free play of the imagination, which as free reaches beyond any limit to unlimit, knows no limit except the excesses of its powers. Yet the creativity of the imagination is its free conformity to law (Kant, *CJ*, § 22, p. 77), and taste clips the wings of genius, which without taste's order overwhelms its design (Kant, *CJ*, § 50, p. 163). Through imagination and genius design outstrips order, outstrips limits. Kant insists that they be returned to order, to nature's harmony, that *poiēsis* return to *technē*.

Yet it has never left it, and we need not insist on law. Dionysus and Apollo are both gods.

The third moment of taste denies the presence in taste of purposes, insisting on a purposiveness *without any representation of a purpose* (Kant, *CJ*, § 17, p. 73; Ross, *AIS*, 111). Nature and its objects have no intrinsic ends, are not ruled by measures of the good, but must be apprehended under design, even a Grand Design, without measure. Order, harmony, purposiveness, finality without measure all are apprehended with delight, and we call that beautiful. Why not disorder, cacophony, chaos, anarchy, also apprehended with delight, to be called sublime, or something else, the good? Because harmony in nature is law.

Harmony, unity, synthesis take precedence in purposiveness and design, leading to natural order and natural law. "*An organized product of nature is one in which every part is reciprocally purpose [end] and means.* In it nothing is vain, without purpose, or to be ascribed to a blind mechanism of nature" (Kant, *CJ*, § 66, p. 222). The good whose beauty disrupts the hierarchies of natural kinds under which Aristotle and Spinoza claim the right of human beings to use anything whatever to their purposes—a right God does not take as belonging to the sacred—undermines the distinction between purposiveness and purpose. No such distinction can be found in general economy. Artistic design, given as genius, can follow its star only against the wounds taste imposes on it, opening up—in Kant's words, after Aristotle—to a creative and productive imagination, which "is very powerful in creating another nature, as it were, out of the material that actual nature gives it" (Kant, *CJ*, § 49, p. 157; Ross, *AIS*, 132). "As it were," *gleichsam*: as if another nature. And what if it *were* another nature? What if nature, as it were, general economy, gave birth to other natures through *mimēsis*, endless other natures, all competing with actual nature, all displacing nature's design from within? What if nature's design were *mimēsis*, quite without purpose, but plenitude and inexhaustibility, expressed, as it were, in representation, called from the good?

Finally, the fourth moment, according to the modality of satisfaction in an object, the same object we have seen moves in judgment from design to ends, from purposiveness to purpose, claims a necessary satisfaction without a concept, without law, again reaching fruition as law, this time (in the teleology of the world) in ultimate terms. Or rather in terms of two ultimates, two ultimate purposes, laws, of nature:

> we have sufficient cause for judging man to be, not merely like all organized beings a *natural purpose*, but also the *ultimate purpose* of nature here on earth, in reference to whom all other natural things constitute a system of purposes according to fundamental propositions of reason. (Kant, *CJ*, § 83, p. 279)

man is the final purpose of creation, since without him the chain of mutu-
ally subordinated purposes would not be complete as regards its ground.
Only in man, and only in him as a subject of morality, do we meet with unconditioned legislation in respect of purposes, which therefore alone renders him capable of being a final purpose, to which the whole of nature is
teleologically subordinated. (Kant, *CJ*, § 84, p. 286)

Man is the measure under whose ordination all other things are teleologically
subordinated. In this way, man excludes all other natural creatures and
things as not measuring up to his moral status, excluding inorganic things,
natural creatures, and animals, the same structure of thought in relation to
natural purposes and kinds in which women are subordinated to men, slaves
to masters, and all material things to spiritualized human beings.

This is a point of supreme betrayal of the good in Kant. For the purposes
of organized products of nature, of natural things and kinds, are claimed in
order to speak of natural beauties without purposes, where Kant speaks of
flowers as free and independent beauties (Kant, *CJ*, § 16, p. 65), while human
beings and animals (for the use of humanity) have natural purposes (Kant,
CJ, § 16, p. 66). "But human beauty (i.e. of a man, a woman, or a child), the
beauty of a horse, or a building (be it church, palace, arsenal, or summer
house), presupposes a concept of the purpose which determines what the
thing is to be, and consequently a concept of its perfection; it is therefore ad-
herent beauty" (Kant, *CJ*, § 16, p. 66).

Several questions lend themselves for thought. Do animals and human
beings have purposes apart from human instrumental ends, the purposiveness Kant calls *external* (Kant, *CJ*, § 82, pp. 274–75)? Under a theory of natural kinds, with purposes throughout all organized products of nature,
flowers would appear to serve human ends no less than do horses and fields,
evoking representations of human freedom. And under a critical theory of human identity, human purposes have been nefarious, bringing women under
the specular light of men for presentation and subordination. The purpose of
women is to serve men, spectacularly and reproductively.

Kant returns to this view of natural kinds in denying that we are to take
the sublime's testimony concerning nature seriously. For the sublime "displays nothing purposive in nature itself" (Kant, *CJ*, § 23, p. 84; Ross, *AIS*, 115).
Nature is displayed by beauty. In the extreme, "the sublime is not to be sought
in the things of nature, but only in our ideas" (Kant, *CJ*, § 25, p. 88; Ross, *AIS*,
117); yet "Nature is therefore sublime in those of its phenomena whose intuition brings with it the idea of its infinity" (Kant, *CJ*, § 26, p. 94; Ross, *AIS*,
118). If this is not an outright contradiction, then Kant is distinguishing the
things of nature, organized according to design, from nature itself, infinite in
magnitude and might. Things are organized from high to low, exhibited as

beauty; nature is disorganized, unlimited, exhibited as the sublime. The natural question, concerning nature, is why beauty takes privilege in our relation to nature rather than to this and that natural thing. Or further, how any privilege, hierarchy, subordination, can withstand the force of the sublime. Nature through art extends itself as form beyond knowledge,beyond domination and oppression, called by the delight they give to nature's chaos, disorder, wildness, and desolation (Kant, *CJ*, § 24, p. 84; Ross, *AIS*, 115).

The corrective Kant offers is a deep one. For what constitutes humanity as the ultimate purpose of the world is freedom:

> The moral law, as the formal rational condition of the use of our freedom, obliges us by itself alone, without depending on any purpose as material condition, but it nevertheless determines for us, and indeed *a priori*, a final purpose toward which it obliges us to strive, and this purpose is the *highest good in the world* possible through freedom. (Kant, *CJ*, § 87, p. 301)

This freedom under law constitutes morality. This freedom as the highest good in the world entails God. This idea of good in the world, high or low, belongs to *technē*, to restricted economies. And so does this freedom under law, nature's highest purpose constituting morality a restricted economy, under measure, rule, and law. This freedom reaches to the stars but remains within rule and measure even in relation to God:

> Hence moral theology alone can furnish the concept of a *unique* author of the world, which is available for a theology.
> In this way theology leads immediately to *religion*, i.e. *the recognition of our duties as divine commands*, because it is only the recognition of our duty and of the final purpose enjoined upon us by reason which brings out with definiteness the concept of God. (Kant, *CJ*, § 91, p. 334)

For we know that freedom, God, and immortality are beyond sense, beyond measure, belong to general not restricted economy. Or belong to restricted economy only as wild intermediary movements of general economy. Kant releases freedom and the angels to fly to God, but God belongs to law. Intermediary movements are irresistible in Kant. Intermediary movements must be curbed if we are not to fall into the abyss.

Something similar happens in relation to the sublime, the place at which the good may most forcefully appear, together with God, beyond sense and form. For beauty in nature is tied to form and boundaries, while the sublime is formless, boundless (Kant, *CJ*, § 23, p. 82; Ross, *AIS*, 114); natural beauty brings purposiveness in form, while the sublime appears to violate purpose (Kant, *CJ*, § 23, p. 83; Ross, *AIS*, 114). Beauty recalls us to purpose and harmony as nature's design; the sublime destroys purpose, destroys harmony, in the name of design. This principle of *mimēsis* is of immeasurable importance, that the sublime is no less a representation of design than beauty, in a quarrel, a *diaphora*, with beauty's harmony, a representation I have associated with *mimēsis* and *poiēsis*.

Kant associates beauty with form and order, the sublime with chaos and disorder. Beauty delights in measure; the sublime delights in immeasure. Both fall into time and sensibility, though one repeats sensibility's measure, the other measure's immeasure, beyond measure. This impossibility in the sublime replays Kant's governance under law. For the idea of the sublime is contradicted in its characterization. The mathematically sublime is absolutely great, great beyond all comparison (Kant, *CJ*, § 25, p. 86; Ross, *AIS*, 115); and the "infinite is absolutely (not merely comparatively) great. Compared with it everything else (of the same kind of magnitudes) is small" (Kant, *CJ*, § 26, p. 93; Ross, *AIS*, 118). Yet how can anything (or everything) be small against something great beyond all comparison? How can the sublime be great (that is, large rather than small) beyond all measure? Finally, if *"the sublime is that, the mere ability to think which shows a faculty of the mind surpassing every standard of sense"* (Kant, *CJ*, § 26, p. 89; Ross, *AIS*, 117), if the sublime surpasses sense, how can it be large, or great, or surpass, exceed, go beyond? Where is it to go, and how can it be anywhere without measure, large or small?

Beauty and the sublime compose a binary opposition, the one this, the other that, the one superior to the other. What if, like *poiēsis* and *technē*, general and restricted economy, they composed an intermediary movement without opposition, again to suggest an unlikeness without measure, an immeasurable space of entwining within and around which we move in intermediary figures. Or rather, in which they move immeasurably and uncontainedly, in every container, place, and envelope. But there is no surpassing, greatness, or largeness. The colossal does not haunt the margins of the sublime with what Derrida reminds us (Derrida, *P*, 119–47; Ross, *AIS*, 416–19) is a size "almost too great for any presentation" (Kant, *CJ*, § 26, p. 91; Ross, *AIS*, 118). The colossal is large, the sublime is immeasurable. The monstrous can "by its size . . . destroy the purpose which constitutes the concept of it" (Kant, *CJ*, § 26, p. 91; Ross, *AIS*, 118), because monstrosity, unlike sublimity, has everything to do with size. The infinite is not large, nor monstrous, nor colossal, nor approached by any of these, all terms belonging to restricted economies, halted by the measures and magnitudes that control their limits. The sublime in nature does not require security, does not require containment and safe borders, though it may be inseparable from them. "[T]he sight of them [threatening rocks, clouds, hurricanes, the boundless ocean] is the more attractive, the more fearful it is, provided only that we are in security; and we willingly call these objects sublime, . . . " (Kant, *CJ*, § 28, p. 100; Ross, *AIS*, 120). War is sublime when "it is carried on with order and with a sacred respect for the rights of citizens" (Kant, *CJ*, § 28, p. 102), as if these limits establish safety against the chaos of the sublime:

> War itself, if it is carried on with order and with a sacred respect for the rights of citizens, has something sublime in it, and makes the disposition of the people who carry it on thus only the more sublime, the more numerous are the dangers to which they are exposed and in respect of which they behave with courage. On the other hand, a long peace generally brings about a predominant commercial spirit and, along with it, low selfishness, cowardice, and effeminacy, and debases the disposition of the people. (Kant, *CJ*, § 28, p. 102)

As if the sublime were reserved entirely for men, against the domesticity of the home, of women. The immeasurability of the sublime imposes at its limits measures against which domestic, bourgeois, and private life falls short, at the edge of colossal monstrosity. The sublime overshadows peace with war without giving up security. The domus, where women are kept for men, is the place of security for women, who know nothing of the sublime, enabling men to carry on war.

In all these cases, and many others, Kant brings us to the verge of a supersensible that is immeasurable by sense and appears throughout sense, only to withdraw into containment. In perhaps the most notorious example, he speaks of beauty as touching unlimit without measures of good and evil, only to impose a boundary—indeed, two boundaries—at the very point at which I have argued, Aristotle brought down the pillars holding up the temple of restricted economy:

> Beautiful art shows its superiority in this, that it describes as beautiful things which may be in nature ugly or displeasing. . . . There is only one kind of ugliness which cannot be represented in accordance with nature without destroying all aesthetical satisfaction, and consequently artificial beauty, viz. that which excites *disgust*. (Kant, *CJ*, § 48, 154–55; Ross, *AIS*, 131)

Why not disgust? Derrida speaks of this moment as the place where Kant imposes a restricted economy at the point where he has called our attention to general economy and the sublime (Derrida, *E*). Nature cannot be represented as beautiful by representations that excite disgust: vomit, excrement, blood. But these belong to nature, without a doubt. Are they forbidden from representation? From art? From the sublime? Doesn't the sublime touch these taboo places everywhere in nature? Yet beauty is superior to the sublime, artificial beauty is superior to natural beauty, in this reach beyond the limits of sense.

Finally, Kant speaks of genius and the productive imagination as if they touched the infinite directly, without limits, anarchy and chaos, but he withholds praise from genius unless delimited by the strictures of taste:

> We thus see (1) that genius is a *talent* for producing that for which no definite rule can be given; . . . (2) But since it also can produce original nonsense, its products must be models, i.e. *exemplary*, . . . (3) It cannot describe or indicate scientifically how it brings about its products, but it gives the rule just as nature does. . . . (4) Nature, by the medium of genius, does not prescribe rules to science but to art, and to it only in so far as it is to be beautiful art. (Kant, *CJ*, § 46, 150–51; Ross, *AIS*, 128)

> The imagination (as a productive faculty of cognition) is very powerful in producing another nature, as it were, out of the material that actual nature gives it. . . . Thus we feel our freedom from the law of association (which attaches to the empirical employment of imagination), so that the material supplied to us by nature in accordance with this law can be worked up into something different which surpasses nature. (Kant, *CJ*, § 49, p. 157; Ross, *AIS*, 132)

Nature gives material to the imagination and gives rule to art. Kant's narrative of genius and the imagination is one of gifts. Yet taste clips the wings of genius: "If, then, in the conflict of these two properties in a product something must be sacrificed, it should be rather on the side of genius" (Kant, *CJ*, § 50, p. 163); and the productive imagination is free conformity to law (Kant, *CJ*, § 34, p. 129; Ross, *AIS*, 125).

Everywhere in Kant we touch the limits of limits, reaching to unlimit, only to be brought back to law, brought back to purposes and ends within a discourse that delimits these within restricted economies. Two examples remain, so to speak on two sides of this concern. One is Lyotard's favorite example: "The idea of good *[Guten]* conjoined with affection *[Affekt]* is called *enthusiasm*. This state of mind seems to be sublime, to the extent that we commonly assert that nothing great could be done without it" (Kant, *CJ*, § 29, p. 112). Nothing great can be done without the idea of the good in mind, bound to feeling. Indeed. Though perhaps we might be as wary of enthusiasm as of war, cautious about the limits Kant imposes on war. But he imposes none on enthusiasm, at least the way he limits war by order and sacred respect. Yet he knows that enthusiasm has its limits. "Now every affection is blind" (Kant, *CJ*, § 29, p. 112). And he follows his claim that "aesthetically, enthusiasm is sublime" (Kant, *CJ*, § 29, p. 112), remarking that "the *absence of affection* . . . in a mind that vigorously follows its unalterable principles is sublime, and in a far preferable way, because it has also on its side the satisfaction of pure reason" (Kant, *CJ*, § 29, p. 113). He insists, first, that he is speaking of great work, demanding an idea of the good joined with powerful emotions, without which no great work can be done. He then suggests that to follow unalterable principles without emotion is sublime, because closer to reason.

Two related questions arise: (1) Is the idea of the good equivalent with following unalterable principles? I have questioned this equivalence from the beginning, equating unalterable principles with restricted economy. General economy knows no principles, alterable or otherwise. Moreover, Kant cannot equate the good with principle, not in relation to freedom. Instead, I suggest, the idea of the good in enthusiasm is an idea of freedom, not law. The idea of the good is not an idea of work. (2) Is the emotion that joins the idea of the good what we call enthusiasm, that of the French Revolution, for example, or does the good challenge the hold of even this enthusiasm, asking that it remember its injustices?

I have spoken of cherishment as the idea of the good everywhere, the emotion associated with the good. Cherishment knows that injustice must be opposed. It hopes to avoid further injustices. Even so, as Lyotard suggests, "[h]istorical-political enthusiasm is thus on the edge of dementia, it is a pathological outburst, and as such it has in itself no ethical validity" (Lyotard, *DPD*, 166). The question of validity is the issue in question. In its dementia, enthusiasm touches the good as an intermediary figure. It touches the good with joy and destruction.

The second example from Kant to supplement the discussion of the good in art, an intermediary figure known as beauty, is at the point at which we make our transition to another place in our discussion of art. For the idea associated with Hegel of the end of art emerges powerfully in Kant. Again, he warns us of the dangers of genius, warns us not to be carried away by enthusiasm for creativity. Humanity works better, strives for progress more effectively, where reason rules rather than enthusiasm or genius. Or art:

> In science, then, the greatest discoverer only differs in degree from his laborious imitator and pupil, but he differs specifically from him whom nature has gifted for beautiful art. And in this there is no depreciation of those great men to whom the human race *(Geschlecht)* owes so much gratitude, as compared with nature's favorites in respect of the talent for beautiful art. For in the fact that the former talent is directed to the ever advancing perfection of knowledge *(Erkenntnisse)* and every advantage depending on it, and at the same time to imparting this same knowledge to others—in this it has a great superiority over those who deserve the honor of being called geniuses. For art stands still at a certain point; a boundary is set to it beyond which it cannot go, which presumably has been reached long ago and cannot be extended further. (Kant, *CJ*, § 47, p. 152; Ross, *AIS*, 129)[6]

We have arrived at the end of art, the boundary beyond which it cannot go, perhaps beyond which we cannot go, casting shadows over our memories and projects under which we still work. This question of the end (or End, of art, or philosophy, or the West, or Man) calls from us a new beginning. Yet before beginning again, as we seem endlessly called upon to do, to begin again, and end, and begin, we may pause and dwell upon this passage beyond the theme of art's exhaustion. I dwell in several brief moments, all casting our attention toward the end, entered upon in the next chapter:

1. This theme of the end of art is told by Kant in memory of the human race, Our "menschliche *Geschlecht*," touched upon briefly in my Introduction, where the gift of language shows itself as the mark of The Human over and above, superior to, The Animal, humans over animals, so that we can use them in any way whatever, to our profit, as if human profit were the final purpose of all things, the highest. Freedom justifies tyranny. At this point of the end of art, we confront the end of humanity in a different but related sense of end, one end in time, the other end as *telos*, suggesting that the two ends, temporal and teleological, cannot be separated, as purpose and purposiveness remain entwined, intermediary figures, where the theme of the end of art, or philosophy, or humanity, is always toward Man's Dominion over nature. All this is to suggest that we are led by the question of the end of art to questions of the end of humanity, the purpose of the kind we call human, to questions of kinds, and purposes, and ends, where time meets the good. The end of art, the end of science, the end of humanity, purpose or design, all come to us as given from the good. And in reverse, we Westerners have always, Kant included here, responded to the gift of the good under the measure of Man, the sign of human history—for there is to us no other.

And still we are haunted by the end, by the fragility of life, and art, and natural things. Could it be that to think this end, this fragility, is to respond diaphorically to the good? Could it be as well that we come up to this end in the fragility of art?

2. Kant imagines that art reached its boundary long ago, but science continues to progress forever, at least indefinitely. By way of contrast, I write, and perhaps you read, in a time in which all that is fundamental about the world, knowable to science, has seemed to many on the verge of exhaustion, while the productive imagination of art seems to move on forever, if not advancing. This question of the boundaries of work touches on the different themes of knowledge, truth, nature, and the good, which our work here has unearthed. All, without exception. And more. Intermediary figures. For science and art touch nature in two different ways, perhaps at different points, both also touching nature's truth, and the good, and our relation to both, mediated by or moved by nature. For we may owe to science immense gratitude

for advancing forever toward the perfection of knowledge, owe to science a debt for bringing nature under its purview, where science and nature manifest both perfection and inexhaustibility, two apparently incompatible ends, intermediarily. And we may revel in the play of nature's gifts, given to the artist, only to the artist, nature's favorite, but imperfectly and brought to an end, exhausted. Nature's plenitude is not given to the favorite but to the toiler; artists, in the free play of their productive faculties, do not mimetically reproduce that plenitude, fail to reach perfection. And still they work. And still we compare their work to science, as if we might abandon reason for art. And why not?

3. The productive faculty of the imagination reaches toward and surpasses nature, produces another nature, opening the possibility that nature's abundance is not enough for art, but art in the free creativity of genius produces another nature, and another, adding to nature's inexhaustible plenitude other plenitudes, other inexhaustibilities. Do we teeter on the edge of the abyss, facing endless possibilities of nature's work, or do we restore ourselves to nature's plenitude, understanding finally that *mimēsis* is inseparable from nature, that nature does its work as representation, that this work of representation is endless, nature's endless work?[7] This would mean, however strange, that art fulfills nature's promise, that nature promises from itself, moving, flowing, without cease, to represent itself in art, and that this *mimēsis* expresses, fulfills, and shows nature's inexhaustibility. Heidegger says something close, for example, that *"[t]he work lets the earth be an earth"* (Heidegger, *OWA*, 46; Ross, *AIS*, 266); more extremely, that "[t]rue, there lies hidden in nature a rift-design, a measure and a boundary and, tied to it, a capacity for bringing forth—that is, art. But it is equally certain that this art hidden in nature becomes manifest only through the work; because it lies originally in the work" (Heidegger, *OWA*, 70; Ross, *AIS*, 278). Heidegger speaks of nature's gifts as art, given as a rift-design from the good, working through art. The *other nature* produced by art belongs to nature, moving within nature's own mobility. Put another way, nature is the circulation of intermediary figures, a gift that moves them more quickly, fluidly, resists any attempt to bring them up short. Here nature's mobility may be compared with truth's perfection, the latter halting the movement of intermediary figures as if truth were not intermediary, not itself in movement. Here art's productivity is compared with science's purposes to halt the movement of nature in an endless movement that mirrors nature's mobility. Here as well, the endlessness of science's movement repeats the productivity of nature's *mimēsis*. Nature's *mimēsis* is science, and philosophy, and art.

4. In science, the greatest discoverer is no different in kind, only in degree, from those who imitate the greatest discoveries. Some would doubt this claim. Some would like to think that Galileo and Newton, Einstein and Bohr,

Gauss and Fermat, surpassed their imitators, indeed that imitation here fails to touch scientific genius. Yet Kant withholds the touch of genius to art, where productive imagination does its work. Some would speak of scientific imagination as productive. Heidegger explicitly denies originariness to science:

> Science is not an original happening of truth, but always the cultivation of a domain of truth already opened, specifically by apprehending and confirming that which shows itself to be possible and necessarily correct within that field. When and insofar as science passes beyond correctness and goes on to a truth, which means that it arrives at the essential disclosure of what is as such, it is philosophy. (Heidegger, *OWA*, 62; Ross, *AIS*, 275–76)

He mentions several such ways, several gifts of truth in the opening of beings, especially art: "One way in which truth establishes itself in the beings it has opened up is truth setting itself into work" (Heidegger, *OWA*, 61–62; Ross, *AIS*, 275). He does not consider that science might dwell in the open, might be given as Being's gift, might interrupt the familiar. To the contrary, science dwells within the familiar, already opened, while art interrupts the hold of history. "The setting-into-work of truth thrusts up the unfamiliar and extraordinary and at the same time thrusts down the ordinary and what we believe to be such" (Heidegger, *OWA*, 75; Ross, *AIS*, 279).

But that is exactly what Kant says, with a peculiar and perhaps indefensible inversion. Art interrupts the advance of history, while science contributes to its endless movement. And science does so without interruption, even of great men, but by laborious imitation. The figure of greatness here, however heinous, the mark of genius, excluding everything familiar and ordinary, everything below the highest, is also a figure of interruption. If we were to give up the highest, as Kant himself does in the service of another greatness, if we abandon greatness and highness but keep genius, we keep a productive imagination that interrupts the movement of nature and history, denies any advance toward perfection, without coming up against a barrier—instead, turns the barrier into another interruption.

The perfection toward which science strives denies the possibility of interruption of its advance in the name of the good. If there is perfection, if history is progress, then interruption impedes the arrival of the good. This is true even in Hegel, for whom the advance is interruption—transmuted into the arrival of the good: a necessary impediment to be passed over and beyond, included within its own demise. But art will pass from the scene having met its end, will reach its boundary—if it has not reached it long ago.

The boundary of art is the end of interruption, a truly incredible idea within a writer who interrupts himself constantly to speak of the good.

5. We owe to science and its great men, who are not geniuses, immense gratitude for advancing toward perfection, however endlessly and inexhaustibly, and for imparting this knowledge to others. In this contrast another thought emerges I have not considered to this point at all, a thought of the gift of learning—not knowledge, but learning, acquiring, growing, interrupting. Learning, we may say, falls under two signs, perhaps the two signs of greatness: one advancing toward perfection, the other the mark of genius, under the sign of the example.

Under the mark of science, learning is laborious imitation; under the mark of art, learning is breaking and founding rules. Under the mark of genius, we learn to produce a work in an originary and founding event that repeats creation, breaking, founding, overcoming, conforming to example. But science advances through its laborious work by imitation. Two forms of imitation here parallel the two forms of learning: by rote and by example. Yet we may remember that virtue cannot be taught in *Meno*, but comes as a gift from the gods. And Socrates, in that same dialogue, teaches Meno by paralyzing his understanding. Here learning is an event beyond both of Kant's examples, something Plato suggests we cannot labor to achieve, either in science or art, but acquire as a gift, provided—I believe this is *Meno*'s point—that the gift keeps moving. Here it is the gift of virtue, neither science nor art, given from parents to children without reliability, without security or safety, either by imitation or example, but a gift that moves from parents to children without stopping, perhaps without stopping at the children, moving on to others.

Here is no advance, no genius, though there are models, examples, and stories, all swirling in confusion, bearing gifts wherever we wish to find them, bearing them beyond us to others, circulating. Kant speaks of such gifts as talents, but holds them back from circulation. The boundary for art beyond which it cannot go is mirrored by the boundary of science's advance, a channel out of which it cannot leap.

We must be able to impart knowledge to others, precisely what Plato repeatedly suggests we must and cannot do. Rather, knowledge moves as a gift; like art, but not the art of *technē*. We learn from others, from the world, in ourselves, we give our learning to others, who also learn from the world, given their learning and the possibility of learning as gifts. But the gift of learning never stops, and I do not mean never stops advancing. I mean that it moves from others to us and from us to still others, and they learn what they will and choose, and what they do not choose. Learning is a gift that moves and does not stop. But the learning Kant calls science stops moving even within its endless advance toward perfection, stops with imitation, with pupils who imitate by rote, who labor to reproduce their mentors' learning.

The superiority of science is that it advances toward perfection, end-lessly, and imparts its truth to others. This imparting, in the shadow of per-fection, halts the endless movement of knowledge toward the unknown, freezes it within the known and familiar. Thus Heidegger can say that in the work of art, the unfamiliar and extraordinary juts up within the ordinary, that the strange thrusts up and the ordinary goes down. I say the same of science, against labor and imitation. The work of science is to bring forth the strange into the light of the ordinary and to make the ordinary strange. Not to bring one up high, the other low, but to light the familiar and ordinary with the glow of strangeness. This work is art, and science, and philosophy, and more. No work can fail to make the familiar strange.

As a consequence, art is not superior to science, nor science to art. In this domain of work, in this deep and circular movement, superiority and in-feriority do not pertain, nor high and low. Greatness, if there be such, is the unfolding of strangeness, the production of a free and creative imagination, unfolding another nature, strange to us, still nature, belonging to nature. In this light, genius, greatness, strangeness, all work in the heterogeneous strangeness of the good, calling to us to respond, demanding that we work against injustice, work to free ourselves from the injustices of prior work, of every advance toward perfection. This work of resistance is art, and science, and more, perhaps all the ways in which truth establishes itself in the Open—that is, as a gift from the good: "truth setting itself into work. . . . the act that founds a political state. . . . The nearness of that which is not simply a being, but the being that is most of all. . . . the thinker's questioning . . . " (Heideg-ger, *OWA*, 62). Also *technē*; and science. For only in a certain light of perfec-tion, defining both science and *technē*, can science fail to call from the good.

And only in a certain light of perfection, perhaps that which defines both science and *technē*, can we come up against the limits of art, the end of the productive imagination. Only in relation to the endless advance of science to-ward perfection can we think the end of art. And perhaps the end of science and philosophy. And Man (if not humanity or men). For it is certain that there will be an end to humanity, to women and men, and other creatures, if not perhaps all creatures and things. It is as certain as can be. Yet this end is not the end of Man, not a purpose and not a finality, but death. Death is certain, but Kant and Hegel do not speak of the death, the extinction, of art. The boundary it has reached long ago it continues to traverse, continues to move next to that boundary. That is what we might say within Kant. Outside, we may remember twentieth-century modernism, where art strives toward nei-ther perfection nor boundary, but upheaves every boundary until that very upheaval imposes another ennui. Heidegger says of the possibility of the end of art that "we have seen the rise of many new art works and new art move-ments. Hegel never meant to deny this possibility. But the question remains:

is art still an essential and necessary way in which that truth happens which is decisive for our historical existence, or is art no longer of this character?" (Heidegger, *OWA*, 80). This is Heidegger's reading of Hegel's question concerning "the highest manner in which truth obtains existence for itself" (quoted in Heidegger, *OWA*, 80), a question of the highest. If we were to relinquish to history once and for all (if we could) the question of the highest, and with it reading history as destiny, would we no longer face the question of the death of art? And is the death of science also a death within the highest?

With this question, we may turn away from Kant to Hegel and Heidegger, perhaps to Nietzsche, again in the highest, even as we know he will break down its resistance: "I am convinced that art represents the highest task and the truly metaphysical activity of this life" (Nietzsche, *BT*, 31–32). Or without this obeisance to god: "art, and *not* morality, is presented as the truly *metaphysical* activity of man . . . the existence of the world is *justified* only as an aesthetic phenomenon" (Nietzsche, *ASC*, 22; Ross, *AIS*, 171).

I turn away into another interruption, in the highest, if not in German. I close returning to the sublime, in English, Blake's *The Book of Urizen*, spoken of with fear and trembling:

> 1. Lo, a shadow of horror is risen
> In Eternity! Unknown, unprolific,
> Self-clos'd, all repelling. What Demon
> Hath form'd this abominable void,
> This soul-shudd'ring vacuum? Some Said,
> "It is Urizen." But unknown, abstracted,
> Brooding secret, the dark power hid.
> (Blake, *BU*, 44; plate 3)

I cannot show you Blake's work here, let you see Urizen or the Eternals or anything else; nor read Blake's handwritten words. Yet I would say the words are still sublime, if not Blake's sublime, the sublime as intermediary movement.

For what horror is Urizen, the "adversary" (Easson, commentary to Blake, *BU*, 68–101)? "Blake understood that Urizen, the adversary, originates in dualism and that dualism originates in failure to acknowledge the relationship of reciprocal contrary states. Each individual, Blake believed, is composed of two eternal kinds of consciousness, which he characterizes in *The Book of Urizen* by the Eternals and Urizen, who is also an Eternal" (Easson, commentary to Blake, *BU*, 67). These words are anything but sublime, in a double sense. Blake's own words are overwhelming:

> 2. Times on times he divided & measur'd
> Space by space in his ninefold darkness,
> Unseen, unknown; changes appear'd
> In his desolate mountains, rifted furious
> By the black winds of perturbation.
> (Blake, *BU*, 44)

Urizen's words:

> 5. First I fought with the fire, consum'd
> Inwards, into a deep world within:
> A void immense, wild, dark, & deep,
> Where nothing was, Nature's wide womb.
> (Blake, *BU*, 46)

> 7. Lo! I unfold my darkness and on
> This rock place with strong hand the Book
> Of eternal brass, written in my solitude:

> 8. Laws of peace, of love, of unity,
> Of pity, compassion, forgiveness.
> Let each chuse one habitation,
> His ancient infinite mansion.
> One command, one joy, one desire,
> One curse, one weight, one measure,
> One King, one God, one Law.

Urizen, himself an Eternal, brings forth order from the void, replaying the story of God's Creation, establishing the law and the obligation to choose: one dwelling, one command, one measure. Urizen is the god of measure, demanding that we choose. He insists that we choose against the infinite in every thing, nature's abundance (Easson, commentary to Blake, *BU*, 67). In a supremely sublime voice, Blake returns us to the diaphoric, intermediary movement one pole of which demands that we choose, represented by Urizen. I must disagree with the Eassons that the adversary may be defeated. "The Eternals [who] represent those eternal forces of existence which, in their variety, stimulate the protean and dynamic motion of human life" (Easson, commentary to Blake, *BU*, 68) know nothing of choice, resist measure in their plenitude.

If Urizen represents dualism, measure, binary opposition, the Eternals do not reinstitute an opposition against him. The Eternals move in endless intermediary movements including Urizen, participating with him, riven by him. Here we may note a point of language where these diaphoric intermediary movements meet, the word "of" in *The Book of Urizen*, about Urizen, written by Urizen, issuing from Urizen's world, for the sake of Urizen, in all the senses of "for the sake of." These junctures are diaphoric; the relation expressed by "of" is intermediary, recalling the relation expressed in gift of the good. Together with the sublime, judgment, nature, and art. The movement has neither origin nor end, exceeds any end or origin, circulates in general economy, another gift of the good, another intermediary movement. In Blake's sublime.

CHAPTER 5

End

"I am convinced that art represents the highest task and the truly meta-physical activity of this life" (Nietzsche, *BT*, 31–32). Or without obeisance to God: "art, and *not* morality, is presented as the truly *metaphysical* activity of man . . . the existence of the world is *justified* only as an aesthetic phenome-non" (Nietzsche, *ASC*, 22; Ross, *AIS*, 171). If we believe that art comes as a gift, whether from God or nature, these words, youthful and impetuous—Nietzsche's words—speak of art giving us the good of the world, of being, but not the moral good, speak of something higher.

These words evoke another thought, one that I must lead to rest, seek to displace, that other thought with which the preceding chapter came to a close before its sublime interruption. For Nietzsche never says so, but surely must be read with Hegel in mind, and with Hegel recalling Kant's words of the end of art, leading us to Heidegger and beyond. For a theme of modern aesthet-ics, the thought of art from Descartes or before up to the present and after, circulates in the idea of the end, or beginning, perhaps the endless beginning of the end. I am speaking of the beginning of modernity, and perhaps its end in postmodernity, if that is its end rather than, as Lyotard suggests, a moment within the modern: "the postmodern . . . is undoubtedly a part of the mod-ern"; it "is not modernism at its end but in the nascent state, and this state is constant" (Lyotard, *WPM?*, 562; Ross, *AIS*, 562). This provocative paradoxi-calization bears a double truth, less of the postmodern than of the modern, of its endless beginning again and its projection of endlessness, endless modernity, endless advance, as if it would abolish time, but with endless be-ginnings and endless endings. The endlessly new requires incessant endings. Derrida speaks of this as iterability, as endless repetition joined with origina-tion. I speak of it as general economy. Lyotard speaks of it as the endless ar-rival of the event, the *arrive-t-il?*, of the *différend*.

But within the endless general circulation are endless restricted economies, and if the postmodern is resistance to these, is resistance to genres, if the postmodern is what Lyotard calls political,[1] then we always belong to restricted economies which may come and go, however strong they make their foundations. Within the thought of the *différend* is the very modern thought of endless beginnings and endings, events, all in the name of the good or politics.

And among the beginnings and endings of which we may speak, among those most telling for our time and culture, is the beginning and end of art. For as we have seen, philosophy, and later, science, began at the very moment art began, not with the first work of art or philosophy or science, as if there were ever a time at which something alike did not precede, of which the later was a repetition, an originary repetition, but with the naming of art in the ancient *diaphora* with philosophy, opening the modern intermediary movement between philosophy and science.

Art began at a diaphoric moment, perhaps in Plato, where philosophy began. For before that moment, in Heraclitus and Parmenides, for example, there was no philosophy, not a philosophy that [k]new its place apart from poetry, knew poetry's place. The birth of philosophy was the birth of poetry, the one brought into the home and state in an act of domesticity, the other exiled to wander in an act of expulsion. This too traditional reading has been supplemented here by a reading of that birth as a double expulsion and double restitution, where philosophy and poetry (and art) wander forever in each other's proximity, supplemented by science and ethics|politics, where ethics and politics also wander forever in each other's proximity, intermediary movements of like-unlike, as if one might become victor, the other victim.

The endlessly nascent state of postmodernism in the modern is another sign of iterability, the endless oscillation of repetition and origination I understand as general economy. And within this endless circulation are happenings, births, events, and deaths, losses, ends. General economy is the circulation of births and deaths, beginnings and ends, beyond any limits, any genres. And here we may return to the idea of the origin and end of art, an idea that we may take to express the idea of philosophy, or rather, to express the idea of the other born together with art. The thought of art, as a thought of beginning and ending, is the thought of philosophy, also a thought of beginning and ending as science, and more. In the extreme, this thought of beginning and ending, especially the beginning and ending of art, and philosophy, and scientific rationality, and more, is philosophy, Western philosophy, Western thought, and life, and culture. The culture of the West, long before modernity and long after, is and will be the thought of beginning (with the Greeks?) and ending (with the end of history?). Or rather, at this time in late and postmodernity, the culture of the West, the culture of "our age," shows itself in endless questions of beginnings and endings of truth and art. Supplemented, I believe, by the deepest and most far-reaching addition, questions of sexual difference, still questions of the beginning and ending of truth and art, and more, under a sign that has haunted Western life and thought from the beginning, leading to a new beginning.[2]

With this recognition, we may understand our diaphoric beginning between poetry and philosophy as the beginning of an endless circulation of beginnings and endings, within restricted economies circulating as more beginnings and endings. The identities of things, together with questions of identity, all are questions of beginnings and endings. And at the core of these circulations is the question of the beginning and ending of art, which began with philosophy, as a gift from the gods, and which may come to an end, together perhaps with the gods. The gods too may die, together with the death of God, the death of what we know cannot die. And in the same ways, perhaps, we face the death of nature, together with the end of art, though we know that nature cannot die, will not die even in the Great Collapse that may follow, finally, the Great Expansion. Some things cannot die; yet their deaths are always in question. In the West. For the West similarly cannot end, yet its end is always in question, called forth by its others.

I have examined the beginning of art at great length at that moment at which philosophy began. I have just begun to examine the end of art. We came to Kant's astonishing understanding that while science and, perhaps, philosophy, is "directed to the ever advancing perfection of knowledge" (Kant, *CJ*, § 47, p. 152; Ross, *AIS*, 129), "art stands still at a certain point; a boundary is set to it beyond which it cannot go, which presumably has been reached long ago and cannot be extended further" (Kant, *CJ*, § 47, p. 152; Ross, *AIS*, 129).[3] I have understood this remarkable understanding of art to cast a long shadow over our understanding of art, and science, and philosophy, a shadow stretching from Kant to the present. I am tracing the edges of this shadow.

The most famous responses to this understanding are Hegel's and Nietzsche's. I have suggested that we read *The Birth of Tragedy* as a response to Hegel and Kant against the idea that truth belongs to science, a response within the call of the good. I have not undertaken an examination of Hegel, nor of Heidegger's return to Nietzsche's refusal. I return for a moment to Kant's understanding of history. For Kant explicates "the ever advancing perfection" of history as teleology in a system where no purpose can be ascribed to nature. In the *Critique of Judgment*, man *(Menschen)* is "the *ultimate purpose* of nature here on earth, in reference to whom all other natural things constitute a system of purposes according to fundamental propositions of reason" (Kant, *CJ*, § 83, p. 279). All other things constitute a system of purposes for Man, for freedom, as we have seen available for human use in any ways whatever,[4] grounded on reason itself. I note without further comment here that every such claim has led to the subordination of women. And animals. I will return to these suppressions later:

> If now things of the world, as beings dependent in their existence, need a
> supreme cause acting according to purposes, man is the final purpose of cre-
> ation, since without him the chain of mutually subordinated purposes
> would not be complete as regards its ground. Only in man, and only in him
> as a subject of morality, do we meet with unconditioned legislation in re-
> spect of purposes, which therefore alone renders him capable of being a fi-
> nal purpose, to which the whole of nature is teleologically subordinated.
> (Kant, *CJ*, § 84, p. 286)

Kant extends the force of this teleological claim to say that the purpose of the universe is human freedom, that this freedom grounded in the supersensible has implications for the world, that it "obliges us to strive, and this purpose is the *highest good in the world* possible through freedom" (Kant, *CJ*, § 87, p. 301). This imperative, to strive for the highest good in the world, leads Kant to what Lyotard calls "the sign of history," to hold that enthusiasm for a political event marks humanity's progress under the Idea, toward culture. Kant claims to predict "from the aspects and precursor-signs of our times . . . the progressive improvement of mankind, a progress which henceforth cannot be totally reversible": that "a phenomenon of this kind in human history *can never be forgotten (vergisst sich nicht mehr)*" (Lyotard, *SH*, 408; quoted from Kant, *CF*).

Kant suggests that he can tell from the signs of his times that progress henceforth will be irreversible. The possibility of progress comes on the scene and can never be reversed. What, we may ask, dies with this birth? Kant understands the advancing perfection of humanity and the world to rest in freedom, not art. This leads to Hegel. Yet we must pause to consider that this end of art, in Kant, is a curtailing of freedom, restricting it to knowledge and science, where it cannot possibly belong, and to the teleology of nature, however inappropriately. Human freedom becomes the purpose of the world. Yet for many Romantics, based on Kant, that freedom belongs to art. In the name of freedom, under the good, Kant imposes humanity as nature's highest purpose. In the name of the good, and freedom, I hope to resist this domination.

If Hegel silenced Schelling, triumphed for a moment in the war of Spirit, he suppressed a thought of art, the possibility, which would not return until Nietzsche, that the ultimate purpose of the world lay in art, where freedom's anarchic movement could be found. Hegel claims that art is "not the highest way of apprehending the spiritually concrete. The higher way, in contrast to representation by means of the sensuously concrete, is thinking" (Hegel, *PFA*; Ross, *AIS*, 146). And since Spirit moves toward its highest realization, art will no longer express the highest truth—*if it ever did so*. For I wonder, even within the dream of archaic Greek supremacy, whether Greek tragedy outstripped the truths of Heraclitus, Parmenides, and Plato, for those who take Greek thought as supreme.

And here we come to Nietzsche and Heidegger. First Heidegger's reading of Hegel on this subject of the truth of art. In his Epilogue to "The Origin of the Work of Art," Heidegger names three propositions to which he understands himself to respond:

> Art no longer counts for us as the highest manner in which truth obtains existence for itself.
> One may well hope that art will continue to advance and perfect itself, but its form has ceased to be the highest need of the spirit.
> In all these relationships, art is and remains for us, on the side of its highest vocation, something past. (Heidegger, *OWA*, 80)

Heidegger adds:

> we have seen the rise of many new art works and new art movements. Hegel never meant to deny this possibility. But there remains: is art still an essential and necessary way in which that truth happens which is decisive for our historical existence, or is art no longer of this character? If, however, it is such no longer, then there remains the question why this is so. The truth of Hegel's judgment has not yet been decided. (Heidegger, *OWA*, 80)

Several issues arise here before we undertake an exploration of the origin and end of art. These concern the highest, the truth, the role of spirit, and what is decisive for our historical existence. I would add sensuousness and thinking. Put in briefest form: Shall we continue to think of humanity from the standpoints of spirituality and truth, must we think of humanity in relation to the highest, even in relation to history, and where do sensuality and materiality belong in this understanding of the highest? Shall we understand Hegel and Heidegger to continue to work within the frame of Kant's teleology of nature, where the question put to nature, and to humanity, is of the historical realization of the highest?

Art is not the highest way, Hegel tells us. "[A]rt has the task of presenting the Idea to immediate perception in a sensuous shape and not in the form of thinking and true spirituality as such" (Hegel, *PFA*; Ross, *AIS*, 146). The higher way is thinking. We may read Nietzsche as opening the possibility, foreclosed from the beginning in the quarrel between art and philosophy, that art is the highest way. Or we may read him to open the possibility, present for us from the beginning, that the *diaphora* is not an opposition, undermining the idea of the highest way. Poetry, art, do not order being from high to low, do not order representation or experience, but cherish every nuance, every detail, every loss and every gain, perhaps as a mother cherishes every gesture of her child, perhaps in a more masculine way. Perhaps. Art and poetry show us, perhaps, that cherishment is possible for those who are not mothers, that maternal care extends beyond the child and mother, that nature everywhere, and humanity everywhere, may cherish and may be cherished, together with loss, with sacrifice, aware as Hegel may not be of its contamination.

In the close of *The Phenomenology of Spirit*, Hegel speaks of sacrifice ambiguously:

> Knowledge is aware not only of itself, but also of the negative of itself, or its limit. Knowing its limit means knowing how to sacrifice itself. This sacrifice is the self-abandonment, in which Spirit sets forth, in the form of free fortuitous happening, it its process of becoming Spirit, intuitively apprehending outside its pure self as Time, and likewise its existence as Space. (Hegel, *PM*, 806–7)

The highest way is Absolute Knowledge: Spirit sacrificing itself into time and space, emptying itself into nature. "This last form into which Spirit passes, *Nature*, is its living immediate process of development. Nature—Spirit divested of self (externalized)—is, in its actual existence, nothing but this eternal process of abandoning its (Nature's) own independent subsistence, and the movement which reinstates Subject" (Hegel, *PM*, 807). The movement reinstates subject as master, owner, of the world: "returning into self-consciousness. It thus discovers this world in the living present to be its own property; and so has taken the first step to descend from the ideal intelligible world, or rather to quicken the abstract element of the intelligible world with concrete self-hood" (Hegel, *PM*, 802). It empties, sacrifices, externalizes itself not into unlike but like. "Spirit is the movement of the self which empties (externalizes) itself of self and sinks itself within its own substance, and qua subject, both has gone out of that substance into itself, making its substance an object and a content, and also supersedes this distinction of objectivity and content" (Hegel, *PM*, 804). All this as thought, not art. Spirit alienates itself into nature, but not a material, sensuous nature, not a heterogeneous, perhaps feminine, Other Nature, makes the world its own, makes nature subject in the shapes of history, emptied into its own time: "The other aspect, however, in which Spirit comes into being, *History*, is the process of becoming in terms of knowledge, a conscious self-mediating process—Spirit externalized and emptied into Time" (Hegel, *PM*, 807), spiritual recollections: "The goal, which is Absolute Knowledge or Spirit knowing itself as Spirit, finds its pathway in the recollection of spiritual forms *(Geister)* as they are in themselves and as they accomplish the organization of their spiritual kingdom" (Hegel, *PM*, 808).

Emptying, abandoning, externalizing, sacrificing. But never embracing, caressing flesh, bodies, materiality. Yet the world that Spirit makes its own, against every possibility touched by Hegel himself, that world whose materiality and heterogeneity might be "our own," cannot be our property, our mastery, but is our heterogeneity. We spirits are other to others and ourselves, heterogeneous, which has to mean in relation to nature, other in the flesh. And this thought of materiality is doubled, that matter is other to our spirituality, heterogeneous, and that we as spirits and material things are heterogeneous to ourselves and to each other. And the others. Which is to say that different kinds are heterogeneous to each other, and heterogeneous to themselves, in themselves, marked by spirituality and materiality, each heterogeneous to the other and itself heterogeneous.

Here art touches gender. For the thought of art we have seen in Plato is a thought of the heterogeneous, understood as love, sexuality, madness, spirit, body, soul, space, time, nature, and so on and on, all intermediary figures. Absolute Spirit seems to move by intermediary figures toward a nonintermediary goal. And where intermediary figures circulate heterogeneities, place and displace their envelopes, Absolute Knowledge gathers up the world in another figure of exclusion, excluding sensuousness and materiality, excluding women and animals (but not always, not always consistently) from the highest. We are exploring the possibility that Absolute Spirit may place intermediary movements into endless circulation, lacking any hierarchy from high to low.

Such a possibility is set aside by Hegel in Spirit's rise to its truth. And we have seen that what is decisive for our historical existence, in Heidegger remains spiritualized in relation to the gift of language. Spirit demands a higher form than art, which remains embedded in its sensuous materiality. Like women and animals. And men, who remain sensuous and material in their most spiritual work, striving toward but always failing to become God. How, we may ask, except in art, do we overcome the abyss between Man and God? How, we may ask, except in love, do we overcome the abyss between Man and Woman? I speak of the Woman who I suppose to know, and love, the Woman whose knowledge and truth and identity I do not know. And I speak as well of animals who I suppose to know, and love, who possess a knowledge and truth and life I do not know. All heterogeneous. All heterogeneous in the flesh.

The incredible thought to which we are led by Hegel is that Spirit, finally, in its gathering of all things together, sacrifices, excludes their materiality, and together with this exclusion of art from the highest come endless other exclusions: women, animals, nature's sensuous materiality. The content is a spiritual, airy content, a universality that cannot belong in the flesh to sensuous, material things, or if belonging there, cannot reach its highest form. The idea of the highest is the ultimate sacrifice, as humanity was the ultimate purpose of things, both sacrifices, exclusions, not of humanity, but of everything else to Humanity as God. In Kant and Hegel, where God includes all things together in their differences. And in Heidegger. The difference between Being and beings, "difference *as* difference [die Differenz *als* Differenz]" (Heidegger, *OTLCM*, 47, 113), shows itself in the difference between *poiēsis* and *technē*, which we have questioned from the beginning as an intermediary movement that does not exclude but bears the burden of exclusion endlessly throughout time. Yet difference as difference excludes. Heidegger excludes science from the "essential" as "not an original happening of truth" (Heidegger, *OWA*, 61–62; Ross, *AIS*, 274–75) as Hegel excludes art from the highest. And Heidegger excludes animals from the gift.

Could it be that difference as difference remains with Spirit in the light of the highest, the glory of God, the onto-theo-logical constitution of metaphysics as positioning Being (ontology) together with God (theology) as the highest form of thought and truth *(logos)?* Could it be that the thought of the "highest need of the spirit" is onto-theo-logical? Could it be that these two thoughts, what is "essential" and what is "highest," together or apart, bring us to onto-theo-logy?

Finally, another question, perhaps a repetition: What of the past, especially the essential and highest way of truth passing away? Could this thought of history, could any thought of history, save us from onto-theo-logy? Assuming we wish to be saved. I mean to speak of history in intermediary movement with art, understanding them as intermediary figures, like truth and flesh, intermediaries without exclusion. Can there be a history, a thought or memory of time, without exclusion? Can there be a thought of European, Western history that does not exclude, subordinate, the primitive, barbaric Others in the name of the higher civilization? And returning to art, can there be a thought of art that does not enforce the highest and most civilized sensibility and taste at the same time that it inhabits the margins of civilization, which always promote something higher than art? This, I suggest, is the thought and life of the aesthetic in Western history, that art should promote the work of the highest while always subordinate to something else.

Like women. Together with women. Portraying women, veiled and unveiled. I have noted Lacoue-Labarthe's reading of Hegel to say that "[i]f woman alone needs to be veiled, it is because she alone expresses—and arouses?—*sensual* desire" (Lacoue-Labarthe, *SP*, 141). This is because, or in consequence of, Hegel's understanding of the highest as another exclusion that puts things in their place:

> Man therefore has his actual substantial life in the state, in learning, etc.,
> and otherwise in work and struggle with the external world and with him-

self, so that it is only through his division that he fights his way to self-sufficient unity with himself. In the family, he has a peaceful intuition of this unity, and an emotive and subjective ethical life. Woman, however, has her substantial vocation in the family, and her ethical disposition consists in this *piety*. (Hegel, *A*, vol. 2, p. 745; quoted in Lacoue-Labarthe, *SP*, 133)

How can we read *Menschen* and *hommes*, not to mention man and mankind, and history, without suspecting such a piety? Could the gathering of Spirit into difference, the gathering of Being into its differences, the belonging-to-gether *(Zusammengehörigkeit)* of Being and beings, in the name of piety, exclude women and animals, all onto-theo-logical?

And what does the critique of onto-theo-logy exclude? What in the name of history? What in the name of art? For art is not the highest way, but even so, the highest does its work in art. In Hegel, and Heidegger:

Only in the highest art are Idea and presentation truly in conformity with one another, in the sense that the shape given to the Idea is in itself the absolutely true shape, because the content of the Idea which that shape expresses is itself the true and genuine content. (Hegel, *PFA*; Ross, *AIS*, 148)

It is precisely in great art—and only such art is under consideration here—that the artist remains inconsequential as compared with the work, almost like a passage way that destroys itself in the creative process for the work to emerge. (Heidegger, *OWA*, 40; Ross, *AIS*, 262)

Only great art. Only poetry. Only thinking. Only humanity. Only man. Only only.

This ordination of the highest, complete with subordination, appears and reappears in Hegel's view of art, a fulfillment of a Western view of art. Only great art is highest. But thinking is higher. And among the arts, the classical is highest; symbolic art is filled with "its fermentation, its mysteriousness, and its sublimity" (Hegel, *PFA*; Ross, *AIS*, 150), while classical art is "the free and adequate embodiment of the Idea in the shape peculiarly appropriate to the Idea itself in its essential nature" (Hegel, *PFA*; Ross, *AIS*, 150). The classical form of art is the highest, but the romantic expresses "the infinite subjectivity of the Idea, which as absolute inwardness cannot freely and truly shape itself outwardly on condition of remaining moulded into a bodily existence as the one appropriate to it" (Hegel, *PFA*; Ross, *AIS*, 151). The romantic is a decline of art, representing the deficiency in art, that it cannot realize the inwardness of the Idea for Subject. And in this double deficiency, of romantic art as art, expressing the defect of art, humanity finds its infinite superiority over animals, by an abyss of essence:

Man is an animal, but even in his animal functions, he is not confined to the
implicit, as the animal is; he becomes conscious of them, recognizes them,
and lifts them, as, for instance, the process of digestion, into self-conscious
science. In this way man breaks the barrier of his implicit and immediate
character, so that precisely because he *knows* that he is an animal, he ceases
to be an animal and attains knowledge of himself as spirit. (Hegel, *PFA*; Ross,
AIS, 151–52)

What, we might ask, are animals aware of if not that they are animals, cats
and ants? What of this struggle of human beings to elevate themselves? Hegel
virtually says that the struggle to elevate oneself in knowledge is that elevation. Perhaps this too Western, too masculine struggle for the height is the
origin of endless disasters.[5]

   Art belongs in Hegel to the struggle of Spirit to elevate itself from the
abstract to the concrete, where art achieves its fulfillment at a certain age,
within a certain history of Spirit. Spirit's history is one of elevation. Art's history is one of elevation. History is elevation. Thinking is elevated over art.
Classical art is elevated over symbolic art, Greek over Egyptian, Chinese, and
African, European over indigenous native peoples, in their arts as well as sciences, but passed over in the romanticization of the (European) subject,
where the Ideal, fulfilled in concrete and sensuous embodiment, passes into
free concrete spirituality (Hegel, *PFA*; Ross, *AIS*, 152).

   Freedom is an endless round of hierarchization where we have seen
it in Kant as the very possibility of judgment. In Hegel, judgment's hierarchies and exclusions are founded on hierarchy and exclusion, repeated
endlessly in time as history. History knows nothing other than itself,
nothing other than hierarchy, nothing other than exclusion, knows
nothing of cherishment, nothing of heterogeneity, of a difference than resists hierarchization.

   The idea of spirit is an idea of hierarchy and development.[6] The idea of
history is an idea of hierarchy and development. The idea of man is an idea
of hierarchy and development. In this context of domination and exclusion,
Hegel names the end of art, and poetry passes away into philosophy: "at this
highest stage, art now transcends itself, in that it forsakes the element of
a reconciled embodiment of the spirit in sensuous form and passes over
from the poetry of the imagination to the prose of thought" (Hegel, *PFA*;
Ross, *AIS*, 158).

   After Hegel, Nietzsche names the end of Christian morality as revaluation of all values. After Nietzsche, Heidegger names the end of metaphysics
as the beginning of thinking. The end of art repeats the hierarchies and subordinations of Western life and thought from the Greeks. What of the end of
Western morality, of Western metaphysics? What of the end of the West?

I hope now to pursue the thought of the end as an intermediary figure, a threshold. With the end of the old, we embark upon a new beginning. If we cross the threshold, we leave it behind, leave it, abandon its role as intermediary figure. From the beginning, I have understood art as an intermediary figure, moving between *poiēsis* and *technē*, and have understood as well each of these as intermediary figures. The thought of art, in its *diaphora* with philosophy, moves each of them, together with the others, in intermediary figures of heterogeneity.

From this point of view, perhaps when Heidegger tells us that "[t]he truth of Hegel's judgment has not yet been decided" (Heidegger, *OWA*, 80), the thought for us to think is not the origin and truth of art, another essence that threatens to divide by an abyss, but the indecision of the end regarded as an intermediary figure of history, resisting advancement, progress, and development as closing off the circulation. Spirit in Hegel closes the circulation of the dialectic. Perhaps the dialectic itself is such a closure. Art replays and resists that circulation, not because it continues to produce new works, but because it no longer represents the fulfillment of Spirit. Spirit's hegemony is threatened by art, if not powerfully or effectively. Or perhaps art is effective in its own ways, having nothing to do with Spirit's decisiveness. Perhaps Spirit, in its decisiveness, replays the *diaphora* between *poiēsis* and *technē* from one side, that of prose, philosophy, and *technē*, refuses the possibility that *poiēsis* and with it, art, may open up something beyond the horizon of Absolute Spirit, something beyond the absolute. All this in the figure of the end as figure of the not-yet-decided, perhaps never-to-be-decided, impossible-to-decide, irrelevant-to-decision.

I think of Nietzsche as an event in Western history, an event whose arrival leaves nothing in that history unchanged, arriving with a hammer, but whose changes remain triply indeterminate, and more. For (returning to the opening thought of this chapter) we may think of modernity as the endless advance of events of discovery and transformation, endless events in endless progress, described and ordered by Kant and Hegel under the sign of history, under the idea of cultural authority, where culture means authority. This is not Lyotard's thought precisely, because it holds the unpresentable in abeyance—for example, in Hegel, for whom, I would say, Spirit is present everywhere as history. But it is Lyotard's thought if we recognize that the unpresentable, the Other, is the Law (Lyotard, *HJ*, 89), the authority of Law and the law of authority. I speak of it as the giving of the good. Modernity's idea of progress rests in forgetting the law of authority, forgetting that authority has no law, that the good of authority resists authority, especially, after Western imperialism, cultural authority, the authority of one culture over others. Culture is authority; authority and the reign of culture are to be resisted. And the advance of history.

I interrupt the discussion of Nietzsche's arrival to contemplate another event of modernity. I suggest that we think of modernism as an event in Western modernity where cultural authority was resisted in the name of the author and the signifier. The tyranny of culture's authority over the signified, mastery of nature, was replaced by the tyranny of the artist and the supremacy of the signifier. This did not diminish mastery over nature, but replaced *technē*'s instrumentality by assigning mastery and authority to *poiēsis*, by technologizing *poiēsis*. The transformation of art by technology, a vital and dynamic historical event, became the perpetration of authority derived from mastery over technique, no less tyranny.

We may think of postmodernism and other "posts" as the arrival of an event in which this continuing crisis of cultural authority as mastery, heralded by Nietzsche, encountered others, other cultures, other worlds, some within its spheres of control, so profoundly that, in Owens's words, after Ricoeur, who speaks of wandering on an "interminable, aimless voyage" through civilizations:[7]

> Pluralism, however, reduces us to being an other among others; it is not a recognition, but a reduction to absolute indifference, equivalence, interchangeability (what Jean Baudrillard calls "implosion"). What is at stake, then, is not only the hegemony of Western Culture, but also (our sense of) our identity as a culture. (Owens, *DO*; Ross, *AIS*, 592)

Our idea of our identity is of singular individuals, apotheosized in modernism, resting on Western history and its cultural authority.

Postmodernism or poststructuralism, the Western movement of thought critical of itself and its endless advance, repudiates Western cultural authority. But it does not as deeply criticize cultural authority as such, either in relation to endless progress, all endings producing new beginnings, or in relation to other cultures, whose claim to cultural authority is quite different, for most—Islam may be an exception—do not claim authority over other cultures, do not insist upon the authority of progress or the progress of authority. Even Jews wander endlessly, chosen to wander. In Western, Greek and Christian civilization, wandering is exile. In our time, these figures of what Owens calls the crisis of cultural authority have been supplemented by political and national disasters, exiles, wandering, and ruin.

Can we find another home amid the ruins? Can we find another place to call home? Or does the arrival of this crisis permit us to think of something different, giving up the themes of alienation and loss in wandering, thinking instead of wandering and traveling as finding ourselves among the others? Lugones speaks of world-traveling, something possible perhaps only for those at the margins: "As outsiders to the mainstream, women of color in the U.S.

practice 'world'-travelling, mostly out of necessity. I affirm this practice as a skillful, creative, rich, enriching and, given certain circumstances, as a loving way of being and living" (Lugones, *PWTLP*, 3). This may be anything but postmodern because it carries within itself not loss of faith but joy in wandering.

This interruption of the event of Nietzsche's arrival, itself interrupting the endless advance of Western civilization, may itself be interrupted by a return. For I have not done with Nietzsche or with Heidegger, two events of interruption of the flow of Western thought that have since been taken up into its authority. That is one of the themes I meant to mark by this brief interruption, interrupted now by Trinh, who speaks of the crisis of the recognition of the other as no recognition at all, interrupting the discourses of Ricoeur and Owens. What Owens speaks of is no recognition of the other, no recognition and no other, but wandering among others as a loss of faith. Trinh speaks of wandering in quite different terms, those painfully forced to wander. But she faces the crisis of cultural authority, using Ricoeur's and Owens's words, faces its suffering and pain, supplemented by the suffering of others:

> What is at stake is not only the hegemony of Western cultures, but also their identities as unified cultures. Third World dwells on diversity; so does First World. This is our strength and our misery. The West is painfully made to realize the existence of a Third World in the First World, and vice versa. The Master is bound to recognize that His Culture is not as homogeneous, as monolithic as He believed it to be. He discovers, with much reluctance, He is just an other among others. (Trinh, *WNO*, 98–99; Ross, *AIS*, 617)

Why painfully, and with much reluctance? Perhaps because cultural authority anchors us safely, whoever we are, and we cannot live together with others at risk of our own cultural safety. Perhaps because Western cultural authority is founded on authority, founded in its monotheism and a monolithic representation of rational authority.

To which Trinh adds: "As long as words of difference serve to legitimate a discourse instead of delaying its authority to infinity, they are, to borrow an image from Audre Lorde, 'noteworthy only as *decorations*'" (Trinh, *WNO*, 101; Ross, *AIS*, 619). The event in which the West was brought to face the task and possibility of delaying authority to infinity, including the authority of that delay, is named Nietzsche, in the Western World. It is not the name of the event in which the Third and Fourth and other, endless Worlds made their claims to belong to history. And the ambiguity remains of whether all these questions are Western, whether, in our world, all authority remains Western, in crisis, in critique, in development.

All this addresses another ambiguity, present in our discussions of the end, which paradoxically was the same subject as that of endless progress. Kant and Hegel speak of the end of art in the context of the endless advance of reason in history, which excludes art from its sphere. Art is too sensuous; the productive imagination is too limited. The end is the mark of endlessness. The remarkable paradox continues past Hegel into Nietzsche's revaluation of all values, which began on September 30, 1888, but which appears to go on forever, endlessly re-marking its repetition, not unlike the endless repetition of scientific rationality. And it continues into Heidegger, for whom the question of the decisiveness of art for our historical existence has not yet been decided, and perhaps will never be decided, so that it will remain with us forever. Does delaying cultural authority to infinity mean bringing something to an end, perhaps cultural authority?

This is a question of art, but it is also a question of culture. On my reading here, culture is the name of this question of authority and end, so that all questions of the end of art, or metaphysics, or science, or philosophy are questions of the authority of culture, where we have no idea whatever what cultural authority means on a world or historical stage. I offer, by way of contrast, another reading, another interruption.

Vattimo speaks of Western destiny, after Nietzsche and Heidegger, as *Verwindung*: "an overcoming which is in reality a recognition of belonging, a healing of an illness, and an assumption of responsibility" (Vattimo, *EM*, 40). This image of an appearance, an event, without historical destination, is supplemented by the thought of destiny, a repetition of history's truth, all given from Being, the giving of Being, bearing a responsibility in oblivion to the good:

> This unveiling and disclosing is at once the final moment, the culmination, and the beginning of the crisis of metaphysics and humanism. Such a culminating moment is not the result of an historical necessity nor of a process guided by some sort of objective dialectic; rather, it is *Gabe*, the giving and the gift of Being, whose destiny exists only as a sending-forth, a mission, and an announcement. For these reasons, in essence, the crisis of humanism is not an overcoming but a *Verwindung*, a call for humanity to heal itself of humanism, to yield itself up and resign itself to humanism as something for which humanity is destined. (Vattimo, *EM*, 40–41)

The final moment, the culmination, the beginning of a crisis in which humanity will fulfill its destiny, not as an achievement, but as a healing, yielding, and resignation. But still destined, historically. History remains the destination of humanity and culture. Nature's abundance remains unthought.

Put another way, more radically, the idea of the end of history is still the idea of history. "The history of events—whether political, military, or theoretical—is but one history among many" (Vattimo, *EM*, 8). Even so, "the true substance of the crisis of humanism is the death of God. It is no coincidence that this should be announced by Nietzsche, the first radically non-humanistic thinker of our age" (Vattimo, *EM*, 32). In a disturbing insight, still caught within the grip of history, Vattimo raises the unsettling thought that non-Western thought remains Western, that the truly other thought will never think of history after Nietzsche and Heidegger, as advance, or progress, or teleology, or destiny. "[W]hat we see today is an ensemble of contemporaneous 'swerves' of the primitive, 'hybrid traces and residues contaminated by modernity, the margins of the present which embrace both Third World societies and the ghettoes of industrial societies.'" (Guidieri, *SPA*, 60; quoted in Vattimo, *EM*, 158). Our world remains Western, marginalizing every other culture.

Returning to Nietzsche: "But why should we take seriously and conform to the development of Western thought in which, ultimately, God is dead? Precisely because this development has dissolved any other point of reference, any other basis of certainty except the cultural heritage" (Vattimo, *EM*, 177). The cultural heritage returns in greater authority, ruling over a wasteland in which all other authorities have been vanquished. Except perhaps for the Church. And other churches and temples.

We return to the question of the relation between judgment and the good, dividing the world into good and bad; between *poiēsis* and *technē*, *diaphora* or *polemos*. From the beginning I have argued that the good cannot judge judgment as good or bad, that *poiēsis* knows nothing and cares less for the work of *technē*, that only Apollo can insist on ruling over Dionysus. Dionysus is the god of music, and music cannot speak of high and low, cannot represent up and down. Up and down, high and low, are places where music does its work. But music cannot judge, though we judge music repeatedly. And perhaps this feature of music is why we have so much difficulty speaking of our musical judgments in discourses other than its own. We judge what works without judgment.

What I have said of music belongs to other arts. I have not cut music off from the other arts, as higher, or lower, even as different, at least in this respect. The respect in which music is different, I believe, is medial: the materiality of sound. This is a supreme but empty difference, because every art and every form of art can mimick the others. But what matter anyway? Art makes everything matter. Art knows nothing of what matters more than something else. All art, including music, chooses and selects with an absolute preference that can be given no ground or legitimacy whatever, nothing historical. The exemplariness of which Kant speaks is Apollinian, not Dionysian. Dionysus makes examples of us, but offers none as exemplary, paradigmatic.

According to Aristotle, tragedy is supremely paradigmatic, presents us with tragic figures who serve as examples for us and make examples of us for others. The tragic hero is a model, leading to Kant's view of genius. Well, we may say, a model or example is a better authority than a rule or law. Yet we are still within the hold of authority. Where we understand tragedy to belong to Dionysus as much as to Apollo, in memory of music and dance, perhaps, nothing may be exemplary, not men or women, nothing stands for anything else. Intoxication and ecstasy model nothing.

The Apollinian art is sculpture. In Hegel, sculpture mirrors the ultimate purpose of the world described by Kant, man the supreme measure of things; Man the Example, leading to God. We also recall, by way of contrast, "the non-imagistic, Dionysian art of music" (Nietzsche, *BT*, 33; Ross, *AIS*, 162). Perhaps it is the imagelessness of music that frees it from exemplariness. It can be an example of nothing but itself, not even of genius. We may think of modernism, in painting, dance, and even architecture, as opening the possibility that all the arts of image and depiction might be as free from exemplariness as music, free to be Dionysian rather than Apollinian.

Such a view would recall Socrates' arguments concerning painting, as if the imagination broke down before the authoritative grip of images, while we know that poetry must struggle with the authority of language, the tyranny of syntax, in the name of God. Such a view of the image is perhaps a bit outdated; we know that images can be free from their Apollinian illusions, the illusions of the unveiling of truth, to intoxicate us without unveiling. But we also know, in our own time, that images grip us with representational authority, described by Owens within the tyranny of the signifier: "that system of power that authorizes certain representations while blocking, prohibiting or invalidating others" (Owens, *DO*; Ross, *AIS*, 593).

Owens speaks of this structure of representation that authorizes some and prohibits others as a system of power, suggesting a separation between the system of power and its representations. I have followed a more Foucauldian path, where the system of power and its representations work by exclusion, but where the system in both guises is productive and everywhere, inseparable from resistance. In other words, representation blocks, prohibits, excludes, and produces. To emphasize production is to be complicit in the destructions. It is to emphasize the Apollinian, orderly, and productive side of systems that exclude and destroy.

Dionysus is not free from destruction. Nor is nature or music. They are free from the pretense that some authority can justify their destructions, and that such an authority defines the sign of history. Nietzsche insists that we understand both Apollo and Dionysus as frenzy, one toward light, the other

toward intoxication. But their divinity expresses two things: that both are driven by desire, and that desire can be beyond all limits, uncontained by limits.
Both are mad, excessive, as gods. Both are figures of the sublime. Not just
Dionysus. Apollo's light is as sublime as Dionysus's revelry. But Dionysus recalls earthly things that Apollo calls upon us to forget in our dreams. Nietzsche speaks of these as gifts of the earth:

> Under the charm of the Dionysian not only is the union between man
> and man reaffirmed, but nature which has become alienated, hostile, or sub-
> jugated, celebrates once more her reconciliation with her lost son, man.
> Freely, earth proffers her gifts, and peacefully the beasts of prey of the rocks
> and desert approach. The chariot of Dionysus is covered with flowers and
> garlands; panthers and tigers walk under its yoke. (Nietzsche, *BT*, 37; Ross,
> *AIS*, 165)

All this reminds us of Diotima's speech. The Apollinian and Dionysian "burst
forth from nature herself, *without the mediation of the human artist*"
(Nietzsche, *BT*, 38; Ross, *AIS*, 165). Yet lest we be overcome with edenic
solemnity, Nietzsche elsewhere reminds us of asses. The reconciliation of humanity with nature appears to forget the flood's disaster. The walk of
humanity with animals under human yoke recalls Eden but not the flood.
Even so, such a harmony may set us a good example. Or it may offer a dream,
an intoxicated revel, that can proffer nothing exemplary. Nature offers gifts
that do not set examples. Rather, Apollo and Dionysus call forth gifts from
us as exchanges between them, under their rule (Nietzsche, *BT*, 39; Ross,
AIS, 167).

Fourteen years later, Nietzsche described *The Birth of Tragedy* as a
"questionable" work, "badly written, ponderous, embarrassing, image-mad
and image-confused . . . a book for initiates" (Nietzsche, *ASC*, 19; Ross, *AIS*,
170). This romantic suffusion of imagination, this impossible book that spoke
of tragedy addressed something different, a different problem than that of
Dionysian art. The "phenomenon of the Dionysian" had to do less with art
than science:

> And science itself, our science—indeed, what is the significance of all sci-
> ence, viewed as a symptom of life? For what—worse yet, *whence*—all sci-
> ence? (Nietzsche, *ASC*, 18; Ross, *AIS*, 169)

> What I then got hold of, something frightful and dangerous, a problem
> with horns but not necessarily a bull, in any case a *new* problem—today I
> should say that it was *the problem of science itself*, science considered for
> the first time as problematic, as questionable. (Nietzsche, *ASC*, 18; Ross,
> *AIS*, 169)

Surely science has always been questioned, from within and without, for example in relation to faith and God. Perhaps by the time Nietzsche wrote, by the time of Kant and Hegel, science could no longer be questioned from the standpoint of faith. Perhaps that is what we mean by the secularization of the world. We lose the sacred, Apollo and Dionysus together as gods, when all that we know is Apollinian. Where one god triumphs—be it Zeus or Apollo or Jehovah or Reason—nothing is left of the sacred, nothing is left of the mobility of the gift. What is left is no longer questionable from without, and rules triumph over truth from within.

Science must be questioned from the standpoint of life, which can ask as science cannot, What good is science and what is its destination? Yet we have seen throughout our exploration of the good as gift that the gift has no destination and the good displaces every place. Nietzsche's question is a double question, a double displacement, of the authority of science, science's rational truth, as if science's authority were supreme; and of the authority of any other god, as if that might be supreme, including life and art. For the first time, science may be considered questionable in the sense that truth's authority is questionable. Whatever its origin, perhaps, the authority of truth is questionable. On this reading, life is not, perhaps, another origin of truth, but of questionableness. I have called it the good. On this reading, also, the questionableness of authority cannot emerge from within; science cannot recognize itself as the problem. *The Birth of Tragedy* questions science "in the context of *art*—for the problem of science cannot be recognized in the context of science" (Nietzsche, *ASC*, 8; Ross, *AIS*, 169). "[T]his audacious book dared to tackle for the first time: *to look at science in the perspective of the artist, but at art in that of life*" (Nietzsche, *ASC*, 8; Ross, *AIS*, 170).[8]

The questions from art and life addressed to science concern the limits of truth and rationality. Derrida suggests that the historical task of thought, especially philosophy, is to think at the limit, understanding that thought to control and to unleash the limit, the surplus of the limit, beyond any containment.[9] In this sense there is no outside of the work, no other place, not that there is no other to science—art, life, or nature—but that others frame the limits of science, and in that sense cannot be thought autonomously. The limit divides diaphorically, intermediarily.

I understand this idea of limit, diaphorically and intermediarily, to address Nietzsche's claim that science cannot question itself. Perhaps every truth can question itself, but only toward limits that exceed both that truth and its questions. Perhaps this is true not only of truth, and science, and art, but of life and nature understood now as limit and excess. And perhaps even more the impulse to question, described by Nietzsche as the will to truth, the will to power, perhaps this will, understanding both truth and power as engendering endless movements from within and without, is what I mean by the good. The art that questions science and the art questioned from the standpoint of life—such a demand to question is from within the will to truth that divided art from philosophy so long ago, giving birth to science, and is a displacement of the hold of that will upon the truth of art. The will to truth is named Apollo. The will to undermine that will to truth is named Dionysus. Both inseparable, diaphorically, at the limit of scientific rationality and art.

Where we find music and where we experience ecstasy. For what is Dionysian (Nietzsche, *ASC*, 20; Ross, *AIS*, 170) joins the craving for beauty with the craving for ugliness, with madness and ecstasy, against "the triumph of *optimism*, the gradual prevalence of *rationality*" (Nietzsche, *ASC*, 21; Ross, *AIS*, 171). At this point, Nietzsche reminds us of his words to Wagner, that "art, and *not* morality, is presented as the truly *metaphysical* activity of man" (Nietzsche, *ASC*, 22; Ross, *AIS*, 171), described as another theology. "Indeed, the whole book knows only an artistic meaning and crypto-meaning behind all events—a 'god' " (Nietzsche, *ASC*, 22; Ross, *AIS*, 172). To which we may add another "crypto-meaning," another "god" (but not a goddess) required at the birth of tragedy. For "the continuous development of art is bound up with the *Apollinian* and *Dionysian* duality—just as procreation depends on the duality of the sexes" (Nietzsche, *BT*, 33; Ross, *AIS*, 162). And, moreover, these gods "appear coupled with each other, and through this coupling ultimately generate an equally Dionysian and Apollinian form of art—Attic tragedy" (Nietzsche, *BT*, 33; Ross, *AIS*, 162). Apollo and Dionysus are two male gods whose union repeats the engenderment of the world. And which, we ask, is female?

We may understand Dionysus to represent ecstasy, Apollo to represent illusion. Yet both inspire imagination, and imagination carries within itself both repetition and production. In their coupling, in their procreation, these gods give rise to ecstasy—I say together. Dreams and intoxication give birth to ecstasy, where each god is sexual, sexually differentiated. Dreams and intoxication replay sexual difference, passing to the sexual differentiation within and without of art, science, philosophy, and technology. And the good. The unveiling of truth is a sexual figure, because the figure of unveiling has always been woman. Women wear the veil, in European and non-European societies. Apollo is no less mad, ecstatic, than Dionysus. Or rather, in their coupling we find ecstasy, the ecstasy of life and tragedy that gives birth to the questions of science. This ecstatic, sexual, engendered coupling of Apollo and Dionysus is the gift of art in the name of the good. It belongs to nature.

Why then does Nietzsche speak of questioning science from the standpoint of art, art from the standpoint of life? Why not speak of questioning science and art and life from the standpoint of nature? And why not speak of questioning as given from the good? All these questions, I believe, are questions of the end. Art, science, and even life may be thought of as coming to an end, but neither nature nor the good. The idea of the end of art, the advance of knowledge, the ultimate purpose of nature, all are linked. The new question of science, which arrived on the scene, which was not present before, is the question of the end of art: questions of its mission, purpose, and destiny and of its coming to a close all are linked.

In Nietzsche, they are linked with the end of God. "The greatest recent event—that 'God is dead,' that the belief in the Christian God has ceased to be believable—is even now beginning to cast its first shadows over Europe" (Nietzsche, *GS*, 447). Not the pagan gods, and perhaps not the Islamic God. The end and origin are linked not because whenever something ends, something else begins, but because origin, end, and destiny are all intermediary terms, touching the limits of science and rationality, where these are understood to touch themselves, their limits, only by the use of instruments. "Man needs an instrument to touch himself with: a hand, a woman, or some substitute" (Irigaray, *VF*, 232). But "woman is neither open nor closed. She is indefinite, in-finite, *form is never complete in her*" (Irigaray, *VF*, 229). An ecstatic, Nietzschean thought.

The Birth of Tragedy is "against morality" (Nietzsche, *ASC*, 24; Ross, *AIS*, 173), against "[h]atred of 'the world,' condemnations of the passions, fear of beauty and sensuality, a beyond invented to slander this life, at bottom a craving for the nothing, for the end, for respite" (Nietzsche, *ASC*, 23; Ross, *AIS*, 172). Against a morality of fear and disgust, affirmation of life in the name of life and art: I call it given from the good.

All in the name of music, concluding with what may be Nietzsche's most telling question: "What would a music have to be like that would no longer be of romantic origin, like German music—but *Dionysian*?" (Nietzsche, *ASC*, 25; Ross, *AIS*, 174). The answer, from *Zarathustra*, is "*learn*—to laugh" (Nietzsche, *ASC*, 27; Ross, *AIS*, 175). I wonder if this is not still Romantic, if we can laugh today after concentration camps and African disasters. And if we cannot, do we repeat the hold of a Christian morality that asks us to resign ourselves to nothing in the name of salvation? Could every salvation be our ruin? Could the death of God be the death of salvation?[10] Could this laughter be another absolute comfort, or perhaps its refusal? And what of the Eternal Return, an absolute refusal to an ultimate purpose to the universe, its ultimate destiny—but an ultimate figure notwithstanding?

Do we know how to laugh? Could that be our new dawn, a new dawn that offered no comfort whatever, no ultimate comfort? And those who suffer, can they be refused restitution in the name of "against morality"?

I do not think we can learn to laugh, perhaps laugh at laughter, without recollecting Kant's thought of laughter, with music in mind. He speaks of the "essential difference between *what satisfies simply in the act of judging it* and that which *gratifies* (pleases in sensation)" (Kant, *CJ*, § 54, Remark, p. 175), reminding us that "the pure judgment of taste is independent of charm and emotion" (Kant, *CJ*, § 13, p. 58), and, more forcefully, "[t]hat taste is always barbaric which needs a mixture of *charms* and *emotions* in order that there may be satisfaction, and still more so if it make these the measure of its assent" (Kant, *CJ*, 58). The pure judgment of taste is free from interest and the empirical, transferred to the sensuous body:

> music and that which excites laughter are two different kinds of play with aesthetical ideas, or of representations of the understanding through which ultimately nothing is thought, which can give lively gratification merely by their changes. Thus we recognize pretty clearly that the animation in both cases is merely bodily, although it is excited by ideas of the mind, and that the feeling of health produced by a motion of intestines corresponding to the play in question makes up that whole gratification of a gay party which is regarded as so refined and so spiritual. (Kant, *CJ*, § 54, Remark, pp. 176–77)

The animation in both cases, laughter and music, moves from and returns to the intestines. "Merely bodily," Kant tells us, of both laughter and music. If we learn to laugh, do we also learn to sing?

"Laughter is an affection arising from the sudden transformation of a strained expectation into nothing" (Kant, *CJ*, § 54, Remark, p. 177). Into nothing. The merely bodily presents an affection that dissolves into nothing, means nothing, leaves no residue. And music? Music and laughter are Dionysian: Kant calls laughter's remains "nothing." He calls music, with color, a "beautiful play of sensations" (Kant, *CJ*, § 51, p. 168), almost nothing, almost indistinguishable from "a play of *pleasant* sensations" (Kant, *CJ*, § 51, p. 169). The sensuous body destroys the possibility of aesthetic judgment, leaving nothing behind.

Perhaps when we learn to laugh, we will learn that sensations are not to be dismissed or despised. Perhaps when we learn to laugh, we will laugh at nothing, laugh at dismissing something as nothing and at nothing itself. We will laugh—for what else can you do with nothing? But the sensuous body is not nothing, nothing to be dismissed, but Dionysian. And more.

For nothing is not nothing, nothing to be dismissed, but Dionysian. Or rather, as Bataille says, and he claims to be Nietzsche himself, "sovereignty is nothing" (he says NOTHING) (Bataille, *AS*, III, p. 430). Nothing, nothing, nothing, is sovereignty. No thing. Like laughter, and music, and intermediary figures, movements, general economy. But this nothing, this sovereignty, is the abundance or excess of nature, of the world, useless expenditure, useless giving. In laughter, we expend energies without use. In music, something moves without utility. In sovereignty, excess is useless, nothing, thereby everything. Perhaps the play of sensations is this useless excess, an expenditure of nothing. Perhaps Kant tries to make something of nothing.

We come to another set of questions, posed by Nietzsche himself, that may bring us to closure, though not too quickly:

What is Dionysian?
Why music?
Why laugh, surrounded by disasters?
Do the idols still march?
What is good, at the end of morality?

To the question, What is Dionysian?, Nietzsche gives several answers. One is from within *The Birth of Tragedy*: "This book contains an answer: one 'who knows' is talking, the initiate and disciple of his god" (Nietzsche, *ASC*, 20; Ross, *AIS*, 170). I have considered another: he speaks of the "craving for beauty," "privation, melancholy, pain"; of the "craving for the ugly"; of "joy, strength, overflowing health," and of "Dionysian madness," "degeneration, decline, and the final stage of culture"; of "ecstasies," "visions and hallucinations shared by entire communities or assemblies at a cult"; finally:

> Could it be possible that, in spite of all "modern ideas" and the prejudices of a democratic taste, the triumph of *optimism*, the gradual prevalence of *rationality*, practical and theoretical *utilitarianism*, no less than democracy itself which developed at the same time, might all have been symptoms of a decline of strength, of impending old age, and of physiological weariness? These, and not pessimism? Was Epicurus an optimist—precisely because he was afflicted? (Nietzsche, *ASC*, 21–22; Ross, *AIS*, 171).

And we, could we be optimists, rational and utilitarian, because we are afflicted? Nietzsche adds: "It is apparent that it was a whole cluster of grave questions with which this book burdened itself. Let us add the gravest question of all. What, seen in the perspective of *life*, is the significance of morality?" (Nietzsche, *ASC*, 22; Ross, *AIS*, 171). This is the question of music. Why music?

Postponing this question for a moment longer, I would reply to the question what is Dionysian? today, after Nietzsche and those who followed him, after events Nietzsche could not have known, but with him in mind, with another cluster of questions, issues, topics, problematics. I list these in successive paragraphs, with intervening comments and associated problematics. Music, laughter, Dionysian revelry, the march of idols, all remain as good. I list them in no hierarchical order, without measure.

What is Dionysian? Music, laughter, revelry, all pessimisms, all refusals of the optimism of the endless advance of reason's truth.

What is Dionysian? Memories of endless and recurrent questions of the end of art, and with those questions others, of the victory of science, the endless march of rational truth, the ultimate purpose of history; or instead, the same in reverse, questions of the end of philosophy, science, and history. We have seen that the question of the origin is the question of the end, and in our post-Nietzschean time, the question of the end of art raises questions of the origin of thought, perhaps in Greece, as a disaster. Origins and ends, all disasters, against the endless advance of unbroken scientific rationality. Another disaster.

The disaster of the death of god, the secularization of a world that still dreams of gods (or Gods). Secularity and sacrality, all questions of the Dionysian. For perhaps secularity produces monsters after Christian and Greek monsters, all killing god. The tragedy of the death of god. The comedy, the way he died. And the laughter.

The overman offers another laughter, perhaps laughing at the idea that we have given up the advance. If we face a new dawn, if we philosophize with a hammer, smashing Greek, Christian, Jewish, German, and endless other idols, if we rise again over the ruins of the idols, do we advance?

Zarathustra tells the world: "*I teach you the overman.* Man is something that shall be overcome. What have you done to overcome him?" (Nietzsche, *Z*, 124). Do we overcome him by something better, better than man, better in man? Or is there no overman in reality? "We have invented the concept of 'end': in reality there is no end" (Nietzsche, *TI*, 500). There is no man; there is no end; there is no overman; nothing is better. Perhaps and maybe. In reality there is no reality:

> The word "overman," as the designation of a type of supreme achievement, as opposed to "modern" men, to "good" men, to Christians and other nihilists—a word that in the mouth of a Zarathustra, the annihilator of morality, becomes a very pensive word—has been understood almost everywhere with the utmost innocence in the sense of those very values whose opposite Zarathustra was meant to represent—that is, as an "idealistic" type of a higher kind of man, half "saint," half "genius." (Nietzsche, *EH*, 717)

"Overman" is a very pensive word, but Nietzsche has been read to institute a higher kind of man. That higher kind is not the overman.

What is Dionysian? What is the overman? Against man as the ultimate purpose of the universe; against man the supreme measure: in reality there is no end, there is no purpose, there is no measure. Most of all, man is immeasure.

What alone can be our doctrine? That no one gives man his qualities—
neither God, nor society, nor his parents and ancestors, nor he himself. . . .
No one is responsible for man's being there at all, for his being such-and-
such, or for his being in these circumstances or in this environment. . . . It
is absurd to wish to devolve one's essence on some end or other. (Nietzsche,
TI, 500)[11]

Man is an intermediary figure.

What is Dionysian? Against the ultimate purpose of the universe, man is
without qualities. Against the ultimate purpose of the universe, there is no
purpose and no end, but Eternal Recurrence of the Same. And within this recurrence, always the same, everything is different. Within this pessimism we
hear laughter.

What is Dionysian? Something beyond: beyond good and evil; beyond
morality; fearful and horrible. Something beyond the security of the sublime, beyond the effeminacy of peace, beyond good and evil, beyond morality. And to where, how far, does this beyond reach? With this question we
return to questions of the immeasurability of the sublime, here the immeasurability of the Dionysian, always caught in the toils of work.
For where Kant admires danger and war, so long as we are safe and they are
kept in order, Nietzsche reverses the priority, still maintaining the relation
of proximity. The Dionysian is unsafe, and we must risk our safety to be
great, for Kant, provided we remain within morality's limits. And why, if
greatness is our due, shall we acknowledge such limits? What if that limitation cost us greatness? What if in sacrificing excess, we sacrificed mystery,
ecstasy, music?

The Dionysian is the question of the deepest sacrifices we must make to
be safe, to be secure. Do we give up too much to be safe? And on the other
side of that question, are we safe? We men. And what of women, who are not
safe in the home? And the others, strangers, barbarians among us and abroad.
Are they safe in their homes? Or ours? Do we care about their safety in seeking our own? Or is our greatness at the expense of strangers? Against ourselves? Against women? And others.

And more. For in asking if we give up too much of greatness to be safe,
to Apollo, we grant that we desire safety. And no doubt we do. But we may also
desire ugliness, and disgusting things, and horrible events. We may revel in
these, finding that our deepest loves and needs remain empty without grue-
someness and horror. Safety is domestic, tame; we veil our craving for evil,
for ugliness, for horror, for vomit and excrement, to be domestic, safe. We veil
our craving for disgust, veiling women. For women always wear the veil, have
the veil draped over them. But it is our craving that we hope to tame, we men.
Or rather, gathering up Kant's idea of security into Nietzsche, it is always

some particular people and things, some places, where we demand safety, imposing the burden of our own hatefulness and ugliness on someone or something.

In this light, the "beyond" of the Dionysian, the "beyond" of good and evil, opened by the sublime, is "beyond all measure" at the same time that it imposes a measure unequally and harshly on some more than others. And not some individuals, but peoples, genders, classes, races, some kinds of people rather than others, historically and systematically imposed on women more than men, who suffer violence, or on minority men, strangers, who suffer violence upon them and commit violence among them, destroying their bodies and spirits in the name of some "beyond." The beyond named as sublime, Dionysian, returns to kill and destroy unless we release its hold upon us in a revelry beyond good and evil.

What is Dionysian?, then, works unequally, differently, in different places. The question, asked by Nietzsche in memory of Kant, and Hegel, asks what is Dionysian for us, we men, we Germans, we Europeans. And what of others, Jews, women, Africans? What of slaves, tortured in the name of truth in Greece? (duBois, *TT*). From the beginning of *The Birth of Tragedy*, in "the Greek world" (Nietzsche, *BT*, 33; Ross, *AIS*, 162), Dionysus far more than Apollo delimited the Greek, marked "the immense gap which separates the *Dionysian Greek* from the Dionysian barbarian" (Nietzsche, *BT*, 39; Ross, *AIS*, 166), the gap between the Greeks and Babylonians (Nietzsche, *BT*, 39; Ross, *AIS*, 167). Dionysian cults and rites marked initiates and strangers. Here Dionysus at one and the same time works to mark the inner and outer and to threaten our safety within.

In this way, the Dionysian brings us face to face with strangers, threatens our safety by threatening them. The question, What is Dionysian?, is one of our safety, in our own places, threatened by others, by everything foreign, where the Dionysian marks our inner ecstasy and the possibility of other strange and foreign ecstasies. The first is what Nietzsche refers to as the perspective of life. The second touches barbarians and women by the same gesture, that life demands safety by a demand so far beyond anything we may be able to acknowledge that we can come to know ourselves in this demand only by insisting that we move beyond it.

The question is whether "the triumph of *optimism*, the gradual prevalence of *rationality*, practical and theoretical *utilitarianism*, no less than democracy itself which developed at the same time, might all have been symptoms of a decline of strength, of impending old age, and of physiological weariness?" (Nietzsche, *ASC*, 21–22; Ross, *AIS*, 171). All these questions of the very core of our life, the conditions of political and ethical safety, are questions of life and morality, understanding by morality the question of how we are to live and how well. Could ethics and morality be symptoms of a

desire for safety that contradicted at its very heart the possibility of a rich
and demanding life?

This question may be divided in two. For on the one hand, the dangers,
threats, and wars against which we have built morality appear to belong to
men, while women have been kept safe in the home, where they suffer violence and degradation. When we criticize morality as effeminate, we must
consider that this critique repeats the diminution of women. On the other
hand, the bonds that strangle European women traditionally are bonds of
Christian morality, of hearth and home, where women will be kept safe to
bear God's children, but will not be allowed to interfere with the sublime genius of men or to fulfill their own, whatever it may be.

Here the domicile is a double or triple figure, of men's safety in a world
where safety is both impossible and self-denial; of safety which bears differently on men and women and slaves; of what lies beyond the gates of the
domicile: strangers, barbarians, war, the sublime, and women. For Nietzsche
extols war in the voice of Heraclitus: "Not contentedness but more power; not
peace but war; not virtue but fitness. . . . " (Nietzsche, *AntiChrist*, 570). But
the ellipsis speaks of "Renaissance virtue, *virtù*, virtue that is moraline-
free"—that is, of binary oppositions. Like Heraclitus, Nietzsche extols a war
against binariness, against a morality of hierarchy, in the voice of hierarchy
and war. Nietzsche speaks of war, but not a war that is better than peace.
Nietzsche speaks of peace, but not an ethical peace.

Here questions of science, cheerfulness, optimism, rationality, utilitarianism, and democracy, all questions of the Dionysian, reach beyond festivity
to the conditions of life, to the unsafe conditions of life denied, hidden, and
imposed unequally on some rather than others. The Dionysian touches, as it
bears upon morality, all the forms of human social and ethical life, but in a
gesture beyond any of its configurations. It takes us back to the possibility of
founding a state, founding a home, founding sexual relations, founding anything human, and more, beyond the idea of founding. To art.

What is Dionysian?, then, touches the idea of humanity, and with that
touch, the idea of men and women, individuals and groups, all the ideas with
which we define the human. "No one gives man his qualities." Or women. Or
whatever. Or put another way, humanity is given qualities to bring us to safety
against the possibility of something beyond. And also, when "we" are brought
to safety, others are harmed: women, children, strangers. The subject is a
principle of safety. The Dionysian reaches to the founding of safety with
recognition that the optimism at the heart of all the categories and classifications we produce give us a safety that is death: ours and others.

At this point, we may accelerate our examination of the reach and depth
of the Dionysian. The question "What is Dionysian?" touches the following,
and more:

The disgusting, excremental, painful side of our material existence in a revelry that resists the hierarchization of mind and spirit over bodies. Materiality and sensuousness, in Dionysian rites, reveal the possibility of ecstasy beyond anything known to rational optimism.

The animal side of humanity resists the institution of The Human against nature and from within reason. Man—perhaps humanity, perhaps the warlike gender rather than the other—is the ultimate purpose of the world, ruling over nature and animals in the name of freedom. This freedom, morality's freedom, is what the Dionysian questions at its heart: whether this "highest" possibility for man is weakness and old age:

> We no longer derive man from "the spirit" or "the deity"; we have placed him back among the animals. We consider him the strongest animal because he is the most cunning: his spirituality is a consequence of this. On the other hand, we oppose the vanity that would raise its head again here too—as if man had been the great hidden purpose of the evolution of the animals. Man is by no means the crown of creation: every living being stands beside him on the same level of perfection. And even this is saying too much: relatively speaking, man is the most bungled of all the animals, the sickliest, and not one has strayed more dangerously from its instincts. But for all that, he is of course the most *interesting*. (A, p. 580)

To us. Perhaps. But the animal side of humanity also touches nature in a way that Christianity has disallowed, at least in its spirit of morality. For that morality has raised man above animals and nature in the spirit of Apollo: Dionysus reminds us of something else, of "nature which has become alienated, hostile, or subjugated, celebrates once more her reconciliation with her lost son, man. Freely, earth proffers her gifts, and peacefully the beasts of prey of the rocks and desert approach" (Nietzsche, *BT*, 37; Ross, *AIS*, 165). The Dionysian reminds us of gifts, of nature giving, and of animals, without celebrating war. The Dionysian reminds us of what we have put away in the name of peace. Here we encounter the Dionysian in its enigmatic splendor. For in the name of security we have built an optimistic rational structure that glorifies war and oppresses women and strangers, and more.

The privilege we grant to truth: Could that be another expression of sickliness, another glorification of war, another oppression? Especially of women. Yet women wear the veil, and must be unveiled in the name of truth. Truth is a woman, mistreated as women are mistreated. The Dionysian is a figure of women in the name of a male god, indeed two male gods. The Dionysian is a memory of women, of sexual difference, between Apollo and Dionysus, the intermediary figure of truth:

Supposing truth is a woman—what then? Are there not grounds for the suspicion that all philosophers, insofar as they were dogmatists, have been very inexpert about women? That the gruesome seriousness, the clumsy obtrusiveness with which they have usually approached truth so far *[bisher]* have been awkward and very improper methods for winning a woman's heart? What is certain is that she has not allowed herself to be won. (Nietzsche, *BGE*, 192)

The *bisher* of revaluation, of the beyond, touches truth and women in the name of Dionysus. The Dionysian reminds us of where we have taken truth so far, perhaps too far in some directions, veiling and unveiling women without a thought of sexual difference or of what it takes to win a woman. As if winning and losing were all that mattered with women. Or truth.

Supposing truth is a woman. What kind of supposition is this for truth? Perhaps that we must not let objectivity blind us to the erotic dance. We treat truth as a thing, an object. What if it were more like women? What kind of supposition is this for women? That is more problematic. For perhaps we men treat women as an object, our object, where we are the subject. For, in Irigaray's words, "Any Theory of the 'Subject' has Always Been Appropriated by the 'Masculine'"; and "what if the 'object' started to speak?" (Irigaray, *ATS*, 135; Ross, *AIS*, 580). What if truth began to speak? Perhaps we humans should not treat truth, nature, knowledge, or women as if we were the subjects and they the objects to be mastered. Perhaps truth is not an object to be mastered, to be stripped bare. Perhaps the exposure of which I have spoken repeatedly is anything but the bachelors stripping the woman bare, anything but nudity, or, if nudity, is my own, our own. We who know, who seek truth, are exposed to it face to face, beyond any measure, any mastery, any objectivity. We are exposed to it, exposed to women, as if we were nude, exposing our sexual difference.

In Nietzsche's words: " 'All truth is simple.' Is that not doubly a lie?" (Nietzsche, *TI*, 467). But truth is not a complex thing, to be mastered with more effort. Truth is more like a woman, whose essence remains to be determined. By her. Truth (and lie) is not unveiling but more veiling; and not even veiling, where women alone wear the veil. In marriage, entering service to men.

Put another way, *"What* in us really wants 'truth'?"* (Nietzsche, *BGE*, 199). Something in us wants truth held against the threat of death, like women who bear our children. I say this in the name of another truth, still something we really want.

We really want truth, beyond anything truth can offer. And why? Could truth be life's movement against life? "[O]ne should ask oneself carefully: 'Why don't you want to deceive?' especially if it should appear—and it cer-

tainly does appear—that life depends on appearance; I mean, on error, simulation, deception, self-deception" (Nietzsche, *GS*, 449). That appearance is
another appearance of life, another deception.

The Dionysian is the free circulation of nature's gifts, given in the name
of a god. I have called it general economy. I ask if it could be called "capitalism" under another understanding, after revaluation. But that is the task of
another chapter.

The Dionysian is challenge to the optimism of rationality, resistance to
reason's authority, perhaps to every authority. Science's rationality demands
taxonomies and hierarchies, all in the name of truth, all institutions of morality. "Thus the question 'Why science?' leads back to the moral problem, 'For
what end any morality at all' if life, nature, and history are 'not moral'?"
(Nietzsche, *GS*, 450). The moral problem is the problem of life. Or rather, the
Dionysian asks us to reexamine every identity and every distinction from the
standpoint of what within us demands that identity, the truth of that identity.
This Dionysian demand is what I understand as the good.

The ultimate purpose of the universe, in Kant and Hegel, is human freedom. The name of that freedom is culture. Human culture is the highest realization of the universe against which everything else is measured. In the
name of the Dionysian, Nietzsche reminds us of the "degeneration, decline,
and the final stage of culture"; of "ecstasies," "visions and hallucinations
shared by entire communities or assemblies at a cult" (Nietzsche, *ASC*, 21;
Ross, *AIS*, 171). In this image of the final stage of culture, its decline, we find
another possibility of community based on visions and hallucinations. The
Dionysian is the question of community freed from the degeneration of rational politics, the decline of cultural ecstasy. There is no ultimate purpose of
the universe, a degenerate idea of culture. There is the possibility of ecstasy,
and it gives rise to community. Here community is the limit of culture, what
brings every idea of Culture down to culture.

The ultimate purpose of the universe is an idea of history. The ultimate
purpose of the universe is an idea of the end and beginning of history. The repeated idea of end—of art, of science, of philosophy, of Christian morality, of
modernity—is replaced by a memory against any possibility of absolute fulfillment or final end. The Dionysian is the end of the end as purpose. The eternal return is the end of the end in repetition. Can we face the most terrible
questions with laughter? Which are the most terrible questions? And for
whom?

I return to the five questions with which I began:

What is Dionysian?
What is good, at the end of morality?

Do the idols still march?
Why laugh, surrounded by disasters?
Why music?

The answer to the question, What is Dionysian? is: the most extreme questions, and more. The answer to the question, What is good, at the end of morality? is: it remains. The answer to the question, Do the idols still march? is:
always. Always another self-deception. The answer to the question, Why
laugh, surrounded by disasters? is: we know the weaknesses of crying. We have
given in to the deceptions and lies of truth. In the name of truth, let us swear
to lies and deceptions. In the name of truth we laugh: another lie. A double,
triple, and more lie. But still, to laugh at heterogeneity, at horror, at our monstrous cravings, is not to foster hatred, perhaps, but to come face to face with
the other, alterity and heterogeneity, without recoiling in the name of truth
and morality. We laugh to let the other be an other, another lie. We laugh in
and at our own heterogeneity. We laugh at nothing, at nothing to laugh at.

　　Finally, now, we come to music, perhaps again to laugh. Why music?
Surely not because music is better than the other arts. The overman is not
better than man; humans are not better than animals; men are not better
than women; *poiēsis* is not better than *technē*; Dionysus is not better than
Apollo, laughter is not better than crying, nor worse. We do not choose between Dionysus and Apollo; each is a god. But we move between them, intermediary movements. The overman is man over, human—otherwise,
touched by a difference that resists the better and higher as dominations and
destructions. As weakness in the name of strength.

　　All betters belong to *technē*, belong to art and music under the sign of
Apollo. Unlikeness becomes better and worse. On this account, in Plato, music is known as order, by parts and wholes, under *technē*, forgetting music's
ecstasy. Music is Dionysian as overwhelming, as passion, charm, and feeling,
put away in the name of order. Yet this overwhelming is not better than music's form, because without that form, without *technē*, music could not be
music, could not be anything. The ecstasy of music is an infection, and we are
all diseased. Tolstoy almost says so, though he hesitates. "If a man is infected
by the author's condition of soul, if he feels this emotion and this union with
others, then the object which has effected this is art" (Tolstoy, *WA*; Ross, *AIS*,
179); "*The stronger the infection the better is the art*, as art" (Tolstoy, *WA*;
Ross, *AIS*, 179). He hesitates at the enormity of this Nietzschean revelation,
bounding the infection with criteria: individuality, clarity, and sincerity (Tolstoy, *WA*; Ross, *AIS*, 180). The infection must be cured, or if not cured, held
in bounds.

　　And what if the infection of music were incurable, unboundable? What
if that were the Dionysian in music, and art, and truth, and science, and life,

and nature, and more? Nature, with the rest, is immeasurable, general economy. As art. In music. Dionysian. Immeasurable, overwhelming, carrying us away in ecstasy, frenzy, madness. And more. All in work.

Why music? Surely not because music is different from the other arts, different by an abyss of essence. The overman is not different from man, but man again, touched by something different, otherwise, man as intermediary figure. The overman allows humanity to move intermediarily. The contemporary name of that allowance is woman. At least, that is what Irigaray says. And she is Nietzsche's marine lover *(amante marine)*. Another interruption.

Irigaray's marine lover—perhaps a mermaid, but no seductress—interrupts the march of the overman—perhaps another idol—with love:

> How I should love you if to speak to you were possible?
> And yet I still love you too well in my silence to remember the movement of my own becoming. Perpetually am I troubled, stirred, frozen, or smothered by the noise of your death. (Irigaray, *ML*, 3)

How should a woman love Nietzsche? How should she, or we, love others by whom we are betrayed? "I am coming back from far, far away. And say to you: your horizon has limits. Holes even" (Irigaray, *ML*, 4).

Woman—perhaps not women; certainly not *the feminine*, "engendered by the father alone" (Irigaray, *ML*, 94); "the father's indispensable intermediary in putting his law into force" (Irigaray, *ML*, 95)—she is not one, not closed, not binary, but incalculable, excessive:

> She does not set herself up as *one*, as a (single) female unit. She is not closed up or around one single truth or essence. The essence of a truth remains foreign to her. She neither has nor is a being. And she does not oppose a feminine truth to the masculine truth. Because this would once again amount to playing the—man's—game of castration. If the female sex takes place by embracing itself, by endlessly sharing and exchanging its lips, its edges, its borders, and their "content," as it ceaselessly becomes other, no stability of essence is proper to her. She has a place in the openness of a relation to the other whom she does not take into herself, like a whore, but to whom she continuously gives birth. (Irigaray, *ML*, 86)

Who is "she," we may ask, "who" neither has nor is a being? That would be enough to deny any binary essence of feminine versus masculine, woman versus man. The openness of woman opens binary opposition to the other, gives birth continuously to alterity and heterogeneity. It is an openness of endless questions, openings, disclosures, all resisting closure. In this passage, questions arise of setting up, institutionalizing, building; of openings and closures; of foreigners as aliens and as others, even ourselves; of castration as the wound of identity and of ceaselessly becoming other; of sharing and exchanging with others and ourselves; of birth and death; of nature, generation, and regeneration; and so on and on. All opened in Nietzsche, within an extreme forgetfulness, of women.

"Women" touch themselves; "men" touch others, need instruments to touch themselves, instruments of mastery. "Men" know their desire as mastery. "Women" do not, know their desire by embracing themselves, their lips touching. This figure of auto-embrace and self-touching emerges from female biology and women's *jouissance*. To which I respond with several thoughts from Lacan: that the woman "whom I suppose to know, I love" (Lacan, *GJW*, 139); but I suppose that "she" knows what I do not, will never, know, her *jouissance*, "A jouissance beyond the phallus" (Lacan, *GJW*, 145), "of which she herself may know nothing, except that she experiences it" (Lacan, *GJW*, 145). Within the other, beyond the "thought" or "idea" or "sign" of the other, I suppose a knowledge, a desire, that I do not and perhaps cannot know. And perhaps "she" does not and cannot know it either. Or perhaps she can. And I. The "perhaps" remains open.

It opens around intermediary figures of love and desire, permeating the body, figures of bodies embracing, touching, lost figures of belonging to the world of desire, reemerging in the figure of woman, whose body embraces, touches itself, at the seat of her desire. We suppose in loving the other that "she" knows and desires something unknown to us, touches something we do not touch, touches something within herself. Perhaps.

Something unknown, forgotten in Western thought and life after the Greeks, and perhaps before, reemerges in Nietzsche as the Dionysian. Endless figures of Western authority circle around the Dionysian. Something unknown, forgotten in Nietzsche, reemerges from his marine lover as Woman. Endless figures of Western authority circle around the woman, disturbing, dis-placing, and re-placing the Dionysian. Endless.

I note a few such intermediary movements, all touching bodies, bodies touching with love, erotically. Irigaray speaks of bodies, "different bodies" (Irigaray, *ML*, 5), and "membranes" (Irigaray, *ML*, 7, 21); of "the boundaries of your body" (Irigaray, *ML*, 21); of "forgetting the body where it ['my birth'] takes place" (Irigaray, *ML*, 31); of man, or the overman, becoming lava, roaming and destroying the earth: "never will you give birth to a solid body" (Irigaray, *ML*, 55). She speaks of bodies as "veiled," sites of "dissimulation" (Irigaray, *ML*, 78) and castration (Irigaray, *ML*, 80), the perhaps supreme mark of simulation and bodily destruction: "A repetition, then, with signs. . . . Fulfilling the master's desire" (Irigaray, *ML*, 81). Most of all, perhaps, the idea of the body as submission to the idea, the coming of Christ "as a redemptory submission of the flesh to the Word? Or else: as the Word's faithfulness to the flesh?" (Irigaray, *ML*, 169), tyranny of the Word, the sign, the signifier, over the body, overcoming women's bodies.

This figure of the word that imposes God the Father's authority over human and other bodies, over the world, the word upon the world, echoes another birth, of touching, caressing, embracing, not the other as repetition of mastery, but of first touching oneself and then the other, with love. "Surely the lightest, liveliest caress means more than thick layers of hoarded possessions" (Irigaray, *ML*, 7), watered by the sea that enfolds and moves and touches, that cannot forget its bodily embrace as can the air.[12]

Man, Nietzsche, lives on the heights. Zarathustra descends from the mountains to the land below. Not to the sea. "But you never say: the superman has lived in the sea. That is how he survives" (Irigaray, *ML*, 13). "It is always hot, dry, and hard in your world" (Irigaray, *ML*, 13). Hard and hot and contoured, with edges that divide and rule. In the sea are fluidity and rapture (Irigaray, *ML*, 13): "In me everything is already flowing, and you flow along too if you only stop minding such unaccustomed motion, and its song. Learn to swim, as once you danced on dry land" (Irigaray, *ML*, 37). Learn to swim, and sing. "These fluids softly mark the time. And there is no need to knock, just listen to hear the music. With very small ears" (Irigaray, *ML*, 37). Sing the song, listen to the music. You do not need a hammer except on dry land. And what good is a hammer in the sea? That other hammer, heard on the piano, echoes the song of music. Why music? Another delay.

We are still in the sea, getting wet, touched by waves, touched and touching. We are still in the figure of woman as marine lover. "And when, in her abundance, she is not giving waters—those supple, living envelopes for specular alchemy—she gives forth airs. And, according to the weather, she can become ice or restless waves" (Irigaray, *ML*, 46). Reminding us of waves at the birth of philosophy in Plato, the birth that traditionally silenced women.[13] "The sea is too deep" (Irigaray, *ML*, 47) for man, for men, "shines with myriad eyes" (Irigaray, *ML*, 47). Even so, the child-god, Dionysus, "still lives in the wet" (Irigaray, *ML*, 135). A bit later, "the women from the sea will soon be immortal flowers" (Irigaray, *ML*, 142): Apollo is born.

With this thought we return to Nietzsche from the depths of the sea, with his lover. For the woman-lover from the sea loves Nietzsche because the possibility of love of the one for the other shows itself in Nietzsche beyond any other. Yet without love as sexual difference. Perhaps:

> Nietzsche—perhaps—has experienced and shown what is the result of infinite distance reabsorbed into the (male) same, shown the difference that remains without a face or countenance. By wishing to overcome everything, he plunges into the shadows—lit up and with no perspective. As he becomes the whole of the world's time, he has no point of view left that would allow

> him to see. Ariadne, or Diotima, or . . . no longer even return his mask or
> his gaze. . . . he preferred the Idea to an ever provisional openness to a
> female other. . . .
>   And what would Ariadne's or Diotima's or anyone else's "yes" have
> changed? Nothing in his thinking. (Irigaray, *ML*, 188)

"A love that knows no other" (Irigaray, *ML*, 189). A love that knows no other
that can say yes. All yeses are mine, says Zarathustra. Irigaray reads Nietzsche's beyond as the same, bearing no touch of the other.

Returning to our remaining question, repeating Nietzsche: why music?
And with it art, and song. For Irigaray speaks of music with the other. "Such
is the failure of the man who does not make his own boundary out of the skin
of the other. He is turned back to the other side of his limit. A catastrophe
that would have no place to be if he obeyed the music of that female other. If
he let her carry him along without forcing her to follow his rhythm alone"
(Irigaray, *ML*, 36). The other calls to us with skin and touch and flesh and music. All wet. All fluid. "These fluids softly mark the time. And there is no need
to knock, just listen to hear the music. With very small ears" (Irigaray, *ML*,
37). Perhaps music allows us to mark the time without contours, fluidly,
softly, with small ears, without a hammer. Perhaps Nietzsche carries too
heavy, too harsh, a hammer. Knocks too loudly.

Reminding us of the cicadas and their song,[14] Irigaray explains how the
hammer hurts the ear. "For I have learned at least this much from your wisdom: when the other does not hear you, it is better to be silent. By doing violence to the ear, one loses the music" (Irigaray, *ML*, 39), returning us to lips
that touch the music. "The sound of lips pressed together being sweeter harmony for you than all the fine speeches that merely sicken the appetite. And
when she sings endlessly, filling the air with plenteous profusion without ever
speaking or breaking, could this be your nostalgia?" (Irigaray, *ML*, 39). Music disperses philosophical speeches that sicken us to death.

Perhaps into a harmony. And flesh. Music and flesh meet in Dionysian
marriage:

> In order to make marriage, there must be a harmonious passage from
> external to internal, from the interior to the exterior of bodies. One arrives
> at the other without violently breaking down barriers, without jumping over
> the river, without being carried brutally into the abyss below or on high. Let
> the two be here and there at the same time, which is not to say that they are
> indistinguishable. (Irigaray, *ML*, 116–17)

Music, bodies, between, inside, outside, without violence. Music is a figure of
the otherwise without violence, as is sexual difference but has not been allowed to be. Or art, or beauty. All intermediary figures. For "the ultimate

beauties in a work" (Nietzsche, *GS*, 339; quoted in Irigaray, *ML*, 92) require an unveiling of gold, "sparkling with promise, resistance, bashfulness, mockery, pity, and seduction. Yes, life is a woman!" (Irigaray, *ML*, 92–93). Reminding us of Persephone who like Teiresias lived in both worlds, an intermediary figure, we are led back to art. For as woman, "enslaved to a mirage technique that separates her from herself. . . . Which makes her— perhaps?—still absent from it. Makes her not have a place there" (Irigaray, *ML*, 114).

Imagistic arts imagine woman in her place, and deny her a place of her own. Music is something else.

"Stop, dead stop, without end" (Irigaray, *ML*, 119).

Stop. Begin. Again.

CHAPTER 6

Origin

What is the origin of the work of art? Why origin? "Origin here means that from and by which something is what it is and as it is. What something is, as it is, we call its essence or nature. The origin of something is the source of its nature" (Heidegger, *OWA*, 17; Ross, *AIS*, 254). With these doubly questionable words, Heidegger famously opens his most famous essay on art. Doubly questionable and more. Because the origin is a source of questions, and because we cannot read Heidegger without questions of our own. Still, why origin? Why seek the *from* and *by*? Why ask after what something is, as it is, its essence or nature? Why pursue the essence? And finally, by no means irrelevant, What of fame: the philosopher's or artist's? What is the role of fame in relation to the origin?

I have pursued the thought that origin and end are linked, that questions of the end of art, or philosophy, or science, questions of the endless advance of spirit, are intimately linked with questions of origin, of the beginning, and of essence. I now suggest that origin and end are linked with greatness, at least in the West—in Kant, for example. For he proclaims the end of art, the boundary beyond which it cannot go, speaking of artistic genius on the one hand, which nevertheless reaches its end, its culmination, and of the greatest discoverer, who participates in the ever-advancing perfection of science. Questions of origin and end concern greatness. The origin of the work of art is the founding of great art. The work of art in question is great, and so is the artist who might be its origin.

Heidegger says this explicitly: "It is precisely in great art—and only such art is under consideration here—that the artist remains inconsequential as compared with the work, almost like a passageway that destroys itself in the creative process for the work to emerge" (Heidegger, *OWA*, 40; Ross, *AIS*, 262). In great art the great artist remains inconsequential. That is why Heidegger chooses a painting by Van Gogh, why Derrida speaks of the "famous picture" (in quotation marks) (Derrida, *R*, 262; Ross, *AIS*, 422) and, in Schapiro's words, of "the famous thinker, author of *The Origin of the Work of Art*" (Derrida, *R*, 276; Ross, *AIS*, 422). The famous Derrida, writing on the two famous writers, Meyer Schapiro and Martin Heidegger. More on this famous coupling later.

I understand this foregrounding of greatness in art as unfolding within gifts from the good, raising several questions bearing upon Heidegger's opening words. I understand that art strives for the good, but perhaps not good over bad, greatness over mediocrity. Fame contaminates the circulation of the good, stocks up reputation against the movement of time, resists the interruption of being. Fame and greatness repeat the hold of *technē*'s binary distinctions over the gifts of the good, where that giving touches every place and every thing. Fame and greatness do *technē*'s work, reminding us of another good, associated with *poiēsis* or madness or the gods, interrupting hierarchies and superiorities.

Heidegger speaks of the essence or nature of a thing, and of the origin of what it is. He does not speak of the good. But he speaks of letting things be *(sein lassen)*: "What seems easier than to let a being be just the being that it is? Or does this turn out to be the most difficult of tasks . . . ?" (Heidegger, *OWA*, 31). Why, I ask, might we do so? Why should we do so? Except that things call upon us and each other to let them be, a call I understand as given from the good. I understand, after Levinas, being as a gift, echoing the good, but where that gift interrupts the assembling of being under categories and essences, by nature. Nature's giving interrupts the categories whereby we order things into taxonomies and hierarchies.

We might wish to say that the origin of the work of art is not the artist, or art, or being, but the good. Yet the good is no origin or end. Rather, it interrupts every origin and end, every essence and form, unends every end. And that is what Heidegger says of truth: "Truth, in its nature, is un-truth" (Heidegger, *OWA*, 54; Ross, *AIS*, 271). On my reading, this "un" is given from the good. Truth cannot give untruth to us except within a hierarchical opposition. The reason is that in its nature, truth reserves the circulation of goods. In its nature, truth is a reservation, along with untruth. But truth and untruth circulate together in art, as art, gifts from the good, circulate as beauty and, I would say, halting that circulation as fame and greatness. Fame and greatness halt the circulation of gifts, including the gift of beauty, the good as art. The ideas of origin and essence, like fame and greatness, may express a contaminated idea of nature and good, may constitute a betrayal of the call of the good.

But I am so far ahead of myself that I must halt my own circulation of ideas to return to the beginning. I do so against the flow of ideas and gifts, halting their anarchic movement, channeling my thoughts so that you will travel with me in an orderly fashion.

Origin and end are linked, as we have seen: beginnings and endings. Heidegger begins his essay with questions of origin. But he ends it recalling Hegel's understanding of the end of art, an understanding we have seen in Kant, repeating a beginning perhaps in Plato, with the supplement, perhaps also in Plato, that the end of art was marked but never began. Rather, what began was philosophy circulating together with art in an intermediary movement. And perhaps we are continuing this movement, this unlikeness into that of beginning and end, another unlikeness that cannot be broken apart. The end of art is linked in Kant with the endless advance of science, whose recognition is the beginning of a certain kind of philosophy, critical philosophy. Philosophy begins in a certain place, in a certain way, with the death of art, and with the endless advance of science, possibly with science become philosophy. Or the reverse.

Heidegger ends his essay, writes an Epilogue to his essay on origins, an epilogue which is still not the end, for it is followed by an Addendum, as if every end might give rise to another addendum, with the question of the end of art. He lists three statements from Hegel's *Lectures on the Philosophy of Fine Art*, haunting and terrifying statements, summarizing them by the single question: "[I]s art still an essential and necessary way in which that truth happens which is decisive for our historical existence, or is art no longer of this character?" (Heidegger, *OWA*, 80). The essential and necessary repeat origin and essence, repeat the possibility that art has a nature, and within that nature bears the burden of coming to an end, at least in relation to the happening of truth, another essence and origination, within our historical existence, perhaps an expression of the Essence of The Human. All these essences may be Essences, of Art, or Truth, or History, or Humanity, however divided any of them may be. All appear not to question the idea of the essential and necessary, even within the historical, returning us to threats of destiny.

Heidegger comments on this question that "[t]he truth of Hegel's judgment has not yet been decided" (Heidegger, *OWA*, 80), suggesting two things: one that we have not yet understood this truth about the end of art, the other that we may decide this truth within our historical existence. Perhaps I am overreading. Perhaps Heidegger leaves open the possibility that the truth of Hegel's judgment may never be decided, along with the truths of essences and natures, and origins. These have not been and may never be decided, not because we seek a decision and have not yet found one, but because the thought of decision overwhelms the truth in question. Perhaps the intermediary question of Hegel's judgment of the end of art touches intermediary questions of beginnings and origins and natures, so that the emergence of truth and being must leave that question open. In the *diaphora* between *poiēsis* and *technē*, now between a truth of disclosure and a truth of essence, decision belongs to one member of the pair and not the other. It does not belong to *poiēsis* or disclosure. In the same way, we cannot decide to let things be because that or any decision is antagonistic to letting. We touch the limits of decision at this point in the name of truth and art. We touch the good.

What is the origin of the work of art? "The artist is the origin of the work. The work is the origin of the artist. Neither is without the other. . . . [A]rtist and work *are* each of them by virtue of a third thing which is prior to both, namely that which also gives artist and work of art their names—art" (Heidegger, *OWA*, 17; Ross, *AIS*, 254). Within this movement of artist and work, where none is prior, we find priority. Yet from the beginning we have seen that the claim of priority in relation to art—the *diaphora* between poetry and philosophy—belongs to philosophy and not art. Does art know or care about the nature or essence of art or work or artist? Does art care about its name, the name given to it by others?

This question of priority reaches toward origin within a hierarchy of primordiality. Within the distinctions of contemporary life between art and science, artists and philosophers, artworks and laboratory experiments, we may find another, deeper distinction, before all the others, leading back to being and truth in the name of art. Or could it be that the very idea of another distinction, in the name of depth, before or higher than or more truthful or better than the others, repeats the play of distinctions, disciplinary and taxonomic distinctions with which we began? Art is not prior to artist and work, nor equal to or equiprimordial with them. Art belongs to them together and they to it, a relation named by a word Heidegger uses frequently: *Zusammengehörigkeit*. I take it to speak of intermediary movements. I understand it as the touch given from the good. I take it to interrupt the gathering of being.

We can see this touch at work in Heidegger as letting-be, though perhaps the idea and possibility of interruption touches something unknown to being. Perhaps. We are to let things be; while historically we have done everything but. The traditional idea of a thing is not a letting-be but a naming that holds and checks. Art originates (or works) in this space of letting-be, where things historically have been counted and contained.

Art allows the work of art to be a work (Heidegger, *OWA*, 18; Ross, *AIS*, 255). But a work is a thing, at least presents itself as a thing, has a "thingly character." We pause in our pursuit of the work of art to explore this thingly character. We pause to take up the being of things before the being of works. What is a thing? "The work of art is also a thing" (Heidegger, *OWA*, 21) in the sense that "all beings that in any way are, are called things" (Heidegger, *OWA*, 21). But "we hesitate to call God a thing. In the same way. . . . A man is not a thing" (Heidegger, *OWA*, 21). "Only a stone, a clod of earth, a piece of wood are for us such mere things. Lifeless beings of nature and objects of use"

Origin 199

(Heidegger, *OWA*, 21). God, human beings, and works of art are not *mere* things, where everything at stake turns on the *mere.*

Heidegger questions whether these all are things, all beings together, to be let be together, each and every one of them and all of them together, anything that in any way is, all things that in any way are, only to retreat to mere things, never to return, retreating from the everywhere and everything to mere things on the one hand, on the left perhaps, and works of art, God, and human beings on the other hand, perhaps on the right. "We thus see ourselves brought back from the widest domain, within which everything is a thing . . . including even the highest and last things, to the narrow precinct of mere things" (Heidegger, *OWA*, 21). The narrow precinct of mere things, of the *mere,* reflects the highest and last, in another exclusion, "an almost pejorative sense" (Heidegger, *OWA*, 22).

He does not consider the possibility that the highest and last is things themselves, that returning to things themselves might be the primordial return beyond all other returns, the most difficult of tasks. He does not examine to its depths the possibility that the very idea that God, humanity, and works of art are higher than things themselves, things in their thingness, appropriates them to our use. He does not consider that the highest is the thing, and that God, humanity, and art diminish the good in things, restricting their range of possibility, delimiting their abundance. I do not say that they do so. I say that it is not a thought to be ignored.

A work of art is not a mere thing. In "the almost palpable reality of works . . . something else inheres" (Heidegger, *OWA*, 22); "the art work is something else over and above the thingly element" (Heidegger, *OWA*, 20). Why "over and above"? Why not under and below, beside, if not within, intermediarily? Why not thing and work and god and humanity together and otherwise, none above or over the others? But then, "a thing is not merely an aggregate of traits" (Heidegger, *OWA*, 22). This entire discussion of things turns repeatedly on merely and only. Every exclusion is marked by only, or merely, or but: this but not that. And every only and merely becomes a higher and lower. It is within this ethics that I have spoken of the good, a good that interrupts binary exclusions, that resists high and low, only, merely, and but. The good includes all things everywhere. The good touches all things everywhere with gifts given from the good. I think that Heidegger touches this good as *sein lassen,* touches it and recoils, for it is We who Let Be, not things that touch each other and let each other be. Mere things are not high enough.

What is a thing? Heidegger offers three traditional answers: (1) "that around which . . . properties have assembled" (Heidegger, *OWA*, 22–23). We call that substance with its properties. (2) "[N]othing but the unity of a manifold of what is given in the senses" (Heidegger, *OWA*, 25).

(3) "Matter and form" (Heidegger, *OWA*, 27). The first allows him to speak of the "appropriation of Greek words by Roman-Latin thought" (Heidegger, *OWA*, 23), where "*hupokeimenon* becomes *subiectum*; *hupostasis* becomes *substantia*; *sumbebekos* becomes *accidens*" (Heidegger, *OWA*, 23). This becoming, this translation, is a betrayal. "Beneath the seeming literal and thus faithful translation there is concealed, rather, a *trans*lation of Greek experience into a different way of thinking. *Roman thought takes over the Greek words without a corresponding, equally authentic experience of what they say, without the Greek word*" (Heidegger, *OWA*, 23). Translation in French, *traduire*, is transgression, violation. In German, *Übersetzung* is a crossing, another violation. In his writing of rifts and thresholds, Heidegger ignores the possibility that translation is a threshold activity, an intermediary movement, in that way close to the good. But this is because between Greek and Latin something greater is at stake. "I am speaking of the special relationship, inside the German language, with the language of the Greeks and their thought. It is something which the French are always confirming for me today. When they begin to think they speak German: they say definitely that they would not manage it in their language" (quoted in Derrida, *OS*, 69; from Sheehan, *HMT*, 62).

The highest spirit of the Germans. We remember Nietzsche. "Germans—once they were called the people of thinkers: do they think at all today? The Germans are now bored with the spirit, the Germans now mistrust the spirit; politics swallows up all serious concern for really spiritual matters. *Deutschland, Deutschland über alles*—I fear that was the end of German philosophy" (Nietzsche, *TI*, 506). Still the language of the "really spiritual," the realm of art. Could we approach the gift of art more closely when we give up the spirit? I do not mean to become bored with it while it continues to haunt us, but to fear and resist it.

Between Greek and Latin the spiritual height of the German language is at stake. And in the twentieth century, the century of National Socialism and concentration camps, when the German language was contaminated so deeply, perhaps, that nothing could save it. Nietzsche spoke of this contamination seventy years before, still however reaching for the height.

I have spoken repeatedly of this height at which humanity makes itself god, at least mirror of god, looks down on the world from a height, named *Geschlecht: unser Geschlecht*, always ours, we humans, Germans.[1] It is the height from which Kant and Hegel speak of the end of art, the height from which human freedom and spirituality define the ultimate purpose of the world, the endless advance of spirit, the end of everything less spiritual, less human. The word *Geschlecht*, in German, touches race, stock, nation, and gender, all contaminated terms of opposition and domination whereby we and our *Geschlecht* are better, purer, higher than the others, including Christians over Jews, whites over coloreds, Europeans over Africans, Germans over French (at least, one language over the other), men over women, heterosexuals over homosexuals, God's chosen over the others, civilization over barbarians, in the end every We over They.

We come to the first interruption in this chapter, recalling the circulation of Jews, whose movement was instituted under coercion in Heidegger's time, leading to their murder, in the extreme, never recalled by him as evil. In Lyotard's words, addressing "jews" rather than Jews, perhaps another disturbing displacement of ethical responsibility, yet without doubt related to justice:

> how could this thought (Heidegger's), a thought so devoted to remembering that a forgetting (of Being) takes place in all thought, in all art, in all "representation" of the world, how could it possibly have ignored the thought of "the jews," which, in a certain sense, thinks, tries to think, nothing but that very fact? How could this thought forget and ignore "the jews" to the point of suppressing and foreclosing to the very end the horrifying (and inane) attempt at exterminating, at making us forget forever what, in Europe, reminds us, ever since the beginning, that "there is" the Forgotten? (Lyotard, *HJ*, 4)

He adds something of the good against the forgetting that still remains within Heidegger's thought of the forgetting of Being. "But remaining anchored in the thought of Being, the 'Western' prejudice that the Other is Being, it has nothing to say about a thought in which the Other is the Law" (Lyotard, *HJ*, 89); "Heidegger's thought reveals itself, quite despite itself, as, in its turn, the hostage of the Law. This is its real 'fault'" (Lyotard, *HJ*, 89). Heidegger's thought remains hostage to the Law (perhaps the good) in forgetting that the Other in Being is ethical|political, hostage to its own oblivion. I add the possibility that this may be something deeper and more insidious, beyond the ontological priority of Being over the good, that Western thought itself remains rooted in its own superiority.

Nothing in Heidegger frees us from this insistent superiority in the name of the highest spirit, reaching toward the hand through the gift of language. "The hand is infinitely different from all the grasping organs—paws, claws, or fangs—different by an abyss of essence. Only a being who can speak, that is, think can have hands and can handily achieve works of handicraft. . . . " (Heidegger, *WCT*, 357).[2] The origin of the work of art originates in a frame, *Gestell* or *parergon*, of superiority under the sign of *Geschlecht*, reiterating the superiority of Man within a refusal of the superiority of the subject. Heidegger does not acknowledge that the movement in which *hupokeimenon* becomes *subiectum*, the institution of the subject, is within a frame of domination, where the subject is from the first, in its inception, thrown down abjectly under authority, subjected to rule. I say "from the first" because *hupokeimenon* also means submission, including submission to a rule. From the very beginning, in Greek and later Roman thought, the subject of predication, underlying identity and order, is brought to order by subjection to authority and rule, by submission to rule.

This link between identity and authority recalls the good, not a repetition of that authority, but interrupting the submission, subjection, and subordination that defines the subject who thinks linked with the subject with qualities, the thing. From the beginning, the good calls upon us to know that the thing has been brought to law in an act of subjection, calls upon us to know this subjection and resist it. From the beginning the good calls upon us to resist every superiority.

Including the superiority of art and of humanity. For the thought of art emerges, for Heidegger, in this place of superiority, marked by the recurrence of the work of art over the mere thing, and of the thing beyond its representations. These representations are things as subjects with properties, the unity of a manifold of sense, and matter and form. All express the transposition by humans of their "propositional way of understanding things into the structure of the thing itself" (Heidegger, *OWA*, 24), something that can occur only with "the thing having already become visible" (Heidegger, *OWA*, 24).

At this juncture where the precondition of representation is a visibility, a lighting, we touch the possibility that Heidegger's ontology reads only one side of Greek thought, the visibility of ideas and forms, as coming into presence, a relation to being and truth that works at a distance. And this is so despite his reading of these ideas of things in relation to distance and proximity. "Whereas the first interpretation keeps the thing at arm's length from us, as it were, and sets it too far off, the second makes it press too hard upon us" (Heidegger, *OWA*, 26). It presses upon us too hard in our manifold of sense, still, perhaps, within the paradigm of sight, or sound, but not of touch. For sight and sound, perhaps unlike taste and smell and touch, present us with fragmentary and episodic data to be assembled into a manifold. The assembling of being works in the light and echoes of sight and sound. The "lower" senses are diffuse, pervasive, like emotion, already infused and dispersed, ecstatic, closer to the good. This thought requires extended consideration.[3]

I mean that we see being and truth at a distance, as if representation maintains remoteness, in the guise of vision and light, rather than in the proximity of touch and the exposure of skin. More intensely, visibility and light keep the good at a distance, against the possibility that we are touched by and exposed to the good as a gift. The giving of the good is an exposure so close as to call for endless response. We respond to things from our exposure.

In this sense, we do not let things be, passively; nor do we throw them under our humanity or throw ourselves under authority. We respond to things from within an immeasurable exposure, an immeasurable responsiveness and sensitivity. This relation of the one to the other is what I understand as the giving of the good.

I understand art from within this immeasurable exposure. Traditionally, Heidegger tells us, we understand art from within the ideas of matter and form. "The distinction of matter and form is *the conceptual schema which is used, in the greatest variety of ways, quite generally for all art theory and aesthetics*" (Heidegger, *OWA*, 27). I read this as giving Aristotle precedence over Plato, for whom we have seen that art bears the touch of the gods and the heavens bear the touch of beauty. And it gives precedence to only one side of Aristotle, who I have suggested may also be read as understanding art in an ethical way much closer to the good through a *mimēsis* without domination or authority.

I have passed over the "already" in "already become visible," though we might have encountered it before. Heidegger speaks against our coming to know what art is from works of art by insisting that we must "know beforehand what art is" (Heidegger, *OWA*, 18). We already know what art is, already touch the world, already see its visibility. This gesture against empiricism appears to resist its atomisms. I understand all post-Kantian rejections of empiricism as an attempt to tame the wildness of experience, understand empiricism itself as such an attempt. The view that we know only from experience, however wild its circulation, has become the idea that experience's contents are finite and repetitive. What if we added iterability to empiricism? We would face experience as an absolute wager, in its fearsome abundance, a profusion without repose or reliability. We would have to learn to trust in our mistrust.

We "mistrust this concept of the thing, which represents it as formed matter" (Heidegger, *OWA*, 27) because it assimilates the thing to usefulness. "As determinations of beings, accordingly, matter and form have their proper place in the essential nature of equipment. This name designates what is produced expressly for employment and use. Matter and form are in no case original determinations of the thingness of the mere thing" (Heidegger, *OWA*, 28). I pass over the reiteration of the *mere* thing, as if usefulness rose above and beyond the thing rather than its diminution.[4] But I cannot neglect it, for Heidegger returns to it explicitly. "We speak of things in the strict sense as mere things. The 'mere,' after all, means the removal of the character of usefulness and of being made. The mere thing is a sort of equipment, albeit equipment denuded of its equipmental being. Thing-being consists in what is then left over" (Heidegger, *OWA*, 30). Things *strictly speaking* are less than equipment, something left over to which equipmentality is added, rather like the way in which form is added to matter to make a thing. Again, if matter can take on any form, beyond limits, then forming it situates it, places it within limits, reduces its infinity to finiteness. And usefulness and even art, added to the infinite and immeasurable possibilities of things, frames them within the limits of human experience. We might call this a disaster. For the thing, I mean, for others, subjected to our appropriation.

Yet within Heidegger's understanding of things as appropriated within a matter-form structure, perhaps unlike the others—substance with qualities and the unity of the manifold—lies one of his most important insights. The idea of the thing in Aristotle and in all Western post-Aristotelian thought assimilates the thought of being to the thought of use, to *technē*. The idea of formed matter belongs to *technē*, to the bringing of form to matter as if from without, while nature moves from within. Within the idea of *technē*—that is, of art—we find nature brought under human subjection. And we must consider the possibility that our account of art, within the *diaphora* of *poiēsis* and *technē*, replays the appropriation of the thing—that is, of nature and natural things—to human usefulness, to reliability. And this despite the opening onto *poiēsis*. Here man the subject rules over nature with his demand for objects ready to hand. Here, I have suggested, man subjects himself to the imposition of objects ready to hand, makes himself ready to hand for others, to be ruled. Even within *poiēsis*.

"What seems easier than to let a being be just be the being that it is? Or does this turn out to be the most difficult of tasks . . . ?" (Heidegger, *OWA*, 31). This difficulty may emerge from the idea with which it is contrasted, that of letting-be, an idea that touches the heart, except that it seems to suppose the possibility of a letting-go, a remoteness akin to the paradigms of sight and sound, whereas if we touch things, if we are entangled everywhere with things in and through our skin, no possibility remains of disentanglement, of untouching. We touch and cannot leave things untouched. But we can touch them without using them. We can touch them in our movements from within ourselves toward them and in return. We can touch them and they touch us in a circulation that does not halt the movement, our movement and their movement, any movement, stocking up reserves for future use. To let things be as if we do not touch them is not difficult, but impossible. To give ourselves to the circulation as if we stored up nothing against future use is also impossible, for we could not let ourselves be without reliability and use. To enter the circulation to which we hope to give ourselves and other things in wild and excessive movement is impossible but also more than possible: it is true and real. Things circulate as gifts in wild and excessive movement, gifts from the good, circulating from one restricted economy to another, calculated use, outstripping every use. Things ready to hand are not all that reliable.

Here we enter a dark and dismal place, a familiar place trodden down by shoes, familiar shoes—"a common sort of equipment" (Heidegger, *OWA*, 32; Ross, *AIS*, 256)—in a "well-known painting by Van Gogh" (Heidegger, *OWA*, 33; Ross, *AIS*, 257), a doubly familiar pair of shoes belonging to a peasant woman. The shoes are equipment, and "[t]he equipmental quality of the equipment consists indeed in its usefulness. But this usefulness itself rests in the abundance of an essential being of the equipment. We call it reliability" (Heidegger, *OWA*, 34; Ross, *AIS*, 257). I hope to speak of abundance in relation to reliability in a more challenging and demanding way. But for a moment let us remain within Heidegger's frame. Equipmentality is reliability. It was discovered "only by bringing ourselves before Van Gogh's painting. . . . The art work let us know what shoes are in truth" (Heidegger, *OWA*, 35; Ross, *AIS*, 259). It shows that "[t]his equipment belongs to the *earth*, and it is protected in the *world* of the peasant woman" (Heidegger, *OWA*, 34; Ross, *AIS*, 258).

We are on the cusp, crossing the threshold, entering the rift between world and earth. The work of art inhabits these divided and mobile regions, dividing and joining like and unlike regions, diaphoric places. The word in which I wish to dwell for just a moment, before undertaking a departure, an interruption or journey away from where we are, is that of *abundance (Fülle)*. The repose of equipment consists in its reliability, its usefulness, an overflowing abundance of usefulness. "The repose of equipment resting within itself consists in its reliability" (Heidegger, *OWA*, 35; Ross, *AIS*, 258). How are we to think of this abundance and repose? As *Reichtum*, affluence? As *reichlich vorhanden*, ample, copious things? As *Fülle*, profusion, solidity, fullness, but also (with *Hülle*) shelter? Or as *Überfluss*, overflowing, surplus, excess? Abundance and repose link diaphorically in reliability and elsewhere, indeed as *Fülle*, but also as excess, between general and restricted economy.

Does reliability rest in its place? Instruments break, give false readings; bridges collapse. We may demand reliability of our equipment, may even expect reliability, but we do not get repose. To the contrary, perhaps. We hope for an orderly world but find it disrupted from within and without, find that our instruments break down unreliably, and find new uses for old tools. The abundance within equipment and thing—the abundance within the thing of the reliability it needs to be equipment—is anything but repose, everything but repose, resting quietly without disruption in its place. Rather, in every place rest (in English; *reste* in French) reminds us of supplements, remains, death, and displacement, of movement and mobility. I speak of general economy and of the hope within a restricted economy that it will remain stable, where it is, under its restrictions. But every restricted economy belongs to general economy, in an abundance of things everywhere, in nature and among human places and tools, that cannot be contained. The containment of reliability, in repose, rests in an abundance beyond containment, reliability, and repose. It rests in the rift between world and earth, in the opening of the stability of the world in the abundance of the earth. It rests in the opening of truth in this rift, an opening that is a concealing.

The art work lets us know what shoes are in truth. What is this truth, this unconcealment? "The Greeks called this unconcealedness of beings *alētheia*" (Heidegger, *OWA*, 36; Ross, *AIS*, 259), an abundance beyond any measure or containment, an abundance of reliability. Truth, unconcealedness, rests in nature's abundance, an abundance in things. *In things*, giving rise to equipment. Abundance in things may go beyond equipment and art, an abundance beyond measure from which the abundance in the world of instruments and works of art springs. The origin of the work of art is the abundance of things beyond any calculation, in proximity to their truth. This is an abundance beyond any repose, an event, a happening of truth in abundance, "a happening of truth at work" (Heidegger, *OWA*, 36; Ross, *AIS*, 259), an abundance of moving, happening, circulation, giving. This happening of truth reminds us of the eventfulness of the event, the mobility of things as their abundance.

Truth sets itself into work in its abundance. Why in work? Why not let abundance be without work? "What truth is happening in the work" (Heidegger, *OWA*, 38; Ross, *AIS*, 260); and more, "What is truth itself, that it sometimes comes to pass as art?" (Heidegger, *OWA*, 39; Ross, *AIS*, 261). Heidegger addresses these questions later, as will I. Why, I ask here, must "the thingly feature in the work . . . be conceived by way of the work's workly nature" (Heidegger, *OWA*, 39; Ross, *AIS*, 259)? Here, as he opens a new section on "The Work and Truth" Heidegger undertakes an extraordinary departure. I say departure though perhaps others may understand it as a repetition of what we Europeans have learned to say of art, that the only art of which we speak, we Westerners, the only art worth attention, is *great*, and "only such art is under consideration here" (Heidegger, *OWA*, 40; Ross, *AIS*, 262). He cancels the possibility without examination that anything and everything called art, whatever we bring our attention to as if it were art, high and low, fine and popular, enduring or fleeting, canceling all these binary distinctions, invidious distinctions, might open the world to us, a world of abundance and unexpected happenings, open a world by disturbing the repose of things in their familiar places. Or rather, that all art, art itself, anything called art and anything called not-art, might cross a threshold delimiting what is familiar and reliable, making it strange, opening its truth, and this may have nothing to do with greatness. Popular, folk, native, indigenous arts touch us in familiar and unfamiliar ways.

Heidegger goes on immediately to speak of "the art industry," of "public and private art appreciation," of "connoisseurs and critics," "art dealers," and "art-historical study" (Heidegger, *OWA*, 40; Ross, *AIS*, 262). "[I]n all this busy activity, do we encounter the work itself?" (Heidegger, *OWA*, 40; Ross, *AIS*, 262), the great work. We might ask in return, do we encounter the work itself anywhere, especially under the label of great? Who defines the work as great but this art industry; who defines the other works as "must-buys"? If we understand that an art industry plays a crucial role in the production of the label of greatness, a Western art industry I would add, which appropriates non-Western art as it sees fit, as primitive, ungainly, and distorted; as remarkable, exotic, sometimes beautiful, depending on the market.

Works of art may open up their worlds, including the worlds of the art industry, museums, and markets, may open them to other and deeper possibilities, to abundance and truth. But they cannot do so away from that industry, not in this or any other world. They cannot do so by themselves, though Heidegger suggests they can. "The work belongs, as work, uniquely within the realm that is opened up by itself" (Heidegger, *OWA*, 41; Ross, *AIS*, 262). Nowhere in the art industry is the work itself. Nowhere in the world is anything itself. I wonder if the work itself is another domination.

At this point I interpose another interruption. I interrupt Heidegger twice, with two questions, one concerning the owner of the shoes, the other concerning the reliability of ownership. The first question comes from Schapiro, the second from Derrida, directed at Heidegger and Schapiro. And more. It all comes down, we might say, to what Heidegger understands of reliability: "The repose of equipment resting within itself consists in its reliability" (Heidegger, *OWA*, 35; Ross, *AIS*, 258). Does this repose work against the abundance in things, including things ready to hand? Does reliability work against the abundance of nature, its general circulation, not as reliability, but as a certain idea, expressed as repose? Or, if repose refers to reliability, to the equipmentality of equipment, something we hope to take for granted in things ready to hand, the security of their reliability, does this work against their abundance and, by extension, against the abundance of other things? What of abundance do we deny in insisting on the repose of things, on their stability, on the sheltering of the earth (Heidegger, *OWA*, 46; Ross, *AIS*, 266)?

This question traces several other interruptions of this repose of reliability within the shoes. Heidegger tells the truth of Van Gogh's shoes, a truth of unveiling, *alētheia*, as the equipmentality of a peasant woman's shoes. Schapiro objects that these are neither a peasant's nor a woman's shoes, but Van Gogh's shoes, who was living in the city at the time (Schapiro, *SLPO*). Schapiro and Heidegger, two famous men, maintained a "secret correspondence" as the well-known Derrida points out, over the rightful owner of Van Gogh's shoes.

These references to fame and secrecy address Heidegger's remark that only great art deserves our attention in the name of truth and his choice of a

famous painting by a famous artist, seen by Heidegger on a visit to Amsterdam in 1930, perhaps at the Vincent Van Gogh National Museum, perhaps at
the Rijkmuseum, we are told by Derrida reading Schapiro (Derrida, *R*, 276;
Ross, *AIS*, 422). This world of titans, is it ours? Is it the art industry's world?

Derrida traces so many entanglements within the secret correspondence
between Schapiro and Heidegger that I must restrict myself to one, if we are
to remain within our interrupted interruption, rather than reassembling our
discussion under Derrida's authority. He speaks of this authority in his Introduction as the question, among other questions of the truth in painting,
as "[t]ruth of truth still, with the two genitives, but this time the value of adequation has *pushed aside [écarte]* that of unveiling" (Derrida, *PP*, 5; Ross,
AIS, 405). This force of adequation, able to push and shove unveiling to the
side, echoes in English while remaining silent in French. For *écarter* suggests more an opening, an intermediary movement, between adequation and
unveiling, perhaps two models of truth. Even so, we may wonder, are there
truly *two* models of truth, two *models* of truth, two models of *truth* (three
times three questions rather than two times two within the genitives of the
truth of truth)?

Or to return to the question haunting us from the beginning in the
name of the good, must we choose in the name of truth (or the good) *between*
adequation and unveiling? Must we choose? Are they things to choose? And
in whose or in which name, that of adequation or unveiling? All choice, I have
repeatedly suggested, belongs to *technē*, to adequation. Whatever unveiling
may open onto, it does not open a choice. The good brings us to choice by an
intermediary passage from something that does not choose, does not know
choice. The good is given to ethical choice from beyond choice. We choose
within a memory of something that cannot be chosen, that knows nothing of
choosing. By analogy, adequation belongs to truth through its proximity to
unveiling, not within a choice of the one or the other. In the ethical relation
of the one to the other, there is no choice. Neither is pushed aside. In that relation. But in every other relation, one is chosen over the other.

Nor should we leave aside the truth that women wear the veil, only
women, in most Western and non-Western countries. This recognition opens
the possibility that *alētheia* names truth as a woman in virtue of this unveiling, has something to do with sexual difference at its core. The possibility is
that within the choice we may hope to refuse between adequation and unveiling, within *alētheia*, we have already made at least two choices, one Greek
(over Latin, Heidegger says, later German over French); the other within the
traditional sign of sexual difference, men over women. It is odd, perhaps, that
if truth is veiled and unveiled, and we privilege truth as our opening to
Being, that men might dominate women in the name of truth. Unless we are
reminded of Nietzsche's suggestion that philosophers—dogmatists—

approach truth as if something to be won, like a woman, linking two moments of domination: men over women, and Western reason over truth. Nietzsche adds that such a domination may not be a winning, not something bearing and receiving love.[5] Within unveiling we find domination. Within adequation and unveiling, within each and in relation to each other, perhaps, we find "the endlessly repeated play of dominations" (Foucault, *NGH*, 150). This finding is given from the good.

Derrida asks why the truth of painting, perhaps its unveiling, imposes the obligation to return something, in this case the shoes, "to their rightful owner" (Derrida, *R*, 258; Ross, *AIS*, 421). Heidegger returns the shoes to the peasant woman—and why a woman, Derrida asks? Why, I ask, if not a repetition of the sexual difference in unveiling? Schapiro returns them to Van Gogh himself, from the country to the city.

To which Derrida brings a number of questions:

1. What if the shoes were not a pair, but *two shoes*? What would that do to their return? What would that do to their usefulness and the reliability of equipment? What do we—what do they, Heidegger and Schapiro—assume in taking for granted that the shoes are a pair? (Reminding us that when Heidegger speaks of the gift of language embodied in the hand, Derrida notes that it is never two hands, never a pair of hands.) What do we—what does Heidegger—assume in taking for granted the usefulness of the shoes, a usefulness more utilitarian in a pair rather than two independent shoes? We are addressing the uselessness of the useful, the unreliability of reliability, the profusion of repose. Derrida speaks of this uselessness as follows:

> Heidegger is interested in this garment only by virtue of its *usefulness*, and in its usefulness only by virtue of walking and working . . . (Derrida, *R*, 332; Ross, *AIS*, 424)

> by not insisting on . . . uses *other than* walking, or on using what is useless, one can be immobilized before two limits that are at least virtual. First, that of not understanding how the uselessness which will soon be in question can be "useful". . . . Second, the so-called fetishization of the produced *and* the worked, of the shoes and the painting, cannot be *thematically* questioned in its already coded problematical zones. . . . The pair inhibits at least, if it does not prevent, the "fetishizing" movement; it rivets things to use, to "normal" use; . . . (Derrida, *R*, 332; Ross, *AIS*, 424-25)[6]

Usefulness is taken for granted, but it is not the truth of either painting or shoes. Perhaps nothing (or "nothing," or No-thing) is this truth, the truth of unveiling, *alētheia*. Of which Derrida also says: "The 'truth' of the useful is not useful, the 'truth' of the product is not a product. The truth of the product 'shoe' is not a shoe—" (Derrida, *R*, 346). Truth as *alētheia* is not "of" anything or anyone, is not to be returned to an owner. And this despite Heidegger's charging the shoes, as a pair, to peasantliness and womanliness.

I postpone the truth of truth for a moment, until the end of this list, to go further with uselessness. Derrida speaks of uselessness in two ways, both useful here. One is that in order to attribute the shoes, Heidegger and Schapiro must prejudge their usefulness, as a pair of shoes, to someone or in some place, and presuppose as well the usefulness of the painting in presenting the usefulness of equipment. Usefulness is presumed, prejudged, all over the place. Yet in every place is abundance, the abundance of usefulness, and this abundance is not a repetition of usefulness, but profoundly useless. Derrida speaks of the usefulness of the useful, but he calls attention to the uselessness of the useful, the abundance of its other possibilities. In the truth of usefulness lies the unboundedness of abundance, borne by uselessness.

What of the possibility that the truth of painting is a uselessness beyond all uselessness, beyond the opposition of usefulness and usefulness, utter nonuse? This is not a repetition of the autonomy of the aesthetic, away from life and experience, but testimony to an experience in art of something beyond use, beyond *technē*, intermediary. This experience of abundance, experienced as excessiveness of desire, plays out as fixing works and things repeatedly in their places at the same time that these places are displaced. The fetish is an intermediary figure of the movement of desire, filled with seduction and fascination.

2. With what surplus value do we assign these shoes to a woman, a peasant woman, a country woman, or whatever? With what surplus value, with what fascination, do we assign any representation, a painting here of shoes, to any place whatever? With what excess? Derrida speaks of the fetishization that belongs to representation, to truth itself, of the seduction, fascination, snares of the laces (more audible in French).

3. Derrida speaks in *Truth in Painting* of Kant's rejection of the "merely empirical" from art, resisting the seductions, fascinations, and charms of objects and things in the name of universal communicability and reason. What of the abundance within two "merely empirical" things, two shoes found, perhaps, on the beach, in the forest, in the street, found by a homeless man or woman, or child. How would they taste? The empirical is contained by empiricism within repetition. But if repetition were iterability, as Derrida says, original as reproductive, original and reproductive, nothing could contain its wandering. Nothing could contain desire. The empirical is contained by those who despise empiricism, perhaps for its monstrosity, its seductions, fascinations, excesses. Put another way, how can the empirical, an abundance of inclusion, so quickly become a category of exclusion?

4. What force of proof do we demand in returning the shoes to some-one, somewhere? That they are a pair of shoes? That they are not two of three shoes? Or more. That if the shoes were painted in the city all peasantliness is excluded? That if they are Van Gogh's shoes, they are not also a woman's shoes, and more?

Derrida speaks of proof in perhaps too solemn, too constabulary, a voice, one that still "smells of the police" (Derrida, *R*, 363; Ross, *AIS*, 425):

> I did not say, like Heidegger, *they are* peasant shoes, but against him: *nothing proves that they are peasant shoes* . . . ; and I did not say, like Schapiro, they are the shoes of a city dweller and even of Van Gogh, but against him: nothing proves or can prove that "they are the shoes of the artist, by that time a man of the town and city." Each time you read "they are clearly . . . ," "this is clearly . . . ," "are evidently . . . ," it does not signify that it is clear or evident, very much the contrary, but that it is necessary to deny the intrinsic obscurity of the thing, its essential crypt, and that it's neces-sary to make us believe that it is clear quite simply because the proof will al-ways be lacking. (Derrida, *R*, 364; Ross, *AIS*, 426)

With what proof does Derrida say that nothing can prove? With what clarity does he claim that the proof will always be lacking. Always. Lacking. How can such an address not hold up the movement of the future against the other stockmen?

There is more, the same again:

> Thus Schapiro is mistaken about the primary function of the pictorial reference. He also gets wrong a Heideggerian argument which should ruin in advance his own restitution of the shoes to Van Gogh: art as "putting to work of truth" is neither an "imitation," or a "description" copying the "real," nor a "reproduction," whether it represents a singular thing or a gen-eral essence. (Derrida, *R*, 312; Ross, *AIS*, 423)

Right, wrong; correct, mistaken; *Fort, Da* (Derrida, *R*, 363; Ross, *AIS*, 425). Freud returns to remind us of the disappearance within the veils, whether of women, or safety; and of the appearance of truth: the play of appearance and disappearance. With what assurance does Derrida know that Schapiro is wrong, mistaken? With what assurance does Derrida know that "putting to work of truth" in art does not return something to its owner?

5. What then is the truth of unveiling, *alētheia*, if it might be beyond return? I began this interruption with the *écarte* or *diaphora* between ade-quation and unveiling, an unlikeness that might be without opposition. But the entire correspondence between Schapiro and Heidegger imposes an

opposition, choosing between unveiling and adequation, country and city, choosing an attribution. Yet *alētheia* is not a choosing or an ascribing; nor is *poiēsis*. Heidegger's "mistake" (if we can speak this way; I would not) is to ascribe what cannot be ascribed to usefulness and to a peasant woman on the way to the earth, to Being. He returns to the world what touched the depths of Being. He restricts the abundance of the gift. Derrida asks us to consider the possibility that this restriction lies coiled within unveiling as inescapable refusal. "The fact is that the step backwards from a truth of adequation to a truth of unveiling, whatever its necessity and its 'critical force,' can also leave one practically disarmed in the face of the ingenuous, the precritical, the dogmatic, . . . There's a law here" (Derrida, *R*, 318; Ross, *AIS*, 422). The law is a law of gifts, perhaps where we cannot find a law of giving.

For Heidegger speaks of gifts, as we have seen, the gift of language, under restriction, refused to animals and plants, and other things. He speaks of the gift of Being within "the originary and fundamental experience of the Greeks" (Derrida, *R*, 290), refused to Romans and, presumably, to others, non-Europeans, non-Westerners. He ascribes and returns the giving of abundance as the gift of Being to some and not to others. This is his "mistake," his crime, not to know that gifts are always held in reserve for some and denied to others, not to know that giving and withholding come from and respond to the good.

But we may understand the truth of which he speaks as opening onto the gift. And that is how Derrida proposes that we read the essay:

> Now it seems to me that *The Origin* can also be read as an essay on the gift *[Schenkung]*, on the offering: one of the three senses, precisely in which truth is said to come to its installation, its institution, or its investiture *[Stiftung]*. One of the two other senses, the "founding" *[Gründen]*, is not without its links with the ground. On the other hand, *The Origin* also says of this truth which is, Heidegger says, "nontruth" which "comes about *[geschieht]* in Van Gogh's picture" (a statement on which Schapiro exercises his irony), that its essence rather opens onto the "abyss." (Derrida, *R*, 261–62)

The truth of painting, *alētheia* joined with *poiēsis*, comes as giving, in abundance, is given as three moments together: institution, founding, and untruth, all giving onto the abyss. Of these only the first, perhaps, concerns attribution, demands an owner. But the truth of institution, in general, the possibility of installation, the falling of *poiēsis* into *technē*, as a gift, belongs to no one, comes from and to no place, but is found in place in the installation of a world.

Derrida speaks of abundance against the demand he ascribes to Schapiro to fix the essence of the owner (Derrida, *R*, 365; Ross, *AIS*, 427):

> As if Van Gogh could not be from town *and* country, as if he could not keep in himself something of the peasant (or keep with him some peasant shoes; what exactly is that?) once he had become provisionally a city dweller! As if he could not paint peasant shoes while wearing town shoes! As if he could not paint, with his brushes, in bare feet! As if one painted shoes with one's shoes! (Derrida, *R*, 365–66; Ross, *AIS*, 427)

As if we could limit, fix the essence, through representation or anything else, in painting, proof, or unveiling. As if we could. We. Within the opening to abundance of "As if" Derrida interposes a fixation, inherent perhaps in iterability, that the abundance can be held in check, shown in the truth of abundance in the form of a wager, something we bet, something bet, not something in the good, belonging to nature.

This is to remark, once again, of an abundance of gifts from the good which includes within itself, within its giving, the restriction and curtailment and blockage of that movement of giving and abundance, also in the name of the good. We do indeed, as do Heidegger and Schapiro, bring the truth of painting back to its rightful owner, against the opening of world and earth disclosed within that painting. We bring the truth of painting back to its rightful owner, truth's truth, as if art were the owner, but in a truth that does not belong to painting—I mean its restoration. We could say that no one, nothing, owns truth, is its owner. And nothing, no one, owns art. Both move, give themselves as gifts, everywhere, continuing to move. The gift continues to move: art, truth, and the others. For as truth, the movement halts. As art and as the movement shows.

The giving of abundance moves as art, and slows down. The abundance flows as truth, and slows. The abundance gives itself in its slowing and stoppage. Which is to say that we cannot increase it and cannot decrease it, for it flows and gives in its abundance no matter what we do. But we can think that we can increase and decrease it, and in that effort, we leave our mark. We leave our marks on nature's abundance, especially in our works, we scratch the soil of Being. We are part of nature's abundance in our works and in our scratchings. As are pigs, the wind, and dinosaurs. At least, they were. Dinosaurs left their works and scratchings, along with Carthage, left marks in the abundance of general circulation. We cannot help but leave our marks. We may hope to mark the good.

In this context, I interrupt my reading of Derrida's reading of Heidegger with another reading of Derrida, this time writing to Eisenman. For the wager may be, in Lyotard's language, on the Law, in my language here, on the good, though I resist the possibility of betting on the good. But in relation to architecture, Derrida raises a number of questions, all of which I would read as given from the good. I consider just a few:

1. Eisenman's work has "authorized many religious interpretations, . . . what distinguishes your architectural space from that of the temple . . . ?" (Derrida, *LPE;* Ross, *AIS,* 430). This question of God cannot be recognized of itself as bearing upon the good, bearing upon gifts, though the Western God with his temples has always been thought to define the Good and to bring the Law. But within this thought of the good as law, under the authority of God, Derrida asks us to think of architecture, an art that would disturb the authority of God's presence in relation to institutional figures that historically pertain to social-political edifices: houses, where women are dominated; museums, which control the circulation of art; research laboratories, housing instruments and animals as if they were instruments (and as if instruments were fit for only the tasks we assign them).
2. "What relations . . . does architecture, particularly yours, carry on, must it carry on, with the voice, the capacity of voice, but also therefore with telephonic machines of all sorts that structure and transform our experience of space every day?" (Derrida, *LPE*; Ross, *AIS,* 431). We may read this difficult question as pertaining to a truth of architecture understood as an institutional performance within the advance of modern technology, the organization of space and time. For Derrida also speaks of history: "This question of history, as the history of spacing, like the spacing of time and voice, does not separate itself from the history of visibility (immediately mediate), that is to say, from all history of architecture" (Derrida, *LPE*; Ross, *AIS,* 431. We recall that this is a history of dominations and oppressions, of disasters. What is the place of architecture among disasters? What is its politics?
3. That is, what of glass? Modern architecture rose over the world in the transparency of glass. "What terms do we use to speak about glass? Technical and material terms? Economic terms? The terms of urbanism? The terms of social relations? The terms of transparency and immediacy, of love or of police, of the border that is perhaps erased between the public and private, etc?" (Derrida, *LPE*; Ross, *AIS,* 432). I think of *Reichskristallnacht,* the night in 1933 in which the breaking of glass marked the opening of a genocide. Shall we build architectural works, of glass, without glass, without a memory of genocide? In 1933 Benjamin wrote of glass. Derrida reminds us. "Things made of glass have no 'aura' " (Benjamin, *EA*; Derrida, *LPE*; Ross, *AIS,* 432). Quoting Scheerbart, "we can easily speak of a 'culture of glass.' The new environment will completely change man" (Benjamin, *EA*; Derrida, *LPE*; Ross, *AIS,* 432–33). In this context of glass and the "impoverishment of the new Man," Derrida reminds us (and Eisenman) of "a poverty that *should* not cause

another one to be forgotten" (Derrida, *LPE*; Ross, *AIS*, 434), an art that builds on wealth while people are so poor that they have too little to eat, of building private homes while people live in public housing, of building at all while there are homeless (Derrida, *LPE*; Ross, *AIS*, 434).

4. Thinking of Kristallnacht, perhaps, of 1933, Derrida asks us to think of a Jewish museum built in Berlin, to think of this as an architectural possibility, and of something else, Kristallnacht perhaps, and of the Holocaust. Think of building a Holocaust museum, in Germany. As a work of architecture, a work of art? As a building to house works—of art? Of death? And while our history contains buildings memorializing events of such disaster, what kind of building does architecture give? What kind of art? And what of housing other works, including works of art? Can we admire works of art as art in a world that has cost so much to procure them, to give them?

This last question brings us to the good as we have not been brought before. And we need to confront it in its enormity. For this reason, I stop right here in pursuing Derrida's questions to Eisenman, and us, to stand face to face with this question of gifts from the good. Art is a gift from the good, and it must always move. What, in a world in which these movements, including the movement of art, especially arts, like architecture, bound tightly to technology, wealth, and development, bound to the production of disasters, what of art? Does it save us? And if it does, does its salvation circulate the good or does it halt the movement, is it complicit in the activities that would halt the movement of goods, building up a world of ruin?

We cannot abandon this question of the good, the most urgent question of the good in art, the good of art. Benjamin asks us to remember that Marinetti glorifies war (Benjamin, *WAATR*, 241; Ross, *AIS*, 537). "All efforts to render politics aesthetic culminate in one thing: war" (Benjamin, *WAATR*, 241; Ross, *AIS*, 537). And perhaps, to render aesthetics political, art political. The good calls upon us to know the disaster of political art and aesthetic politics. The question of the good in art touches us with ruins.

But I will postpone this question, returning from our interruption of "The Origin of the Work of Art" to think of Heidegger at the time of Kristallnacht, his rectorship under Hitler, think of his life and works, then think of his writings in memory of glass. What did Heidegger think of the smashing of glass? What did Heidegger know or think of God? What did he think of the political world in which his works unfolded? What of homeless people, new men, and Jews? What memory did Heidegger have of Jews? What thought in his work of disasters? What contribution did they make to disaster?

What thought did Heidegger have of the good? Does he mark the good? This question will provoke other interruptions. For the moment, I remain within the question. Does Heidegger mark the good in art or being? I return to "The Origin of the Work of Art." We left the work, before our interruption, in the happening of its truth, revealing the equipmentality of equipment, the reliability of a peasant women's shoes, between world and earth. "This equipment belongs to the *earth*, and it is protected in the *world* of the peasant woman" (Heidegger, *OWA*, 34; Ross, *AIS*, 258). The work, Van Gogh's painting, reveals the belonging and protecting of world and earth, the happening of truth at work, where "the work belongs, as work, uniquely within the realm that is opened up by itself" (Heidegger, *OWA*, 41; Ross, *AIS*, 262); "to be a work means to set up a world" (Heidegger, *OWA*, 44; Ross, *AIS*, 264). Now I wonder at the protecting of equipment in the world of the peasant woman, where some worlds disturb and threaten. And here, perhaps, we may come before the good in a way that brings Heidegger to task. Perhaps. For some worlds protect things ready to hand, and people: some worlds, some things, some people. In every world, some things are destroyed, some people are threatened, harmed, oppressed. The protection of world for some is at the expense of others. The world of the peasant woman is a difficult and dangerous world, at times, more frequently than not.

We might wish to say that the world that protects people and equipment—but perhaps not animals, plants, and rocks—is an ethical world, a world that grants freedom and nurturing to human beings, if not others. Except that the world that protects some does not protect others, suggesting that perhaps protection, belonging, setting up a world, may be a contaminated movement. Shelter is an exclusory figure where only some find shelter. To give a world, to be given a world, is to be given something from the good, but this good is neither good nor bad, unfolds the possibility of good and bad, works in contaminated spaces. Good and bad, right and wrong, unfold in the realm of law, of *technē*, within a world opened up. But the good interrupts this opening to call upon us not to respond with repose at the reliability of equipment, but with agitation and injustice, destruction, and violence, intermediary movements.

Heidegger speaks of a Greek temple work "that first fits together and at the same time gathers around itself the unity of those paths and relations in which birth and death, disaster and blessing, victory and disgrace, endurance and decline acquire the shape of destiny for human being" (Heidegger, *OWA*, 42; Ross, *AIS*, 263). He speaks of a world-historical work, a world-historical building that builds a world for posterity, for more than those who lived in its vicinity. Even this worlding is for others. Van Gogh's shoes, whoever's shoes they were, the world opened by the painting is not world-historical though the painting is famous. Neither work, however world-historical, belongs to its world uniquely, but dominates its world along with the gods and kings, some of whom were tyrants. Can a world-historical work avoid dominating its world? Can it avoid a world of domination by others? Does it reproduce and repeat such a domination, in Greece and today, in our century in Germany, for example, where the arts were ruled by fascism? "The temple-work, standing there, opens up a world and at the same time sets this world back again on earth" (Heidegger, *OWA*, 42; Ross, *AIS*, 263). "The *world worlds*" (Heidegger, *OWA*, 44; Ross, *AIS*, 264). Earth is the ground "on which and in which man bases his dwelling" (Heidegger, *OWA*, 42; Ross, *AIS*, 263); the Greeks called its emerging and rising *phusis* (Heidegger, *OWA*, 42; Ross, *AIS*, 263). I understand *phusis* as abundance, giving, moving, circulating: nature's general economy. I understand world as worlding, happening, the erecting of structure upon the earth. What in the world lets the earth be an earth? "*The work lets the earth be an earth*" (Heidegger, *OWA*, 46; Ross, *AIS*, 266).

The world comes forth from the earth as *phusis*, emerging and rising, *giving*. The giving comes from the earth as the ground on which man dwells, man and his world, the abundance of the earth given into the human world, with one return: the world's works, at least as art, let the earth be an earth. Only human works of art, and only great works at that, let the earth be an earth. And what of the rest? What of the others, first other works of art, popular, mediocre, loved, works that circulate everywhere, works that give rise to famous works by famous workers because everyone knows them? Do folk and common works not establish and open a world? What of other creatures and things than human beings and human works? What of animals and plants? "Plant and animal likewise have no world, but they belong to the covert throng of a surrounding into which they are linked" (Heidegger, *OWA*, 45; Ross, *AIS*, 265). And this despite the recognition that "men and animals, plants and things, are never present and familiar as unchangeable objects" (Heidegger, *OWA*, 42–43; Ross, *AIS*, 263. Human beings, animals, plants, and things are not unchangeable objects, but emerge and rise, circulate in nature's forthcoming. Yet animals, plants, and things have no world, and this deficiency marks man as ruler, from whom the others derive their essences, linked to man.

The world worlds. The work lets the earth be an earth. To which I add, the earth earths, in its abundance, so that each thing, plant and animal and thing, earths, touches, unfolds in and enriches the abundance of things. Against this, we might say that world destroys, dominates, wounds, restricts this abundance. We might also say that it is human tragedy to know this wound as the human world, the world that is opened by works of art, including beautiful Greek temples. Animals were sacrificed there. Women held no property, were restricted to the home. Slaves were bought and sold.

The good appears here in a double interruption, one marked by Heidegger as the interruption of world by earth. No world comes forth from earth, even in the light of the greatest and most beautiful works of art, without a wound. The work wounds. The work betrays. It betrays the earth that gave it forth. It betrays the earth in founding a world, in belonging to a world, in finding itself already in many worlds. Beauty is a betrayal. But it is a betrayal in the work of the good, among the gifts from the good. A world halts the circulation of goods of the earth, slows down general economy into restricted economy. This halting is an interruption. And in reverse, the earth interrupts the worlding of world, as if without betrayal, interrupts the smooth and familiar possibilities of world with whatever has been neglected, hurt, and damaged. Halting and interrupting are ethical relations, given from the good. The inexhaustible variety and abundance of the earth is interrupted repeatedly, building good and bad upon abundance, building law, even in the work of art.

"The world is the self-disclosing openness of the broad paths of the simple and essential decisions in the destiny of an historical people" (Heidegger, *OWA*, 48; Ross, *AIS*, 267), a destiny that everywhere, not least in Germany, meant war, destruction, violence, inwardly and outwardly. Destiny is an ethical relation intimately related to violence. It is mirrored in Heidegger in the relation between world and earth. "World and earth are essentially different from one another and yet are never separated" (Heidegger, *OWA*, 48–49; Ross, *AIS*, 267), an intermediary movement and more, for "[t]he opposition of world and earth is a striving" (Heidegger, *OWA*, 49; Ross, *AIS*, 267), a struggle, "and "in the struggle, each opponent carries the other beyond itself" (Heidegger, *OWA*, 49; Ross, *AIS*, 267). Each opponent.

When Heraclitus says that "justice is strife," *polemos*, does he mean that we are at war over justice, in justice? Or does he mean something closer to *diaphora*, that unlikeness belongs to justice at its heart, pervades justice, so that we can never overcome, resolve, dissipate that unlikeness in any moment of justice? When Anaximander speaks of the injustice of things composing the ordinance of time, does he mean war? Or does he mean that *diaphora* so pervades justice that every just work falls back, repeats, injustice. The aporia is that justice is injustice; injustice in justice, inseparably. Yet this unlikeness and proximity need not be war, strife, *polemos*, death to one over the other.

Anaximander tells us that justice cannot triumph over injustice. Nor does world triumph over earth. Nor is there a truce between bloodthirsty opponents. The Greek sense of opposites is a belonging-together, *Zusammengehörigkeit*, in unlikeness, intermediary movements. This is something Spirit discovers in the *Phenomenology* only after demanding and imposing a war to death. But if this opposition is our model, what does it mean to overcome it, to sublate it? It has to mean that what we have taken as *polemos* is closer to *diaphora*. The quarrel between poetry and philosophy is a shared proximity of unlikeness, not a harmony in which strife and injustice vanish, but a belonging-together of differences in endless memory of injustices. That is in part what abundance means, in memory of "subjugated knowledges" together with their insurrection (Foucault, *2L*, 81). Within historical memories of struggles and subjugations is an insurrection given from the abundance of unlikenesses.

The language of "The Origin of the Work of Art" is oppositional, conflicted, violent, more so, perhaps, than almost any other of Heidegger's writings. Against the repose of letting-be and *Gelassenheit*, world and earth belong together in a striving, a strife. Heidegger does not read this proximity between world and earth in ethical terms, not even in relation to letting-be and abundance. He understands the gift as given from Being, not from the good, as if his recognition embodies a double refusal: of the ascendancy of humanity as the measure of Being together with a refusal of the good as this measure. He does not consider the possibility that the refusal of the ascendancy of humanity over Being is a refusal in the name of the good, given from the good. The refusal is of the assembling of Being under any single sign, a refusal given from the good.

Leading to a brief interruption, speaking from the heart of the good, brief because the remaining chapters will pursue this thought within other interruptions. It is said by Levinas early in a voice that does not seem to recognize Heidegger. "Being is exteriority: the very exercise of its being consists in exteriority, and no thought could better obey being than by allowing itself to be dominated by this exteriority" (Levinas, *TI*, 290). It is this exteriority no matter how divided, rifted, or concealed, no matter how striven or polemic. It is assembled under the sign of difference without interiority, intimacy, or remainder. Later, Levinas calls this remainder *otherwise*, and associates it with subjectivity: "in subjectivity an exception putting out of order the conjunction of essence, entities and the 'difference' " (Levinas, *OB*, xli). "Not *to be otherwise*, but *otherwise than being*" (Levinas, *OB*, 3). An otherwise beyond being to "a God not contaminated by Being" (Levinas, *OB*, xlii), to "a non-origin, an-archical," to "the Good" (Levinas, *OB*, 11).

The abundance of the gift comes for me in an intimacy without subjectivity, without privileging the human, as Levinas does, speaking of animal breath and the breathlessness of the spirit. "It is the longest breath there is, spirit. Is man not the living being capable of the longest breath in inspiration, without a stopping point, and in expiration, without return?" (Levinas, *OB*, 182). I ask, in response, why would a creature that touched the world, touched things intimately, in their being and their goodness, received their intimate gifts, proclaim his superiority? What in spirit demands superiority, and with what betrayal?

But I must interrupt this interruption to return to Heidegger where we saw this same claim of human superiority coupled with oblivion to the demands and touches of the good. I return to "the setting up of a world and the setting forth of earth" (Heidegger, *OWA*, 48; Ross, *AIS*, 267) in "the destiny of an historical people," to strife. "The world, in resting upon the earth, strives to surmount it. As self-opening it cannot endure anything closed. The earth, however, as sheltering and concealing, tends always to draw the world into itself and keep it there" (Heidegger, *OWA*, 48; Ross, *AIS*, 267). I questioned the contamination of the destiny of history, an idea too close, perhaps, to its ultimate purpose amid countless historical peoples and the abundances of things. World seeks to bring forth into the open; earth strives to conceal. We may be reminded of the conflict Freud describes between Eros and Thanatos, a striving to build against a striving to destroy. I add the Nietzschean thought somehow lacking from this picture of conflict, that Eros and Thanatos each strive, but their striving within themselves need not be a conflict between them, but a belonging-together. The unconcealing and concealing of world and earth is an intermediary movement, not perhaps an opposition, certainly not an opposition in which one can win.

Perhaps what I just said is false. If we think that humanity is the source of world, the only source of unconcealment, then we know with certainty that earth will win, will finally triumph, on Thanatos's ground. Death may be withheld for but a cosmic moment. But if we think, with Lyotard for example, that linking belongs to earth, that nothing can stop its movement; or think of unconcealment as touch rather than sight or sound, then all things touch each other, open each other at their skin, face each other in proximity. The flow of life, but more, the flow of movements in nature is from one to the other, not only ingestion and respiration but osmosis and mitosis, and more, every motion by contact, every touch of waves across space and time, every contact in proximity and remotely, is a contact, a caress, an opening, an unconcealment. Earth for humanity is an oblivion that calls it from the depths and reaches of nature, not just in its animality, for animality touches things with prehensile grasp, paws, claws, and fangs, touches with fur as well as skin, with whiskers and tentacles, and more; and other things touch each other with surfaces and edges, all shaping their identities and shaping the movements in their surroundings. Every shaping, every influence, every touch opens; and every one conceals.

If human beings set up worlds in the destiny of historical peoples, animals and plants set up ecological worlds in the movement of natural systems, planets and their debris, stars and suns, set up worlds of galactic scale, all composing and measuring space and time, all exceeding any measure. The setting up of a world is the building of a structure within which measure holds, opening that world to revelation. Worlds compose our natural surroundings, not just human worlds, all measurable, orderly, structured worlds, all beyond measure, with hidden crevices and obscurities. This is the point of the striving between world and earth, that earth does not strive to conceal but to show, and world does not strive to open but to conceal its striving. Concealment and unconcealment do not mark the rift between world and earth, but belong to each and to both.

"The opposition of world and earth is a striving" (Heidegger, *OWA*, 49; Ross, *AIS*, 267), but to be confounded with neither "discord nor dispute," with "disorder and destruction" (Heidegger, *OWA*, 49; Ross, *AIS*, 267). "In the struggle, each opponent carries the other beyond itself" (Heidegger, *OWA*, 49; Ross, *AIS*, 267), still opponents. The work of art—returning to the work and its truth—works "so that the strife may remain a strife" (Heidegger, *OWA*, 49; Ross, *AIS*, 268). "The work-being of the work consists in the fighting of the battle between world and earth" (Heidegger, *OWA*, 49; Ross, *AIS*, 268). And more. The work allows this battle "in the simplicity of intimacy" (Heidegger, *OWA*, 49; Ross, *AIS*, 268), in the "repose of the work" (Heidegger, *OWA*, 50; Ross, *AIS*, 268). Striving, strife, battle; intimacy, repose: two sets of terms that define the belonging-together of unlike.

I have added that each and all of these belong to world and earth in themselves and in their relation—that is, in every place. Place is a place of unlikeness, otherness and otherwise, in moving, striving, desire, in intimacy and repose, in public and private intermediary figures, public and private figures of the good.

How else can we understand world and earth as war and strife, as intimacy and repose, except in relation to the good, as ethical gifts? How else can we understand the work of art in relation to world and earth except as a gift bearing unlikeness from the good, displacement and dispersion, to the world? The gift borne from earth to the world is a gift emerging from the abundance of the earth in all its profusion and multiplicity, divided, disrupted, mobile; a gift to and from being otherwise.

In this context, at this place, Heidegger speaks of gifts. "Things are, and human beings, gifts, and sacrifices are, animals and plants are, equipment and works are" (Heidegger, *OWA*, 52-53; Ross, *AIS*, 270). We may read this as a repetition of all the ways that things are in general, except that it is not a general list. Rather, after things in general, it is a list of the essential ways in which things are in the Open, spoken of a few lines later. "In the midst of beings as a whole an open place occurs. There is a clearing, a lighting"; "[t]hat which is can only be, as a being, if it stands within and stands out within what is lighted" (Heidegger, *OWA*, 53; Ross, *AIS*, 270). What stands out, stands in this open place, are human beings, gifts, sacrifices, animals and plants, and human works. And the others, other things, things in general? Do they remain dark? Or is the very lighting a darkening? "Each being we encounter and which encounters us keeps to this curious opposition of presence in that it always withholds itself at the same time in a concealedness" (Heidegger, *OWA*, 53; Ross, *AIS*, 270). Each being we encounter presents and withholds itself. I call this presenting|withholding the gift of touch. Everything we touch reveals and conceals itself in that touch, and everything that touches us, and more: everything that touches something else, presents and withholds itself. World worlds for everything in touch, and in this worlding we touch the gift of the good.

Heidegger almost says this, and recoils, for the gift must be held in reserve for us. He reinstates a powerful sense of opposition—"world and earth are always intrinsically and essentially in conflict, belligerent by nature" (Heidegger, *OWA*, 55; Ross, *AIS*, 271). This "belligerence," appearing for the first time, gives rise to what I take to be the most dogmatic thought in this essay, that truth "happens in a few essential ways" (Heidegger, *OWA*; Ross, *AIS*, 271) and not others, listed a few pages later:

> One essential way in which truth establishes itself in the beings it has opened up is truth setting itself into work. Another way in which truth occurs is the act that founds a political state. Still another way in which truth comes to shine forth is the nearness of that which is not simply a being, but the being that is most of all. Still another way in which truth grounds itself is the essential sacrifice. Still another way in which truth becomes is the thinker's questioning, which, as the thinking of Being, names Being in its question-worthiness. By contrast, science is not an original happening of truth, but always the cultivation of a domain of truth already opened, specifically by apprehending and confirming that which shows itself to be possible and necessarily correct within that field. When and insofar as science passes beyond correctness and goes on to a truth, which means that it arrives at the essential disclosure of what is as such, it is philosophy. (Heidegger, *OWA*, 62–63; Ross, *AIS*, 275–76)

The abundance of the earth shows itself (essentially) only in some places and not others, is to be ascribed to some places, persons, and activities and not others. And why not the others? Why are the others not sites of the struggle between world and earth? Why is Heidegger's exclusion not another event in the history of concealment?

"*Beauty is one way in which truth occurs as unconcealedness*" (Heidegger, *OWA*, 56; Ross, *AIS*, 272). Beauty is one way in which being gives its gifts. Heidegger lists four (or five) others. I speak of countless others. His project is the specific way in which art gives truth. First, "[t]he establishing of truth in the work is the bringing forth of a being such as never was before and will never come to be again" (Heidegger, *OWA*, 62; Ross, *AIS*, 276). Yet we may suppose that every being meets this condition in its uniqueness. Second, "truth establishes itself as a strife . . . brought into the rift-design" (Heidegger, *OWA*, 63; Ross, *AIS*, 276), understanding rift *(Riss)* as "the intimacy with which opponents belong to each other" (Heidegger, *OWA*, 63; Ross, *AIS*, 276), in intermediary movements. Intimacy again, returning to men and women, sexual difference, friendship, children, and the home, all places of intimacy—shall we say among opponents? Or does that presume too much?

The tracing of the rift-design in work gives something unique to art, recalling the installation, institution, and investiture of truth. Truth must be installed, instituted, in the world. It cannot remain in earth. It comes forth in the rift, traced as a design. That is what Heidegger says, in work. I have spoken of the skin.

But as I speak of the skin, and remember caresses and embraces, I also recall Kafka's penal colony, and masters and slaves. We have not been able to arrive this far without remembering Hegel's account of masters and slaves. Now we encounter Heidegger's. For immediately before he unfolds the rift-design, he speaks of slavery. "As a world opens itself, it submits to the decision of an historical humanity the question of victory and defeat, blessing and curse, mastery and slavery" (Heidegger, *OWA*, 63; Ross, *AIS*, 276). Are these ethical questions? Are victory and defeat the same as slavery? Or is that a Greek idea? Is it ethical? Does Heidegger know anything of oppression written on the soul, the skin, the heart of those oppressed, or oppressors?

From which we turn back to the design in the rift, just named as slavery, also named as *"figure, shape, Gestalt"* (Heidegger, *OWA*, 64; Ross, *AIS*, 277). "Thought cuts furrows into the soil of Being" (Heidegger, *NL*, 70), as figure, shape, design (Heidegger, *WL*, 121), cuts into skin. I read this moment in Heidegger's writing as among the most vital in his work, addressing two burning questions for him and for us: (1) the relation—difference—between Being and beings (for us between the good and its works); (2) why art? Why does the rift between world and earth call for the work of art? Heidegger's answer is that the striving between world and earth gives shape as design, the rift-design, traced on the surface of Being, freeing the earth to be earth. "In the creation of a work, the conflict, as rift, must be set back into the earth, and the earth itself must be set forth and used as the self-closing factor. This use, however, does not use up or misuse the earth as matter, but rather sets it free to be nothing but itself" (Heidegger, *OWA*, 64; Ross, *AIS*, 277).[7]

We recall that the frame of this entire essay is given in its Epilogue, Hegel's theses on the end of art. Art will come to an end because its service to Spirit will be sublated by thought. Art's sensuousness diminishes its spirituality. Against this figure of a spirit, *Geist*, that diminishes itself in falling into the world, a figure of Christ incarnate but sacrificing spirituality and divinity, Heidegger gives us art *as* sensuous, tracing, figural, in that way in the rift, in that way belonging to Being, to the earth, remaining in that belonging, not using it up. On this reading, Hegel speaks of Spirit sacrificing itself in space and time, into the material and natural world, still Spirit but sacrificing its spirituality. It must rise again to overcome that alienation. Heidegger understands this difference—no longer alienation—not to be overcome. It cannot be overcome; it must not be overcome, must not be used up. For that overcoming is to sacrifice any memory of Being.

Here Being, *phusis*, earth, gives rise to intermediary figures of threshold, rift, and design. The sensuousness of art allows it as design to be intermediary, and as intermediary to remain in the Open, another intermediary figure. The truth of unveiling remains open, intermediary. We might go so far as to consider Being as intermediariness—not intermediary, but intermediariness, giving rise to endless intermediary movements, figures, thresholds, designs. On this reading, Christ incarnate is the intermediary figure, never to be forgotten in his intermediariness, with the Father and Holy Ghost the remaining figures of that intermediariness, of the circulation. But they do not circulate, and in that way they are themselves not in the Open. Christ is the holy figure of openness.

On this reading, the good is not intermediary, but it is intermediariness, makes intermediariness possible, gives intermediariness to the world, in every place and for every thing, so that they are intermediary, every thing and every place. Where Heidegger speaks of the opening and clearing of truth, I speak of the work of the good. The intermediariness of truth emerges into the open as design, as figure, shape, frame.[8] Yet he does not speak of the good, of care for the other. He does not understand the rift-design as touch, an ethical relation given from the good. He does not understand intermediariness as ethical as well as ontological. "Figure is the structure in whose shape the rift composes and submits itself. This composed rift is the fitting or joining of the shining of truth" (Heidegger, *OWA*, 64; Ross, *AIS*, 277). Composing and submitting are figures of touch, of the good, too much, perhaps, echoing mastery and slavery. Intermediariness is interruption.

Perhaps Heidegger speaks of design, of composing, fitting, joining, and submitting, in memory of mastery and slavery. Perhaps of matter and form. But earth is not matter but *phusis*, coming forth and emergence, circulation; and world is not form but shaping, joining, intermediary movements of work. The work of art is a working, designing, tracing, building in the intermediariness between world and earth, refusing to pass to mastery, refusing to form according to an idea, but giving itself over to the abundance of the earth in its working. This is touch; this is in memory of, given by, the good. It is not submission, nor is composition mastery.

I add one thought to this intermediariness of design and truth before undertaking another interruption. The bringing forth of the work in rift-design is more deeply present the more solitary the work. "The more solitarily the work, fixed in the figure, stands on its own and the more cleanly it seems to cut all ties to human beings, the more simply does the thrust come into the Open that such a work *is*, and the more essentially is the extraordinary thrust to the surface and the long-familiar thrust down" (Heidegger, *OWA*, 66).

What overcomes this solitude is preservation. Heidegger responds to Kant's suggestion that taste clips the wings of genius, the wings of the soul Plato describes as caring for things everywhere, a supreme intermediary figure, by a figure of preservation and conservation that does not curtail the thrust of the created work into the open. "Just as a work cannot be without being created but is essentially in need of creators, so what is created cannot itself come into being without those who preserve it" (Heidegger, *OWA*, 66), where preserving is "letting the work be a work" (Heidegger, *OWA*, 66). Preserving "is a knowing" and "[h]e who truly knows what is, knows what he wills to do in the midst of what is" (Heidegger, *OWA*, 67). We come before an unmistakable figure of the good.

I interrupt this discussion, perhaps the most crucial discussion till now of the intermediariness of Being, the good, and earth, giving forth the intermediariness of works of art and more, to consider a less radical reading of Heidegger, perhaps of art. It is a reading I admire, and I will say why. But in this intermediary movement, it halts, I believe, and of that too I will say why, as I understand it.

I am speaking of Gadamer's view of art as play, more radically, of art in time as play, giving from this temporality the timelessness of (great) art. For the point of Gadamer's analysis is to understand the timelessness of art, and only great art is timeless in the same way that, for Heidegger, only in great art is the artist inconsequential. Time and artist disappear in great art. As for the rest, ungreat works of art and mere things, they are another matter. And why, we might ask, are not great works of art "un-great" as truth is un-truth; and conversely, is there no greatness, no truth, in every work of art, ungreat works of art, in untruths? Or are we still within the conviction that truth happens in only a few essential ways—a conviction that halts the circulation and refuses intermediariness?

Gadamer speaks of art in the context of his view of the universality of hermeneutic understanding. All understanding is interpretation, including art and science—though he does not offer a detailed hermeneutic chemistry or physics, and at times suggests that the natural sciences offer a different model. He understands the hermeneutic circle as a relation of whole and part despite profound qualifications. "The totality of meaning that has to be understood in history of tradition is never the meaning of the totality of history" (Gadamer, *TM*, xxiii). Understanding posits a totality for meaning in history and tradition, posits universality. Gadamer worries about the relativization of finite truth, "how one can do justice to the truth of aesthetic experience and overcome the radical subjectivisation of the aesthetic" (Gadamer, *TM*, 87;

Ross, *AIS*, 358); how we can overcome "untenable hermeneutic nihilism" when no outside point of view exists.

The paradigm in which art shows itself to represent hermeneutic consciousness is in play. In play the game is primary over the players engaged in it, as art is something beyond or over artist and audience. Play "plays something" (Gadamer, *TM*, 96), the players give themselves over to something else, "[p]lay is structure" (Gadamer, *TM*, 105). Most important, art expresses radical temporality as timelessness within continuity, as originary repetition. "Every repetition is equally an original of the work" (Gadamer, *TM*, 110; Ross, *AIS*, 362). And speaking of the festival, the celebration, which "exists only in being celebrated" (Gadamer, *TM*, 110; Ross, *AIS*, 362), "regularly celebrated": "[a]n entity that exists only by always being something different is temporal in a more radical sense than everything that belongs to history. It has its being only in becoming and in return" (Gadamer, *TM*, 110; Ross, *AIS*, 362). This is an account as close to Derrida's idea of iterability as can be imagined, except for the continuity posited as temporality, the continuity of history, tradition, and work, "the fundamental continuity of the whole" (Gadamer, *TM*, 217).[9]

Heidegger speaks of time as "ek-static," out of place. To be somewhere in time is to be elsewhere. *"Temporality is the primordial 'outside-of-itself' in and for itself"* (Heidegger, *BT*, 377). Do the continuity and return of difference in time speak deeply enough of temporal ek-stasis, of the solitariness of the work in the Open? "To be present is to share" (Gadamer, *TM*, 111; Ross, *AIS*, 363), a festival is a communion, not witness to the solitary thrust of earth into the Open. We find both moments in Gadamer. The appearance of the work of art is an absolute moment, a parousia, a detachment and distance in which the spectators are reconciled with themselves, given back their being, in a "proper and comprehensive sharing" (Gadamer, *TM*, 113; Ross, *AIS*, 365). He does not consider the possibility that the solitary, the distinct, the liminal, all may appear in a work of art, thrust up into the shared and familiar world as the unshared and unshareable upsurge of Being, of the earth. He does not consider that although this upsurge may be preserved and conserved in the life of a people, such a preservation is incompatible with universality. He understands radical subjectivization in Kantian terms, within the immediacy of subjective experience, rather than as the radicalization of culture, universality, or communicability—the possibility, for example, that art's supreme achievement may be, in its culture, to deny to other cultures accessibility to it, that radical cultural diversity shows that lack of universality may be the only universal. Even so, we learn and live and understand together— in some cases, understanding that we do not understand, and that that understanding is the best available. The work of art unfolds a world, we might say, precisely so that we might have such an understanding, of what we do not understand and share, not of what we do. What is its unfamiliarity and uncanniness otherwise?

Here we come to the emphasis on great art, where greatness speaks both of the values we share, we Westerners, and of the Westernness of its idea. For many cultures know nothing of greatness in art, but still produce works that open up worlds and places. And many places in Western cultures produce works of art in abundance that come and go with little sense of greatness. In all these works, something strange and uncanny joins with familiarity, in disturbing and disorienting ways.

The question Gadamer brings before us is from Kant. It is the question of community. What creates community? The answer in Kant is universal communicability displayed in art. The answer in Gadamer is totality of meaning and shared experiences, posited and realized in dialogue, however uncanny and unfamiliar. I pursue the possibility that community may be born of encounters in which we touch each other; the possibility that we live and die together under shared and unshareable conditions. What, more than art, might express the possibility of an abundance surrounding us in which something quite different might emerge? And why call our experience of the origination of repetitions *nihilism*, rejecting a community of what we do not share, when we encounter unshared experiences everywhere, even after destroying countless cultures and languages to make them *ours*?

Gadamer's rejection of this possibility that we live together, participate in the world together, in virtue of not sharing, not understanding, each other rests on a familiar yet extraordinary article of faith, analogous with Kant's universal communicability. "All that is asked is that we remain open to the meaning of the other person or of the text. But this openness always includes our placing the other meaning in a relation with the whole of our own meanings or ourselves in a relation to it" (Gadamer, *TM*, 238; Ross, *AIS*, 368). And what if cannot do so, are brought up short? What if our placing the other meaning in relation to our own meanings is an act of colonization? To what extent does our living among others and their other meanings allow us to form a whole, a totality, of our own meanings, rather than a collection of dispersions and discontinuities? Gadamer speaks of "the fusion of the horizons of understanding, which is what mediates between the text and its interpreter" (Gadamer, *TM*, 340; Ross, *AIS*, 376). What if we cannot *fuse* other horizons with our own within our heterogeneity? And why should we do so except within the idea of a heterogeneity hostile to the hegemony of Western culture and community?

And where, if we allow it, do we encounter this heterogeneity more than in art? And what, I add, if this abundance were not over and above, against, the art industry of which Heidegger speaks, but fostered by it, despite its appropriation of works for the market? With this question I return from this interruption to Heidegger's unfolding of the truth in work, to the point we left it, preserving the work. The work cannot remain in the Open, cannot remain in its truth, cannot stay in the rift-design, without preservers, who hold it resolutely in the rift. But preserving:

> is far removed from that merely aestheticizing connoisseurship of the work's formal aspects, its qualities and charms. . . .
>   As soon as the thrust into the extraordinary is parried and captured by the sphere of familiarity and connoisseurship, the art business has begun. (Heidegger, *OWA*, 68)

Again, Heidegger distances himself from the *mere*: the merely aesthetic, the sphere of familiarity, the art business. As we might distance ourselves from museums, who belong to the same business, and whose business is to make works of art familiar. Perhaps. I wonder at the possibility that we experience unfamiliar, strange, and uncanny works in museums and galleries, among other places, that without such places only those who owned the works could encounter them in any way, familiar or extraordinary. Museums, galleries, and dealers control the circulation of works, and this is to be resisted in the name of the good. But they circulate works that present themselves as extraordinary, as worth paying for because they are extraordinary. Some of the abundance of art and the earth is sacrificed to the art market; some of it perhaps shows itself, circulates more widely, because of the market's efficiency.

And perhaps the same is true of connoisseurship, of any similar exclusion, suggesting the better, the truer, the finer, the more uncanny, primordial, or extraordinary preserving of the extraordinary work. The connoisseur more than any other person has a stake in the extraordinariness of the work. He insists on construing that unfamiliarity exclusively in the realm of taste. And perhaps we resist his construal. It has traditionally been the business of men to construe and control the taste that defines great art, one of the considerations relevant to abandoning the idea of greatness. Still, the unfamiliar in art can be used to define greatness—I would say in a familiar and tired way. Or it can be used to open art away from the exclusions that have controlled it, together with the stake of the market, which is torn between adding to the market value of a small number of works and adding more and more works to the market, increasing the total market value of art. If not all works can be marketable, for that would dilute the value of any, then only some extraordinary works can be bought and sold.

Heidegger interposes another exclusion:

> *Art then is the becoming and happening of truth.* Does truth, then, arise out of nothing? It does indeed if by nothing is meant the mere not of that which

is, and if we here think of that which is as an object present in the ordinary way, which thereafter comes to light and is challenged by the existence of the work as only presumptively a true being. Truth is never gathered from objects that are present and ordinary. (Heidegger, *OWA*, 71; Ross, *AIS*, 278)

This exclusion marks a theme that runs throughout Heidegger's writings, beginning with *Being and Time*. Familiar objects, objects ready to hand, useful things, have nothing exceptional in them, nothing of truth, nothing worth paying attention to. They are exhausted, used up, in their familiarity. It seems that these familiar and ordinary things are not to be let be, not to be liberated in their truth, incapable of being revealed in their truth. Only a few essential ways show truth, one of which is art. Present and ordinary things are—whāt? Untrue? Too dead to be true? Mere things?

In the abundance of the earth of which Heidegger speaks, all things, including first of all perhaps familiar and ordinary things, are to be let be, to be revealed in their unfamiliarity and extraordinariness. Yet Heidegger sharply and dogmatically restricts the abundance, an abundance he described somewhat differently a page before. "True, there lies hidden in nature a rift-design, a measure and a boundary and, tied to it, a capacity for bringing forth—that is, art. But it is equally certain that this art hidden in nature becomes manifest only through the work, because it lies originally in the work" (Heidegger, *OWA*, 70). Hidden in nature and everywhere, especially perhaps in familiar and ordinary objects, in which something extraordinary always exists. We recall that "at bottom, the ordinary is not ordinary; it is extra-ordinary, uncanny" (Heidegger, *OWA*, 54; Ross, *AIS*, 271). Yet "equally certainly" art hidden in nature becomes manifest only through the work. With what certainty might we say this, refusing things of nature (in virtue of their darkness) and things ready to hand the possibility of opening in their rift-design?

Without certainty, I think that everywhere in nature things touch each other, opening by this touch, the touching of their skins, membranes and edges and surfaces, the abundance of possibilities in nature. I think that familiar and ordinary things are extraordinary, uncanny. Art tells us this, shows us this. But it does not exhaust the extraordinariness and uncanniness. The works that reveal the play of light and shadows around ordinary things, that caress the surfaces of things with pigments and words, touch the surfaces of their surfaces, showing how abundant and uncanny they are in countless other ways, because of those before us we can count. Art is inexhaustible and shows the inexhaustibility of things. But it does not give us those things in their abundance. Nor does anything do so, even the most familiar things in familiar places.

Heidegger's essay does not end before another exclusion: "language alone brings what is, as something that is, into the Open for the first time"

(Heidegger, *OWA*, 73; Ross, *AIS*, 279). Language alone, not painting, dance, or architecture. It is as if within his critique of Hegel on nature's materiality, Heidegger cannot let himself let go of spirit and spirit's language. Why *language* alone? Or is language not a restriction? Why language *alone*, when where language is not a restriction, it belongs to and opens everywhere?

For a moment, I pass over the reference to the first time, to the origin and beginning, closing the circle the essay opens around the work of art. I pursue for a moment longer the beginning and opening as language. For language in art calls us to poetry, in two different voices. One is the unmistakable voice of *poiēsis*:

> The nature of art is poetry. The nature of poetry, in turn, is the founding of truth. We understand founding here in a triple sense: founding as bestowing, founding as grounding, and founding as beginning. (Heidegger, *OWA*, 75)

> Genuinely poetic projection is the opening up or disclosure of that into which human being as historical is already cast. This is the earth and, for an historical people, its earth, the self-closing ground on which it rests together with everything that it already is, though still hidden from itself. (Heidegger, *OWA*, 75)

And what for an unhistorical people, a people that give up history, a people that do not care to remember, Nietzsche's people, perhaps? And what for an historical or unhistorical nonpeople, animals and plants, other things? Do they not belong to and disclose the earth, though it always remains hidden from itself? It seems that an historical people are linked inextricably with their name, with a name they or others give as language. "Language, by naming beings for the first time, first brings beings to word and to appearance. Only this naming nominates beings *to* their being *from out* of their being" (Heidegger, *OWA*, 73). This nomination, this nominal naming, is language in its exclusion, not its abundance.

But we have come again to the beginning, to the first time and the origin. Language, it seems, as naming, brings truth into being for the first time, *as poetry*. This second voice of language in art as poetry is *as poetry*, in words, not *poiēsis*, which opens wherever and however it does. *Poiēsis*, we may say, emerges in unfamiliar ways, in extraordinary things and places. Language, however unfamiliar it remains, becomes all too familiar, if not ready to hand.

This first time is repeated, in a different voice:

> Bestowing and grounding have in themselves the unmediated character of what we call a beginning. . . .

> A beginning, on the contrary, always contains the undisclosed abundance of the unfamiliar and extraordinary, which means that it also contains strife with the familiar and ordinary. (Heidegger, *OWA*, 76)

We return to the origin and beginning as the gift of abundance, a gift that carries on the unfamiliar and extraordinary, returning us to strife. The unfamiliar and extraordinary—the *great*—contains strife with the ordi-nary, fights against the ordinary in a war (even unto death?). Is this abundance or its simulacrum, that which must kill in the name of greatness? Is nature's abundance, given everywhere and in every place, a war to destroy?

I speak of the gift of abundance, but elsewhere Heidegger says something I must borrow:

> In the beginning of Western thinking, Being is thought, but not the "It gives *[es gibt]*" as such. The latter withdraws in favor of the gift which It gives. That gift is thought and conceptualized from then on exclusively as Being with regard to beings.
>
> A giving which gives only its gift, but in the giving holds itself back and withdraws, such a giving we call sending. According to the meaning of giving which is to be thought in this way, Being—that which It gives—is what is sent. (Heidegger, *TB*, 8)

Being is what is sent, the gift, and it is thought and conceptualized as itself, Being, in the Western tradition. But the giving, the giving that withholds in giving, the abundance of giving and withholding, remains to be thought, neither as Being, which is the gift, nor as It, which is not to be thought at all, but as an intermediary figure of abundance. We can think of abundance only as giving, not as given, and we can think of abundance only as withdrawing.

I think we may think of language as we think of being, as the gift, as given. As given, it is exclusive, restrictive, and destructive. It is also, as given, too familiar. It is, as abundance, giving, extraordinary and uncanny, along with works of art and everything else. Everything let be is let be, freed, in its abundance, an abundance of giving and withholding composing the earth. With an additional qualification. The abundance and withholding are given from the good, calls to be and to respond, to care, to touch. It is from this cherishment that we can resist the coercion of the gift, named as Being, named in language, the coercion of language as poetry, the coercion of *poiēsis* by poetry. It is from this call and care that we can resist the oppression of the origin, of the first time and the beginning.

Heidegger ends the essay with a question foreshadowing the Epilogue. "Are we in our existence historically at the origin?" (Heidegger, *OWA*, 78).

This question of the origin is a question of the end, of art, of us, questions we must resist in the name of giving and abundance. In the remaining two chapters, I will give my attention to abundance and giving. With two supplementary interruptions.

Irigaray resists the edges and cuts of solid volumes with the fluidity and mobility of water, resists the domination of identity. Woman, fluidity, water are intermediary figures. She responds to Nietzsche's hammering on land with love from the sea. She responds to the spiritualization of Being and language with air, speaks of the forgetting of air, insists on the materiality of intermediary movements, from the beginning:

> "In what" *is* it for it to work before all knowing . . . ? Before the possibility of separate "things." In what "is" it to found being and presence while disappearing in the act of founding? To have already been "used"—and using?—without any birth attributed to it. To have already given place to being without a beginning of being. . . .
>
> In what *is* it? Diaphanous, translucid, transparent. Transcendent? Intermediary, fluid medium in contact with itself without obstruction, with certain of its parts following their customs: real or decreed "trues." . . .
>
> What *is* it in? In air. (Irigaray, *OA*, 11–12: my translation)[10]

What view of art, what poetics, might we pursue if we never forgot the materiality of being, the abundance of materiality?

Charlotte Salomon was born in 1917 in Berlin. She died in Auschwitz in 1943. To escape the increasing persecution of Jews in Germany, she escaped in 1939 to southern France to stay with her grandparents. During her years in France, she completed an immense cycle of pictures with words, gouaches overlaid with tracings, the "story" of her "life" (?): *Life? As Theater?* The autobiography is composed of 769 pictures, 32.5 × 25 centimeters, with accompanying painted texts, preliminary studies, and unused compositions totaling 1325 sheets.

The work is exceptional, composed of over 700 gouaches with overlays, words effacing images and words, all separable and recoverable, palimpsests of memory and forgetting. It is comparable to *Remembrance of Things Past* and *The Man Without Qualities* in its relation to time, its scope and breadth, the worlds it inhabits and portrays, including the Germany of anti-Semitism and swastikas. It far exceeds them in its pictorial materials, tracings, and text interwoven with music, a theme highly present in Proust and Musil. I do not mean in presenting such a comparison to suggest that Salomon's work is "as great" as Musil's and Proust's. Nor to deny that possibility. I mean to suspend the question of greatness in relation to her work and theirs as an intermediary figure. I mean to suggest that greatness is less to be thought of as a culmination or end of art than an intermediary movement in which art responds to the good. Salomon's work belongs to the good.

I do not offer you a few gouaches with tracings. Most of the books on Salomon omit the overlays. One, *Charlotte: Life or Theater?* offers the entire autobiography, translated into English. The German, sometimes French, text is entirely visible. I bring each drawing under erasure to say that the entire book—it is indeed a book, visible and readable—presents a powerful and sweeping experience.

I would rather speak of what is only barely present in the book, tracings on tracings. Salomon's life? as theater?, with two question marks, as if her life, and art, and ours, can appear, in our time perhaps, only with question marks. This life, this autobiography, is named *LEBEN? ODER THEATER?: EIN SINGESPIEL*, where "THEATER" is almost written "TELEATER," which may be read as from a distance,[11] but which I read as the end of the earth *(telos/terre)*, with a question mark. And of Salomon. Perhaps of the world we know. This *Singespiel* is a play with music, in three colors (Salomon, *CLT*, 3). Music echoes in every moment, recalling Nietzsche. "Do you know these words of Nietzsche, 'Learn to sing, O my soul?' What does that mean if not the urge to freedom?" (Salomon, *CLT*, 235). Life?, and the (possible) end? of life as theater?, can only be sung, with abundance. Described by Salomon at the beginning:

> The creation of the following paintings is to be imagined as follows: A person is sitting beside the sea. He is painting. A tune suddenly enters his mind. As he starts to hum it, he notices that the tune exactly matches what he is trying to commit to paper. A text forms in his head, and he starts to sing the tune, with his own words, over and over again until the painting seems complete. (Salomon, *CLT*, 5)

I add two moments before I cease this interruption. First, from the beginning of Act Two:

> The swastika—a symbol bright of hope—
> The day for freedom and for bread now dawns—
>
> Here you see how this affected a number of different souls that were both human and Jewish!

> *"Der Stürmer*; organ of popular enlightenment.
> "The Jew has made only money from your blood. The Jewish bosses financed the world war!
> "The Jew has deceived and betrayed you, so—German men and women! Take your revenge!!!"
> (Salomon, *CLT*, 152–53)

And from the end, after contemplating suicide:

> And with dream-awakened eyes she saw all the beauty around her, saw
> the sea, felt the sun, and knew: she had to vanish for a while from the hu-
> man plane and make every sacrifice in order to create her world anew out
> of the depths. (Salomon, *CLT*, 782)

I conclude with two thoughts interrupting this interruption. One is from Griffin, who calls our attention to Alfred Wolfson, the singing teacher who taught Salomon's stepmother and who inspired Salomon herself (in *Leben? oder Theater?* he is named Amadeus Daberlohn). The *Singespiel* portrays him with a fiancée, longing for Charlotte's stepmother, and at the same time having an affair with Charlotte, who credits her memory of love for him with inspiring her work. In Griffin's words: "A woman who becomes an artist is a kind of thief. Like the Jewish artist who is seen by the anti-Semite as stealing culture, she breaks the trance of domination by the very practice of her art. It follows then that a young woman who tries to become an artist would also become the object of a sexual conquest" (Griffin, *CS*, 301). We must not forget that Salomon was a woman, and that European women artists were erased as artists in a world of men, nor that Salomon's work will never allow itself to become a monument to history, because of its materials, its complexity.

We must not forget that Salomon died because she was Jewish. What memory does that bring of the origin of art?

My final comment is ethical|political. It is said that the Holocaust—the one Holocaust alone, or one of many disasters—cannot be represented, that with the gas chambers the possibility of innocence vanished from European life. Perhaps. But Salomon represents something of that disaster, her disaster among others, and of the end, of art, of herself, and of her world. She asks us to awake, to touch the abundance of nature, to create our worlds. If this is not a representation of disaster, what would one be? What would we ask one to be? If it is not a representation of abundance, however famous or unknown Salomon remains, what else would one be? Especially, by a woman, who was not expected to be great, but good, who responded to the good. To the end.

CHAPTER 7

Abundance

We have seen in Heidegger's understanding of art an abundance of things, spoken of first as the abundance of reliability, then of the unfamiliar and extraordinary, repeatedly given as a gift, but not given by or from Being. Being is the gift that we may think of as giving, the abundance of things and the earth. I hope to explore the abundance in this chapter, the giving in the next, in relation to art, and in relation to the good. For I call Heidegger into question where the gift is Being with no mention of the good, of the exposure of things to each other in their being together and in their giving to each other. The good gives abundance to nature from which, for various reasons in ourselves and things, we select and destroy, still in memory of the good, still exposed to its abundance. I call this abundance general economy. The phrase is from Bataille. I understand it somewhat differently. I understand many of the ideas I take from Bataille somewhat differently. I hope to show these differences here.

Bataille calls abundance "accursed" *[maudite]*, in part because there is too much—too much abundance, energy, imposing a debt, an obligation, a curse, in part because the form the abundance takes is destruction: we must waste and destroy what we cannot use. This is true of all systems that hope to build and survive, all organisms. All must destroy their excess energy; the abundance is met by a curse, gives rise to violent destruction. Humanity defines itself as given by a curse, as accursed, as "nature transfigured by the *curse*" (Bataille, *AS*, I, 78). Humanity is *The Accursed Share* at the same time that some—the victims—are chosen to be destroyed. Humanity separates itself from things by singling out some as victims:

> The victim is a surplus taken from the mass of *useful* wealth. And he can only be withdrawn from it in order to be consumed profitlessly, and therefore utterly destroyed. Once chosen, he is the *accursed share [part maudite]*, destined for violent consumption. But the curse tears him away

from the *order of things*; it gives him a recognizable figure, which now ra-
diates intimacy, anguish, the profundity of living beings. (Bataille, *AS*, I, 59)

The key term for me is *intimacy*; I hold it in abeyance for a while.

It is crucial to my understanding of general economy that even the curse
is too much a measure of general economy, even the universe is not, nothing
can be general economy. I follow what Bataille says in the end of sovereignty,
"[t]he main thing is always the same: sovereignty is NOTHING" (Bataille, *AS*,
III, 430). I hold sovereignty in abeyance for a moment, together with intimacy, noting that "[w]hat distinguishes sovereignty is the consumption of
wealth, as against labor and servitude, which produce wealth without con-
suming it" (Bataille, *AS*, III, 198). Sovereignty, which Bataille says is nothing,
is the consumption demanded by general economy, which I say is nothing. I
hold this nothing in abeyance for a moment.

Bataille associates general economy with the universe, which, whatever
it may be, is not nothing:

> I will begin with a basic fact: The living organism, in a situation deter-
> mined by the play of energy on the surface of the globe, ordinarily receives
> more energy that is necessary for maintaining life; the excess energy
> (wealth) can be used for the grown of a system (e.g., an organism); if the sys-
> tem can no longer grow, or if the excess cannot be completely absorbed in
> its growth, it must necessarily be lost without profit; it must be spent, will-
> ingly or not, gloriously or catastrophically. (Bataille, *AS*, I, 21)

This necessity belongs to the universe, belongs somewhere. Excess belongs
to the universe if it does not belong to restricted economies. "Beyond our immediate ends, man's activity in fact pursues the useless and infinite fulfillment of the universe" (Bataille, *AS*, I, 21); "On the surface of the globe, for
living matter in general, energy is always in excess; the question is always
posed in terms of extravagance" (Bataille, *AS*, I, 23). Such a view of the universe is not Bataille's alone, but has appeared within the metaphysical tradition, in Spinoza and Whitehead for example. I interrupt this movement
through Bataille to speak of Spinoza's and Whitehead's universe, for just a
moment, interrupting the circulation.

Spinoza's God is absolutely infinite, in infinite ways. If this is unlimit, it
is an abundance of infinites, inexhaustible excesses, beyond any measure:

> By God I understand Being absolute infinite, that is to say, substance
> consisting of infinite attributes, each one of which expresses eternal and in-
> finite essence.
> *Explanation.* I say absolutely infinite but not infinite in its own kind
> *(in suo genere)*, for of whatever is infinite only in its own kind *(in suo*

genere), we can deny infinite attributes; but to the essence of that which is absolutely infinite pertains whatever expresses essence and involves no negation. (Spinoza, *E*, Part I, Def. 6)

Each attribute is infinite in its own kind, an infinite measure, but this is not absolutely infinite. For what is absolutely infinite is infinite in infinite numbers of infinite kinds, whatever expresses kinds, essences, qualities. Spinoza speaks in and of abundant kinds, inexhaustible kinds, each infinite, each a restricted economy, limited but infinite in its kind, together in God beyond any measure. As plainly as can be said without the idea of economy, Spinoza describes a world and God composed of infinite numbers of restricted economies, each abundant and infinite, together in another abundance, absolutely infinite, beyond any restricted economy. Being absolutely infinite is general economy, associated with God. Things circulate under God beyond any restriction.

Spinoza does not stop with this. For *"The more reality or being a thing possesses, the more attributes belong to it"* (Spinoza, *E*, Part I, Prop. 9). Each kind of being possesses an abundance of reality, but nature and God possess infinite numbers of infinite attributes, expressing inexhaustible and abundant reality. God or substance exists in infinite abundance. *"God or substance consisting of infinite attributes, each one of which expresses eternal and infinite essence, necessarily exists"* (Spinoza, *E*, Part I, Prop. 11). This abundance includes infinite numbers of things in infinite ways. *"From the necessity of the divine nature infinite numbers of things in infinite ways (that is to say, all things which can be conceived by the infinite intellect) must follow"* (Spinoza, *E*, Part I, Prop. 16).

I keep repeating what I take to be the most provocative aspect of Spinoza's understanding of nature's abundance, what I call general economy, that God's absolutely infinite nature is not an unspeakable and unmentionable unlimit, but expresses and is expressed in infinite numbers of ways and kinds, each of which is infinite, each circulating among the others beyond measure. God and nature are abundances of abundance, beyond all essence and kind, expressed in kinds. General economy is composed of restricted economies, expressed in kinds, circulating among individuals and kinds throughout nature.

Whitehead speaks of abundance as Creativity, apparently without withholding, in relation to the good:

> "Creativity" is the universal of universals characterizing ultimate matter of fact. It is that ultimate principle by which the many, which are the universe disjunctively, become the one actual occasion, which is the universe

conjunctively. It lies in the nature of things that the many enter into complex unity. . . .
. . . The many become one, and are increased by one. In their natures,
entities are disjunctively "many" in process of passage into conjunctive
unity. This Category of the Ultimate replaces Aristotle's category of "primary
substance." (Whitehead, *PR*, 21)

The universe is composed of countless individuals, individual actual entities,
each a drop of experience, each a drop of process, always creatively becoming
anew. The universe is a creative process in which countless multiplicity
passes into another countless multiplicity of novel togethernesses, each a
concrescence of experience. Where Aristotle's primary substance is in motion
but governed by its idea, Whitehead's primary substance is abundantly creative, giving itself to form in passing, always passing over to other kinds, circulating beyond itself. The universe is creative and abundant.

This creative abundance is at heart aesthetic, for each individual entity
strives to achieve subjective intensity of feeling (Whitehead, *PR*, 27). Whitehead calls this intensity "Beauty," first defined as "the mutual adaptation of
the several factors in an occasion of experience" (Whitehead, *AI*, 324), later
joined with conflict. "Thus the contribution to Beauty which can be supplied
by Discord—in itself destructive and evil—is the positive feeling of a quick
shift of aim from the tameness of outworn perfection to some other ideal with
its freshness still upon it. Thus the value of Discord is a tribute to the merits
of Imperfection" (Whitehead, *AI*, 331). Imperfection returns us to abundance
in the form of Adventure: "namely, the search for new perfections" (Whitehead, *AI*, 332). All the qualities Whitehead ascribes to civilization—"Truth,
Beauty, Adventure, Art, Peace"—name abundance. In this way, perhaps,
Whitehead expresses general economy everywhere, circulating even where
governed by restrictions.

Imperfection leads this aesthetic sense of abundance to the good. Each
actual entity striving for an ideal unique to it; actual entities together, giving rise to abundance and intensity of feeling, giving rise to evil. First the
ideal:

> every definite total phase of "givenness" involves a reference to that specific
> "order" which is its dominant ideal, and involves the specific "disorder" due
> to its inclusion of "given" components which exclude the attainment of
> the full ideal. The attainment is partial, and thus there is "disorder"; but
> there is some attainment, and thus there is some "order." There is not just
> one ideal "order" which all actual entities should attain and fail to attain. In
> each case there is an ideal peculiar to each particular actual entity, and aris-
> ing from the dominant components in its phase of "givenness." (Whitehead,
> *PR*, 83–84)

Each actual entity, each becoming, event, or concrescence, arises within a world that gives to it the conditions from which it emerges and defines for it an ideal peculiar to itself. This ideal peculiar to each individual entity White-head calls "Platonic." Order is individual, multiple, and ideal, bearing within itself valuation and selection according to an aim of fulfillment. What White-head calls Platonic is the good, not an idea that rules over all things together, but an ideal within each thing for its becoming, derived from the world from which it emerges. In this endless and abundant becoming, givenness is a gift among countless other gifts, given as ideal under the good. But givenness is not the only gift, though it names the giving as ideality.

We may call this ideality a multiplicity of ideals, of goods, where the good is never one for all. The good is multiplicity, pluralized but still ideal. Moreover, it is never attained, for the environing world forbids its full attain-ment, so that the ideal exists for each entity in its impossibility. And further, this impossibility depends on selection, incompatibility, exclusion, on what Whitehead calls *evil*. "Selection is at once the measure of evil, and the process of its evasion" (Whitehead, *PR*, 340).[1] We may read this evasion as overcoming. By selection, by higher experience, we triumph over the ob-structions and destructions of evil. This is Apollinian. And Whitehead can be read as Apollinian. But he can also be read in memory of Anaximander, per-haps Dionysian, so that the possibility of being, of life, of abundance, de-mands selection and exclusion, demands sacrifice and death. There is joy in death and sacrifice, joy in life and being. But it cannot be enjoyed without injustice. Selection is evil, and selection opens the possibility of avoiding evil, of caring about it. The Apollinian understands all of this, I believe, but its own evil, its own injustice.

Creativity belongs to individuals, actual entities, not kinds. Whitehead says this explicitly. He understands that creativity is not restricted to given kinds. From the ideal order pertaining to individual actual entities, from "the notion of 'order' [which] is primarily applicable to the objectified data for in-dividual actual entities" (Whitehead, *PR*, 89), we come to "a derivative sense of the term 'order,' " "speak of the 'order of nature,' " where "the term 'order' evidently applies to the relations among themselves enjoyed by many actual entities which thereby form a society" (Whitehead, *PR*, 89), a kind. If societies are "derivative," it is not because they are peripheral. Societies pervade the universe in virtue of the striving of individual actual entities for intensity.[2] Creativity gives rise to inexhaustible kinds of kinds. Abundance is an abun-dance of kinds, individuals and kinds, identities upon identities upon identi-ties, none holding firmly against the movement of creativity, all expressing inexhaustible ideals.

With this sense of abundance we may return to Bataille's account of general economy and abundance in terms of the universe and energy. Both,

I would say, are restricted economies, not because I think the universe and energy are finite. But if they are infinite, they are infinite in their kind. And they are infinite without ideals. This may seem perverse if we understand energy as whatever does work in any place, and if we understand nature and the universe to coincide. Yet I mean that no individual or kind, be it nature or God or the universe or energy, named as an essence, expresses the abundance of abundances, general economy. Abundance belongs to nature beyond any restriction, exceeds all boundaries and measures, exceeds anything—any thing or kind—we might call "nature." It marks "everywhere" and "every thing" and "nowhere" and "no thing."[3]

Bataille associates general economy with the following conditions, each crucial to my understanding of the good, though he does not himself discuss the good. He does discuss the curse. And animals and animality. These are not the same, but cannot be separated from the curse or each other, in Bataille. I will hold these in abeyance for just a moment, together with intimacy, sovereignty, and nothing. For the moment, I remain with expenditure, with consumption.

We may read Bataille on consumption as a mad and extravagant resistance to capitalism, to accumulation, the transformation of the world into commodities, including human beings. This resistance expresses a double madness, one that squandering can resist the hegemony of capitalist production, of the market, the other that profits can be squandered, spent extravagantly, without utility. The madness consists in taking commodification, utility, and profit as all-inclusive except for squandering. He does not consider the possibility that within the reign of the market, utility and profit must undermine themselves, must do so if they belong to general as well as restricted economy. In the extreme and most radical possibility I can think of, that the capitalist market economy, if it becomes the only economy, must be both general and restricted. Commodities—not just "things" or human beings ("sovereigns")—resist commodification, for example, as objects of desire, becoming fetishes. The desire that allows things to be turned into commodities is excessive, beyond measure, evoking abundance.

Put another way, I take Bataille's understanding of squandering and extravagance without consumption not to be abundant enough to reach general economy. Extravagance remains restricted. This can be seen in one of his most interesting claims concerning consumption. "If a part of wealth (subject to a rough estimate) is doomed to destruction or at least to unproductive use without any possible profit, it is logical, even *inescapable*, to surrender commodities without return. Henceforth, leaving aside pure and simple dissipation, analogous to the construction of the Pyramids, the possibility of pursuing growth is itself subordinated to giving" (Bataille, *AS*, I, 25). What is logical belongs to a restricted economy in which a part of wealth will be destroyed. If we must destroy wealth profitlessly, let us then destroy it to our benefit, destroy it by giving it away, provided something is given in return.

Bataille speaks of gifts and giving, speaks of Mauss, but understands giving as ultimately always toward something in return, always working in restricted economy. "Potlatch is, like commerce, a means of circulating wealth, but it excludes bargaining. More often than not it is the solemn giving of considerable riches, offered by a chief to his rival for the purpose of humiliating, challenging and obligating him" (Bataille, *AS*, I, 67). "The problem posed is that of the expenditure of the surplus. We need to give away, lose or destroy. But the gift would be senseless (and so we would never decide to give) if it did not take on the meaning of an acquisition. Hence *giving* must become *acquiring a power*" (Bataille, *AS*, I, 69). Yet he recognizes a giving without return, though he must turn to natural things and processes for his examples. "The origin and essence of our wealth are given in the radiation of the sun, which dispenses energy—wealth—without any return. The sun gives without ever receiving" (Bataille, *AS*, I, 28). Even here we may respond that natural processes are reciprocal, follow the second law of motion. This reciprocity is not, however, utilitarian.

The sun gives energy without requiring return, though if it did not receive any return, it would die out sooner. It accumulates matter falling into it as a result of its attraction, given by the same conditions as its expenditure. The sun gives without a curse, gives and destroys without prohibition. But it makes good things possible, belongs to the abundance, demands responses in return, if not accumulations. Bataille calls this abundance *exuberance*. Abundance gives rise to abundance, especially in relation to life (we may say, but mountains, valleys, glaciers, and galaxies speak of other abundances), in wild exuberance, containable only for the moment, then bursting forth in unexpected ways. Some of the deadest things in the sky are the most lively and exuberant in terms of the energy and things they squander—I speak of dark galactic clouds and black holes.

This account of expenditure and excess suggests a nature without ethics, certainly an abundance without exclusion. And here we must think of the good. Bataille speaks of it repeatedly, speaks of squandering excess while avoiding war and destruction. He speaks of ethics in conventional terms, yet also speaks of ethics transformed by general economy, a thought I associate with the good. Giving can take precedence over growth, circulation over accumulation. Even so, the giving that marks another acquisition is not the giving that circulates without return, or circulates with or without return, where return is another circulation.

With this idea of general economy as circulation, related to the gift, I begin my detailed reading of Bataille, under a number of explicit headings related to the good as art.

General economy. Bataille speaks of "the useless and infinite fulfillment of the universe" and "the play of energy on the globe." He speaks in a binary relation, an opposition, between restricted and general economy. The places where we live and work are restricted economies, economies of growth, accumulation, and production. We accumulate to grow and produce. But such activities are servile. They submit themselves exclusively to use (Bataille, *AS*, II, 14–15). One pole of the binary, restricted economy, is servile, organized entirely around use. I hold this binary in abeyance for a moment, suggesting that if one pole is usefulness, the other is uselessness; if one pole accumulates to use, the other spends uselessly. In Bataille, we see the fulfillment of Heidegger's critique of equipmentality and reliability understood in a binary relation. But Heidegger does not understand the binary relation in quite this way. For in reliability there is abundance.

Restricted economy is where work is done, understood by Bataille in terms of use. It is servile for human beings (typically men) to think that accumulation and use are all there is. There is useless expenditure, consumption, and squandering. General economy is this useless expenditure, extravagance, linking those rich enough to spend, powerful enough to give away, to production and consumption. Bataille speaks of general economy in a binary relation, as if we might choose to accumulate or to squander. And in another binary, if we choose to spend, we may choose to do so "gloriously or catastrophically" (Bataille, *AS*, I, 21). General economy is a surplus of wealth, energy, or forces that must be spent.

I understand all "musts" to belong to restricted economy. If we must spend or die, accumulate or die, consume or be destroyed, we are under the rule of limits, of life and death. General economy as I understand it is not restricted economy, but in the sense of otherwise, something very different from restriction and limit, belonging to unlimit, otherwise, immeasure. Abundance is not too much of this or that, too much energy to spend, but perhaps not energy at all, perhaps nothing. Abundance, like sovereignty, is NOTHING. Energy and wealth are not nothing, but too much something, restricted economies, beyond measure, evoking abundance. Extravagance remains within the restricted economy of profit and loss, accumulation and expenditure, however excessive. Extravagance belongs to accumulation, another return. Extravagance is closer to what Spinoza calls "infinite in its own kind" rather than "absolutely infinite," in all kinds, abundance and inexhaustibility.

I do not take extravagance to express the excess and abundance of the earth for two reasons: because it retains the names of energy, wealth, and squander; and because it remains in a binary relation. It remains so throughout, from consumption through eroticism to sovereignty. Two additional examples, both glorious:

Beyond need, the object of desire is, *humanly*, the *miracle*; it is sovereign
life, beyond the necessary that suffering defines. This *miraculous* element
which delights us may be simply the brilliance of the sun, which on a spring
morning transfigures a desolate street. (Bataille, *AS*, III, 200)

May we not say of death that in it, in a sense, we discover the negative ana-
logue of a miracle, something we find all the harder to believe as death
strikes down the one we love, the one who is close to us, something we could
not believe, *if it, if death were not there.* (Bataille, *AS*, III, 206–7)

Miracle and death are extraordinary experiences. Sovereignty is not everywhere or in every moment. Yet the unfamiliar, strange, may appear at any
time and in any place. This is the sense of the good I bring to Bataille especially, and to Heidegger, if more sporadically.

For Heidegger speaks of the abundance of reliability so that the very idea
of use bears within itself an excess beyond use. Within the restricted economy of reliability and equipmentality the earth gives forth its abundance.
Even so, Heidegger can say that in equipment matter is used up, against the
call of its abundance. Yet if we think that matter is used up in equipment, if
we think that reliability dissolves its abundance into equipment and use, all
of experience testifies against it. Commodities continue to move, move from
one place to another, are only rarely destroyed, changing their uses and their
directions. They are not destroyed as a matter of course, but circulate as different kinds of objects.

I understand the binary opposition in which Bataille works, between
accumulation and expenditure, to remain within restricted economy. All
binaries are restricted economies. I understand the abundance of which Heidegger speaks to open away from restricted economy toward the general
economy of the earth, but as neither energy nor wealth, something other, excessive, toward possibilities and goods without a name. I think of nature as
abundant, moving from itself toward itself in a circulation without categories
and distinctions, always circulating individual things and kinds, so that the
circulation of general economy, beyond measure, takes place everywhere, not
just in relation to individuals and singulars. We have seen it marked in Spinoza and Whitehead, naming kinds, an absolutely infinite general economy
composing infinite numbers of infinite kinds. Spinoza touches something
only dimly present throughout the metaphysical tradition, that infinity bears
doubly on kinds, each infinite, together infinite beyond the infinity of each,
together composing general economy.

Spinoza speaks of human profit and of the striving within each thing to
persevere. "Each thing, in so far as it is in itself, endeavors to persevere in its
being" (Spinoza, *E*, Part III, Prop. 6). "The effort *[conatus]* by which each
thing endeavors to persevere in its own being is nothing but the actual

essence of the thing itself" (Spinoza, *E*, Part III, Prop. 7). "By good, I under-stand that which we certainly know is useful to us" (Spinoza, *E*, Part IV, Def. I). And in what I take to be the most heinous passage in Spinoza, which I understand entirely within restricted economy, and have mentioned before, we may use anything "except men" "in any way whatever" (Spinoza, *E*, Part IV, Appendix, XXVI).[4] I take this despicable sense of the good to belong to re-stricted economy and not to nature or God because it falls entirely under what is useful to us where "[n]ature has set no end before herself" (Spinoza, *E*, Part I, Appendix), and "we neither strive for, wish, seek, nor desire anything because we think it to be good, but, on the contrary, we adjudge a thing to be good because we strive for, wish, seek, or desire it" (Spinoza, *E*, Part III, Prop. 9, Schol.). I understand one good, that which profits humanity, to be-long to restricted economy. I understand the other to belong to general econ-omy, that which pertains to God's abundance. That is how I understand Spinoza.

General and restricted economy compose the good together. Nature's, Being's, abundance is beyond fulfillment, opposition, measure, at the same time that nature's work is done in restricted economies. Restricted economies do work against the abundance from which they emerge, oblivi-ous to the abundance of their emergence. That is how I understand, at least for the moment, the gift of Being, holding the giving in abeyance for a mo-ment. *Es gibt* Being, where the gifts belong to restricted economies and the giving comes from Being, belongs to nature's general economy, to abun-dance. I understand the abundance of Being as giving, from the good, un-derstanding that "*the gift must always move*" (Hyde, *G*, 4). The gift of Being never stops giving, never stops circulating. The wild and excessive circulation of goods, of kinds of things, commodities circulating beyond commodifica-tion, things circulating beyond objectification, is general economy. It is abundance, given from nature and the earth and elsewhere, everywhere, given I insist from the good, as the good, plenishment in the earth, "a nature of wondrous beauty" (Plato, *Symposium*, 210–211a).

This nature of wondrous beauty is given in memory of the good to all things in their restricted economies. It is circulation beyond the limits of bi-nary oppositions, inexhaustible possibilities and heterogeneities. It is circu-lation in the flesh, of things in their bodies and materialities, in the sensuousness of art and language, for example, *mimēsis*, expressing general economy, the circulation of general economy in every restricted economy, in every place and frame. General economy is circulation without purpose, be-yond purpose, calling in the name of the good for work, giving rise to things with purposes, ends, and goods of their own.

Cherishment is responsiveness to every thing in every place, every thing and every kind, circulating beyond any measure, called in the name of the good, a good beyond measure. But in their places, in every place, each thing belongs to kinds that cannot work together without conflict. In its place, every good conflicts with others, giving rise to sacrifice. Bataille associates sacrifice with the sacred, and the sacred with abundance, with general economy. But sacrifice belongs to cherishment, pertaining to every economy. The conflict among goods in circulation belongs not just to each individual thing's purposes and goods for itself, but reflects a good beyond that thing to its kind, and beyond that to other kinds, endlessly. The possibility of individual goods bears a memory of general economy and the good exceeding the hold of every good in every place. In Spinoza, it comes from nature and God, whose call works in every individual thing beyond its profit and the uses it makes of other things. This is not extravagance and uselessness, nor a use passing for uselessness, but something beyond use.

Restricted economy. I think of general economy as the circulation of goods beyond measure, setting aside all considerations of profit and loss, accumulation and expenditure, acceptability and unacceptability, good and bad as belonging to restricted economy. In this way I set aside as well extravagance as a form of expenditure, but not as exuberance. The general circulation of things is wild, anarchic, exuberant in its wildness.

If general economy is the exuberant circulation of goods beyond measure, it finds itself endlessly falling into restricted economies of work and measure, promoting conflict and sacrifice. We can escape binary oppositions no more than we can take them to define the good, knowing that every binary opposition destroys. Bataille speaks of restricted economies as accumulation and use, describes those who believe that there is nothing but use and accumulation as *servile*. In addition to binary oppositions organized around utility and use, we have binary oppositions between accumulation and expenditure, servility and sovereignty, restricted and general economy, humanity and nature.[5]

I have resisted reading general and restricted economy as another binary, associating binarities with restricted economy. We cannot add another binary to restricted economy because it includes all binary oppositions within itself. To resist servility, we cannot think of it as opposed to sovereignty, restricted economy opposed to general economy, humanity opposed to nature. Bataille's exclusion of nature, of animals, is another oppression. Humanity and nature are inseparable, and general and restricted economy intertwine diaphorically, though they do not integrate (another term of restricted economy), do not unify, are not mediated. In every binary circulation, in place, something exceeds that circulation, expresses the wild and unmeasured circulation of general economy, the abundance of nature.

Bataille speaks of restricted economy as accumulation in a strongly Nietzschean voice. And perhaps this brings us to the point where we may understand his ethical relation to the good. For what he objects to in the modern world, objects to in its servility to use, is democracy:

> I call attention to the immense hypocrisy of the world of accumulation. In principle, it is completely contrary to archaic society's two main forms of activity, to the positing of *rank*, established by some form of ostentatious expenditure, and *war*, which is assuredly the most costly form of the destruction of goods. . . . The world of accumulation cannot use up its wealth except through differences of rank and through war. (Bataille, *AS*, III, 424)

I do not mean to suggest that democracy resists rank and war. That is a mythology we need not support—though democracies may go to war infrequently with other democracies. But democracy understands that the rank that belongs to it, to democracy, is never intrinsic, inward, or sovereign. Rather, accumulation imposes the rank of wealth from itself at the same time that it democratically suggests that anyone may become rich, may achieve rank. And the same may be said of war. The surplus here is surplus value, the gap between one value and another, use and exchange. The surplus here belongs to restricted economy. General economy circulates goods away from one value to another, circulates them democratically without rank or war. Rank and war, like restricted economy, stock up, withhold the circulation.

A brief interruption. Heidegger speaks of modern technology as within the frame, the *Gestell*, of *Bestand*, translated as standing-reserve, associated with reliability and durability (Heidegger, *QT*, 298). I have associated abundance with general economy, including the abundance of reliability of which Heidegger speaks, the abundance of standing-reserve, however strange that may seem, the general economy in every restricted economy. Restricted economy here is standing-reserve, holding up the circulation, holding the future hostage. Lyotard speaks of it as time "stocked-up" *(stocké)* (Lyotard, *DPD*, 176), in the "economic genre." Stocking time, gaining and deferring time, holding the future hostage, all belong to the economic genre, to restricted economy. But the event, the *Ereignis* in Heidegger, the *arrive-t-il? (is it happening?)* in Lyotard (Lyotard, *DPD*, 181), circulates regardless of restrictions, through restrictions, not as if the restrictions do not exist, not as if free of all restrictions, but beyond and through them. "The *is it happening?* is invincible to every will to gain time" (Lyotard, *DPD*, 181).

I add Lyotard's account of general economy, of which he says three things:

1. We are "to bear witness to the differend *(temoigner du différend)*" (Lyotard, *DPD*, xiii) where *Le différend* "(through the generic value of the def-

inite article) [suggests] that a universal rule of judgment between heterogeneous genres is lacking in general" (Lyotard, *DPD*, xi).
2. "The witness is a traitor" (Lyotard, *I*, 204).
3. [I must say it in French]: *La réalité comporte le différend* (Lyotard, *D*, 90).[6] Reality is composed of *différends*, of events, of heterogeneities beyond restricted economies.

This is an account of general economy, made up of *différends*, of heterogeneous events, where every restricted economy, like the economic genre, hopes to stock up time against the event, against the *différend*, against reality and nature. And every witness to general economy, to what Bataille calls sovereignty, betrays it. Restricted economies continually betray general economy while at the same time bearing witness within themselves to its circulation.

The reality—nature, Being, the earth—made up of *différends* is the earth's general economy, the endless circulation of heterogeneities that restricted economies are composed to hold, hold back, against the circulation, understood now as time, there as heterogeneity. The *arrive-t-il?*, the happening, the event, arrives and happens heterogeneously, circulating within general economy even when always caught in restricted economy. The earth's abundance belongs no less to restricted economy than to general economy, belongs everywhere, resists binary opposition and division as repetitions of restricted economy, but not by unifying the earth under totality. Totality is as restricted an economy as any. General economy is not totality, interrupts totality. The betrayal of the witness to general economy is essential to its circulation and heterogeneity beyond measure, undercuts the possibility of any measure even as it imposes measure.

Bataille associates restricted economy with accumulation, with growth, and general economy with expenditure, with surplus and excess, as if we can choose to accumulate or expend, to grow or exceed. I understand such a choice to belong to restricted economy, understand every choice to belong to restricted economy, where general economy knows nothing of choice or measure, but always falls into choice while at the same time disturbing and displacing measure. On the one hand, general economy in restricted economy exceeds every restriction. On the other hand, every testimony to general economy betrays it by imposing measures. Goods circulate underground and in hidden pathways, exceeding every channel and accumulation. Things are always more than any law under which they can be sorted. Things and kinds circulate in ways unimaginable and unknown in any system of restriction, any system of ends and rules.

Bataille appeals to Lévi-Strauss and his idea of culture to define restricted economies as systems of exchange. This includes gift economies in which gifts are given in exchange, either trading gifts or acquiring rank by giving without a gift in return. I have contrasted such an understanding of gifts in restricted economies with a view of giving where gifts always move without return, exemplifying general economy. I will hold giving in abeyance for a moment. But the most telling and pervasive condition of human culture, perhaps, is the exchange of women:

> The father must bring the wealth that is his daughter, or the brother the wealth that is his sister, into the circuit of ceremonial exchanges: he must give her as a present, but the circuit presupposes a set of rules accepted in a given milieu as the rules of a game are. (Bataille, *AS*, II, 41)

> Thus, women are essentially pledged to *communication*, which is to say, they must be an object of generosity of those who have them at their immediate disposal. The latter must give them away, but in a world where every generous act contributes to the circuit of general generosity. (Bataille, *AS*, II, 42–43)

General generosity comes close, we may suppose, to general economy, at least on Bataille's view, with two sweeping qualifications: (1) that women have been accumulated, are at men's "immediate disposal"; (2) that the general generosity composes a circuit. I understand general economy to circulate without accumulation and to compose no structure, not even a circuit, to be anarchic and immeasurable. This system of culture Bataille accumulates from Lévi-Strauss rests on the accumulation of women, the restricted economy of sexual difference and sexual reproduction, as if women were objects rather than subjects, measurable commodities rather than beyond measure. I will have more to say of this in a moment. Even so, in this restricted system of the oppression of women upon which culture is said to rest, the exchange of women exceeds any regulation, and the circulation of women also circulates men. We can see general economy circulating within the restrictions of the exchange of women. To give women (or anything, anyone else) away as a gift is to place something in circulation that cannot be controlled or mastered. This can be seen in play in Lévi-Strauss and Bataille:

> The prohibition of incest is less a rule prohibiting marriage with the mother, sister or daughter, than a rule obliging the mother, sister or daughter to be given to others. It is the supreme rule of the gift. (Bataille, *AS*, II, 44)

> On the one hand, the exchange, or rather the giving of women brings into play the interest of the one who gives—who gives only on condition of a return gift. On the other hand, it is a function of his generosity. (Bataille, *AS*, II, 47)

The supreme rule of the gift is defined by the contradiction that the gift, the woman, is given away, on condition of a return, another woman, while the gift must be given away to be a gift, must express generosity without return. In fact, women given away always complicate, for themselves and for those who give them, the reciprocity. As with all things.

I halt the circulation at this point to pursue this heinous and, perhaps, incredible idea of the circulation of women, doubly incredible once we think about it. I halt the circulation in the name and voice of women:

> The society we know, our own culture, is based upon the exchange of women. Without the exchange of women, we are told, we would fall back into the anarchy (?) of the natural world, the randomness (?) of the animal kingdom. The passage into the social order, into the symbolic order, into order as such, is assured by the fact that men, or groups of men, circulate women among themselves, according to a rule known as the incest taboo. (Irigaray, *WM*, 170; her question marks)

> [Lévi-Strauss, Lacan, and their epigones] call upon unconscious processes, for example, which require the exchange of women as a necessary condition for every society. . . . The symbolic order, without which there can be no meaning, no language, no society, depends on it. But what does women being exchanged mean if not that they are dominated?" (Wittig, *SM*, 31–32)

Every human society must propagate itself, must bring men and women together in conditions of intimacy and kinship. But it is said that women are circulated among men, ruled by men, as the essential condition for language, meaning, society, culture. The essential condition described by Lévi-Strauss and Bataille is the domination of women against the threat to culture of animality. This threat pervades Bataille:

> Lévi-Strauss opposes the state of culture to that of nature, much in the way that it is customary to contrast man with animals. . . . There would thus be in the horror of incest an element that marks us out as *human beings*, and the resulting problem would be that of *man* himself, insofar as he adds humanity to the universe. *What we are*, hence *all* that we are, would be involved in the decision that sets us against the vague freedom of sexual contacts, against the natural and undefined life of the "beasts." (Bataille, *AS*, II, 31)

I hold animals in abeyance for a moment. But at this point we may see in the idea of culture, of restricted human economies, themes of domination and exchange that in a single gesture oppress human beings—women and members of other races, classes, and kinds—and animals, based on the idea of a humanity opposed to their "natural and undefined life," all the while continuing to circulate beyond any capacity to regulate and control the relations between men and women, women and women, men and women and animals, and more.

I will explore these different themes of culture and restricted economy. I add a reminder of two themes that pervade the discussion. The first is that of art, for the gift of the good circulating in general economy is for our discussion here focused on art. The culture that circulates and exchanges women against the threat of animality requires animality in order to survive, must return to nature. In this way, art both expresses culture and belongs to this return to abundance, in Bataille. More of that later. The second is that of knowledge, truth. For knowledge, like art, belongs at once to restricted and general economy:

> To know is always to strive, to work; it is always a servile operation, indefinitely resumed, indefinitely repeated. Knowledge is never sovereign: to be *sovereign* it would have to occur in a moment. (Bataille, *AS*, III, 202)

> We could not reach the final object of knowledge without the dissolution of knowledge, which aims to reduce its object to the condition of subordinated and managed things. The ultimate problem of knowledge is the same as that of consumption. No one can both know and not be destroyed; no one can both consume wealth and increase it. (Bataille, *AS*, I, 74)

Knowledge is servile, useful, but it posits from within itself something beyond work, beyond consumption. More of that later as well.

Nature. The idea of servility in restricted economy and culture is so strong in Bataille that it depends throughout on systematically rejecting nature, and with nature, animals and animality. Yet he associates nature with general economy, with surplus and freedom from accumulation. Humanity defines itself by curse and prohibition. I hold animals in abeyance for a moment, though much of Bataille's account of nature and human resistance to it turns on recoil from animality, including women. Resistance to nature is resistance to oneself, to one's nature, to humanity in general circulation:

> I submit that man is an animal who does not simply accept the natural given, who negates it. In this way, he changes the natural external world; he derives from it tools and manufactured objects that form a new world, the *human* world. Concurrently, man negates himself; he trains himself; . . . (Bataille, *AS*, II, 52)

> Man is the animal that negates nature; he negates it through labor, which destroys it and changes it into an artificial world; he negates it in the case

of life—creating activity; he negates it in the case of death. (Bataille, *AS*, II, 61)

Yet he must return to nature as infinite object of desire. With a difference: "nature transfigured by the *curse*" (Bataille, *AS*, II, 78), by prohibition, giving rise to the sacred.[7] Nature is the wondrous beauty of which Diotima speaks, sacred and divine, containing within itself the transformations given by prohibition and curse, the sphere of the forbidden. These two natures are divided by an abyss, one resting on the domination of women and the consumption of animals. This abyss, marked by the curse and prohibition—not just restriction— bears within itself several immeasurable excesses: nature, the general economy in which things, goods, circulate beyond measure; a curse, a law, a prohibition, under whose sign culture comes into existence, a hatred and prohibition beyond measure; two excessive and unmeasurable desires, to be human and not natural, animal, to belong to nature in its sacredness and divinity.

Three (and more) excesses, beyond measure, all represented as nature, the play or clash of nature as general economy with nature as object of prohibition, defining restricted economy. The curse defines the sacred, therefore the mark in human culture of the divine, of general economy. All these movements, linked by the curse, nature transfigured by the curse, express the relation of general economy to the good, to sacrifice. The curse is the contaminated, desperate, horrific side of general economy, that in our excessive desire and endless relation to nature, the inexhaustible circulation of ourselves and things in nature, we can do no work, can create no culture, cannot live, propagate, care for ourselves and others, cannot even care for the earth and its kinds, without sacrifice, without rules, without marking some to die that others may live, some to be destroyed that others may grow. Growth and accumulation is sacrifice. Restricted economies are economies of growth and sacrifice. But sacrifice is excessive. The desire to grow and accumulate excessively is beyond measure—that is, divine—marked by general economy, beyond measure. Nietzsche calls it the will to power, but it is immeasurable and it works in the name of the good. The curse, like the witness's betrayal, is the visible mark of the good.

This may be the most important thought I would gather from Bataille, though he does not quite say it. The nature to which we return in the name, I say, of general economy, is nature transfigured by the curse. For us there is no other nature, no other general economy. We cannot relate to nature without memory of the curse—that is, of prohibitions, dominations, oppressions, subjugations. The thought of general economy is given from the good in multiple ways, but two are striking here: general economy disturbs the hold of restricted economies of domination, subjugation, and exclusion; and the thought, the idea, of general economy comes for us from restricted economies of domination and exclusion.

We may see this in several important places. One is that when we think of abundance and heterogeneity beyond measure, we always impose a measure. We always betray the good; the good works in our betrayal. This is the truth from the good that resists every utopian gesture, not by halting the gesture—utopia comes from the good—but by calling us to be witness to our own betrayal. Humanity's unique and special role in this interaction, unlike other natural things that also work in the light of the good, is to claim superiority in the name of totality, of being and the good, so that this claim demands betrayal. Those who claim rational superiority over others in the name of the good betray it repeatedly. Those who must sacrifice others to flourish, and who engage in local sacrifices do not bear the same responsibility. A second place where humanity encounters the mark of its own historical subjugations and oppressions is in relation to the idea of humanity, which is neither one over all human beings nor divided into enclaves under incommensurate rules, but dispersed into kinds, under measure, with different prohibitions and exclusions, frequently excluding each other, strangers to each other. We flourish and we suffer under the curses that define "us" as who we are, human, animal, natural, social.

A third place lies, I believe, in materiality and historicality. We human beings—at least, Western human beings, but perhaps more—possess and strive for a certain spirituality. Human beings, however secular, strive for something beyond measure, frequently in the name of the sacred and divine, sometimes in the name of spirituality, or truth, or the good. All are riven by the curse, repetitions of prohibitions and oppressions, even where they would be insurrections against subjugation. To be riven by the curse is to be historical creatures struggling against the rules and prohibitions that both make us who we are and impose obstacles to our fulfillments. This curse falls upon us no matter who we are, though it curses oppressors and victims in different ways. To be riven by the curse is also to be spiritual creatures struggling with material bodies marking humanity as human. With all the talk in our time of different bodies and truths of embodiment, it seems to me that we struggle continually with the curse, the prohibition, of taking bodies as the mark of humanity.

A fourth place pertains to desire, the evident mark of general economy, of something immeasurable, beyond calculation, in every restricted economy. Bataille speaks of the erotic; I have spoken of love as mad, frenzied, beyond comprehension or limit. Lovers face to face touch the limit of general economy. Yet the mark of inexhaustible desire is always, in every restricted economy, a repetition of accumulation, of wealth, sexual domination, political rule. Every restricted economy bears the mark of excessive authority, in different places and under different rules.

Finally, then, a fifth place at which nature's general economy continues to show itself in every restricted economy, perhaps the one that includes the others, is found in every natural thing, which enters restricted economies to be governed and ruled, treated as an object, only to exceed every rule repeatedly. We do indeed in restricted economies treat things and people as commodities, but in that very treatment we presuppose an abundance beyond any use. Things are treated as different kinds of commodities, like people, who find their roles as producers changing in any system of accumulation. A multiplicity of productive roles is as disturbing to commodification as excessive desire and excessive prohibition of bodily functions.

Worlds. Heidegger speaks of art and truth happening in the rift between world and earth, between restricted and general economy. Bataille speaks of human worlds, sometimes of the world:

> We often speak of the world, of humanity, as if it had some unity. In reality, humanity forms *worlds*, seemingly related but actually alien to one another. Indeed, sometimes an immeasurable distance separates them. . . . The most striking thing is that in each of the worlds to which I allude, ignorance, or at least disregard, of the others is the rule. (Bataille, *AS*, II, 21)

> Even if he has lost the world in leaving animality behind, man has nonetheless become that *consciousness* of having lost it which we are, and which is more, in a sense, than a possession of which the animal is not conscious. It is *man*, in a word, being that which alone matters to me and which the animal cannot be. (Bataille, *AS*, II, 133)

Human worlds, restricted economies, form themselves in binary oppositions: human world against natural and human world; approved against disapproved worlds; world of thought against world of things.

I have spoken of restricted and general economy, and of the curse. I am interested here in marking a profusion of worlds and kinds, different places where human beings and other creatures and things carry on their work. Bataille marks different worlds, perhaps as Heidegger does, with the difference that all human worlds are marked by the curse, by prohibition. The founding of a world is more than a struggle over dark and light, between earth and world, but belongs to the good in the name of the curse. We may read this in somewhat traditional terms, as a struggle for domination, reminded of Foucault's extreme words in memory of Nietzsche:

> Humanity does not gradually progress from combat to combat until it arrives at universal reciprocity, where the rule of law finally replaces warfare; humanity installs each of its violences in a system of rules and thus proceeds from domination to domination.
> The nature of these rules allows violence to be inflicted on violence and the resurgence of new forces that are sufficiently strong to dominate those in power. (Foucault, *NGH*, 151)

Even so, the curse of domination does not preclude the domination of domination, does not prohibit the possibility of working toward the good. It does
not preclude ethics but precludes a restricted economy without betrayal,
curse, and domination. In relation to his own reading of the curse of self-
consciousness, Hegel understands a struggle for domination and control, to
the death if necessary, to pass away into universal reciprocity, retaining traces
of the struggle, but relinquishing the curse. Most of those who write after
Hegel, who remember atrocity after atrocity, holocausts and genocides, remember the curse. Worlds are cursed by domination, betrayed by oppression.
Victims are the mark of the curse.

Bataille speaks of the sacrificial victim as marked by humanity as accursed. If we must expend and destroy the surplus, under the curse, we may
choose to do so in different ways: "it must be spent, willingly or not, gloriously or catastrophically" (Bataille, *AS*, I, 21). The sacrificial victim gains
something glorious in destruction, something exuberant. Traditional victims, women and Jews, members of other races in Western societies, of lower
castes in non-Western societies, and poor, are silent, oppressed, less than glorious, less than human. I cannot imagine that those who suffer, who are oppressed, would regard themselves as fulfilled if they were destroyed in
glory—though that is one way to understand terrorism. I leave aside without
further comment Bataille's refusal to think of the victim from the victim's
point of view.

Even so, however, the mark of the curse—that is, of prohibition and
repression—belongs to human worlds. For the moment I am exploring the
relation between the curse and the good. I understand the curse, like Nietzsche's and Foucault's understanding of the will to power and domination,
as ethical, intermediary, between the general economy of the circulation of
goods that cannot be stocked or held—desire, power, things, the earth—and
restricted economies of work and culture inhabited by human beings, also including stable ecological systems. Human worlds are multiply cursed under
the good, responsible for destruction, creating victims and destructions
wreaked by members of these worlds on others and themselves. The curse
builds the restricted economy. The curse returns us to nature betrayed, transfigured by the curse.

Culture knows the curse. And at this point I must begin to resist the as-
sociation of the curse with sovereignty in Bataille, at least of sovereignty with
sovereign rule, with political domination:

> The sovereignty I speak of has little to do with the sovereignty of States,
> as international law define it. I speak in general of an aspect that is opposed
> to the servile and the subordinate. In the past, sovereignty belonged to those
> who, bearing the names of chieftain, pharaoh, king, king of kings, played a

leading role in the formation of that being with which we identify ourselves, the human being of today. (Bataille, *AS*, III, 197)

The common feature among these rulers is that they belonged to institutional systems of domination, under whose dominion some were oppressed and many destroyed. It is essential in thinking of general economy to remember the curse of restricted economy, the betrayal of the witness. It is essential in thinking of the curse and betrayal to remember that the ideas of curse and betrayal and culture, not to mention general economy and restricted economy, are all cursed, all betrayals. No thought, no witness, to catastrophe fulfills it, does its work under the good. The good circulates beyond any attempt to hold it, stock it up, including every witness to its circulation.

Heterogeneity. I must join an additional thought to the idea of human worlds in Bataille. For if the idea of culture and worlds, restricted economies, is cursed, it is also multiple, inexhaustible, and more. Human worlds are "seemingly related but actually alien to one another. Indeed, sometimes an immeasurable distance separates them: . . . " (Bataille, *AS*, I, 21). And so, I insist, with kinds, though I might complicate their relation and that of human worlds a bit more. Bataille suggests that human worlds seem to be related but an immeasurable distance may separate them. They may also seem distant but bear an immeasurable kinship within them. Human and other worlds, natural kinds and kinds of kinds, things of the earth, are related in inexhaustible ways and also alien, are distant in inexhaustible ways and also related. Kinship contains this immeasurable belonging together and departing within itself: members of families, villages, communities, all related to and different from each other. Community works around the orderings and heterogeneities of kinship, and so does nature, around the orderings and heterogeneities of natural kinds, and kinds of kinds. Domination and victimization all work within this space of heterogeneous kinds. General economy here is the circulation of heterogeneous kinds, and kinds of kinds, among systems of kinship, each of which diminishes, betrays, curses the heterogeneity, attempts in vain to halt the circulation, slows it down in certain ways, as it must slow down to remain in circulation.

I am speaking of two things under this heading of heterogeneity: the abundance of kinds, and the specificity of certain kinds, in particular, sexual difference and human and animal kinds. These last kinds are linked in Bataille and elsewhere. The human is defined by a consciousness of having left the animal behind, within its impossibility. "Our" dignity, we humans—men—is defined in relation to heterogeneity, to other kinds, women and animals, and more, all transfigured by the curse. This is evidently true in Bataille of animals, within the binary pair human-animal. It is less evident in relation to women, who we may suppose are human, and who in their exchange define humanity—for men. Heterogeneity here works in two different but related ways, one the exclusion of animals, the other—despite Bataille's rejection of utility—the *use* of women. Women—not men—are exchanged in kinship rituals and incest taboos. The curse touches men and women differently, humans and animals differently. Nature transfigured by the curse is a heterogeneous nature, made of different kinds and different worlds. Curses, prohibitions, and taboos, also dominations and subordinations, are the ways humanity marks heterogeneity.

I return to nature's heterogeneity as the abundance of kinds, not to pursue abundance further but to speak of kinds. General and restricted economy pertain to individuals but especially to kinds, women and animals, humans and nature, and all the other kinds. General economy is the endless circulation of heterogeneous kinds; restricted economy is the governance and rule of kinds. These cannot be separated, cannot be divided. Moreover, our relation to such kinds, heterogeneously, is face to face, erotic. We cannot escape from restricted economies of domination and prohibition to general economy, but every restricted economy exceeds itself, sometimes in the violence of its dominations and prohibitions. And general economy circulates in restricted economies of prohibition and domination, face to face, sometimes but not always or necessarily in domination and prohibition. The risk cannot be eliminated.

Bataille speaks of returning to nature transfigured by the curse. The nature from which culture emerges, before the curse of sacrifice, is a nature of heterogeneous kinds without exclusion. The nature to which culture returns, after sacrifice, is a nature filled with exclusions defining the human world. These represent our relations to heterogeneity. I understand our relation to nature as cherishment toward multiply different kinds, cursed by sacrifice, by the impossibility that all these different kinds may endure together, giving rise to plenishment, the union of cherishment and sacrifice. It is not a relation to self but to others, not sovereignty but work in the memory of sacrifice, of the curse.

Sovereignty. We have seen two meanings of sovereignty in Bataille, linked in ways that undermine the binarity of general and restricted economy. One is of the sovereign as ruler, destroyer and squanderer. Speaking of the Aztecs: "One of the functions of the sovereign, of the 'chief of men,' who had immense riches at his disposal, was to indulge in ostentatious squander" (Bataille, *AS*, I, 63). In perhaps a Nietzschean thought, sovereignty belongs to sovereigns, but also to others: "it belongs essentially to *all men* who possess and have never entirely lost the value that is attributed to gods and 'dignitaries'" (Bataille, *AS*, III, 197). I associate sovereignty with authority more than with expenditure, though those with authority have always expended it, frequently without profit. While authority is useful, it exceeds all use in desire and power. Desire's authority over us, our authority over others in the exercise of power, our subjection to the authority of truth and law and *polis* all exceed any possibility of use.

This is the second meaning of sovereignty, much closer to cherishment: the immeasurability of authority and value, closely linked with intimacy. Bataille associates this with subjectivity, with avoiding being a thing. *"[B]eing in a sovereign manner"* is "man's not becoming merely *a thing"* (Bataille, *AS*, I, 131). He also associates it with consumption, another binary:

> What distinguishes sovereignty is the consumption of wealth, as against labor and servitude, which produce wealth without consuming it. The sovereign individual consumes and doesn't labor, whereas at the antipodes of sovereignty the slave and the man without means labor and reduce their consumption to the necessities, to the products without which they could neither subsist nor labor. (Bataille, *AS*, III, 198)

Because he works so much within binaries, he runs the risk of making sovereignty idle rule rather than what I take it to be, cherishment. "Life beyond *utility* is the domain of sovereignty" (Bataille, *AS*, III, 198). I believe that nothing can be lived "beyond" utility; life is utility and work. But within the authority of use and growth, something always exceeds the hold of authority, is in this sense "beyond" authority. But it is not a life we can live, or live wholly, or live by expending and destroying.

Bataille is much closer, perhaps, to the experience of sovereignty when he speaks of miracles. I would speak of something in every experience of authority that marks its miraculousness, the delight we experience not in what he calls "sovereign moments" as if these were not ordinary moments, but the "sovereignty" within every moment. I recall Heidegger's description of *poiēsis* as the unfamiliar within the everyday: I questioned whether the everyday could become wholly familiar, whether strangeness might remain in the most familiar, everyday things. "[A]t bottom, the ordinary is not ordinary; it is extra-ordinary, uncanny" (Heidegger, *OWA*, 54; Ross, *AIS*, 271). Things in Bataille are of the same nature as the subject—that is, immeasurable, uncanny, extraordinary.

But sovereignty belongs to instants, for Bataille, another binary exclusion of the temporality—the future projection—that belongs to utility. He resists the stocking-up of time as use through sovereignty in the instant, the pure moment of subjectivity. I resist it in the circulation of general economy, understanding the moment and its subjectivity as another restricted economy. He treats knowledge within the same opposition. "Knowledge is never sovereign: to be *sovereign* it would have to occur in a moment" (Bataille, *AS*, III, 202). Yet knowledge and truth exceed any possibility of use, of work. The binarity of servility and sovereignty destroys the possibility of living in echoes of sovereignty, of singing the song of the earth, its general economy.

Intimacy. Bataille speaks of sovereignty, related to intimacy, where intimacy is eroticism and more. Things apart from use are in intimate participation with the subject (Bataille, *AS*, I, 55), perhaps in intimate relation with each other, not requiring subjects for intimacy. Things can be restored to their intimacy to themselves and each other, overcoming the sense that they have intimacy only for humanity. "The animal or plant that man *uses* (as if they only had value *for him* and none for themselves) is restored to the truth of the intimate world" (Bataille, *AS*, I, 57–58). It is a world of madness, immoderation, Dionysian frenzy:

> The world of *intimacy* is antithetical to the *real* world as immoderation is to moderation, madness to reason, drunkenness to lucidity. There is moderation only in the object, reason only in the identity of the object with itself, lucidity only in the distinct knowledge of objects. The world of the subject is the night: that changeable, infinitely suspect night which, in the sleep of reason, produces *monsters*. (Bataille, *AS*, I, 58)

Again, history marks order and utility. Bataille does not seem to know the intimacy and madness of reason and history. In the same binarity: "Intimacy is not expressed by a *thing* except on one condition: that this *thing* be essentially the opposite of a *thing*, the opposite of a product, of a commodity—a consumption and a sacrifice" (Bataille, *AS*, I, 132).

I understand cherishment as intimacy, face to face. Things touch each other, we touch them and they touch us, and in this touch, this intimacy, is love, *erōs*. Intimacy and general economy, cherishment and earth, cannot be separated. Intimacy, face to face, is how things circulate, touching each other, skin to skin, face to face. Bataille knows this in the form of the embrace, holding it firm in humanity's restricted economy. "In a word, the object of desire is the universe, in the form of she who in the embrace is its mirror, where we ourselves are reflected" (Bataille, *AS*, II, 116). This is the restricted economy of the curse, no doubt that of men rather than women, humans rather than animals:

> The moment comes when my attention in the embrace has as its object the animality of the being I embrace. I am then gripped with horror. If the being that I embrace has taken on the meaning of the totality, in that fusion which take the place of the subject and the object, of the lover and the beloved, I experience the horror without whose possibility I cannot experience the movement of the totality. There is horror in being: this horror is repugnant animality, whose presence I discover at the very point where the totality of being takes form. But the horror I experience does not repel

me, the disgust I feel does not nauseate me. Were I more naive I might even imagine, and moreover I might even claim, that I did not experience this horror and this disgust. But I may, on the contrary, *thirst for it*; far from escaping, I may resolutely quench my thirst with this horror that makes me press closer, with this disgust that has become my delight. For this I have *filthy* words at my disposal, words that sharpen the feeling I have of touching on the *intolerable* secret of being. I may say these words in order to cry out the uncovered secret, wanting to be sure I am not the only one to know it; at this moment I no longer doubt that I am embracing the totality without which I was only *outside*: I reach orgasm. (Bataille, *AS*, II, 118)

Orgasm, eroticism, intimacy face to face, is where things touch each other beyond any order or measure. Under the curse, we human beings are filled with horror, horror at the immensity and terror of nature, horror filled with desire, horrible desire. In the name of the curse Bataille reaches orgasm. But this is not the only orgasm we know. And orgasm, genital contact, is not the only intimacy we know. We human beings know many loves and intimacies. And things may know others, many know more, other *jouissances*. Things may embrace themselves erotically in joys beyond any joys human beings may know.

Animals. At this point we come to something monstrous, contrary to general economy's heterogeneity in Bataille: the destruction of animals. To an extreme. I offer a tiny representative sample of an overwhelming din. I am referring to two related themes, one the curse laid on nature and on the animal side of human beings, the other, denial to animals of all the traits that make humanity human with no regard whatever for other possibilities:

> Essentially, eroticism is the sexual activity of man, as opposed to that of animals. Not all of human sexuality is erotic, but it is erotic often enough not to be simply animal sexuality. . . . But to begin with, its object is the passage from the simple sexuality of animals to the cerebral activity of man, which is implied in eroticism. I am referring to the associations and judgments that tend to qualify sexually objects, beings, places and movements that by themselves have nothing sexual about them, or anything contrary to sexuality: the meaning attached to nudity, for example, and the prohibition of incest. (Bataille, *AS*, II, 27)

> What marks us so severely is the *knowledge* of death, which animals fear but do not *know*. (Bataille, *AS*, II, 82)

> Animals lack an elementary operation of the intellect, which distinguishes between action and result, present and future, and which, subordinating the present to the result, tends to substitute the anticipation of something else for that which is given in the moment, without waiting. (Bataille, *AS*, II, 83)

> It is always a matter of going beyond the limits allowed: there is nothing
> erotic in a sexual game like that of animals. . . . Man's sexual life developed
> out of the accursed, *prohibited* domain, not the licit domain. (Bataille, *AS*,
> II, 124)[8]

And this despite recognizing the exuberance of the animal body. "The
fragility, the complexity, of the animal body already exhibits its luxurious
quality, but this fragility and luxury culminate in death" (Bataille, *AS*, I, 34).

And this despite recognizing that the aversion to animality, the category
of animality and nature here, has served the most heinous practices, still spoken of by Bataille in terms of animals.

And this, finally, despite the return to nature and animality in sovereignty, marking a difference, for Bataille, that repeats the entire course of hatred and domination:

> There is no question that primary prohibitions concerning the races have
> the most *inhuman* consequences (on the more or less human scale, noth-
> ing is more *animal* than Auschwitz). It is humiliating for the species to find
> in contempt for the other's animality an opportunity to slide toward a
> lower—and the least pardonable—brutality. . . . From the bottom to the top
> of the scale, the impulses are of the same nature: it is never a question of
> anything else but putting a check on animality everywhere it appears.
> (Bataille, *AS*, II, 334–35)

Instead, we might say, humanity and nature were always within this play of
contradictions and transgressions:

> The human world is finally but a hybrid of transgression and prohibition, so
> that the word *human* always denotes a *system* of contradictory impulses,
> some depending on those that they neutralize but never entirely eliminate,
> and others delivering a violence mixed with the certainty of peacefulness
> that will follow. Hence the word *human* never denotes, as simpleminded
> people imagine, a stabilized position, but rather an apparently precarious
> equilibrium that distinguishes the human quality. The word *man* is always
> connected with an *impossible* combination of movements that destroy one
> another. (Bataille, *AS*, III, 342)

At stake is the human under the sign of the curse, a curse that wounds
and destroys many different kinds of victims—I emphasize *kinds*: women,
animals, members of other races, members of "other kinds," "other tribes,"
strangers. I forbear taking up Bataille's *anthropology*, leaving that to others,
the possibility that this account after Lévi-Strauss is a replay of the dominations Bataille asks us to situate ourselves against. The binary oppositions of

civilized and primitive, human and animal, replay in a fundamental and un-recuperable way the oppositions of master-slave against which exuberance and abundance are arrayed. The human *is not* the animal; the subjective *is not* the natural. Except that we return to our animal sides, which we never left, cannot leave, know that we cannot leave, and we return to nature under the sign of the curse. But this curse, I would say if Bataille does not, curses the binary oppositions between humanity and nature, nature given and nature cursed, replaces them with transgressions and abundance.

It is as if we come to know, in our refusal to return to it, that nature given, *merely* natural, including the *merely* animal, is given by a hateful refusal to respond to the good. It is as if the curse, which curses victims and animals and women along with countless others, in the name of the curse of humanity, reveals the possibility that the good haunts being, nature, animals, and humans everywhere, in and as prohibition, in and as victimization, but also in and as love, cherishment, and more. We are cursed to respond to the good, cursed to touch things in the name of the good. This curse is cherishment and sacrifice together, is plenishment in the earth. We discover, in the curse, the collapse of all the binary oppositions into something beautiful everywhere in the earth.

The consciousness in which humanity knows that it has left animality behind, and cannot return, the consciousness of the curse, is the consciousness that humanity works under the sign of the good, not in the neutrality or ethical emptiness of being. With this consciousness, denied at first to animals, to nature, to being, we return together with the curse to know and experience nature, and animals, and being all exposed to the good. All. We cannot aspire to return to *mere* animality, to *mere* nature. But we return to nature, transfigured by the curse, and the good, return seeking sovereignty. Sovereignty now, general economy, the endless circulation of goods, is ethical, the circulation of *goods*. The remaining question, after Bataille and Nietzsche, is whether sovereignty belongs to human beings only. My reply is that just as the word human is not simple-minded, but includes an impossible combination of movements, so with animals, and nature, and every other kind. All gifts from nature, from the good.

Gifts. Bataille speaks of gift-giving as expenditure without return, equates *gift-giving* with "squandering without reciprocation" (Bataille, *AS*, I, 38). This allows him to link the activities of rulers and merchants with the sovereignty of general economy. "The Aztec 'merchant' did not sell; he practiced the *gift-exchange*: He received riches as a *gift* from the 'chief of men' (from the sovereign, whom the Spanish called the *king*); *he made a present* of these riches to the lords of the lands he visited" (Bataille, *AS*, I, 65). And it allows him to link sovereignty with gift economies, though not without a certain return. "To give is obviously to lose, but the loss apparently brings a profit to the one who sustains it" (Bataille, *AS*, I, 70). My concern in this chapter is with abundance, interpreting it as general economy. Like Bataille, and through Bataille, I understand abundance to be related to general economy and heterogeneity, desire and intimacy, all related to giving, the gifts of nature, the gift of beauty.

I will come to art and beauty in just a moment. Here I am exploring the relation between the gift and general economy, on the one hand abundance, profusion, heterogeneity, on the other, expenditure without return, profitlessly. I interpret abundance and heterogeneity as beyond measure—that is, beyond oppositions and relations. But nothing can be, can be thought and gathered, without relation and measure. It follows that general economy is not something we can choose over or instead of restricted economy, but belongs to and circulates within restricted economies, their disturbances and displacements, the interruption of choices where we are surrounded by choices. We cannot choose general economy; we cannot choose not to choose; choice belongs to restricted economy.

I take Bataille to pursue a similar thought but to do so frequently in contexts that restore bininess to the possibility of general economy. For this reason, I take Bataille's account of gift economy to need reworking. Potlatch, gift economies, still retain expectation of return, forcing us to deny their sovereignty. Giving in gift economies is a loss that brings a profit. Against this view, Hyde speaks of the gift as always moving, continuing to move.

Perhaps the issue is as follows: Bataille denies that any thing or economy can be both restricted and general economy at once. "It is contradictory to try to be unlimited and limited at the same time, and the result is comedy. The gift does not mean anything from the standpoint of general economy; there is dissipation only for the giver" (Bataille, *AS*, I, 70). This returns gifts to restricted economies, denies that the circulation of gifts belongs to general economy. Hyde's words are quite different: "It is the assumption of this book that a work of art is a gift, not a commodity. Or, to state the modern case with more precision, that works of art exist simultaneously in two 'economies,' a market economy and a gift economy" (Hyde, *G*, xi); in my terms here, in general and restricted economy.

Heidegger suggests something similar in speaking of the giving rather than the gift—the *es gibt*—of Being, saying that even familiar things are unfamiliar, strange, circulating, I would say, in strange and heterogeneous economies, not just the restricted economies in which we know them. Things, objects of use and natural things, all things we know and experience, move and are held fast in restricted economies, but also, in the name of Being, the gift of Being, are given in strange, uncanny, and unfamiliar movements and circulations. General economy circulates heterogeneity.

What makes a gift economy general economy—and perhaps potlatch was not such an economy—is that the gifts continue to move in circulation, are not stopped and stocked up. I add that all economies, all restricted economies, circulate goods and things that continue to move, that continue to bear the marks of heterogeneity, circulating beyond any boundaries, categories, or measures. We may recall another example from Bataille, a contaminated and dangerous example, recalling that one of the most remarkable gift economies he mentions is the gift economy of women named as the incest taboo. Women must be given away in order that women will be returned. Social rules describe the restricted economy of the exchange of women.

Can one circulate women as if they were things? Can one circulate things as if they were commodities? Here gifts belong exclusively to restricted economies, defined by codes of use and reciprocation, with penalties and expectations. Even so, women circulate in their exchanges beyond any codes and measures, marking the very limit of exchange. Bataille speaks of this in relation to eroticism, in which all codes and rules of exchange vanish into the curse of prohibition, erotic activities still practiced within their prohibition, defying the hold of rules within the forcefulness of the curse.

Against even this reading, I recall Wittig's and Irigaray's rejection of the exchange economy of women. "What does women being exchanged mean if not that they are dominated?" (Wittig, *SM*, 31–32); "the possibility of our social life, of our culture, depends upon a ho(m)mo-sexual monopoly?" (Irigaray, *WM*, 171). Without rejecting the domination and monopoly, I add that the circulation of women in exchange economies always exceeds any restriction, displays the circulation of general economy. Within the domination of women, circulated among men as gifts, where men monopolize the social control of reproduction and kinship, women circulate too quickly, beyond social control—frequently leading to their destruction: women bear the cost of their own excessive circulation, perhaps of other excessive circulations— undermining men's control of the social contract, moving men into other excessive circulations. And other circulations as well, around men and women, perhaps children, and others, animals and others, other excessive circulations within culture and without.

I interrupt this reading of the gift in Bataille to follow Hyde a bit further. For although I read his understanding of the movement of the gift into general economy, he does not go so far. For one thing, he distinguishes between a market economy and a gift economy as if we may (and must) choose one over the other. And he defines a gift in such a way that it is not, for example, a commodity. "There are several distinct senses of 'gift' . . . but common to each of them is the notion that a gift is a thing we do not get by our own efforts. We cannot buy it; we cannot acquire it through an act of will. It is bestowed upon us" (Hyde, *G*, xi). I respond that we can buy it but it exceeds any price. Works of art are bought and sold. We can steal or destroy works of art as we choose. But they, and other things, exceed our accumulations and destructions. Gifts are bought and sold but not as gifts. I might add a reference to grace, given from God, which on some versions comes to us regardless of our efforts, as a gift, but toward which we apply our efforts nevertheless. We cannot place the gift of grace in a binary relation to our will, as if we may sit around placidly hoping to receive grace. Yet the gift does not follow from or produce our efforts. It runs on another track, one that cannot be severed from the world in which we live and work. "Unwork" is not not-work. Gift economy is not not restricted economy, not unrestricted economy, not even restricted economy's other.

The movement of the gift takes place in and joins the gift's circulation regardless of any market or restricted economy. "Regardless" here is a powerful and enigmatic idea. It is not that the gift circulates and moves against the restrictions of restricted economy. Sometimes, as in the market economy of works of art, museums and collectors, restricted economies are the form in which works of art circulate in general economy, circulate beyond any restriction. I add even the stocking up of works of art in museum basements and storehouses, seldom to be seen. Some visitors go down to see them, others remember them, still others seek them. It is impossible to restrict the circulation of works of art, and women, and anything else in such a way as to stop the movement of general economy. The gift that moves is not in this sense *outside* restricted economy but circulates its inner and excessive heterogeneity.

Hyde says something similar in concluding *The Gift*:

> It has been the implication of much of this book that there is an irreconcilable conflict between gift exchange and the market, and that, as a consequence, the artist in the modern world must suffer a constant tension between the gift sphere to which his work pertains and the market society which is his context. . . .
>
> My position has changed somewhat. I still believe that the primary commerce of art is a gift exchange, that unless the work is the realization of the artist's gift and unless we, the audience, can feel the gift it carries, there is no art; I still believe that a gift can be destroyed by the marketplace. But I no longer feel the poles of this dichotomy to be so strongly opposed. (Hyde, *G*, 273)

He presents the relation between gift economy—gift *exchange*, I must note, insisting on a return—and market economy as a dichotomy, if not quite so strong an opposition as he may have suggested earlier. Gift and market economy are dichotomies, binary oppositions, if not quite so strong an opposition as may be supposed. And so with general and restricted economy. But if we understand that goods circulate beyond any restriction although restrictions attempt to hold them fast, if we understand that circulation and restriction are not dichotomies or oppositions, nor even two sides that work together in a relation, but disturbances, displacements, disruptions, then art like everything else, every gift, including grace, falls into and is seized by market and other exchange and restricted economies, always to exceed them in its circulation. What is striking, I would say, about art is not its peculiar and unique circulation, but the mystique and aura it has taken on in the world, Western and otherwise, marking the general and excessive circulation of works of art. Something in art reveals its general economy, its giving, moving, beyond the hold of the market or the academy. And it is this movement, this giving and giving again, that makes those for whom everything is useful find art contaminated beyond measure. Even those who fail to care for it recognize, at least in others, the gift of art. And similarly, even those who fail to care for the good recognize in different places in the world, and others, gifts from the good. Even in their denials.

The gift in Hyde and Bataille—returning from my interruption—remains in both general and restricted economy in a somewhat different sense of *both* than given by the idea of general economy as I understand it. General and restricted economy remain dichotomies, binary oppositions, where the giving—not the exchange of gifts, but their movement—undermines the restrictions, exceeds the restrictions. The difficulty of thinking of gifts as belonging to two economies suggests that both are restricted and the gift reflects both sets of restrictions. Bataille speaks of this as the return in status and power given in return to the giver of the gift. I understand the general economy of the gift as knowing nothing of returns, neither a return nor not a return, neither market nor some other economy, but at the same time every economy, beyond economy, no economy. The gift is given from nowhere, is nothing, circulates goods that already circulate. This will take us back to nothing. For the moment I return to art.

Art. Bataille speaks of art in relation to sovereignty, the sovereignty that is nothing: the sovereign writer and artist in our time. In archaic societies in which sovereignty belonged to sovereigns, the artist, even the sacred artist, could not be sovereign in virtue of art. In our time, however, a consequence of the profaning of art and "The Poverty of 'Art for Art's Sake'" (Bataille, *AS*, III, 418), and perhaps after the transformations wrought by Romanticism, art has become the historical site of sovereignty, for example in Heidegger, perhaps for others. "If art is heir to the sovereignty of the kings and of God, this is because sovereignty never had anything in it but general subjectivity (except for that power over things that was attributed just as arbitrarily to sovereignty as to the operations of magic)" (Bataille, *AS*,

III, 419). Bataille speaks of this sovereignty as pertaining to the moment, the instant, the nothing of subjectivity. Art escapes from the world of accumulation into sovereignty.

I have spoken of the gift of beauty, given from the good, in art. Art is given in the name of something good, possibly without rank, possibly knowing nothing of high or low. Art is given in the name of the good, possibly without exclusion, though certainly with the destructions required to build. And certainly art has served sovereign masters, kings and states, has given itself to corporate powers, has allowed itself to be restricted, has circulated itself in restricted economies. As if it might have done otherwise. The gift of beauty in art does not resist these restrictions, does not assert the sovereignty of the moment against the restrictions of accumulation. The gift in art, of art, of beauty in art is in the work, given as the work, circulates in works, in restricted economies, but bearing within these works an abundance, a general circulation, beyond, exceeding the restrictions, carried in a desire, a love, a cherishment beyond the love for possessions and wealth.

I must add immediately, in case I am understood to institute another binary dichotomy between art and things, that we know in art, we have allowed ourselves to see and feel in art, something of an excessiveness that belongs to all things, even to commodities, everywhere in every place. But art reaches out and touches those things and places, and moves them in general circulation, a circulation beyond the identities of things and places at the same time that the general circulation is restricted to certain classes and kinds of people who are permitted to own and disseminate works of art. General circulation, beyond identity and place, has nothing to do with overcoming restrictions, with escaping from dominations. But it displaces the right with which we impose restrictions.

Nothing. This nothing, which art knows of overcoming restrictions, is the nothing of sovereignty. Sovereignty is NOTHING. (Bataille, *AS*, III, 430). Sovereignty, general economy, the good, all are nothing, all are interruptions. Restricted economies impose the restrictions that make possible and institute the identities of things as the things they are. But art, and general economy in and out of art, know that things are not "the things they are," not "just" the things they are, are always in other circulations beyond any restrictions, intermediary movements. The nothing of general economy is the nonidentity of intermediary figures, with the supplement that every thing in every place is an intermediary figure, circulates in general economy. Art shows that circulation in lifting any thing, or if not a thing, any act or material or configuration, lifting any of these into places we and they and others could not have imagined them to be found: on the canvas or stage, in our ears rather than our eyes, in our dreams. We dream of, we live surrounded by NOTHING. It calls us, touches us, draws us toward and away, leads us to restricted economies. Its touch is the gift of the good. It is linked inextricably with desire. Its name, for me, is exposure.

We are exposed in our being in the world, among things in their places, to a disturbing movement and circulation, exposed to other possibilities, called and touched in our exposure, yet deeply and profoundly touched by, exposed to, nothing. We are exposed to the inexhaustible possibilities in things where at any moment, in any place, these are nothing. This nothing, this exposure, is the good. The gift of this book is the idea that this exposure shows itself in art, happens in works of art. It might be called truth, truth happening in the work of art. I call it the good: in art it is beauty, the gift of the good. Always nothing.

I have spoken of the stocking up of time in works, the holding of the general circulation of things in place, the creating of identities. The creating of these identities is the creation of something, some things in their places. And we can privilege such identities as we must in building works, give precedence to the identities of things as things. Yet general economy is nothing, resists this precedence. I have spoken of this resistance as art, the nothing that is art beyond art, *poiēsis* beyond *technē*.

I interrupt this idea of resistance with two artistic references, two ideas of works in time unknown to the West under the sign of history. One example is that of Australian Aboriginal art, an art produced by peoples who suffered terribly under the destructions of Westerners who themselves had suffered exile from the West but who remained in its shadow. Aboriginal peoples were exterminated, and for a while their glorious painted works were treated as primitive relics, "fetishes." The Western market knows no bounds, however, and tribal art has been exhibited, collected, and produced for consumption on that market (Fry and Willis, *AA;* Ross, *AIS*, 642–43).

I will speak of collection in a moment, within this interruption. But I am concerned with a moment in Fry and Willis's discussion that marks something too little known to Western audiences. "The *right* of a culture, like Australian Aboriginal cultures, to treat many of its artifacts as ephemeral and subordinate to the continuity of symbolic performance (to ceremony, for example) is thus refused in the ahistorical drive to preserve objects as arrested signs of a commodified materiality" (Fry and Willis, *AA;* Ross, *AIS*, 644). Western collecting seeks to hold the artifact fast, collected and preserved, partly for the market—which circulates it beyond any place in which it is collected—and partly in a certain image of art and time. Aboriginal artists produced their works on tent flaps, wintering over in the north of Australia, and when the winter ended, left them behind.

I am interested in collecting, but for the moment I am interested in the temporality at work in Western and Aboriginal life, especially in relation to art. For in the name of art, Western collectors hope to preserve, while

Aboriginal artists had no interest in preservation. But in the name of every-day life, the market or accumulation, Western builders destroy old buildings and places, have little interest in preservation. Western history is a history of destruction, losses of the past, catastrophes, joined with endless struggles to remember and preserve. Death walks the streets of the West. In the name of everyday life, nomadic tribes go on, telling tales of the past in oral narratives, but having little need to preserve the past in artifacts or places.

I offer another example, this time from Bali. Balinese tribal life knew nothing of historical time, nothing of successive time, marked a cyclical time with multiple revolutions, but without a language or culture that could rep-resent years or epochs or generations. Balinese music repeats a similar tem-porality, as if beginning and ending had no artifactual representation. Rather, the music begins in different voices working in different cycles and rhythms, and ends when it ends. Time is not the same for all peoples. The stocking up of time in art, or artifacts, in histories and things, is not universal. Nor is diachrony.

I do not mean to suggest that nomadic and tribal lives take place in gen-eral economies while Western lives belong to restricted economies. These are all restricted. Nor do I mean to suggest that some are better than others, as if I owned a general restricted economy. Rather, I am interested in the rela-tion of art and general economy to nothing, the nothing that Aboriginal peo-ple took artifacts to be, the nothing that Balinese people took time to be, a nothing that reappears in music, a nothing that shows itself in the ephemer-ality of Aboriginal art. In tribal art and life, in Western art and life as well, the nothing that resists the identities of things and tools, the nothing of abun-dance, shows itself especially poignantly in art, though it shows itself else-where, everywhere, in every place.

Here I conclude my discussion of this nothing everywhere in relation to art by ending my procrastination on collecting works of art. For in this con-text, works of art are nothing, and in this nothing we find their gift, the giv-ing of abundance, general economy. The collection of art, I suggest, is the refusal within restricted economy to let art pass away into nothing, into gen-eral economy. The collectors of art—and I mean to include the preservers of whom Heidegger speaks, art galleries and auctions, museums and private col-lectors in the West, but also oral narratives and tribal ceremonies, dances in which artifacts are employed—is always the holding of the nothing, the gen-eral circulation in which art transpires, against its vanishing. I propose an in-version of the Western idea of masterpiece art that works of art resist the play of time in their own atemporality. I have noted this in relation to Gadamer, who understands the temporality of history and art to give rise to the idea of play and art free from the restrictions of time and place: time without time, time as nothing in art. But that is my point, the atemporality of art is nothing. The collection of works of art against the ravages of time holds back nothing in two senses: time will work its destructions no matter what; and what art marks in its collection is nothing. Everything belongs to restricted economies, and collection seeks to take works of art—not things at all—to hold them in restricted economies.

Works of art, we say, are not things. To collect them is to collect them as things. To criticize them, to admire them, to restitute them back to their owners, is to treat them as things. Works of art are nothing. General economy is nothing. All we can do is to work in restricted economies. And in such restricted economies, the gift of beauty, the giving of the good in art, is nothing.

Here I return to Fry and Willis's suggestion that Western collectors impose a certain view of art and things upon a culture that has chosen quite differently. I add that ethnography is a form of collecting: " 'Cultures' are ethnographic collections" (Clifford, *CAC;* Ross, *AIS*, 627). In our time, however, collecting and the places of works are no longer to be taken for granted in Western terms. "The 'proper' place of many objects in museums is not subject to contest" (Clifford, *CAC;* Ross, *AIS*, 639). The proper place of works of art is displaced, unknown, placed back in the circulations from which collecting withdrew them, for a while. But desire, among others, makes it impossible to hold anything fast, especially works of art.

With this recognition that what collecting seeks to gain is nothing, that art-collecting reveals the impossibility of turning nothing into something—an impossibility that takes place everywhere and all the time, for a while. Time can be stocked up against the event for a while, but not for ever. General economy interrupts the restrictions. We are exposed to general economy, and in this way we are exposed to nothing. Always something. Given everywhere. In art.

CHAPTER 8

Exposure

Levinas speaks of subjectivity as *une exposition, sans merci* [a merciless exposure] (Levinas, *OB*, xlii), as "an exception putting out of order the conjunction of essence, entities and the 'difference'" (Levinas, *OB*, xli), as "a passivity more passive than all passivity" (Levinas, *OB*, 14). The good appears—or disappears—in an exposure beyond being, not being-other *(autre)*, but *otherwise (au-delà) than being* (Levinas, *OB*, 3). The good shows itself—speaks or says—in the face, "ordered toward the face of the other" (Levinas, *OB*, 11), calling forth a response from "the responsible one" (Levinas, *OB*, 11).

I speak of the gift of the good as exposure to abundance without exceptional regard to subjectivity. I speak of this exposure to the other, to others, as inexhaustible responsiveness to their touch, in the skin as well as in the face or gaze, a responsiveness everywhere, in every place, where bodies touch, which becomes responsibility for human beings under law. Wherever things are exposed to others they respond, are called upon to respond, respond whenever and wherever they are touched, in their abundance, by the abundance of others.

For Levinas, the responsible one, the subject, is hostage to the other, pervaded by "vulnerability, exposure to outrage, to wounding, passivity more passive than all patience" (Levinas, *OB*, 15). I understand these terms in memory of Anaximander, where all things are hostage throughout the ordinance of time to their injustices toward each other. All things. Every thing in every place is vulnerable to the touch of others, exposed to them in justice and injustice, wounded by others, wounded in itself, in its place, by the others, by the sacrifices it has imposed on others, wounded by the wounds it has imposed on others, exposed to them in a touch, a wounding, a caress more passive than any passivity, than the passivity within the binary of activity-passivity. This is a passivity after Heidegger's letting-be, an exposure to and in abundance, beyond abundance, adding that passivity, exposure, and abundance are all from the good. Letting-be is called forth as a gift from the good in abundance, expressed as exposure to touch, in proximity.

Exposure is the "veracity of saying *[dire]*" (Levinas, *OB*, 15) if not the said *(dit)*. I have understood this privileging of language, of speaking within and before the human subject, as privileging The Hand in Heidegger, and with it repeating the privilege of The Human. I have found the same privilege at work in Levinas while the call of the good makes every privilege suspect.[1] I resist privileges of hands over paws, fangs, and claws, humans over animals, animals over stones, speak of exposure as touch, open to and responding to the touch of others, in proximity, without subjectivity still "a sacrifice without reserve" (Levinas, *OB*, 15), without qualification, a vulnerability beyond measure. I do not leave it at that, however, for I acknowledge the remarkable link Levinas draws in *exposition* between exposure and revelation, truth, representation, expression, if not saying. In exposure to abundance the other shows, presents, displays, expresses itself and its heterogeneities, its abundance. Abundance abounds in exposure. Exposure exposes itself and others in exposition, in rift-design, in work. In this exposition, we come to art, to where this exposure takes us, to work. I delay this movement for a while.

For the moment I pursue some themes in Levinas foreshadowing exposure. For exposure precedes truth, precedes *alētheia*, as *alētheia* precedes familiar and adequate truth. Truth comes forth in response to exposure. The opening onto Being in which truth arises is older, before, that arising, is given from the good. Levinas speaks of this, again in relation to the knowing subject, but also the "soul" *(âme)*:

> It is then necessary, in order that truth come about, that in one way or another this ex-ception of inwardness be recuperated, that the exception enter under the rule, that within the being exposed be found the subject of knowledge, and the pulsation and respiration of the "soul" belong to or come back to being as a whole. Truth can consist only in the exposition of being to itself, in self-consciousness. (Levinas, *OB*, 28)

It is necessary that truth come about, and that this coming emerge from an exposure that shows, reveals, in exposure|exposition *(exposition)*, to the soul in respiration. Truth and knowledge come about from the exposure of things to one another, not just subjects to objects or to themselves, not just consciousness or self-consciousness, but in the exposure of all things to each other, in proximity, in the pulsation and respiration of "souls" everywhere, in memory of *Phaedrus* where *psuchē* has care for all things everywhere. Truth and knowledge come as gifts from a more primordial exposure, the proximity of things to each other, affecting, influencing each other in an abundance before knowledge or truth.

Whitehead speaks of this proximity as prehension, and it carries all the force of Levinas's exposure with the exception of consciousness, a late entry in the circulation of goods in their exposure to one another. And it speaks of souls in every place. "Actual entities involve each other by reason of their prehensions of each other. There are thus real individual facts of the togetherness of actual entities, which are real, individual, and particular, in the same sense in which actual entities and the prehensions are real, individual, and particular" (Whitehead, *PR*, 20).[2] Throughout the universe, things are exposed to one another in the double sense that they are influenced by others, exposed to others, subjects and objects for each other, and that this exposure, this prehension, is both from the one to the other, directly and unmediated, and mediated through every other relevant other, an abundance of abundances. The world is made up of prehensions and their prehensions, prehensions of prehensions, abundances of abundances, exposures to exposure, expositions of exposition. Prehension is an intermediary figure between the one and the other, in circulation, intermediary because it retains its abundance within the circulation, does not presuppose reciprocity or totality.

Dewey speaks of experience as abundance preceding knowledge and truth, speaks of immediate and reflective experience, of things had before they are known. "[T]hings are objects to be treated, used, acted upon and with, enjoyed and endured, even more than things to be known. They are things *had* before they are things cognized" (Dewey, *EN*, 21). They are had in all the ways they may be had, in the ways they may be touched, abundantly and qualitatively, in feeling, before they are known, and knowledge, truth, emerges from this having, touching, from experience's abundance.

He speaks of the "integrated unity" of experience (Dewey, *EN*, 9) to resist the dichotomies of reflection, leading to the idea of an experience underlying art. "In short, art, in its form, unites the very same relation of doing and undergoing, outgoing and incoming energy, that makes an experience to be an experience" (Dewey, *AE*, 48; Ross, *AIS*, 208). The emphasis on unity and integration suggests exclusion, setting aside whatever lacks integration. "In such experiences, every successive part flows freely, without seam and without unfilled blanks, into what ensues" (Dewey, *AE*, 36; Ross, *AIS*, 206). Yet Dewey's words may be read inclusively, expressing abundance: "there are no holes, mechanical junctions, and dead centers when we have *an* experience" (Dewey, *AE*, 36; Ross, *AIS*, 206); "it is experience freed from the forces that impede and confuse its development as experience; freed, that is, from factors that subordinate an experience as it is directly had to something beyond itself. To esthetic experience, then, the philosopher must go to understand what experience is" (Dewey, *AE*, 274; Ross, *AIS*, 219). Art exposes us to abundance, to beauty in nature and experience. We are exposed to this abundance everywhere and in every place, though reflection sometimes blocks abundance, blunts exposure, obscures beauty.

Truth comes about in the circulation of abundances, in havings and prehensions, the exposures of things in proximity, open to the others, revealed and revealing, in a responsiveness without limits that can respond only in limits. That responsiveness is exposure, prehension, exposition, before truth, giving rise to the possibility of truth. Unveiling builds on exposure, proximity. Things must be in the vicinity of each other, exposed to one another, must touch and respond to one another, if the one can emerge in its truth for the other. We touch things inexhaustibly, and in that touch the possibility of truth emerges, a double emergence from exposure.

This exposure is given from the good. If truth is a gift from the good—and that is how I understand it, though I will not pursue truth further here—it is given within being, the exposition of beings to one another, given from the proximity of things to one another, given as touch, exposure, vulnerability. All these are Levinas's terms except touch, resisted by him because exposure, obsession, is not reciprocal, is "non-reciprocity itself" (Levinas, *OB*, 84). He gives up the thought of exposure as touch as slipping toward reciprocity, toward quiddity. "Maternity, vulnerability, responsibility, proximity, contact—sensibility can slip toward touching, palpation, openness upon . . . , pure knowing taking images from the 'intact being,' informing itself about the palpable quiddity of things" (Levinas, *OB*, 76 [his ellipses]). Yet he speaks of contact:

> contact with the other. To be in contact is neither to invest the other and annul his alterity, nor to suppress myself in the other. In contact itself the touching and the touched separate, as though the touched moved off, was always already other, did not have anything common with me. As though its singularity, thus non-anticipatable and consequently not representable, responded only to designation. (Levinas, *OB*, 86)

I fear that singularity, here, reduces abundance in the name of heterogeneity, an alterity without abundance. I understand touch in a proximity beyond singularity toward abundance, exposed to abundance, inexhaustibly.

I come to the exposition of this chapter, the gift of beauty, understanding beauty as abundance and art as exposure|exposition, given toward beauty. Abundance is given as beauty, and more. Here I leave aside the more, remain with beauty and art. I follow Heidegger to speak of the possibility that what happens in the work of art exposes us to abundance, to the general economy of the good, exposes us in art's exposition. I add to Heidegger's rift-design the abundance of the earth coming into the world as traces cut into this abundance, the exposition of *mimēsis*.

But first, I recall Levinas's refusal of the gift of art as from the good. "In the inexhaustible diversity of works, that is, in the *essential renewal* of art, colors, forms, sounds, words, buildings . . . recommence being" (Levinas, *OB*, 40).[3] How, I ask, can the art criticized by Plato as *mimēsis*, whatever *mimēsis* may be—certainly not "imitation"—put itself back into beings without echoes of something beyond, *au-delà*, immeasurable? How can *mimēsis*, even as imitation, repetition, restitution, restoration, how can any of these "re's" reassemble being without exposition|exposure? *Mimēsis* touches, exposes abundance. Art exposes us to things in abundance. Art exposes us to madness, to the anarchy of general economy, to heterogeneity, to ecstasy. To the wandering of exposition in art, as *mimēsis*, to the wandering of exposure, its ineluctable abundance. I insist that *mimēsis*, traditionally read as the contamination of reason's truth by subtraction, adds to things what was already theirs, in their abundance, and does so in virtue of its exposure. *Mimēsis* as exposition exposes us to abundance's abundance, circulates as given from the good.

The good here is not good—that is, better than bad. The good to which we are exposed in every place gives the gift of judging, showing, exposing good and bad, given within abundance, as our exposition of abundance. In this way, abundance is anarchy, anarchic, heterogeneous. What Levinas says of art, including music and song, denies that art exposes us to heterogeneity, remains untouched by Nietzsche's reminders of Dionysian madness and obscurity, exposed in music and dance. We may remind ourselves that music continually fails to be contained under beauty, along with the other arts, which also fail to be contained, reducing their exposure to the world, but repeatedly and in the most accumulative exchange economies open our exposure to abundance.

Levinas relates to art through shame, recalling Kierkegaard, a combination of dislike and disapproval, recalling Hegel. Art is bad; we who enjoy it too much are wicked; What would be more likely, even responsible, than to bring it to an end? Resisting Nietzsche:

> There is something wicked and egoist and cowardly in artistic enjoyment. There are times when one can be ashamed of it, as of feasting during a plague.
> Art then is not committed by virtue of being art. But for this reason art is not the supreme value of civilization, and it is not forbidden to conceive a stage in which it will be reduced to a source of pleasure—which one cannot contest without being ridiculous—having its place, but only a place, in

> man's happiness. Is it presumptuous to denounce the hypertrophy of art in
> our times when, for almost everyone, it is identified with spiritual life? (Lev-
> inas, *RS*, 142)

These words were written in 1948, replying to Sartre's idea of committed literature. Levinas speaks to his time as dogmatic about art when it no longer
seemed to matter. "It is generally, dogmatically, admitted that the function
of art is expression, and that artistic expression rests on cognition. . . .
Where common language abdicates, a poem or a painting speaks" (Levinas,
RS, 130); "One then has the right to ask if the artist really knows and
speaks" (Levinas, *RS*, 130); "The painting then does not lead us beyond the
given reality, but somehow to the hither side of it. It is a symbol in reverse"
(Levinas, *RS*, 136); "And perhaps we are wrong to name art and poetry that
exceptional event—that sovereign forgetfulness—which frees language
from its servitude towards the structures in which the *said* prevails" (Levinas, *SM*, 153). Perhaps we claim too much for art to free us from the world
of law, to take us beyond binary oppositions, goods and bads, to the good beyond the said.

Levinas continues the last passage with a more Hegelian suggestion:
"Perhaps Hegel was right as far as art is concerned. What matters—call it poetry or whatever—is that a meaning should be utterable beyond the confines
of Hegel's completed discourse, that a meaning forgetful of the presupposi-
tions of that discourse should become *fable*" (Levinas, *SM*, 153). What matters is the possibility of a meaning beyond, given from the good. But it will
most likely not be art; art is not spiritual enough.

The completeness of art stands in the way of its commitment, of its ethical responsibility, of its reach beyond:

> a work would not belong to art if it did not have this formal structure of
> completion, if at least in this way it were not disengaged. We have to un-
> derstand the value of this disengagement, and first of all its meaning. Is to
> disengage oneself from the world always to go *beyond*, toward the region of
> Platonic ideas and toward the eternal which towers above the world? Can
> one not speak of a disengagement on the hither side—of an interruption of
> time by a movement going on on the hither side of time, in its "interstices"?
> (Levinas, *RS*, 131)

This direct response to Sartre on the ethical-political commitment of literature is plausible enough: the atemporality of art, its suspension of time in
work, weakens its historical relevance. This is a common complaint, hardly
worth the effort to repeat it. Much more powerful is the claim that art remains on the hither side of time and the good, an interruption without exposure. "Art . . . contrasts with knowledge. It is the very event of obscuring,

a descent of the night, an invasion of shadow. . . . [A]rt does not belong to the order of revelation. Nor does it belong to that of creation, which moves in just the opposite creation" (Levinas, *RS*, 132).

All in terms of a hostile reading of *mimēsis*:

> The most elementary procedure of art consists in substituting for the object its image. Its image, and not its concept. A concept is the object *grasped*, the intelligible object. Already by action we maintain a living relationship with a real object; we grasp it, we conceive it. The image neutralizes this real relationship . . .
>
> . . . the disinterestedness of the artist scarcely deserves this name. For it excludes freedom, which the notion of disinterestedness implies. Strictly speaking, it also excludes bondage, which presupposes freedom. In image does not engender a *conception*, as do scientific cognition and truth; it does not involve Heidegger's "letting be," *Sein-lassen*, in which objectivity is transmuted into power. An image marks a hold over us rather than our initiative, a fundamental passivity. (Levinas, *RS*, 132)

I wonder if the passivity we experience before art might be the passivity beyond passivity of vulnerability and exposure to which Levinas leads us in his later writing. Here, image and vision share the betrayals of art:

> To see is to be in a world that is entirely *here* and self-sufficient. Any vision beyond what is given remains within what is given. The infinity of space, like the infinity of the signified referred to by the sign, is equally absent from the here below. Vision is a relation with a being such that the being attained through it precisely appears as the world. Sound, for its part, appeals to intuition and can be given. This naturally involves the primacy of vision with respect to the other senses. And on the primacy of vision rests the universality of art. By creating beauty out of nature, art calms and quietens it. All the arts, even those based on sound, create silence. (Levinas, *TW*, 147)

Levinas seems not to share Merleau-Ponty's understanding of the painter's task:

> To unveil the means, visible and no otherwise, by which it makes itself a mountain before our eyes. Light, lighting, shadows, reflections, color, all the objects of his quest are not altogether real objects; like ghosts, they have only visual existence. In fact they exist only at the threshold of profane vision; they are not seen by everyone. (Merleau-Ponty, *EM*, 166; Ross, *AIS*, 287)

Merleau-Ponty wrote these words in 1964, perhaps with Levinas in mind. So Levinas could not have seen them when he wrote so unyieldingly of images and beauty. "Beauty is being dissimulating its caricature, covering over or absorbing its shadow" (Levinas, *RS*, 137). Nor when he expressed his shame at boundless pleasure in art, reminding us again of Kierkegaard:

> Art is not serious enough, too charming, irresponsible, brings us un-burdened freedom, recalling us to shame. Art brings into the world the ob-scurity of fate, but it especially brings the irresponsibility that charms as a lightness and grace. It frees. To make or to appreciate a novel and a picture is to no longer have to conceive, is to renounce the effort of science, phi-losophy, and action. Do not speak, do not reflect, admire in silence and in peace—such are the counsels of wisdom satisfied before the beautiful (Lev-inas, *RS*, 141).

But he saw them later, and he read Blanchot, speaking of art's betrayal, dwelling on words. "The poetic word *[verbe]* itself can, however, betray itself, become engulfed in order and take on the appearance of a cultural product, a document or testimony. It becomes encouraged, applauded and rewarded, sold, bought, consumed and consoling, talking to itself in the language of a whole people" (Levinas, *SM*, 157). He speaks of betrayal in a voice full of other betrayals:

> language which gives sign without establishing itself in the eternity of the idea it signifies, discontinuous language, is circumvented by that ancillary language which follows in its tracks and never stops speaking. The coherent language in which being (and even "the Being of beings") stretches and ex-tends, is all memory, all anticipation, all eternity. It is never-fading, and al-ways has the last word. It contaminates with logic the ambiguity inscribed in the trace of forgotten discourse and never gives itself up to enigma. As the speaker of truth, how can she be silenced? She recounts, in a consistent manner, the extravagances of her master and is reputed to love wisdom. She derives triumph and presence from narrating the failures, the absences and the escapades of him she serves and spies upon. She has taken stock of the secret places she cannot open and holds the keys to doors which have been destroyed. She is an utterly reliable housekeeper, who supervises the house she rules over and disputes the existence of secret locks.
>
> Housekeeper of Mistress? A marvellous hypocrite! For she loves the madness she keeps watch over. (Levinas, *SM*, 158)

Always the woman who serves the master; always housekeeper or mistress. No other possibilities for her, for us, for art. Levinas speaks of her master key as if he were master, at least as if some truth were master, in a discourse of exposure, perhaps exposure without abundance.

I speak of art as given from the good, circulating as the gift of beauty, given from nature's general economy, nature's abundance. I speak of the gift of beauty remembering the sublime, remembering ugliness, horror, loathing, repugnance, and disgust, represented in art. I speak of art as given from the good remembering other gifts, especially the gift of exposure, revealing, touching other places than art. Perhaps I speak most of exposure, of the diaphoric places, intermediary figures, in which the good exposes itself, in which we find ourselves exposed to it, places between art and philosophy, poetry and music, art and science, and more. The good circulates in intermediary figures, mad, erotic figures around art. I mean to include sexual difference. And I mean not to avoid the contaminations of exposure.

Art is not the only exposure to the good, nor even the "greatest." The good circulates everywhere, in every place and thing. The gift of beauty is not the only gift from the good, not the only ecstasy. The good gives truth and justice among countless others. Western art is not the only exposure to abundance, even within its "greatness," nor is "great" art more abundant, more of such an exposition. Western art has frequently imposed restricted economies on the general economy in which beauty is given as a gift, has restricted the abundance of art; but also frequently calling forth within its restrictions exposure to abundance.

This phenomenon in relation to art, the ways in which the restrictions to which art is subjected, as all things and works are subjected to restrictions, at least in Western art but perhaps everywhere, are ways in which art and other things and works exceed their restrictions. This shows itself, as we have seen, from the beginning in Western thought, in the *diaphora* between art and philosophy, where *poiēsis* opens the space within *technē* of the sacred, magical, excessive, of unlimit within the limits of *technē*. Art is given from the gods, in the inspiration from the Muses, uncontainable within the limits of restricted economy, opening onto a nature of wondrous beauty. This revelation is exposure to art, exposure in art, opening onto nature's abundance, an abundance so uncontainable and unlimited that we cannot face its alterity except in the name of ecstasy. Exposure is excessive, in general economy, to the abundance of abundance—named as alterity and heterogeneity.

Art exceeds its restrictions. *Poiēsis* exceeds *technē*. But this excess is not the imposition of another category, but the exposition of something in the production and recognition of art, present everywhere, named as art within the most pressing of restrictions. Art here exceeds the limits of its category. Foucault speaks of the creation of literature in the age of classical representation as the appearance and preservation of the excess of language. I speak of the excess, abundance, of nature and general economy, of which language's excess is one disciplinary revelation, somewhere between general and restricted economy. The point is that the name of literature, like the name of art, in the West perhaps because of its Greek history, is the repeated name of nature's excess. The name of art, in the *diaphora* between art and philosophy, *poiēsis* and *technē*, names abundance. This is both trait and condition of art, at least as it has been framed in Western thought, and trait and condition of its framing. But we have seen excess and abundance elsewhere in Western thought, in Spinoza and Whitehead, for example. If in Whitehead, abundance is related to beauty, a beauty related to art, in Spinoza it is related to a beauty given in geometry, still abundance and abundance's abundance.

Art has traditionally in Western thought and practice exposed us to abundance. But it has also and in the same ways and places exposed us in endless restrictions of thought, practice, culture, and representation. This intermediary movement between general and restricted economy in relation to art is expressed in Western thought in the thought and practice of art as excess and in the ways in which restricted economies of art expose abundance from within themselves. This touches the pervasive thesis of my understanding of abundance and general economy: that general economy requires restricted economies for its work; that restricted economies expose themselves from within their restrictions to general economy, expose abundance, circulate in general economy. In relation to art, but not art alone, the historical and cultural conditions imposed on art, capturing the works of artists within the dominant codes of a culture, Western culture especially, reveal and express abundance, not only the abundance of art, but of culture, history, and countless other gifts. The gifts of art touch the immeasurable gifts of abundance circulating in general economy. In the West and elsewhere.

The gift of beauty, then, the giving of the good exposed in art, the abundance of gifts showing in the places of art, does not belong to art alone nor to art especially. Beauty is everywhere in abundance. And perhaps it is abundance and general economy with which I am concerned here, more than art, except that general economy cannot be given in general, only under restriction, if it is given at all. The beauty of nature's abundance shows itself in particular places. I speak of art in this book, and of art's exposure to abundance, in the name of something excessive that cannot be revealed except in place, framed in place, in this place framed in art.

I will speak of art and beauty in a moment. But I must speak first of the frame. Works of art are always framed, framed in place, framed as art. And all works are framed; framed as and in the restricted economies they are and inhabit. But the idea of the frame belongs to art, I would say, at least in the West, works framed for display, framed for hanging and show, in exposition. And the idea of the frame has been exposed in relation to art, in Kant and Derrida for example, the frame as *parergon*. Works of art are framed because the frame, what is inside and outside the work, is always explicitly at stake in art. We respond to works of art as if their abundance were unlimited, except for the frame. In this way the stakes of the frame are present in art as they are not so overtly present in science or philosophy, in other genres, transforming the frame and the work in art into intermediary figures. And art itself, together with the work of art, is a frame, another intermediary figure, from the beginning in its intermediary dance with philosophy, reason's frame, exposing the abundance of reason and the good within their restrictions. In this way, perhaps, we may say that art exposes us to abundance in its framing and in the frame it provides to other restricted economies, exposing us to abundance. But I must emphasize again that this abundance does not belong to art alone, nor does art alone expose us to things in their abundance. The good's abundance shows itself in gifts, circulates as gifts, including the gift of beauty among abundant other gifts.

I now consider some of the ways in which art exposes us to things beyond measure, ways I have characterized as the *poiēsis* in *technē*, both intermediary figures, joined by another intermediary figure, that of *diaphora*. These are ways in which art has been understood in the West, and beyond the West, ways in which art has become familiar, always on this reading, exposed, exposing itself, and us, to things in the world, and those things to us, in itself, all exposures given in the name of the good, all unfamiliar, strange, extraordinary, many spoken of by Levinas, far from art. For the moment I follow his language of alterity, recalling that he seems to know nothing of abundance, of general economy, gifts.

Art is *poiēsis*, and more; *technē*, and more. And both *poiēsis* and *technē* are more than art. Between *poiēsis* and *technē*, art and art, is more, the *diaphora* of more, all intermediary figures. Madness, anarchy, ecstasy circulate around *poiēsis*. I wonder if *poiēsis* might be exposure, and in that exposure if we could find the gift of the good. I wonder if *poiēsis* might expose us in art and elsewhere to an endless abundance of goods.

I have joined *poiēsis* with madness and love against the wisdom of *technē*. Above all, I have distinguished *poiēsis* from *technē* on the basis of choice. *Technē* is choice, decision; *poiēsis* is nothing of choice, nothing to choose. But in every choice, in every restriction, is *poiēsis*, the abundance from which the choice comes forth.

Poiēsis is emergence, coming to be, bringing being forth from nonbeing. In this way it is given from nature as the mobility and heterogeneity of *phusis*, moving from and toward itself, endless restlessness. It is given from the abundance of every place, every restriction and work, as the mobility and heterogeneity of every restriction, which does not stay fast, cannot be held firm against the teeming of its departures. Every movement is wandering, a wandering associated with *poiēsis*. I understand this mobility as a double exposure, of things to each other, including the exposure of nature to

humanity, touching, revealing, moving. Movement here is touch and exposure. And of humanity to nature, to the things we reach out to know, to love,
to build. Together with *poiēsis*—and *poiēsis* is in no exceptional way poetry—as *mimēsis*, all the forms of *mimēsis*, countless forms beyond nature's
movements, moving with, alongside, and beyond nature's heterogeneous
circulation. I include in *mimēsis* all the forms of representation, beyond and
including language. I think of *mimēsis* as representation's frames, the exposure of representation to things through the abundance of its frames.

All these frames, all forms of *mimēsis*, touch the world, touch its abundance, as perhaps other forms of touch, including human senses, may not do.
We do not touch things in their abundance when we see them or even run
our hands over them. We are exposed to them indeed, but within our sensory
limits, exposed to them under restriction. We hold them before our eyes,
grasp them with our hands, locate them with our ears, hold them fast in every
case, open them to abundance. But our senses are restricted economies—if
also much more. We belong to restricted economies, listen to this and not
that, smell this and disregard that, are framed by such restricted economies
as if they allowed no other, all the while opening onto other abundances. Prohibition and the curse of which Bataille speaks seem to me to show something other than profitless expenditure. The curse marks the inverse side of
restricted economy, that we restrict and kill what in some profound way has
touched us with its abundance. That we sense the world in the ways we do,
are cursed by our restrictions, opens onto other exposures, the sensuous materiality of *mimēsis*.

Restricted economies are the economies in which we live and work. They
bear within themselves, in every restriction, prohibition, curse, or exclusion,
an inverse movement toward abundance, exposing those who exclude to what
they include, exposing endless heterogeneous possibilities of inclusion in
every exclusion. Exposure to heterogeneity transpires in every place and for
every thing. This includes *poiēsis* and *mimēsis*, includes the abundance of
representation. In this generic sense, the very possibility of restriction presupposes abundance, and in every such restriction we are exposed to abundance. Heidegger says this of equipment. Instruments, tools, and equipment,
all restricted by use, presuppose an abundance of reliability, expose us in their
use to endless possibilities of use, to unknown and heterogeneous uses. In use
we encounter restriction and abundance. In use we are exposed.

Yet the force of use is immense, and we in our everyday distractions may
not give ourselves over to this exposure but may insist on the utility of restrictions. We hammer nails with hammers, not philosophy. Utility has its
uses, and we bend ourselves to those uses in the interest of utility. And well
we should, for that gives us good rather than bad, benefits us enormously. Yet
even in this production of benefits, we know that we might have chosen dif-

ferently, that such a choice was available even if we did not know it. In every choice we are exposed to abundance. Yet we do not know of abundance in ourselves or things, and must learn to release this abundance, even in utility, the multiple and heterogeneous possibilities of use released and excluded in every use. Utility is abundance, and every tool exposes us to abundance as well as, through restriction.

I am speaking of something more far-reaching than utility, more than *poiēsis* and *mimēsis*, closer to representation, where representation is understood as the divided region, intermediary figure, between general and restricted economy, pervading the human and natural worlds. We can restrict only by representation—at least, that is what I mean by representation. We restrict to repeat, to hold. Representation is stocking up time, allowing for repetition. And repetition is representation, repetition of any act or thing held over from past to future. Yet repetition is iteration, and every repetition differs, repeats by difference. The play of repetition and difference—iterability—is representation. The stocking up in representation is releasement and play, difference and heterogeneity. This is why, I believe, abundance may be invincible against the attempt to restrict it. The restriction presupposes it. The repetition evades capture, wanders off in difference.

On this reading, representation is not the *technē* against which *poiēsis* struggles. *Poiēsis* and *technē* are not in opposition, but in *diaphora*, intermediary movements, circulating in general and restricted economy. Representation is this endless intermediary movement of intermediary figures. It belongs, I believe, to natural things and places, is not produced by human beings. The work of nature, in its abundance, is done through representation, repetition with a difference. Things reproduce themselves, reproduce their acts, reproduce their kinds, live repetitively from day to day, opening vistas of alternative and abundant possibilities of other selves, acts, kinds, and lives. This includes stones as well as insects, all enduring, striving to endure as Spinoza says, through repetition and representation. Representation is the play of mobility and restriction around natural kinds, endless and abundant.

And it shows itself everywhere in human life, but especially in the exposure to abundance we know as *poiēsis* and *mimēsis*. I have spoken of these as gifts from the gods, given in inspiration and heterogeneity. We are exposed to abundance through intermediary figures, all belonging to representation, *poiēsis* and *mimēsis*. Plato's critique of *mimēsis* argues for restriction in the name of simplicity, a restriction that knows nothing of abundance without the complicity of *mimēsis*. To the world we know, *phusis* offers endless abundance, and with it, enriching and repeating its abundance, *poiēsis* offers, produces, different abundances. That is what Aristotle and Kant say of *mimēsis*, opening other abundances of nature. The feigned or represented world of *poiēsis* opens vistas of abundance we would not know nature to have within it unless we were God. In this way, we are exposed to abundance's abundance through *poiēsis*.

We are exposed to nature's abundance everywhere, and every natural thing in every place is exposed to that abundance, within itself and touching others. But the abundance of abundance does not show in a time and place except through representation, through *mimēsis* and *poiēsis*. *Poiēsis* opens nature's abundance to other abundances. *Mimēsis*, criticized for violating nature's givens, violating abundance, adds to nature something wondrous that was always there, requiring a frame. This, I believe, is the link essential to exposure. *Mimēsis* marks within itself the framing of representation, *its* representation, calling our attention in its materiality to the abundance of representation. For *mimēsis* opens onto worlds of *poiēsis*, worlds of unlimit, because *mimēsis* knows no end. The possibility of the end of art always struggles against the abundance of *mimēsis*.

Heidegger speaks of letting-be as if we might let things be without restraint, though we are tempted by the vicissitudes of everyday life not to do so. He also suggests that letting-be might be immensely difficult, that it transpires in a struggle, a rift, between world and earth. One difficulty within this struggle, close to everyday life, is that we live in restricted economies and cannot escape from them to nature's general circulation. Another, however, is the impossibility of following what may be read as Heidegger's suggestion that we can let things be in their abundance by relaxing our hold on the frame, associated with *technē*, the frame in which we live and in which we place the things of our world. We institute worlds by building frames. The frames hold things and us in place. Art emerges in the struggle between the frames of worlds and abundance, emerges in abundance, along with all other works, other emergences.

I insist that the possibility of instituting worlds belongs to nature, and us, in the frames of representation, in the worlds we build and find built around us. We occupy frames that hold us in their places, but that occupation belongs to abundance. In this sense, we cannot release the frame of modern technology to open nature and us to Being's abundance. The frame is given as a gift as much as anything else, from abundance. What is required is to place it in circulation more quickly, more fluidly. And that is what we gain from *poiēsis* and *mimēsis*, from representation. We reframe the frame in its abundance, and in this abundance we are exposed to the abundance of abundance. We release the frame to fluid abundance.

Representation is always framing. But some framing denies its frame, or denies its abundance, imposes edges, cuts, exclusions, denies its gift from the good. Perhaps no framing should do so, should be allowed to do so. Perhaps all framing does so to some extent, all representation. The witness, the frame, betrays. And in this denial, this oblivion, to framing we withdraw from our exposure to the abundance of things, everywhere. This withdrawal from abundance, from heterogeneity, is a withdrawal from exposure at the same time that it is exposure.

Art does not deny its frame, its sensuous exposure to things beyond their surfaces. Art always cuts, but does not cut with so sharp an edge of exclusion as to obscure its *mimēsis*. I mean art that continues to exist in the *diaphora* between *poiēsis* and *technē*, given historically in the West, but not perhaps art as such. I do not know art as such except within another frame, another restriction in the intermediary movements of general economy. Art arose in Greece in intermediary movements, in the gift of abundance from the good, called by different names in different places, *poiēsis*, *technē*, unfolding wondrous beauties and sublimes, all at the very edges of the frame, all nailed in place by arbitrary restrictions. In art, nevertheless, the arbitrariness of the frame repeatedly shows itself. In the West. Elsewhere art is so profoundly integrated into tribal life that the intermediary spaces between art and its others do not emerge. Such a tribal life is filled with other intermediary figures that touch the sacred, prohibited, and natural worlds, exposed endlessly to uncontainable movements.

Perhaps *art* does not exist in tribal societies until their artifacts emerge into Western spaces. In this sense, tribal *art* knows no particular exposure to abundance, to the mad and magical movements in which tribal worlds relate to nature. Art is unframed; but tribal practices produce artifacts that are framed as art upon entering Western life. Historically, such a framing has frequently been disastrous to the works and peoples that produced them, disastrous to their standing and abundance, victimizing works, individuals, societies, and lives. Even so, such works have eventually entered Western collective artistic practices framed as art, effectively reframing and continually reframing the possibility of art, along with possibilities of knowledge, philosophy and science, and more. Tribal knowledge is deep and wide, opening onto abundance, frequently embodied in its arts, undivided as in the West from other knowledges.

In the West, *poiēsis* belongs to art but known repeatedly to emerge in science and philosophy, recognized to mark the possibility of the arising of science. Kant denies that genius pertains to science as he denies that science knows anything of the sublime. That limitation of *poiēsis* to art is both its exposure in Western thought and its arbitrary restriction. Yet even where science is acknowledged to emerge from movements of genius, close to and crossing the limits of intelligibility, we mark its passages, its exposures, through terms traditionally assigned in the West to art: metaphor, creativity, genius, inspiration. Again, such exposures are named in entirely different ways in tribal arts.

Heidegger speaks of five essential ways in which truth happens, excluding science, but including art, politics, nearness, sacrifice, and questioning. I speak of endlessly abundant ways in which abundance happens, everywhere and in every place, including art and science. I associate ethics|politics, like Lyotard, with the circulation of happenings, the movements of general economy within its restrictions. Such an ethics|politics, given from the good, cannot be separated from art, or from philosophy and science, cannot be separated. In this sense, I continue to speak of art as exposure to the good, to things in the name of the good, circulating the gift of beauty, as an ethics|politics, touching the good.

I wish at this point to think more carefully of wandering, of exposure as wandering in general economy, the wandering of gifts that continue to move, in art, as art, art's exposure to nature's general economy. I think again of what Derrida calls iterability, repetition with a difference, founding and conserving. I think of iterability as the general economy of restricted economies and the restrictions of general economy.

Iterability is Derrida's term. Wandering is mine, general economy. Exposure is to abundance, before and in abundance. Exposure is intimacy, face to face in Levinas, before the other. But where intimacy for Levinas is one subject face to face with another subject, intimate in inward subjectivity, it is for me face to face, or skin to skin, as touch, one thing touching another in heterogeneous abundance. Here, iterability is not repetition and its repetition, in difference but not indifference. Iterability is exposure in the skin, material, embodied exposure to the wealth of abundance in oneself and others, in repetition and departure, expressed as wandering. In this sense, exposure does not express iterability, but wandering expresses abundance as exposure. Repetition belongs to touch as memory, thereby to exposure. We repeat others in our exposure to them, repeat ourselves in self-exposure, and in our repetitions we find ourselves exposed to difference, in difference, wandering in our exposure.

Material, embodied exposure is intimate, to ourselves or others, inward or outward. We encounter the world intimately, face to face and skin to skin, as touch, in exposure. In this exposure we face and touch abundance, touch its heterogeneity and familiarity, touch things and ourselves in familiar and unfamiliar ways, wandering. Exposure, then, is within and toward abundance, understanding abundance as the circulation of general and restricted economy, the circulation of goods in dyads face to face, exposure, where dyads become familiar. Lovers are frequently dyads, though love knows no absolute restrictions, wanders in its abundance among other abundances. Yet an abundance, a heterogeneity, is expressed in love, a wandering among the deep recesses and fissures of abundance, face to face and skin to skin, touching the flesh of lovers.

I am following a different wandering here, that of exposure as representation, as exposition. Exposure in the skin belongs, I believe, to representation. That is where I join Derrida's sense of wandering as iterability, as representation, as work. The general economy circulates in restricted economies of work and representation; work and representation circulate in intimate dyads, exposition in the skin. Levinas calls this vulnerability, a passivity beyond passivity. I depart from him through the abundance that forbids the reassembling of being. It is not inward subjectivity which is being's otherwise, forbidding the closure of being around essence, but being's abundance. It is not inward subjectivity that calls us to the good but being's abundance. Exposure to abundance is cherishment, responsiveness to the things of the world in their abundance and abundance's abundance. This abundance, the abundance of abundance, is otherwise than being, general economy, exceeding all restriction. It works in restricted economies—that is, wanders as representation. It works as the framing of representation. It wanders as the excess of framing. It works in art.

I interrupt this concluding discussion to speak of framing and abundance by example. The example is the Marmottan museum, containing Monet's *Water Lily* paintings done at Givenchy. It is one of the most beautiful and peaceful places in the world I know, beauty and peace themselves. The museum is a familiar bustling and noisy place upstairs. Below ground level the rooms are hushed, with places to sit at length, at peace, filled with beauty. I have spent glorious hours there in beauty.

I have wondered why and how the works give such peace, what enables them to bear such gifts. The books of reproductions are pretty, not glorious. The answer, I believe, is that the works are very large, disturbing the viewer's orientation. Their surfaces are recognizably water lilies in water, but with no other objects orienting the viewer's body in space. Finally, the edges of the paintings are unfinished, are framed unfinished, without lines cutting them off from the world. As a consequence, the viewer is suspended in an unknown space beyond all other spaces, thrown in body into strange and unfamiliar places. And I emphasize in body. The peace is a peace of abundance, a glorious beauty, given to us in our bodies, in space, in their abundance and incompleteness, incompleting our bodies, spaces, and being in the world. We are disoriented, but a disorientation without violence, beyond, I would say, touched by the good. We wander in the frame, the absence of the frame, in our bodies, in space, wander into strange and unfamiliar places of abundance, abundance's peace.

Art is wandering par excellence, which is by no means to say that it wanders more quickly or widely than other forms of representation. Rather, it presents exposition as its frame, presents the work wandering in its frame, and other frames, all wandering. The possibility of *mimēsis* exposes other possibilities, endless abundances, of *mimēsis*. In this way, the idea of a representation that represents without *mimēsis* suggests a representation that does not wander, cannot wander, a work without abundance. In this way, exposure is wandering, expressed in art as *mimēsis*. The sensuousness, the exposition and *mimēsis*, of philosophy express its wandering among the general economy of things and representations.

Abundance is not representation, and representation is not abundance. Each is abundance of the other, the other's wandering. Representation's abundance, abundant in art, expresses general economy, other abundances, the abundance of the earth as cherishment. And representation's abundance, as work, abundant in art, expresses restricted economy, still other abundances, the abundance of world (in Heidegger's language) as sacrifice. This means that art is plenishment. It is not only plenishment, nor is plenishment only art. The gift of beauty is among the gifts circulating in nature, circulating as exposure, circulating in touch, where touch opens things to their abundance but also places them in restricted economies.

The gift of beauty is the abundance of things, is given from the good, framed as cherishment. In art, the gift of beauty is restricted, enters restricted economies of work, framed by history and judgment, framed in place. The gift of the good is sacrificed into work, in art, still bearing the mark of the good, witness to the abundance of the good, remembering wondrous beauties and catastrophic disasters. Art is the sacrifice of beauty to hold it in place within its wandering. Art is the sacrifice of beauty to hold the memory, the representation, of wandering in place for its enjoyment, in love, as exposure. Exposure to the good, in beauty, demands a frame, other frames. Heterogeneity requires a frame to encounter it and know it.

Exposure is cherishment, love, of things in their abundance, circulating in general economy. But love demands intimacy, knows abundance intimately, face to face and skin to skin, cherishes things in touch, erotically, in exposure. Love, cherishment, is born in desire, material and embodied. In this way we come to thoughts of art that work against its Western appropriation. I speak of sensuous enjoyment and delight, of fetishes, of *jouissance* and *exubérance*, all exposure. I return to the shame of art.

We have seen that art in Western thought has from its beginnings in Greece presented us with a profound ambivalence around its sensory and emotional power. We are moved by art, moved deeply, moved to tears and love, moved by the material power of words and things, moved in our bodies. And repeatedly, threatened by the power of feelings that threaten to overpower us, Western philosophers have drawn back from this power in art, either placing it away from the good or placing its sensuousness away from the good in art, away from beauty. I have understood these two movements, away from the good in art, as betraying—in the double sense of exposing, showing, and violating—the power of sensory desire to draw us to the good, expressed in art. In this way, the overwhelming force of desire both testifies to the good and calls us to it, if at the same time it distracts us from it. I include women in this overwhelmingness of desire, who represent the excess of desire for men and who are denied their own desire, who as sensuous embodiments of men's desire are denied relation to the good from within the very touch of the good that reveals abundance. I include sexual difference as intimate exposure.

I understand exposure as cherishment, and cherishment as sensuous, and more. But certainly the more is not unsensuous, disembodied, ethereal, and spiritual, but the wealth of abundance in materiality and embodiment, which, whatever spiritual thought may say, remains both source of all spirituality, born in the body, and abundant in countless ways. The abundance of things is abundant in their materiality, filled with inexhaustible abundances, calling for us to know and cherish them in their materiality, exposed in touch, knowing that touch exceeds any embodiment, that embodiment exceeds materiality, that general economy circulates beyond the identities of minds and bodies, spirituality and materiality.

When Kant holds back the empirical delight we experience in our bodies from beauty in art, he restricts the abundance of the world from interest in the highest. And so with all hierarchies: restricted economies that do work too frequently work upon and oppress some kinds of people, women, members of other races and classes, but also animals and other natural things, treat them as lower and therefore as something to be used to profit the higher, without abundance of their own. Yet in holding back empirical delight, Kant acknowledges its reality. We may say that in art this abundance of things and in our feelings toward things shows itself. Not great art, and not art alone. But in art, we experience abundance against any restriction, any domination, at the same time and in the same respects that social codes and market forces impose endless restrictions. In this play of restriction and excess in art, but not art alone, we experience the excess of restriction, experience general economy circulating in restricted economies. We experience this in art because of *mimēsis*, because art's artifice shows us its representativity, because of the emotional power of art, because of art's exposure. Art brings into question all the forces of restriction. It makes us weep, makes us angry, plays with artificiality, competes with memory, falsifies history, toys with truth, and more, endless more. Art revels in the abundance of abundance.

In this way, then, art as art—understanding this intermediary figure to have no determinate meaning, no determinate restrictions, dissociating every disciplinary restriction from its authority—promotes excess, exposes us to abundance. The abundance of which I speak at this moment is that of emotion and feeling. Like philosophy, art warns us of the destructions of excessive desire, of overwhelming feeling. Unlike philosophy, art overwhelms us with feeling. Unlike reason and science, art overwhelms us with whatever might overwhelm us, through *mimēsis*. If Plato warns us about this dangerous side of *mimēsis*, he also grants its gift from the good.

We are overwhelmed by poems, tragedies, and music. We weep. We suffer. And we know that such overwhelming has its dangers, can distract us from what we must do at the same time that it calls attention to other responsibilities. In the overwhelming emotion that transpires in art, in our delight and terror before works of art, we are exposed to abundance, to unfamiliarity and excess, exposed in our places, exposed in virtue of restrictions. Restricted economies lose their hold, if for but a moment, in the circulation of art, in the emotional powers of art, as we weep and love and care. And in this loss we sometimes lose the very possibility of working toward the good, overwhelmed by despair or distracted by delights, or otherwise indifferent. In these cases still, I say, we are exposed to abundance, exposed to the good, overwhelmed by our exposure, exposed in overwhelming. Exposure to abundance, in excessive emotion, not just delight, in pleasure and terror in art, overwhelms us with abundance, with the circulation of things beyond any restrictions, beyond our efforts to work toward the good. For the good and abundance are beyond work, even work in the name of the good.

The sensuous, emotional, material overwhelming of art reflects the abundance of things in our exposure to them, sensuously, emotionally, materially, empirically. Art knows something of the abundance of experience, something of the excesses of emotion and desire, of the materiality of things. Art knows something of love's overwhelming, something that lovers know and experience profoundly, but frequently do not know how to say except through art. I speak again of emotion and intimacy, of love. I speak of exposure as emotional intimacy, of an intimacy beyond any restrictions, permeating the beloved's body and soul, body-soul, permeating and circulating in the abundance of the other, heterogeneously. But we lovers can only love a few in such intimate ways. Through art we love others, love other people and other things, even love those we could not stand to love in the flesh. Through art we encounter the abundance of things beyond the possibility of other encounters.

With this abundance and love we come to *jouissance*, understanding it as the joy, the desire, of the other, from within our own desire. We know, we experience, in our love toward others, our joyful, emotional cherishment of others, something we will never know, never experience, within our own experiences of love. Irigaray and Lacan speak of this as women's *jouissance*. I speak of it as the *jouissance* of the other. In our own *jouissance* something shows of another *jouissance*, beyond any possibility of our experience. In our own desire, our own erotic emotional excesses, we know something of other excesses, still erotic and emotional. In cherishment, we experience the possibility of endless abundances of joys, endless *jouissances*, the abundance of loves in other creatures and things, touching each other in love and cherish-ment. Our exposure exposes us to the abundance of abundance.

The *jouissance* of the other is known in love, as love, erotically and pas-sionately. It is known in its unknowability. In many longstanding restricted economies, those described by Lévi-Strauss and Bataille, it is subordination, domination and oppression of the other. Desire's excess opens onto the abun-dance of other desires, but in its overwhelming may hope to enslave them. Yet this enslavement blinds itself to desire's abundance, blinds itself to its own exposure. Our desire, our *jouissance*, exposes us erotically to the *jouissances* of others, other sexes, genders, kinds.

Exposure to giving from the good is abundance. The abundance of things exposes itself in the abundance of exposure. Exposure as abundance is given as intimacy, face to face and skin to skin, as touch. The circulation of goods in general economy exposes itself in proximity, in the proximity of the other, of others, abundantly and endlessly. In this proximity and abundance, I believe, we find the gift of beauty realized as art. I speak of beauty; Levinas speaks of glory. Both touch abundance, and its abundance. Levinas speaks of glory as responsibility, bearing the debt of subjectivity. "The more I answer the more I am responsible; the more I approach the neighbor with which I am encharged the further away I am. This debit which increases is infinity as an infinition of the infinite, as glory" (Levinas, *OB*, 93). The approach that opens onto the abundance of abundance is glory. I call it ecstasy, opening onto beauty.

I follow Anaximander to understand that this approach, given in the name of the good, bears down upon us as our endless injustice. "The more I return to myself, the more I divest myself, under the traumatic effect of per-secution, of my freedom as a constituted, willful, imperialist subject, the more I discover myself to be responsible; the more just I am, the more guilty I am. I am 'in myself' through the others" (Levinas, *OB*, 112). Indeed, I say, we are in ourselves, where we are, through the others. And through the oth-ers to whose abundance we are exposed, in beauty or glory, we are exposed through cherishment to sacrifice, to injustice, bearing a debt to those others in an abundance of responsibility. But where Levinas calls this guilt, I hold guilt in abeyance in relation to abundance, hold it for circulation in restricted economies. Guilt mirrors by inversion the willful, imperialist subject. We and others touch the world in its abundance, not through guilt, a subject's guilt, but in a glory, or beauty of abundance, the abundance of touch touching abundance.[4] If we cannot avoid sacrifice, and if that sacrifice exposes us to guilt, something of abundance, of cherishment, exposes us beyond guilt to abundance. The debt that increases as it is paid, the responsibilities that mul-tiply in the measure in which they are taken on (Levinas, *OB*, 12), express abundance more profoundly than culpability, responsiveness to abundance.

The abundance of abundance is beauty, given to us everywhere and in every place and thing, showing everywhere as well, no matter how well assembled in place. Assembling is disassembling; placing is displacing; working is undoing; representation is misrepresentation, under masks; desire is beyond itself. All are abundances touching abundances, circulating beyond measure in the places in which they receive their measures. This includes art, which at least in Western thought has always been a place in which unmeasure opens the abundance of measure, in which general economy shows the abundance of restricted economies in the abundance of their restrictions. I speak of the immeasurable will to truth, of the immeasurable unwork of work, the wandering of representations from assembling to dissembling and back again. All these are gifts from the good. All are glory. All are beauty, showing in art.

"The glory of the Infinite is the anarchic identity of the subject flushed out without being able to slip away" (Levinas, *OB*, 144). The beauty of abundance is the anarchic circulation of things beyond the hold of any restriction. "The subjectivity of the subject is persecution and martyrdom. . . . It is by the voice of the witness that the glory of the Infinite is glorified" (Levinas, *OB*, 146). It is by exposure, to which we are all witnesses, all of us and all things everywhere, that the beauty of abundance is given. We are all witnesses; the witness is a traitor. This betrayal is our fate, our sacrifice, our persecution and martyrdom, born everywhere and in every place. "The glory of the Infinite shuts itself up in a word and becomes a being" (Levinas, *OB*, 151). The beauty of abundance passes from general circulation to restricted economy. The gift of the good is closed up into a binary relation of good to bad. But no closure can abolish beauty, or glory, or abundance:

> In the proximity of the other, all the others than the other obsess me, and already this obsession cries out for justice, demands measure and knowing, is consciousness. (Levinas, *OB*, 158).

> All the others that obsess me in the other do not affect me as examples of the same genus united with my neighbor by resemblance or common nature, individuations of the human race, or chips of the same block, like the stones metamorphosed into men by Deucalion, who, behind his back, had to collect into cities with their hearts of stone. The others concern me from the first. (Levinas, *OB*, 159)

The others, all the others in proximity, represent abundance. Abundance circulates in proximity.

This proximity, among all the others, this meeting between all the others who are not totality or universality, but other embodied creatures, individuals and kinds, takes place in proximity, face to face and skin to skin.

Levinas moves too quickly for me from the proximity of the other to justice through all the others. I take the general economy of all the others, in proximity, to cry out against injustice and domination without holding justice and freedom fast. I hesitate to think that the proximity of the other might not know consciousness, but that in the call of others, obsession toward all the others, we and others are led to consciousness, measure and knowing. I take the others in their abundance, an abundance beyond measure and knowing, beyond consciousness, to reach toward the good. All the others impose no limit upon proximity.

Levinas denies that the others that obsess me do so as kinds, united with their neighbors by commonality. The others have nothing to do with genera and kinds. I think this denial is much too hasty. Like the movement from proximity to justice, touched by all the others, the denial never touches the identities of those others as kinds. Yet before the possibility of justice, however impossible justice may be, we must loosen, find loosened, the hold of identities, circulating among individuals and kinds, intermediary figures. Only in relation to kinds do identities become intermediary figures; I add that in Western thought, identities of kinds have been the origin of heinous oppressions.

I am who I am, I who stand before you or the others to say here I am, in virtue of my kinds. The I who stands before the face, in the skin, does not touch the others in their absolute singularity, nor in the absolute singularity of the I. The singular in its absoluteness renders the disturbance of identity impossible, takes all identities to pertain as betrayals to the absolute singularity without identity. Here the identity of the individual is an impossibility. Yet we know in our experience that the difficulty with identity is not that it is impossible, but that it is too much with us, too many identities, too many kinds. The abundance of identities comes and circulates from the good among kinds: humans, animals, insects, stones, and more. But abundance is not the circulation of fixed essences. To the contrary. Abundance is the circulation of unstable and mutable essences, general economy. I stand before you as man, Jew, teacher, and more. Always more. Identities circulating to excess.

Stones speak, they do not fix into unmoving hearts. They touch and remember.[5] They move, and hearts of stone with them. All the others make hearts move in their pain and suffering, in their destructions, including the destructions of stones and the destructions witnessed by stones. Those touched by Medusa wept, continued to weep, as did all the suffering women for whom she rendered justice. Things touch each other, and in their touch bear witness to destructions, to endless injustices. Nothing can fix such an abundance. Everything can witness abundance.

Witness to abundance is *exposition*: exposure|exposition, proximity and intimacy at work, in show, in rift-design. Work and show belong to the said, to restricted economies, yet in their exposition resides proximity, the touch of things in the skin, the deepest recesses of bodies touching at the skin. This touching, this gift of touch, circulates in nature's abundance as beauty, but not beauty alone. As beauty it circulates in art, but not in art alone.

What we call "beauty"—but not beauty alone, or always, or Beauty Itself—interrupts the assembling of the identities of things in restricted economies, under the pressures of everyday experience, under the governance of rules, within the codes of culture, the dominations of authority, exposes us to abundance, nature's general economy. Beauty renders the familiar strange and the strange familiar, interrupts the most elusive of authorities, presents us with enigmatic and mysterious kinds. Beauty is interrupted by ugliness, disgusting and revolting things and experiences, by curses and prohibitions, interrupted and sustained, for they may all be beautiful in time. Beauty is interrupted by the sublime, the terrible, the prohibited, the uncanny, the strange, the unfamiliar, most of all and most terribly by dominations and devastations, where beauty must bear witness to horrible crimes, must bear responsibility for interrupting the assembling of histories that have forgotten the crimes that made them. But not and never beauty alone, though beauty excludes no gift from the good.

What we call *art*—but not art alone, or always, in every work of art, or Art Itself—interrupts the assembling of identities of things and works in restricted economies, under the codes of practices and genres, in disciplinary practices, the oppressions and regulations of authority, exposes us to the abundance of abundance, to representation's and beauty's general economy. Under a variety of names in the West, and other names elsewhere—for example *poiēsis*, *mimēsis*, genius, or the sublime—art has been given responsibility for the excesses of authority and desire, reaching beyond the rules of taste, or beauty, to interruptions from the good. The gifts of the good fall into art as interruptions of other economies, other genres, governed by rules—science, philosophy, ethics, politics—interrupting the economy, genre, or practice, its *technē*, by *poiēsis*, genius, or the sublime, or whatever, perhaps the so-called primitive, non-Western, nonobjective, or unpresentable. Art works at the very limit of work, receiving the gift of beauty in myriad forms, some we hesitate to call beautiful, some so terrible they give us no delight, are not transfigured into artistic pleasure. Art bears witness in the name of beauty, the sublime, or whatever to abundance, to terrible injustices within this abundance, and to excesses of and toward abundance.

Art does not alone expose us to abundance or bear witness to the good, alone circulate intermediary movements of general economy within restricted economies. Nor is art free from restrictions, from social codes and expectations, from market exchanges and political dominations. At times it seems the greatest victim of political powers and economic exchanges, entirely subject to market control. Yet always, in the West and in its imperial reaches toward art elsewhere, incorporating African and Eastern works into its sales, art as we know and label it expresses something beyond any rules and governances, works as an intermediary figure. Art does not alone present monsters, who are found in philosophy and science, in ethics and politics, everywhere. Yet the disciplinary practices of philosophy and science, at least since the rise of modernity, have repeatedly instituted practices designed to keep monsters at bay, to keep them in art and wild nature where they belong, to keep them tamed. And the disciplinary practices of ethics and politics claim to have recognized all the forms of ethical monstrosity and to have instituted channels for their containment, if not their control. Art has never succeeded in the West in any plausible way in controlling or regulating its monstrosities, but has flaunted them on the surfaces and in the crevices of its works and in the ideas that constitute art. Monsters, marking the abundance of nature, belong to the very thought and practice of what we call *art*, within its and nature's beauties. Art bears witness to monsters, savagely attacked for its monstrosities.

In this way, beauty is the gift from the good, nature's abundance, circulating as an intermediary figure everywhere, transforming everything it touches, everything that touches anything anywhere, into other intermediary figures, coming to rest momentarily in art, the wealth of intermediary figures circulating throughout our restricted economies, setting them into motion, transforming them into intermediary figures. When literature was separated from classical representation, *mimēsis* from *diēgesis*, *poiēsis* from *technē*, each of the latter was for a moment, a stretch of historical time, purified, restricted, stabilized, halted in its circulation, only to undergo mobilization again when the former returned from its journeys, touched by endless and abundant intermediary figures. The good returns with gifts, touching stable identities and spinning them into motion, motions they for just a moment of historical time forgot. Art is the disciplinary name of what, in that moment, allowed for that stability, and also the name of what, subsequently, destabilized every disciplinary identity.

Beauty belongs to nature as its abundance, general economy, the circulation of identities among individuals and kinds, but especially among kinds. Nature's abundance is given as beauty dispersed among nature's kinds, restricted and unrestricted kinds. Restricted economies name kinds against the wealth of singularities and individuals. General economy destabilizes these kinds as kinds, but does not return them to singularity. Identities, economies, beauties all belong to kinds, and to individuals who circulate among abundant kinds, circulate excessively in their unstable identities among different kinds.

Art in this way pertains to kinds, turns every kind into an intermediary figure, and every intermediary figure into other intermediary figures. This is what I mean by exposure: to kinds, individuals and kinds, individuals as kinds and kinds of individuals. All this is to speak against the idea of absolute singularities, absolute individuals unrelated to other individuals, subjects or objects. And it is to speak against the authority of any disciplinary stabilization of the identities of kinds, of kinship and families, public and private. Exposure is to the depth and reach of the abundance of kinds, intimately and in proximity, to possibilities of intimacy and love, individual to individual and kind to kind, possibilities of family and familiarity, interrupted by other families and unfamiliarity, always excessive within every restriction, always sedimenting into known families and kinds within the endless movement of abundance.

Here we may compare for just a moment the idea of an instrumentality in which a given practice defines the end, the instrumentality of a hammer, a tool, to be used in one way and no others. If this is the idea of *technē*, then all instruments and tools bear within themselves an abundance beyond any given idea of use. Tools are used in many different ways, and new uses emerge from within their material presence as they circulate into new realms of use. *Technē* is a mark of abundance, even as it is the restriction of abundance. *Poiēsis* is not *technē*'s other, but something within every restriction of abundance, uncanny and enigmatic. Always, we may say, restrictions and abundances pertain to kinds, to the families in which works circulate, in which they live, in which we live together with them, in families and kinds.

Art for art's sake—a betrayal of the good—reflects a truth of abundance, named here by inversion. Art's sake is the sake of the good, but it is no use, not the use described as *technē*, but rather, within that usefulness to reach for abundance: *poiēsis* in *technē*. Art is useless, and within that very uselessness is profoundly useful to the good, to unleash within representation and work the abundance of usefulness. I do not understand this abundance as abundance of reliability if that means more reliability, but understand it as the abundance from which reliability emerges, which it draws upon, the wealth of possibilities of usefulness, and more. Reliability belongs to restricted economies, held in check by ends of use, always exceeding any bonds. Abundance of reliability is the general economy of use, drawing upon usefulness and reliability as intermediary figures, always giving rise to other uses, new and forceful uses, dominations and authoritarian uses, and more. Usefulness is restriction; abundance is the excessive will beyond any possible end to reach for usefulness.

Beauty touches every place, including every restricted place, every reliable and useful place with something in that place—the beauty of usefulness for example, sometimes wonderful and glorious—and something beyond that place—beauty without use, exceeding use, *mimēsis* or *poiēsis*.

If beauty interrupts the authority of restrictions, exposes us to abundance, and if that interruption is interrupted itself, then we need no longer speak of other interruptions, of *poiēsis* interrupting *technē*, *mimēsis* inter-rupting *diēgesis*, genius interrupting taste, beauty interrupted by the sub-lime. Beauty is interruption, and more interruption, peaceful as well as tumultuous interruption, exposing us to interruption in countless ways, na-ture's general economy. The gift of beauty is interruption and exposure, in every disciplinary place, known disciplinarily in the West as art.

Art is the disciplinary name for beauty's interruptions. But beauty in-terrupts restrictions in every place and thing. In that way beauty interrupts the gift of art, calling upon us not to receive that gift as art alone, mindless of the abundance of other gifts. Disciplinary practices in art and literature are frequently as restrictive as disciplinary practices without art and literature. In that way, we are called from the good, by abundance, to refuse disciplinary practices that would relegate exposure to abundance to art at the same time that we continue to pursue disciplinary practices in the name of goods.

And here I come to conclusion, to rest for just a moment, before em-barking on other exposures, other circulations, of gifts in general economy. I conclude that disciplinary practices, genres and spheres of regulation—all the domains of work called science, art, and practice—restrict nature's abun-dance in order to do work, circulate general economy into restricted economies where work is done face to face, skin to skin. And in this move-ment, which retains within itself and its structure, however authoritarian and dominating, traces of general economy, restrictions bring oblivion to abun-dance, to beauty, to nature's excess, to their own excesses, to the excesses of the desires that shape them. They retain traces of intermediary figures within themselves while all their resources are mustered to resist the movement of general economy, of the good. The beauty of a mathematical proof opens onto vistas of something beyond the authority of proof. The beauty of a physical theory opens onto vistas beyond the truth of such a theory. The beauty of the abundance of social codes opens onto vistas of abundance exceeding any pos-sible social codes. And so on. The possibility of restricted economies emerges from a nature, a world, of wondrous beauty beyond any restriction and binary opposition. As Diotima says, who does not belong to the restricted economy of men in drunken discussion at the party, but circulates as an intermediary figure between the gods and the good, setting Socrates, and us, in circula-tion, exposing us to abundance.

Notes

General Preface to the Project

1. I think of the work of the good as occupying restricted economies, goods divided from bads, binary oppositions and exclusions, setting prices. I think of the good as interrupting every restricted economy, circulating in the general economy of excess, unlimit, unmeasure. The gift of the good is the general economy of priceless goods that circulate everywhere in restricted economies as work within an immeasurable exposure. In this way, the good resists every binary opposition, resists every measure, not as another opposition or measure, and not as another place or thing. The good is not a good, neither good nor bad, nor both good and bad, nor neutral, indifferent to good and evil. It is neither transcendent nor immanent, high or low, inside or outside, but interrupts the choice of either/or, the hold of the one or the other, the authority of "or," and "and," and "neither," and "both," all belonging to restricted economies. What I speak of in the name of the good is the exposure borne by every creature and thing within its limits to countless others, and the responsibility they bear to resist the injustices of every limit by a movement interrupting limit. I call this movement the general economy of the good. I think of nature as the general and excessive circulation of precious goods exposed to others giving birth to the work they do in restricted, exchange economies.

I pursue the thought of restricted and general economies found in Bataille, *AS*. See my *PE*, chaps. 5 and 6; and here, chap. 7.

2. I have spoken of it, after Anaximander, as injustice, for which all our works are restitutions. See n. 7, here. Derrida has spoken of it as *justice* (see Derrida, *FL*). Plato speaks of it repeatedly. Again, the good is not a thing, a measure, does not divide, does not exclude, but gives all things to us, places them in circulation, exposes us to them, charges us to respond.

3. Wherever possible I include page references to my *AIS* from which I believe the major part of this study of art and giving may be recovered, frequently with references to the most convenient sources of the complete work in question. Many of the references to Plato's *Ion* and *Republic*, and to Aristotle's *Poetics*, may be found in *AIS*, but page numbers for these works in *AIS* are not listed here.

4. I speak of sonance in my *RR*: the ring of representation. Levinas speaks of *la gloire de l'Infini* (Levinas, *AÊ*, 230).

5. See n. 6, here.

6. "Kata to chreōn didonai gar auta dikēn kai tisin allēlois tēs adikias." The entire fragment from Simplicius is canonically translated as: "Into those things from which existing things have their coming into being, their passing away, too, takes place, according to what must be; for they make reparation to one another for their injustice according to the ordinance of time, as he puts it in somewhat poetical language" (Simplicius *Phys.*, 24, 18 [DK 12 B 1]) (Robinson, *EGP*, 34).

Introduction

1. See General Preface to the Project, here, n. 6.

2. See my *PE*, where the gift of the good is born from the liberation of women. Here the gift is shown as art. Plenishment is the joining of cherishment with sacrifice, where sacrifice names the exclusions demanded by work. Sacrifice is the work of the good; cherishment is the call of the good; plenishment is the work of the good, responsive to its touch.

3. Here I depart from my prior discussion of art in terms of categories and identities, as inexhaustibility by contrast, and contrasts of contrasts (see my *TA*). I now understand my earlier reading as a theory of the abundance of art, a theory to which I still subscribe, but knowing too little of the good.

4. See chap. 8, here, pp. 275–78.

5. "The question of our time," in Irigaray's words. See chap. 1 here, pp. 51–52.

6. See my *RR*, chap. 8, *IR*, chap. 8, and *PE*, chap. 7.

7. See chap. 6, here, pp. 230–32, for the full quotation and further discussion.

8. See chap. 7, here.

9. See my *PE*, especially chap. 5. See chap. 7, here, also.

Chapter One

1. I speak in Greek with two thoughts in mind. One is to retrieve thoughts of art from their beginnings in Greece, crossing the *diaphora* from then to now, across traditional readings and understandings. The other, which I express in transliterated Greek to avoid suggesting that we can return to origins, is to hope to free our thinking from the words into which it has sedimented by crossing that sedimentation with another thought of the words from which it has emerged, crossing another *diaphora*.

I hope to think of *diaphoros* as an intermediary figure of endless crossings. I coin the adjective diaphoric to express intermediary movements (see n. 2, here).

2. Irigaray's phrase for angels, moving between gods and mortals, recollecting Diotima's *daimonic* Eros. Intermediary figures move between like and unlike; they do not choose. How can an angel choose between heaven and earth? Even in William Wenders's *Wings of Desire*.

3. I have discussed *Phaedrus* in detail elsewhere, and shall not repeat that discussion here. (See my *IR*, chaps. 9 and 10.) Here I mean to discuss other dialogues that speak of the gift of the gods. Yet *Phaedrus* is a supreme event, on my reading, making us a gift, from Plato, of the sacred gifts of madness and magic present in all art and everywhere in nature.

4. "All soul has the care of all that is inanimate, and traverses the whole universe, though in ever-changing forms" (Plato, *Phaedrus*, 246c). All soul, and all things, everywhere included, cutting nothing off from care, excluding nothing from the good.

5. Discussed here in chap. 2.

6. Also: "And the same things appear bent and straight to those who view them in water and out, or concave and convex, owing to similar errors of vision about colors, and there is obviously every confusion of this sort in our souls" (Plato, *Republic*, 602c).

7.

> they all journeyed to the Plain of Oblivion, through a terrible and stifling heat, for it was bare of trees and all plants, and there they camped at eventide by the River of Forgetfulness, whose waters no vessel can contain. They were all required to drink a measure of the water, and those who were not saved by their good sense drank more than the measure, and each one as he drank forgot all things. . . . And so, Glaucon, the tale was saved, as the saying is, and was not lost. And it will save us if we believe it, and we shall safely cross the River of Lethe, and keep our soul unspotted from the world. (Plato, Republic, 621abc)

8. See chap. 2, here, pp. 61–62.

9.

> In this matter, then, of the regulation of women, we may say that we have surmounted one of the waves of our paradox and have not been quite swept away by it in ordaining what our guardians and female guardians must have all pursuits in common, . . . (Plato, Republic, 457c)

> Perhaps you don't realize that when I have hardly escaped the first two waves, you are now rolling up against me the "great third wave" of paradox, the worst of all. (Plato, Republic, 472a)

> I am on the very verge, said I, of what we likened to the greatest wave of paradox. But say it I will, even if, to keep the figure, it is likely to wash us away on billows of laughter and scorn. (Plato, *Republic*, 473c)

I thank Deborah O'Connell-Brown for calling my attention to these waves.

10. Irigaray speaks of a new poetics, returning us to *poiēsis*:

> Sexual difference would constitute the horizon of worlds more fecund than any known to date—at least in the West—and without reducing fecundity to the reproduction of bodies and flesh. For loving partners this would be a fecundity of birth and regeneration, but also the production of a new age of thought, art, poetry and language: the creation of a new poetics *[poïétique]*" (Irigaray, ESD, 5).

11. We may consider two touches in the passage in question, one that we are to consider the immortal soul "adequately in the light of reason" [*logismē*], that is, by calculation, as if adequate accounting could pertain to the divine; the second, that this purified soul, in proximity to the divine, will more "clearly" [*henargesteron*: visibly, palpably] distinguish justice and injustice. The question is whether this adequacy and light of reason pertain to the clarity of the distinction between justice and injustice, to the choice between the one and the other, or whether Socrates is raising the thought of another understanding of choice, of judgment, than given by rational art, by *technē*, a judgment intimately related to the divine, an intermediary figure.

For this question of judgment closes the dialogue in the story of Er, preceded by this transition to immortality. The immortal soul will more clearly distinguish justice and injustice. The gods "certainly are not unaware of the true of the true character of each of the two, the just and the unjust" (Plato, *Republic*, 612e); "the one will be dear to the gods and the other hateful to them" (Plato, *Republic*, 612e). In this way, the gods give the gift of the good, the true character of justice and injustice, finding one dear the other hateful. But do they do so rationally?

The reading from *Phaedrus* insists that love without divine madness is lifeless, dead, as are writing and philosophy. The gift of the gods cares for all things, without exclusion, but gives birth from itself without *technē*, the goodness of justice over injustice. In a single life, injustice can pay. In far too many countries of the world in our time, heinous and violent political injustices can be expected to bear fruit. The question that Adeimantus and Glaucon pose, whether injustice or justice is more profitable in mundane experience, has an answer we all know: in one or more mundane lives, in any technical domain, injustice can be more profitable. But in relation to the gods, given by the sacred and the good, justice is not better than injustice, but is wrong. Is this because in "all time" justice is more profitable, by the same norms of justice and injustice? Or does it come as a gift in a different relation to the good?

12. Allusions to Addelson, *IT*, and Harding, *IACFT*. I add Owens's description of the relevance of feminist discourse to contemporary discourse:

> The critique of binarism is sometimes dismissed as intellectual fashion; it is, however, an intellectual imperative, since the hierarchical opposition of marked and unmarked terms (the decisive/divisive presence/absence of the phallus) is the dominant form both of representing difference and justifing its subordination in our society. What we must learn, then, is how to conceive difference without opposition. (Owens, DO; Ross, AIS, 596)

Anarchistically, unstably, I would say, given in the name of the good.

13. See Kant, *CJ*, § 46, 150–51; Ross, *AIS*, 128, discussed in chap. 4, pp. 148–54.

14. "La différence sexuelle représente une des questions ou la question qui est à pense à notre époque. Chaque époque—selon Heidegger—a une chose à penser. Une seulement. La différence sexuelle est probablement celle de notre temps. La chose de notre temps qui, pensée, nous apporterait le « salut » ?" (Irigaray, *ÉDS*, 13).

15. See my *PE*.

16. These allusions to morning and dawn remind us of Heidegger and Nietzsche, profeminists both.

17. Nussbaum suggests that in Greece one might be guilty of injustice despite doing the best one can, the best one can imagine, the best possible (Nussbaum, *FG*). Injustice crosses justice at every turn, reminding us of Anaximander.

18. Teiresias's testimony is diaphoric, opening onto the intermediary figures of *Oedipus at Colonus*, Oedipus' years to come, suggesting that truth itself is diaphoric. See Sophocles, *OK*, 382.

Oedipus' life represents an incarnation of Anaximander's principle that the most just life is filled with injustice. Governance, rule, the institution of laws of justice, is unjust, bears the arrogance of authority at its heart. See Sophocles, *OK*, 396. An evil doom is visited upon all of us who would act in the name of justice, surrounded by hidden, forgotten crimes. The witness, the author, the ruler, is a traitor. That is the diaphoric sacred dance, perhaps.

19. See chap. 3, here, pp. 116–21.

20. And more, at 631, 633, 648.

21. See Sophocles, *OC*, 664–65.

Chapter Two

1. "If you were founding a city of pigs, Socrates, what other fodder than this would you provide?" (Plato, *Republic*, 372d). We may read this as suggesting that the fevered state is more fit for pigs than humans, that Socrates' austere society, whose members

> reclined on rustic beds strewed with bryony and myrtle, they will feast with their children, drinking of their wine thereto, garlanded and singing hymns to the gods in pleasant fellowship, not begetting offspring beyond their means lest they fall into poverty or war . . . living in peace and health, they will probably die in old age and hand on a like life to their offspring, (Plato, Republic, 372cd)

is ideal. But perhaps we should understand that human beings must live in a complex society in order to develop complex virtues. And what is more complex as a virtue than *mimēsis*, than struggling with the relation between truth and the good in sensuous terms?

2. See 338c where Socrates demands that Thrasymachus explain what he means on Socrates' terms.

3. See Plato, *Republic*, 395de–396a. Socrates repeatedly suggests that the gods appear to us in our madness, and that the madness of that representation is *poiēsis*. What we may hope to avoid is representing the gods under *technē*, as if we might make them ready to hand, available for our use. I call attention to the text where Socrates apologizes for giving a speech on love without madness, in simple argumentative form (Plato, *Phaedrus*, 242d).

4. I remind you of Pharmakeia, in all her violence and ambiguity. See chap. 1, p. 25. See also my *IR*, chaps. 9 and 10.

5. See my *TA*. Augustine speaks of the beauty of God's world as an "opposition of contraries, arranged, as it were, by an eloquence not of words, but of things" (Augustine, *CG*, Book 11, chap. 18, 160). This eloquence is *mimēsis*.

6. See also Kierkegaard, *FT*, 96–97.

7. See the Introduction here, pp. 14–17.

8. See the Introduction here, pp. 14–17.

9. See the Introduction here, pp. 16–17.

10. For example:

> Let us now for once compare an ethical and an aesthetical individual. The principal difference, and one on which everything hinges, is that the ethical individual is transparent to himself and does not live ins Blaue hinein as does the aesthetical individual. This difference states the whole case. He who lives ethically has seen himself, knows himself, penetrates with his consciousness his whole concretion, does not allow indefinite thoughts to potter about within him, nor tempting possibilities to distract him with their jugglery; he is not like a witch's letter from which one sense can be got now and then another, depending upon how one turns it. He knows himself. (Kierkegaard, E/O, 262–63)

Here, the either/or divides ethics from aesthetics as good from bad, the one far better, truer, higher than the other, which is to be given up. And more:

> The aesthetic individual views himself in his concretion and then distinguishes inter et inter. He regards some things as belonging to him accidentally, other things as belonging to him essentially. This distinction, however, is exceedingly relative, for so long as a man lives merely aesthetically one thing belongs to him as accidentally as another, and it is merely for lack of energy an aesthetic individual maintains this distinction. The ethical individual has learned this in despair, hence he has another distinction, for he, too, distinguishes between the essential and the accidental. Everything posited by his freedom belongs to him essentially, however accidental it may seem to be; everything else is for him accidental, however essential it may seem to be. (Kierkegaard, E/O, 264)

11. See Derrida, *TP*.

12. See chap. 1, here, pp. 51–52.

13. For the full quotation, see chap. 1, here, p. 51.

14. "[N]ot once *I* swear to you will *I* utter your name" (Wittig, *LB*, 46). "*I* am she who holds the secret of your name. *I* retain its syllables behind m/y closed mouth even while *I* would rather cry them out over the sea so that they might fall and be sombrely engulfed therein" (Wittig, *LB*, 130).

15. See my *RR*, chapter 8, Embodiment.

16. One example:

> I discover that your skin can be lifted layer by layer, I pull, it lifts off, it coils above your knees, I pull starting at the labia, it slides the length of the belly, fine to extreme transparency, I pull starting at the loins, the skin uncovers the round muscles and trapezii of the back, it peels off up to the nape of the neck, I arrive *[j//arrive]* under your hair, m/y fingers traverse its thickness, I touch your skull, I grasp it with all m/y fingers, I press it, I gather *[j//atteins]* the skin over the whole of the cranial vault, I tear off *[j//arrache]* the skin brutally beneath the hair, I reveal the beauty of the shining bone traversed by blood-vessels, m/y two hands crush the vault and the occiput behind, now m/y fingers bury themselves in the cerebral convolutions, the meninges are traversed by cerebrospinal fluid flowing from all quarters, m/y hands are plunged in the soft hemispheres, I seek the medulla and the cerebellum tucked in somewhere underneath, now I hold all of you silent immobilized every cry blocked in your throat your last thoughts behind your eyes caught in m/y hands, the delight is no purer than the depths of m/y heart m/y dearest one *[m/a très chérie]*. (Wittig, LB, 17)

17. How, if we bear endless responsibilities toward the good, if we remember countless violences toward women, can we join the thought of women face to face together in such a violent way? How do we avoid ethical contamination? What are we to make of such sado-masochistic language, when most sado-masochistic events are directed destructively at women?

We may wonder, reading *The Lesbian Body* as opening a truth concerning our belonging in flesh, our materiality and embodiment, not just lesbians' bodies, and understand the theme of violence to be part of that belonging, if we may avoid recapitulating the oppression and subjugation of women, their physical destruction. Perhaps violence belongs to desire. Perhaps we may celebrate its Dionysian side. Yet as we do so, we must wonder if the unnamed woman who narrates *The Lesbian Body* might be celebrating a destruction and violence too conventional, too masculine, too repetitive for us to bear ethically. Yet we cannot read *The Lesbian Body*, in its shocking violence, without a profound and far-reaching sense of cherishing the beloved's body.

18. That is the burden of my *RR*.

306 Notes

Chapter Three

1. That is another topic of consideration, not to be taken up here. For I doubt that anything available to us matches Aristotle's sense of *technē*, even technique, craft, and technology.

2. Or rather, of which we traditionally take it to know nothing. For I think *technē* is a gift from the good. That is the implication of understanding that every restricted economy is a general economy. The mean restricts judgment in relation to virtue, but virtue always exceeds every restriction.

3. This inexhaustibility of representation is at the heart of my *RR*. It touches on the limits of language. See my *LL*.

4. See the Introduction, here, pp. 11–12.

5. See this chap., p. 121.

6. See the reference to Wittig, p. 12.

7. See Derrida, *E*, 22:

> The question what is? already parleys *[arraisonne]* like a parergon, it constructs a framework which captures the energy of what is completely inassimilable and absolutely repressed. Any philosophical question already determines, concerning this other, a paregoric parergon. A paregoric remedy softens with speech; it consoles, it exhorts with the word. As its name indicates.
>
> The word vomit arrests the vicariousness of disgust; it puts the thing in the mouth; it substitutes, but only for example, oral for anal. It is determined by the system of the beautiful, "the symbol of morality," as its other; it is then for philosophy, still, an elixir, even in the very quintessence of its bad taste.

8. The two are spoken of by Lyotard as the two sorts of Inhuman. See chap. 1, here, p. 49.

9. The sublime is neither "greater" nor "lesser" than representation, because greater and lesser belong to representation. That is the fundamental problem of Kant's sublime, to be discussed in the next chapter.

10. See my *IR*, chapter 10, for a more detailed reading of this relation between wisdom and rule.

11. I have Spinoza's *Ethics* in mind, a work written entirely under the call of the good, whatever its limitations.

12. It is translated in other places as "beautiful in its nature" (Plato, *Symposium*, 205); and "wondrous vision," neglecting "*phusin*."

13. Of which Wittig speaks. See chap. 2, here, p. 90.

14. Spoken of in *Phaedrus* where Socrates compares divine *mania* with *manteia*.

15. See chap. 2, here, p. 85, for the full quotation.

16. Within this ellipsis is a supreme *diaphora* between the love of which Diotima speaks and the rest of human life, filled with binary oppositions, good and bad: "for they love not what is their own, unless perchance there be some one who calls what belongs to him the good, and what belongs to another the evil" (Plato, *Symposium*, 205e). Ownership divides the world into mine and yours, but the good has nothing to do with such divisions.

Chapter Four

1. In *The Order of Things* the excess belongs to language, not being or the good:

> In the modern age, literature is that which compensates for (and not that which confirms) the signifying function of language. Through literature, the being of language shines once more on the frontiers of Western culture—and at its centre—for it is what has been most foreign to that culture since the sixteenth century; but it has also, since this same century, been at the very centre of what Western culture has overlain. (Foucault, OT, 44)

This opens another intermediary figure, marking our time as (perhaps continuing to be) a time of language, between language and art, repeating the opposition between spirit and sensuality, marking animals forever with the domination of The Human under the sign of language.

2. I speak of reason's madness, concerning which Foucault says:

> We have yet to write the history of that other form of madness, by which men, in an act of sovereign reason, confine their neighbors, and communicate and recognize each other through the merciless language of non-madness; to define the moment of this conspiracy before it was permanently established in the realm of truth, before it was revived by the lyricism of protest. (Foucault, MC, ix)

He goes to speak of "letting madness speak for itself," of what Derrida describes as "madness itself" (Derrida, *CHM*, 33–34): "We must try to return, in history, to that zero point in the course of madness at which madness is an undifferentiated experience, a not yet divided experience of division itself" (Foucault, *MC*, ix). This undifferentiated madness, experienced at the zero point of division itself, cannot be "madness itself," although it may be quite mad. Such a madness cannot inhabit a binary relation between reason and madness. Nor can reason's conspiracy to institute the merciless language of nonmadness as if it knew no other be "madness." The thought, the face, of the other is quite mad, or if not mad, then not rational either. Nor is it God. It is everywhere without a face.

I have noted that Diotima speaks of it as *phusin kalon*, "a nature of wondrous beauty," everlasting, knowing nothing of oppositions and distinctions, high and low. I have called it the good, but it is inseparable from nature. Nature's beauty is the good, a good that does not know dividedness, yet is filled with endless heterogeneity, in that sense other, giving birth to division itself. Perhaps it is quite mad, the way Dionysus is mad. The god of madness. The good of the world. Or mad. Or good.

3. See my *RR*, especially chap. 3.

4. The final purpose "can be nothing else than *man under moral laws*" (Kant, *CJ*, 296), requiring us to "admit that there is a God" (Kant, *CJ*, 301). See discussion following in this chapter.

5. See the Introduction here, p. 16.

6.

> Im Wissenschaftlichen also ist der grösste Erfinder vom mühseligsten Nachahmer und Lehrlinge nur dem Grade nach, dagegen von dem, welchen die Natur für die schöne Kunst begabt hat, spezifisch unterschieden. Indes liegt hierin keine Herabsetzung jener grossen Männer, denen das menschliche Geschlecht so viel zu verdanken hat, gegen die Günstlinge der Natur in Ansehung ihres Talents für die schöne Kunst. Eben darin, dass jener Talent zur immer fortschreitenden grösseren Vollkommenheit der Erkenntnisse und alles Nutzens, der davon abhängig ist, imgleichen zur Belehrung anderer in eben denselben Kenntnissen gemacht ist, besteht ein grosser Vorzug derselben vor denen, welche die Ehre verdienen, Genies zu heissen: weil für diese die Kunst irgendwo still steht, indem ihr eine Grenze gesetzt ist, über die sie nicht weiter gehen kann, die vermutlich auch schon seit lange her erreicht ist und nicht mehr erweitert werden kann; . . . (Kant, KU, 408)

7. I call this *ergonality*. See my *RR*.

Chapter Five

1. "Politics, however, is the threat of the differend. It is not a genre, it is the multiplicity of genres, the diversity of ends, and par excellence the question of linkage" (Lyotard, *D*, 138).

"Everything is political if politics is the possibility of the differend on the occasion of the slightest linkage. Politics is not everything, though, if by that one believes it to be the genre that contains all the genres. It is not *a* genre" (Lyotard, *D*, 139).

I resist the idea of the necessity of linking, whether *Müssen* or *Sollen*. "For there to be no phrase is impossible, for there to be *And a phrase* is necessary. It is necessary to make linkage. This is not an obligation, a *Sollen* (an ought to), but a necessity, a *Müssen* (a must). To link is necessary, but how to link is not" (Lyotard, *D*, 66). I resist the possibility and necessity of the *différend*. I do not know where we stand to speak of necessity or possibility, in what genre or place. I think we may forget the *différend* because it may disappear, may no longer in certain places be necessary or possible. That is why we are called from the good to witness the *différend*, to witness what may not be possible, to lost possibilities, and actualities, and to deaths and sacrifices.

Yet no restricted economy can close itself off from all other economies, restricted or general. This absence of closure knows nothing of necessity or possibility.

2. See chap. 2, here, pp. 51–52.

3. See chap. 4, here, pp. 149–55.

4. In Spinoza explicitly, but throughout in the European tradition.

5. But see the discussion of the curse in Bataille, chap. 7, here.

6. We find hierarchies of Spirit, subordinating art; hierarchies in forms of art, subordinating primitive, symbolic, and romantic art; hierarchies of arts and works of art. Where there are individual arts, some must be superior. One hierarchy, unifying taxonomy with history as development, is the movement from architecture as spirituality beyond the possibility of material embodiment—with temples and churches the primary examples—to sculpture, again classical, realizing "the ideal forms of the human figure" (Hegel, *PFA* (Ross, *AIS*), 155), to the arts where "is God himself truly spirit, spirit in his community" (Hegel, *PFA* (Ross, *AIS*), 156), leading to another hierarchy of arts, from painting through music to "the most spiritual presentation of romantic art . . . in *poetry*" (Hegel, (*PFA* Ross, *AIS*), 158). One hierarchy after another; one development after another; history as that development, that history, organized around the human figure as God, spirit in community, art as "the universal forms of the self-unfolding Idea of beauty" (Hegel, *PFA* (Ross, *AIS*), 159).

7. Ricoeur's words, quoted by Owens, are, "Suddenly it becomes possible that there are just *others*, that we ourselves are an 'other' among others. All meaning and every goal having disappeared, it becomes possible to wander through civilizations as if through vestiges and ruins" (quoted in Owens, *DO;* Ross, *AIS*, 592).

8. This idea that we may bring forth questions only from without, at least from without science, reason, and *technē*, is deeply questionable. It appears throughout most writings indebted to Nietzsche. I offer two. From Heidegger, "the essence of technology is by no means anything technological" (Heidegger, *QT*, 287). From Foucault:

> it is not possible for us to describe our own archive, "the general system of the formation and transformation of statements" (Foucault, AK, 130)], since it is from within these rules that we speak, since it is that which gives to what we can say—and to itself, the object of our discourse—its modes of appearance, its forms of existence and coexistence, its system of accumulation, historicity, and disappearance. (Foucault, AK, 130)

Nietzsche, Heidegger, and Foucault all interpose something outside, other than scientific and technological rationality whereby we may question that rationality. Reason does not ground itself, cannot ask itself all fundamental questions. On one reading, life is the ground, and art closer to the earth than *technē*, closer to the ground, so that when we interrogate science's truth from the standpoints of life and art, we touch the ground. On another reading, there is no ground, and science must be questioned from the standpoint of art while art must be questioned from the standpoint of life, all points otherwise. And each archive must be questioned from the standpoint of another.

Derrida denies that there is an outside, denies the outside of the work. The outside frames the work; art frames science and technology; life frames art and is now, in today's world, as Heidegger insists repeatedly, framed by science and technology. The frame resists both the inner grounding of science's truth and the outer grounding of science in life and being. Art and *poiēsis*, here, in proximity to the good, do not ground, do not give the primordial essence of truth or Being or *Dasein*, but unground the essence of truth as untruth.

9. "Philosophy has always insisted upon this: thinking its other. Its other: that which limits it, and from which it derives its essence, its definition, its production. . . . Does the limit, obliquely, by surprise, always reserve one more blow for philosophical knowledge?" (Derrida, *T*, x–xi).

10. If not " 'salvation'?" or *"le « salut » ?"* See chap. 1, here, n. 14.

11. More directly and explicitly:

> Man is a rope, tied between beast and overman—a rope over an abyss. A dangerous across, a dangerous on-the-way, a dangerous looking-back, a dangerous shuddering and stopping. (Nietzsche, *Z*, 126)

> What is great in man is that he is a bridge and not an end: what can be loved in man is that he is an *overture* and a *going under*. (Nietzsche, *Z*, 127)

12. Though Irigaray remembers the material touch of air against the ethereal force of spirit in Heidegger, and Levinas. See chap. 6, here, p. 232.

13. See chap. 1, here, pp. 42–43.

14. In *Phaedrus*. See chap. 1, here, pp. 26–27.

Chapter Six

1. In the Introduction here, pp. 14–18, in my *RR*, chap. 8, and *IR*, chap. 6.

2. See the Introduction here, p. 14, for the full quotation and an extended discussion.

3. Postponed to a later volume of this project, *The Gift of Touch: The Good Embodied.*

4. I call attention to Whitehead, for whom actual entities surpass any appropriation into use.

5. See chap. 5, here, pp. 189–93.

6. Summarized in three moments and after as:

> First moment: this usefulness can only allow itself to be apprehended in use, during use, by use. . . .
> Second moment. Only the possibility of this overflowing interlacing [between usefulness and uselessness: surplus value] permits Heidegger to cross the line in both directions, now in the frame, now outside the frame. . . .

Third moment. . . . Usefulness does not really interest Heidegger, in the last instance, therefore the useless does not either. (Derrida, TP, 336–47)

7. In *OWL*, the striving gives language as the trace.

8. *Gestell/Gestalt/parergon.*

9. And more: "Aesthetic consciousness considers to be its experience . . . in the final analysis as the discontinuity of experiences. But we have found this to be unacceptable" (Gadamer, *TM*, 89 (Ross, *AIS*), 360).

10.

« En quoi » ce est pour qu'il opère, antérieurement à tout savoir et méthode de connaissance—identité, omoiôsis, adéquatio, . . . —, la co-existence, co-essence, coprésence de deux ? Avant leur position possible en « choses » séparées. En quoi ce « est » pour avoir un tel pouvoir de fonder l'être et la présence, tout en disparaissant dans l'acte de fondation même ? Pour qu'il ait déjà été « utilisé »—et utilisant ?—sans qu'aucune naissance puisse lui être attribuée. Pour qu'il ait déjà donné lieu à l'être sans qu'aucun commencement de l'être soit.
En quoi ce est ? Diaphane, translucide, transparent. Transcendant? Médiation, médium fluide mettant en rapport sans obstacle le tout avec lui-même, et certaines de ses parties entre elles suivant leurs propriétés : réelles ou décrérées « vraies ».
En quoi ce est ? En air.

11. Salomon, *L?T?*, 31.

Chapter Seven

1. See chap. 1, here, p. 49, for the full quotation.

2. "Thus the problem for Nature is the production of societies which are 'structured' with a high 'complexity,' and which are at the same time 'unspecialized.' In this way, intensity is mated with survival" (Whitehead, *PR*, 101).

3. Whitehead says something similar of the place of actual entities in the extensive continuum, virtually a geometrical account of general economy:

Every actual entity in its relationship to other actual entities is in this sense somewhere in the continuum, and arises out of the data provided by this standpoint. But in another sense it is everywhere throughout the continuum; . . . Thus the continuum is present in each actual entity, and each actual entity pervades the continuum. (Whitehead, PR, 67; see also chap. 3, here, n. 24)

He speaks of "two metaphysical assumptions" in relation to the contemporary world (Whitehead, *PR*, 65):

(i) That the actual world, in so far as it is a community of entities which are settled, actual, and already become, conditions and limits the potentiality for creativeness beyond itself. (Whitehead, PR, 65)

(ii) The second metaphysical assumption is that the real potentialities relative to all standpoints are coordinated as diverse determinations of one extensive continuum. This extensive continuum is one relational complex in which all potential objectifications find their niche. It underlies the whole world, past, present, and future. . . . This extensive continuum expresses the solidarity of all possible standpoints throughout the whole process of the world. It is not a fact prior to the world; it is the first determination of order—that is, of real potentiality—arising out of the general character of the world. In its full generality beyond the present epoch, it does not involve shapes, dimensions, or measurability; these are additional determinations of real potentiality arising from our cosmic epoch. (Whitehead, PR, 66)

We may understand this place of individual actual entities as doubly restricted: somewhere and everywhere; in one place and relevant to every place. We may understand this idea of place as analogous to Leibniz's monads: in the places defined for them by God, somewhere and everywhere, without windows, mirroring everything. But I read mirrors of mirrors mirroring everything, all other mirrors, as opening an abundance of images, repetitions, and representations exceeding all containments and limits. (See my *RR*.) Within each monad are endless mirrors mirroring other mirrors mirroring themselves, endless, excessive, and abundant. This is representation's abundance, representing the abundance of the earth. Similarly, each individual actual entity is in its place and in every place, and every place is displacement and abundance. To be is to be somewhere and both nowhere and everywhere, to exceed every place and every identity. This excessiveness pertaining to every restriction, every identity and place, is abundance. Every restricted economy belongs to, circulates within, general economy, an economy without restriction, exceeding every restriction. This general economy is nature, understood as both the restricted and distinct kinds of nature and their abundance, beyond any restriction. In this latter sense, nature is not the name of general economy but includes its abundance within its panoply of forms and representations.

4. See the Introduction here, p. 11, for the full quotation.

5. "[M]an sets himself essentially apart from nature; he is even vehemently opposed to it, and the absence of prohibition would have only one meaning: that *animality* which men are conscious of having left behind, and to which we cannot aspire to return" (Bataille, *AS*, II, 23).

6. Translated by Van Den Abbeele as "Reality entails the differend" (Lyotard, *DPD*, 55).

7.

Something unfamiliar and disconcerting came into being, something that was no longer simply nature, but nature transfigured, the sacred.

In a basic sense, what is sacred is precisely what is prohibited. But if the sacred, the prohibited, is cast out of the sphere of profane life (inasmuch as it denotes a disruption of that life), it nevertheless has a greater value than this profane that excludes it. It is no longer the despised bestiality; often it has retained an animal form, but the latter has become divine. As such, relative to profane life this sacred animality has the same meaning that the negation of nature (hence profane life) has relative to pure animality. (Bataille, AS, II, p. 92)

8. See other passages on animals in this chapter, pp. 249–51, 256–58.

Chapter Eight

1. See the Introduction here, pp. 14–18, chap. 6, pp. 199–201.

2. Together with Categories of Explanation (x) and (xi):

> (x) That the first analysis of an actual entity, into its most concrete elements, discloses it to be a concrescence of prehensions, which have originated in its process of becoming.
> (xi) That every prehension consists of three factors: (1) the "subject" which is prehending, namely, the actual entity in which that prehension is a concrete element; (b) the "datum" which is prehended; (c) the "subjective form" which is how that subject prehends that datum. (Whitehead, PR, 23)

3. See the discussion in chapter 2, here, pp. 000–000.

4. The cacophony of the earth, in song. See my *RR* and *PE*.

5. "It is said that the close study of stone will reveal traces from fires suffered thousands of years ago" (Griffin, *CS*, 9).

Bibliography

Adams, Carol J. *The Sexual Politics of Meat [SPM]*. New York: Continuum, 1992.

Addelson, Kathryn Pyne. *Impure Thoughts [IT]*. Philadelphia: Temple University Press, 1991.

———. "The Man of Professional Wisdom" [*MPW*]. In *Impure Thoughts*.

Agamben, Giorgio. *Language and Death: The Place of Negativity [LD]*. Trans. Karen E. Pinkus with Michael Hardt. Minneapolis: University of Minnesota Press, 1991.

Aquinas, Thomas. *Basic Writings of St. Thomas Aquinas [BWTA]*. Ed. Anton C. Pegis (2 vols.). New York: Random House, 1945.

———. *Summa Theologica [ST]*. Trans. Fathers of the English Dominican Province. London: Burns, Oates & Washbourne, 1912–36.

Arendt, Hannah. *The Human Condition [HC]*. Chicago: University of Chicago Press, 1958.

Arens, W., and Karp, I. eds. *Creativity of Power [CP]*. Washington and London: Smithsonian Press, 1989.

Aristotle. Ed. Richard McKeon. *The Basic Works of Aristotle*. New York: Random House, 1941. All quotations from Aristotle are from this edition.

———. *Poetics [P]*. Reprinted in part in Ross, *Art and its Significance*, 66–74. From *Basic Works of Aristotle*.

Augustine. *Basic Writings of Saint Augustine [BWA]*. Ed. and int. Whitney J. Oates. New York: Random House, 1948.

———. *City of God [CG]*. In *Basic Writings of Saint Augustine*.

Bakhtin, Mikhail Mikhailovich. *Discourse in the Novel [DN]*. Reprinted in part in Ross, *Art and its Significance*, 484–97. From *The Dialogic Imagination*. Ed. Michael

Holquist. Trans. Caryl Emerson and Michael Holquist. Austin: University of Texas Press, 1981.

Bataille, Georges. *The Accursed Share: An Essay on General Economy [AS]*. Trans. Richard Hurley. New York: Zone Books, 2 vols., 1988 and 1993. Translation of *La Part maudite, L'Histoire de l'érotisme*, and *La Souveraineté (Consumption [I]; The History of Eroticism [II]; Sovereignty [III])*. In Georges Bataille, *Oeuvre Complètes*. Paris: Gallimard, 1976.

——. *L'Expérience intérieure*. Paris: Gallimard, 1954.

——. *Méthode de Méditation*. In *L'Expérience intérieure*. Quoted in Derrida, "From Restricted to General Economy."

Baudrillard, Jean. *Forget Foucault [FF]*. New York: Semiotext(e), 1987.

Benjamin, Walter. *Erfahrung und Armut [EA]*. Passages quoted in Derrida, "Letter to Peter Eisenman."

——. "The Work of Art in the Age of its Technical Reproducibility" *[WAATR]*. Reprinted in part in Ross, *Art and its Significance*, 526–38. Selections from "The Work of Art in the Age of Mechanical Reproduction." Trans. Harry Zohn. In *Illuminations*. New York: Harcourt, Brace & World, 1968.

Bernal, Martin. *Black Athena: The Afroasiatic Roots of Classical Civilization, Volume I: The Fabrication of Ancient Greece 1785–1985 [BA]*. New Brunswick: Rutgers University Press, 1987.

Blake, William. *The Book of Urizen [BU]*. Ed. and comm. Kay Parkhurst Easson and Roger R. Easson. Boulder: Shambhala, and New York: Random House, 1987.

Bowden, Ross. "Sorcery, Illness and Social Control in Kwoma Society" *[SISC]*. In Stephen, *Sorcerer and Witch*.

Bullough, Edward. " 'Psychical Distance' as a Factor in Art and as an Aesthetic Principle" *[PD]*. Reprinted in Ross, *Art and Its Significance*, 458–67. Originally published in *British Journal of Psychology* (1912), 87–98.

Burtt, Edwin A. ed. *The English Philosophers from Bacon to Mill [EPBM]*. New York: Modern Library, 1959.

Butler, Judith. *Gender Trouble: Feminism and the Subversion of Identity [GT]*. New York: Routledge, 1990.

Caputo, John D. *Against Ethics: Contributions to a Poetics of Obligation with Constant Reference to Deconstruction [AE]*. Bloomington: Indiana University Press, 1993.

Card, Claudia, ed. *Feminist Ethics [RE]*. Lawrence: University Press of Kansas, 1991.

Cheal, David. *The Gift Economy [GE]*. New York: Routledge, 1988.

Cheney, Jim. "Eco-feminism and Deep Ecology" *[EDE]*. In *Environmental Ethics* IX (1987).

Christ, Carol P. "Reverence for Life: The Need for a Sense of Finitude" *[RL]*. In Cooey, Farmer, and Ross, *Embodied Love*.

————. "Spiritual Quest and Women's Experience" *[SQWE]*. In Christ and Plaskow, *WomenSpirit Rising*.

Christ, Carol P., and Judith Plaskow. *Womanspirit Rising [WR]*. New York: Harper & Row, 1979.

Cixous, Hélène, and Clément, Catherine. *The Newly Born Woman [NBW]*. Trans. Betsy Wing. Int. Sandra M. Gilbert. Minneapolis: University of Minnesota Press, 1975.

Clark, Cedric X. "Some Implications of Nkrumah's Consciencism for Alternative Co-ordinates in NonEuropean Causality" *[SINC]*. In Ruch and Anyanwu, *African Philosophy*.

Clément, Catherine. "The Guilty Ones" *[GO]*. In *The Newly Born Woman*.

Clifford, James. "On Collecting Art and Culture" *[CAC]*. Reprinted in Ross, *Art and its Significance*, 621–42. From *Out There: Marginalization and Contemporary Cultures*. New York: New Museum of Contemporary Art and Cambridge: MIT Press, 1990, 141–46, 151–65.

Coleridge, Samuel Taylor. *Biographia Literaria [BL]*. Ed. J. Shawcross. London: Oxford University Press, 1949.

Collingwood, R. G. *The Principles of Art [PA]*. Oxford: Oxford University Press, 1972.

Cooey, Paula M., Sharon A. Farmer, and Mary Ellen Ross, eds. *Embodied Love: Sensuality and Relationship as Feminist Values [EL]*. San Francisco: Harper and Row, 1987.

Cole, Eva Browning, and Susan Coultrap-McQuin, eds. *Explorations in Feminist Ethics: Theory and Practice [EFE]*. Bloomington: Indiana University Press, 1992.

Cornell, Drucilla, Rosenfeld, Michel, Carlson, David Gray, eds. *Deconstruction and the Possibility of Justice [DPJ]*. New York: Routledge, Chapman and Hall, 1992.

Curtin, Deane. "Toward an Ecological Ethic of Care" *[TEEC]*. In Warren, *Hypatia* VI.

Curtiss, Susan. *Genie: A Psycholinguistic Study of a Modern-Day "Wild Child" [G]*. New York: Academic Press, 1977.

Daly, Mary. "After the Death of God the Father: Women's Liberation and the Transformation of Christian Consciousness" *[ADGF]*. In Christ and Plaskow, *WomenSpirit Rising*.

————. *Gyn/Ecology: The Metaethics of Radical Feminism [G/E]*. Boston: Beacon Press, 1990.

Danto, Arthur C. "Approaching the End of Art." In *The State of the Art*, 202–18.

————. *The State of the Art [SA]*. New York: Prentice Hall, 1987.

————. *Transfiguration of the Commonplace: A Philosophy of Art [TC]*. Cambridge: Harvard University Press, 1981.

Deleuze, Gilles. *Différence et répétition [DR]*. Paris: P.U.F., 1969.

————. *Logique du sens [LS]*. Paris: Editions de Minuit, 1969.

Derrida, Jacques. "Cogito and the History of Madness" *[CHM]*. In *Writing and Difference*.

————. *Dissemination [D]*. Trans. and int. Barbara Johnson. Chicago: University of Chicago Press, 1981.

————. "Economimesis *[E]*." *Diacritics* 11 (June 1981).

————. "Force of Law: the 'Mystical Foundation of Authority'" *[FL]*. In Cornell, Rosenfeld, and Carlson, *Deconstruction and the Possibility of Justice*. Reprinted from *Cardozo Law Review*, XI (1991).

————. "From Restricted to General Economy: A Hegelianism without Reserve" *[FRGE]*. In *Writing and Difference*.

————. "Geschlecht: sexual difference, ontological difference" *[G1]*. *Research in Phenomenology*, XIII (1983).

————. "*Geschlecht* II: Heidegger's Hand" *[G2]*. Trans. John P. Leavey, Jr. In *Deconstruction in Philosophy: the Texts of Jacques Derrida*.

————. *The Gift of Death [DT]*. Trans. David Wills. Chicago: University of Chicago Press, 1994.

————. *Given Time [GT]*. Trans. Peggy Kamuf. Chicago: University of Chicago Press, 1992.

————. "Heidegger's Ear: Philopolemology *(Geschlecht IV)*" *[G4]*. In Sallis, *Reading Heidegger*.

————. "Letter to Peter Eisenman" *[LPE]*. Reprinted in Ross, *Art and its Significance*, 429–37. From *Assemblage* (12), 7–13.

————. "Parergon" *[P]*. Reprinted in part in Ross, *Art and its Significance*, 411–20.

————. *Of Spirit: Heidegger and the Question [OS]*. Trans. Geoffrey Bennington and Rachel Bowlby. Chicago: University of Chicago Press, 1989.

————. "Passe-Partout *[P-P]*. Reprinted in Ross, *Art and its Significance*, 401–10. Introduction to *Truth in Painting*.

———. "Plato's Pharmacy" *[PP]*. From *Dissemination*.

———. "The Politics of Friendship" *[PF]*. In *Journal of Philosophy*, 85 (November 1988).

———. "Restitutions *[R]*." Reprinted in part in Ross, *Art and its Significance*, 421–28. From *Truth in Painting*.

———. *The Truth in Painting [TP]*. Trans. G. Bennington and I. McLeod. Chicago: University of Chicago Press, 1987.

———. *Writing and Difference [WD]*. Trans. Alan Bass. Chicago: University of Chicago Press, 1978.

———. "Violence and Metaphysics: An Essay on the Thought of Emmanuel Levinas" *[VM]*. In *Writing and Difference*.

Dewey, John. *Art and Experience [AE]*. New York: Putnam, 1934. Reprinted in part in Ross, *Art and its Significance*, 204–20.

———. "Context and Thought" *[CT]*. In *Experience, Nature, and Freedom*.

———. *Experience and Nature [EN]*. 2nd ed. New York: Dover, 1958.

———. *Experience, Nature, and Freedom [ENF]*. Ed. and int. Richard J. Bernstein. Indianapolis: Library of Liberal Arts, 1960.

———. "Nature in Experience" *[NE]*. In *Experience, Nature, and Freedom*.

Dixon, Vernon J. "World Views and Research Methodology" *[WVRM]*. In King, Dixon, and Nobles, *African Philosophy*.

duBois, Page. *Torture and Truth [TT]*. New York: Routledge, 1991.

Dworkin, Andrea. *Intercourse [I]*. New York: Free Press, 1987.

Dworkin, Ronald. "Feminists and Abortion *[FA]*." In *New York Review of Books* XL/11 (June 10, 1993).

———. Review of MacKinnon, *Only Words [OW]*. In *New York Review of Books* XL/17 (October 21, 1993).

Ecker, Gisela ed. *Feminist Aesthetics [FA]*. Trans. Harriet Anderson. Boston: Beacon Press, 1985.

Euripides, *Hecuba*. Trans. E. P. Coleridge. In Oates and O'Neill, *The Complete Greek Drama*.

Feyerabend, Paul. *Against Method: Outline of an Anarchistic Theory of Knowledge [AM]*. Atlantic Highlands: Humanities Press, 1975.

Foucault, Michel. *Archaeology of Knowledge [AK]*. Trans. A. M. Sheridan-Smith. New York: Pantheon, 1971.

———. *The Care of the Self [CS]*. Trans. Robert Hurley. New York: Pantheon, 1986.

————. *History of Sexuality, Volume I [HS]*. R. Hurley tr. New York: Vintage, 1980.

————. *Language, Counter-memory, Practice [LCP]*. Trans. Donald F. Bouchard and Sherry Simon. Ed. and int. Donald F. Bouchard. Ithaca: Cornell University Press, 1977.

————. "Nietzsche, Genealogy, History" *[NGH]*. In *Language, Counter-memory, Practice*.

————. *The Order of Things: An Archaeology of the Human Sciences [OT]*. New York: Vintage, 1973.

————. *Power/Knowledge [P/K]*. Ed. and trans. C. Gordon. New York: Pantheon, 1980.

————. "A Preface to Transgression" *[PT]*. In *Language Counter-memory, Practice*.

————. "Theatrum Philosophicum" *[TP]*. In *Language, Counter-memory, Practice*.

————. "Two Lectures" *[2L]*. In *Power/Knowledge*.

Freud, Sigmund. "Femininity" *[F]*. In *New Introductory Lectures on Psychoanalysis*, vol. 22, 113. From *The Standard Edition of the Complete Psychological Works of Sigmund Freud*. Ed. James Strachey, 24 vols. London: Hogarth Press, 1953–74.

————. "The Relation of the Poet to Day-dreaming" *[RPD]*. Reprinted in Ross, *Art and its Significance*, 500–506. From Sigmund Freud, *Collected Papers*, vol. 4. Article trans. I. F. Grant Duff. New York: Basic Books, 1959.

Fry, Tony, and Willis, Anne-Marie, "Aboriginal Art: Symptom or Success?" *[AA]*. Reprinted in part in Ross, *Art and its Significance*. From *Art in America* (July 1989), 111–16, 159–61.

Fuller, Steve. *Social Epistemology [SE]*. Bloomington and Indianapolis: Indiana University Press, 1988.

Gadamer, Hans-Georg. *Truth and Method [TM]*. New York: Seabury, 1975.

Gilbert, Bil. "Crows by far and wide, but there's no place like home." In *Smithsonian*, 25/5 (August 1992).

Gilligan, Carol. *In a Different Voice: Psychological Theory and Women's Development [IDV]*. Cambridge: Harvard University Press, 1982.

Goodman, Nelson. *Languages of Art: An Approach to a Theory of Symbols [LA]*. 2nd ed. Indianapolis: Hackett, 1976.

————. *Ways of Worldmaking [WW]*. Indianapolis: Hackett, 1978.

Gottlieb, Alma. "Witches, Kings, and the Sacrifice of Identity or The Power of Paradox and the Paradox of Power among the Beng of Ivory Coast" *[WKS]*. In Arens and Karp, *Creativity of Power*.

Göttner-Abendroth, Heide. "Nine Principles of a Matriarchal Aesthetics" *[MA]*. Trans. Harriet Anderson. Reprinted in Ross, *Art and its Significance*, 566–77. From Ecker, *Feminist Aesthetics*.

Graves, Robert. *The Greek Myths [GM]*. Baltimore: Penguin, 1955.

Griffin, Susan. *A Chorus of Stones [CS]*. New York: Doubleday, 1992.

Guidieri, R. "Les sociétés primitives aujourd'hui" *[SPA]*. In *Philosopher: les interrogations contemporarines*. Ed. Ch. Delacampagne and R. Maggiori. Paris: Fayard, 1980.

Hallen, Barry. "Phenomenology and the Exposition of African Traditional Thought" *[PEATT]*. In *Proceedings of the Seminar on African Philosophy/La Philosophie Africaine*. Ed. Claude Sumner. Addis Ababa: Chamber Printing House, 1980.

Hallen, B., and Sodipo, J. O. *Knowledge, Belief & Witchcraft: Analytic Experiments in African Philosophy [KBW]*. Fwd Dorothy Emmett. London: Ethnographica, 1986.

Harding, Sandra. "The Curious Coincidence of Feminine and African Moralities: Challenges for Feminist Theory" *[CCFAM]*. In Kittay and Meyers, *Women and Moral Theory*.

———. "The Instability of the Analytical Categories of Feminist Theory" *[IACFT]*. *Signs*, 11:4 (1986).

———. *The Science Question in Feminism [SQF]*. Ithaca, New York: Cornell University Press, 1986.

———. *Whose Science? Whose Knowledge?: Thinking from Women's Lives [WSWK]*. Ithaca, New York: Cornell University Press, 1991.

Hegel, G. W. F. *Aesthetics: Lectures on Fine Art [A]*. Trans. T. M. Knox. London: Oxford University Press, 1975. In *Art and Its Significance* as "Philosophy of Fine Art" *[PFA]*.

———. *Jenenser Realphilosophie I, Der Vorlesungen von 1803–1804 [JR I]*. Ed. J. Hoffmeister. Leibzig: 1932. Quoted and translated in Agamben, *Language and Death*.

———. *Jenenser Realphilosophie II, Die Vorlesungen von 1803–1804 [JR II]*. Ed. J. Hoffmeister. Leipzig: 1932. Quoted and translated in Agamben, *Language and Death*.

———. *Phenomenology of Mind [PM]*. Trans. and int. James Baillie. London: George Allen & Unwin, 1910.

Heidegger, Martin. *Basic Writings [BW]*. Ed. David Farrell Krell. New York: Harper & Row, 1977.

————. *Being and Time [BT]*. Trans. John Macquarrie and Edward Robinson. Translation of *Sein und Zeit [SZ]*. New York: Harper & Row, 1962.

————. *Discourse on Thinking: A Translation of* Gelassenheit *[DT]*. Trans. John M. Anderson and E. Hans Freund. New York: Harper & Row, 1966.

————. *Identity and Difference [ID]*. Trans. and int. Joan Stambaugh. New York: Harper & Row, 1969.

————. *Introduction to Metaphysics [IM]*. Trans. Ralph Manheim. Garden City, N.Y.: Doubleday, 1961.

————. "Language" *[L]*. In *Poetry, Language, Thought*.

————. "Language in the Poem" *[LP]*. In *On the Way to Language*.

————. "Letter on Humanism" *[LH]*. In *Basic Writings*.

————. "Martin Heidegger interrogé par *Der Spiegel*. Réponses et questions sur l'histoire et la politique" ["Martin Heidegger Interviewed by *Der Spiegel*: Responses and Questions on History and Politics." Trans. William J. Richardson S. J. as " 'Only a God Can Save us': The *Spiegel* Interview." In Sheehan, *Heidegger, the Man and the Thinker*.

————. "The Nature of Language" *[NL]*. In *On the Way to Language*.

————. "On the Being and Conception of *Physis* in Aristotle's *Physics* B. 1" *[OBCP]*. Trans. T. J. Sheehan. *Man and World* IX/3 (August 1976).

————. "On the Essence of Truth" *[OET]*. In *Basic Writings*.

————. *On the Way to Language [OWL]*. Trans. Peter D. Hertz. New York: Harper & Row, 1971.

————. *On Time and Being [OTB]*. Trans. Joan Stambaugh. New York: Harper & Row, 1972.

————. "The Onto-theo-logical Constitution of Metaphysics" *[OTLCM]*. In *Identity and Difference*.

————. "Origin of the Work of Art" *[OWA]*. Reprinted in part in Ross, *Art and its Significance*, 254–80. From *Poetry, Language, Thought*.

————. *Poetry, Language, Thought [PLT]*. Trans. Albert Hofstadter. New York: Harper & Row, 1971.

————. "The Question Concerning Technology" *[QT]*. In *Basic Writings*.

————. "Time and Being" *[TB]*. In *On Time and Being*.

————. *Was ist das—die Philosophie [WP]*, 1955. Quoted in Derrida, "Heidegger's Ear."

————. "The Way to Language" [*WL*]. In *On the Way to Language*.

———. "What Calls for Thinking?" *[WCT]*. In *Basic Writings*.

Hölderlin, Friedrich. *Friedrich Hölderlin Poems and Fragments*. Trans. Michael Hamburger. Ann Arbor: University of Michigan Press, 1966.

———. "Patmos." In *Friedrich Hölderlin Poems and Fragments*.

Hume, David. "Of the Standard of Taste" *[OST]*. Reprinted in Ross, *Art and its Significance*, 78–92.

———. *A Treatise of Human Nature [T]*. London: Oxford University Press, 1888.

Hyde, Lewis. *The Gift: Imagination and the Erotic Life of Property [G]*. New York: Random House, 1979.

Irigaray, Luce. "Any Theory of the 'Subject' has Always Been Appropriated by the 'Masculine' " *[ATS]*. In *Speculum of the Other Woman*.

———. "The Culture of Difference" *[CD]*. In *Je, tu, nous*.

———. *An Ethics of Sexual Difference [ESD]*. Trans. Carolyn Burke and Gillian C. Gill. Ithaca: Cornell University Press, 1993. Translation of *Éthique de la Différence sexuelle* [*ÉDS*]. Paris: Minuit, 1984.

———. "He Risks who Risks Life Itself" *[HR]*. In *The Irigaray Reader*.

———. *The Irigaray Reader [IR]*. Trans. Seán Hand. Ed. and int. Margaret Whitford. Oxford: Blackwell, 1991.

———. *Je, tu, nous: Toward a Culture of Difference [JTN]*. Trans. Alison Martin. New York: Routledge, 1993.

———. *Marine Lover of Friedrich Nietzsche [ML]*. Trans. Gillian C. Gill. New York: Columbia University Press, 1991.

———. "The 'Mechanics' of Fluids" *[MF]*. In *This Sex Which is Not One*.

———. *"La Mystérique" [M]*. In *Speculum of the Other Woman*.

———. *L'oubli de l'air: Chez Martin Heidegger [OA]*. Paris: Minuit, 1983.

———. "The Power of Discourse and the Subordination of the Feminine" *[PDSF]*. In *This Sex Which Is Not One*.

———. "Questions" *[Q]*. In *The Irigaray Reader*.

———. "Questions to Emmanuel Levinas" *[QEL]*. In *The Irigaray Reader*.

———. "Sexual Difference" *[SD]*. In *The Irigaray Reader*.

———. *Speculum of the Other Woman [SOW]*. Trans. Gillian C. Gill. Ithaca, New York: Cornell University Press, 1985; translation of *Speculum de l'autre femme*. Paris: Minuit, 1974.

———. *This Sex Which is Not One [SWNO]*. Trans. Catherine Porter. Ithaca: Cornell University Press, 1985.

———. "Volume-Fluidity" *[VF]*. Translation of "L'incontourable volume" *[Volume Without Contour]*. In *Speculum of the Other Woman*.

———. "When Our Lips Speak Together" *[WOLST]*. In *This Sex Which is Not One*.

———. "Why Define Sexed Rights?" *[WSDR]*. In *Je, tu, nous*.

———. "Women on the Market" *[WM]*. In *This Sex Which is Not One*.

James, William. *Essays in Radical Empiricism [ERE]*. New York: Longman's Green, 1912.

Jung, Carl Gustav. *Modern Man in Search of a Soul [MMSS]*. Trans. W. S. Dell and Cary F. Baynes. New York: Harcourt Brace Jovanovich, 1955.

———. "Psychology and Literature" *[PL]*. Reprinted in Ross, *Art and its Significance*, 507–20. From *Modern Man in Search of a Soul*.

Kafka, Franz. *The Complete Stories [CS]*. Ed. Nahum N. Glatzer. New York: Schocken, 1971.

Kant, Immanuel. *The Conflict of the Faculties; Der Streit der Fakultäten [CF]*. Trans. Mary J. Gregor. New York: Abaris, 1979.

———. *Critique of Judgment [CJ]*. Trans. J. H. Bernard. New York: Hafner, 1951. Of *Kritik der Urteilskraft [KU]*. In *Kritik der Urteilskraft und Schriften zur Naturphilosophie*. Wiesbaden: Insel-Verlag Zweigstelle, 1957.

———. *Critique of Practical Reason [CPR]*. From *Kant's Critique of Practical Reason and Other Works on the Theory of Ethics*. Trans. T. K. Abbott. London: Longman's Green, 1954.

———. *Critique of Pure Reason [CPR]*. Trans. J. M. D. Meiklejohn. Buffalo: Prometheus, 1990. Trans. Norman Kemp Smith *[CPR (NKS)]*. New York: St. Martin's, 1956. Of *Kritik der reinen Vernunft [KRV]*. 2 Band. Berlin: Deutsche Bibliothek, 1936.

———. *Fundamental Principles of the Metaphysics of Morals*. In *Kant's Critique of Practical Reason and Other Works on the Theory of Ethics*.

———. *Lectures on Ethics*. Trans. L. Infield. New York: Harper & Row, 1963.

———. *The Metaphysical Principles of Virtue*. Indianapolis: Bobbs-Merrill, 1968.

Kheel, Marti. "The Liberation of Nature: A Circular Affair" *[LN]*. In *Environmental Ethics* VI/4 (1985).

Kierkegaard, Søren. *Either/Or [E/O]*. 2 vols. Trans. David F. Swenson and Lillian Marvin Swenson. Rev. and fwd. Howard A. Johnson. Garden City, N.Y.: Doubleday, 1959.

———. *Fear and Trembling/The Sickness Unto Death [FT].* Trans. W. Lowrie. Garden City, N.Y.: Doubleday, 1954.

King, Lewis M. "On the Nature of a Creative World" *[ONCW].* In Ruch and Anwanyu, *African Philosophy.*

King, Lewis M., Dixon, Vernon J., Nobles, Wade W., eds. *African Philosophy: Assumption & Paradigms for Research on Black Persons [AP].* Los Angeles: Charles R. Drew Postgraduate Medical School, 1976. Fanon Research and Development Center Publication, Area VIII, #2.

King, Roger J. H. "Caring about Nature: Feminist Ethics and the Environment" *[CN].* In Warren, *Hypatia* VI.

King, Ynestra. "The Ecology of Feminism and the Feminism of Ecology" *[EFFE].* In Plant, *Healing the Wounds.*

Krell, David Farrell. *Daimon Life: Heidegger and Life-Philosophy [DL].* Bloomington: Indiana University Press, 1992.

———. *Intimations of Mortality [IM].* University Park: Pennsylvania State University Press, 1986.

Kristeva, Julia. *The Kristeva Reader [KR].* Ed. Toril Moi. Trans. Alice Jardine and Harry Blake. New York: Columbia University Press, 1986. Published as "Le temps des femmes."

———. "Stabat Mater" *[SM].* In *The Kristeva Reader.*

———. *Strangers to Ourselves [SO].* Trans. Leon S. Roudiez. New York: Columbia University Press, 1991.

———. "Women's Time" *[WT].* In *The Kristeva Reader.* Published as "Le temps des femmes." In *Cahiers de recherche de sciences des textes et documents* 5 (Winter 1979).

Lacan, Jacques. *Feminine Sexuality [FS].* Ed. Juliet Mitchell and Jacqueline Rose. Trans. Jacqueline Rose. New York: Norton, 1985.

———. "God and the *Jouissance* of ~~The~~ Woman" *[GJW].* In *Feminine Sexuality.*

Lacoue-Labarthe, Philippe. *The Subject of Philosophy [SP].* Trans. Thomas Trezise, Hugh J. Silverman, Garmy M. Cole, Timothy D. Bent, Karen McPherson, Claudette Sartiliot. Ed. and fwd. Thomas Trezise. Minneapolis: University of Minnesota Press, 1993; translation of *Le Sujet de la philosophie [SP].* Paris: Aubier-Flammarion, 1979.

Lahar, Stephanie. "Ecofeminist Theory and Grassroots Politics" *[ETGP].* In Warren, *Hypatia* VI.

Langer, Susanne K. *Feeling and Form: A Theory of Art [FF].* New York: Scribner's, 1953.

Leibniz, G. W. F. "The Exigency to Exist in Essences: Principle of Plenitude" *[EEE]*. In *Leibniz Selections*.

———. *Leibniz Selections*. Ed. P. Wiener. New York: Scribner's, 1951. All references to Leibniz are from this edition.

———. "The Monadology" *[M]*. In *Leibniz Selections*.

Levinas, Emmanuel. *The Levinas Reader [LR]*. Ed. Seán Hand. Oxford: Blackwell, 1989.

———. *Otherwise than Being or Beyond Essence [OB]*. Trans. Alfonso Lingis. The Hague: Martinus Nijhoff, 1978. Of *Autrement qu'être ou au-delà de l'essence [AÊ]*. The Hague: Martinus Nijhoff, 1974.

———. "Reality and Its Shadow" *[RS]*. Trans. Alfonso Lingis. In *Levinas Reader*.

———. *Totality and Infinity [TI]*. Trans. Alfonso Lingis. Pittsburgh: Duquesne University Press, 1969.

———. "The Servant and her Master" *[SM]*. In *Levinas Reader*.

———. "The Transcendence of Words" *[TW]*. Trans. Seán Hand. In *Levinas Reader*.

Lévi-Strauss, Claude. *The Elementary Structure of Kinship [ESK]*. Trans. James Harle Bell, John Richard von Sturmer, and Rodney Needham. Boston: Beacon, 1969.

Lugones, Maria C. "On the Logic of Pluralist Feminism" *[OLPF]*. In Card, *Feminist Ethics*.

———. "Playfulness, 'World'-Travelling, and Loving Perception" *[PWTLP]*. In *Hypatia* 2/2 (Summer 1987).

Lyotard, Jean-François. *Le Différend [D]*. Paris: Minuit, 1983.

———. *The Differend: Phrases in Dispute [DPD]*. Trans. Georges Van Den Abbeele. Minneapolis: University of Minnesota Press, 1988.

———. *Heidegger and "the jews" [HJ]*. Trans. A. Michel and M. Roberts. Minneapolis: University of Minnesota Press, 1990.

———. *The Inhuman: Reflections on Time [I]*. Trans. Geoffrey Bennington and Rachel Bowlby. Stanford: Stanford University Press, 1991.

———. *The Lyotard Reader [LR]*. Ed. Andrew Benjamin. Oxford: Blackwell, 1989).

———. *Peregrinations [P]*. New York: Columbia University Press, 1988.

———. *The Postmodern Condition: A Report on Knowledge [PMC]*. Trans. Geoff Bennington and Brian Massumi. Minneapolis: University of Minnesota Press, 1984.

———. "The Sign of History" *[SH]*. In *Lyotard Reader*.

————. "What is Postmodernism?" *[WPM?]*. Reprinted in part in Ross, *Art and its Significance*, 561–64. From *Postmodern Condition*.

MacKinnon, Catharine A. "Feminism, Marxism, Method, and the State: An Agenda for Theory" *[FMMS1]*. In *Signs* 7:3 (1982).

————. "Feminism, Marxism, Method, and the State: Toward Feminist Jurisprudence" *[FMMS2]*. In *Signs* 8:4 (1982).

————. *Feminism Unmodified: Discourses on Life and Law [FU]*. Cambridge: Harvard University Press, 1987.

————. *Only Words [OW]*. Cambridge: Harvard University Press, 1993.

————. *Toward a Feminist Theory of the State [TFTS]*. Cambridge: Harvard University Press, 1989.

Mauss, Marcel. *The Gift [G]*. Glenco: Free Press, 1954. Also *The Gift: The Form and Reason for Exchange in Archaic Societies*. Trans. W. D. Halls. London: Routledge, 1990.

Mbiti, John S. *African Religions and Philosophy [ARP]*. London: Heinemann Educational Books, 1969.

Merleau-Ponty, Maurice. *Eye and Mind [EM]*. Trans. Carleton Dallery. Reprinted in part in Ross, *Art and Its Significance*. From *The Primacy of Perception*, 282–98.

————. *Phenomenology of Perception [PhP]*. Trans. Colin Smith. London: Routledge & Kegan Paul, 1962.

————. *Primacy of Perception [PrP]*. Ed. James M. Edie. Chicago: Northwestern University Press, 1964.

Meyer, Christine, and Moosang, Faith, ed. *Living with the Land: Communities Restoring the Earth [LL]*. Gabriola Island, BC: New Society Publishers, 1992.

Mudimbe, V. Y. *The Invention of Africa [IA]*. Reprinted in part in Ross, *Art and its Significance*, 600–606. From *The Invention of Africa: Gnosis, Philosophy, and the Order of Knowledge*. Bloomington: Indiana University Press, 1988.

Nancy, Jean-Luc. *The Inoperative Community [IC]*. Trans. P. Connor, L. Garbus, M. Holland, S. Sawhney. Minneapolis: University of Minnesota Press, 1991.

Nietzsche, Friedrich. *The Antichrist*, Selection in *Portable Nietzsche*.

————."Attempt at a Self-Criticism" *[ASC]*. In *Basic Writings*.

————. *Basic Writings of Nietzsche*. Trans. Walter Kaufmann. New York: Random House, Modern Library Giant, 1968.

————. *Beyond Good and Evil [BGE]*, in *Basic Writings*.

————. *Birth of Tragedy [BT]*. In *Basic Writings*.

————. *The Gay Science [GS]*. Selection in *Portable Nietzsche*.

————. *Ecce Homo [EH]*. In *Basic Writings*.

————. *Twilight of the Idols*. In *Portable Nietzsche*.

————. *The Portable Nietzsche [PN]*. Ed. and trans. Walter Kaufmann. New York: Viking Press, 1954.

————. *Thus Spake Zarathustra [Z]*. In *Basic Writings*.

————. *The Will to Power [WP]*. Ed. Walter Kaufmann. Trans. Robert Hollingdale and Walter Kaufmann. New York: Vintage, 1968.

Nodding, Nel. *Caring: A Feminine Approach to Ethics and Moral Education [C]*. Berkeley: University of California Press, 1984.

Nussbaum, Martha. *The Fragility of Goodness [FG]*. Cambridge: Cambridge University Press, 1986.

Oates, W. J., and E. O'Neill, ed. *The Complete Greek Drama [CGD]*. New York: Random House, 1938.

Owens, Craig. "The Discourse of Others: Feminists and Postmodernism" *[DO]*. Reprinted in Ross, *Art and Its Significance*, 591–98.

Pagels, Elaine H. "What Became of God the Mother? Conflicting Images of God in Early Christianity" *[WBGM]*. In Christ and Plaskow, *WomenSpirit Rising*.

Parrinder, Geoffrey. *Witchcraft: European and African [WEA]*. London: Faber and Faber, 1970.

Peirce, Charles Sanders. *The Collected Papers of Charles Sanders Peirce [CP]*. (6 vols.). Ed. Charles Hartshorne and Paul Weiss. Cambridge, Mass.: Harvard University Press, 1931–35.

————. *The Philosophical Writings of Peirce [PP]*. Ed. Justus Buchler. New York: Dover, 1955.

Plant, Christopher, and Plant, Judith, ed. *Green Business: Hope or Hoax? [GB]*. Gabriola Island, BC: New Society Publishers, 1991.

Plant, Judith, ed. *Healing the Wounds: The Power of Ecological Feminism [HW]*. Philadelphia: New Society Publishers, 1989.

Plato. *The Collected Dialogues of Plato [CDP]*. Ed. Edith Hamilton and Huntington Cairns. Princeton: Princeton University Press, 1961. All quotations from Plato are from this edition unless otherwise indicated.

————. *Phaedrus*. Trans. Harold North Fowler. Loeb Classical Library. Cambridge: Harvard University Press, 1914. All Greek passages from *Phaedrus* are from this edition.

————. *Symposium*. Reprinted in part in Ross, *Art and its Significance*, 56–63. From *The Dialogues of Plato*. Trans. Benjamin Jowett, 3rd ed. (London: Oxford University Press, 1982). All quotations in English from *Symposium* are from this edition.

————. *Symposium*. Trans. W. R. M. Lamb. Loeb Classical Library. Cambridge: Harvard University Press, 1925. All Greek passages from *Symposium* are from this edition.

Rachels, James. "Why Animals Have a Right to Liberty" *[WARL]*. In Regan and Singer, *Animal Rights and Human Obligations*.

Randall, Jr., John Herman. *Aristotle [A]*. New York: Columbia University Press, 1960.

————. *Plato: Dramatist of the Life of Reason [P]*. New York: Columbia University Press, 1970.

Reed, A. W. *Myths and Legends of Australia [MLA]*. Sydney: A. H. and A. W. Reed, 1971.

Regan, Tom. *The Case for Animal Rights [CAR]*. Berkeley: University of California Press, 1983.

Regan, Tom, and Singer, Peter. *Animal Rights and Human Obligations [ARHO]*. 2nd ed. Englewood Cliffs: Prentice-Hall, 1989.

Rigterink, Roger J. "Warning: The Surgeon Moralist Has Determined That Claims of Rights Can Be Detrimental to Everyone's Interests" *[W]*. In Cole and Coultrap-McQuin, *Explorations in Feminist Ethics*.

Roach, Catherine. "Loving Your Mother: On the Woman-Nature Relationship" *[LM]*. In Warren, *Hypatia VI*.

Robinson, John Manley. *An Introduction to Early Greek Philosophy [EGP]*. Boston: Houghton Mifflin, 1968. All Greek fragments are quoted from this edition unless otherwise indicated.

Rorty, Richard. *Consequences of Pragmatism [CP]*. Minneapolis: University of Minnesota Press, 1982.

————. "Philosophy in American Today" *[PAT]*. In *Consequences of Pragmatism*.

Ross, Stephen David. *Injustice and Restitution: The Ordinance of Time [IR]*. Albany: State University of New York Press, 1993.

————. *The Limits of Language [LL]*. New York: Fordham University Press, 1993.

————. *Plenishment in the Earth: An Ethic of Inclusion [PE]*. Albany: State University of New York, 1995.

————. *The Ring of Representation [RR]*. Albany: State University of New York Press, 1992.

————. *A Theory of Art: Inexhaustibility by Contrast [TA]*. Albany: State University of New York Press, 1983.

————. "Translation as Transgression *[TT]*." *Translation Perspectives* V. Ed. D. J. Schmidt. Binghamton: Binghamton University, 1990.

Ross, Stephen David, ed., *Art and Its Significance: An Anthology of Aesthetic Theory [AIS]*. 3rd edition. Albany: State University of New York Press, 1994.

Ruch, E. A., and Anyanwu, K. C. *African Philosophy: An Introduction to the main philosophical trends in Contemporary Africa [AP]*. Rome: Catholic Book Agency, 1984.

Sacks, Oliver. *The Man who Mistook his Wife for a Hat and other Clinical Tales*, published in four volumes as *Awakenings [A]*; *A Leg to Stand On [LSO]*; *The Man Who Mistook His Wife for a Hat and Other Clinical Tales [MMWH]*; *Seeing Voices [SV]*. New York: Quality Paperback Book Club, 1990.

Sallis, John ed. *Deconstruction in Philosophy: the Texts of Jacques Derrida [DP]*. Chicago: University of Chicago Press, 1987.

————. *Reading Heidegger: Commemorations*. Bloomington: Indiana University Press, 1993.

Salomon, Charlotte. *Charlotte: Life or Theater?: an autobiographical play by Charlotte Salomon [CLT]*. Trans. Leila Vennewitz. Int. Judity Herzberg. New York: Viking Press, 1981.

————. *Levan? of Theater? Life? or Theatre? [L?T?]*. Int. Judith C.E. Belinfante, Christine Fisher-Defoy, Ad Petersen. Amsterdam: Joods Historisch Museum, 1992.

Schapiro, Meyer. "The Still Life as a Personal Object" *[SLPO]*. In Marianne L. Simmel ed., *The Reach of the Mind: Essays in memory of Kurt Goldstein*. New York: Springer Publishing Company, 1968. Discussed in Derrida, "Restitutions," in *Truth in Painting*.

Scott, Charles E. *The Question of Ethics: Nietzsche, Foucault, Heidegger [QE]*. Bloomington: Indiana University Press, 1990.

Selfe, Lorna. *Nadia: A Case Study of Extraordinary Drawing Ability in an Autistic Child*. New York and London: Harcourt, Brace Jovanovich, 1977.

Sen, Amartya. "More than 100 Million Women are Missing" *[MMWM]*. *New York Review of Books* (December 20, 1990).

Sessions, Robert. "Deep Ecology versus Ecofeminism: Healthy Differences or Incompatible Philosophies?" *[DEE]*. In Warren, *Hypatia* VI.

Sheehan, Thomas, ed. *Heidegger, the Man and the Thinker [HMT]*. Chicago: Precedent Publishing, 1981.

Singer, Peter. *Animal Liberation: A New Ethics For Our Treatment of Animals [AL]*. New York: Avon, 1975.

Slicer, Deborah, "Your Daughter or Your Dog" *[DD]*. In Warren, *Hypatia* VI.

Sophocles. *Oedipus the King [OK], Antigone [A], Oedipus at Colonus [OC]*. All trans. R. C. Jebb. In Oates and O'Neill, *The Complete Greek Drama*.

Spelman, Elizabeth V. *Inessential Woman: Problems of Exclusion in Feminist Thought [IW]*. Boston: Beacon, 1988.

Spinoza, Benedict de. *Ethics [E]*. Trans. William Hale White and rev. Amelia Hutchinson Stirling. Ed. and int., James Gutmann. New York: Hafner, 1949.

―――. *A Political Treatise [PT]*. Trans. and int. R. H. M. Elwes. New York: Dover, 1951.

Stephen, Michele. "Contrasting Images of Power" *[CIP]*. In *Sorcerer and Witch*.

―――. "Master of Souls: the Mekeo Sorcerer" *[MS]*. In *Sorcerer and Witch*.

―――. ed. *Sorcerer and Witch in Melanesia [SWM]*. New Brunswick, N.J.: Rutgers University Press, 1987.

Strawson, Peter F. *Individuals: An Essay in Descriptive Metaphysics [I]*. Garden City, New York: Doubleday & Co., 1959.

Sumner, Claude. *The Source of African Philosophy: The Ethiopian Philosophy of Man [SAP]*. Stuttgart: Franz Steiner Verlag Wiesbaden GMBH, 1986.

Tannen, Deborah. *You Just Don't Understand: Women and Men in Conversation [YJDU]*. New York: Ballantine, 1990.

Taylor, Paul. *Respect for Nature: A Theory of Environmental Ethics [RN]*. Princeton: Princeton University Press, 1986.

Theroux, Paul. "Self-Propelled" *[SP]*. In *New York Times Magazine* (April 25, 1993).

Thomas, Elizabeth Marshall. "Reflections (Lions)" *[L]*. In *New Yorker*, October 15, 1990.

Tolstoy, Leo. *What is Art? [WA]*. Reprinted in part in Ross, *Art and Its Significance*, 178–81.

Trinh, Minh-ha T. *Woman, Native, Other: Writing Postcoloniality and Feminism [WNO]*. Indianapolis: Indiana University Press, 1989.

Valiente, Doreen. *Witchcraft for Tomorrow [WT]*. Custer, Washington: Phoenix, 1987.

Vattimo, Gianni. *The End of Modernity [EM]*. Trans. J. R. Snyder. Cambridge: Polity Press, 1988.

Warren, Karen J., "Feminism and Ecology: Making Connections" *[FEMC]*. In *Environmental Ethics* IX (1987).

————. ed. *Hypatia* VI/1 (Spring 1991). Special Issue on Ecological Feminism.

————. "The Promise and Power of Ecological Feminism" *[PPEF]*. In *Environmental Ethics*, XII (1990).

Warren, Karen J., and Cheney, Jim. "Ecological Feminism and Ecosystem Ecology" *[EFEE]*. In Warren, *Hypatia* VI.

Wenders, William. *Wings of Desire*. Screenplay by Wenders and Peter Handke. 1988.

Whitehead, Alfred North. *Adventures of Ideas [AI]*. New York: Macmillan, 1933.

————. *Process and Reality [PR]*. Corr. ed. Ed. D. R. Griffin and D. W. Sherburne. New York: Free Press, 1978.

————. *Science in the Modern World [SMW]*. New York: Macmillan, 1925.

Wittig, Monique. "The Category of Sex" *[CS]*. In *The Straight Mind*.

————. *The Lesbian Body [LB]*. Trans. David Le Vay. Boston: Beacon, 1973. Translation of *Le Corps Lesbien [CL]*. Paris: Minuit, 1973.

————. "The Mark of Gender" *[MG]*. In *The Straight Mind*

————. "One is not Born a Woman" *[OBW]*. In *The Straight Mind*.

————. "The Straight Mind" *[SM]*. In *The Straight Mind*.

————. *The Straight Mind and other Essays [SME]*. Foreword Louise Turcotte. Boston: Beacon, 1992.

Index

Gauss, K., 152

Gaze, 123, 192, 271.

Gender, 12, 15–16, 45, 51–53, 58, 83–85, 88–91, 127, 165, 183, 185, 200, 291, 316, 332. *See also* Sexual difference, Sexuality

Genealogy, 87, 320

Genera, 95, 293. *See also* Kinds

General economy. *See* Economy.

Genius, 21, 50, 74–75, 100–101, 107, 129, 131, 142–43, 148–49, 151–54, 174, 181, 184, 195, 225, 285, 294, 297

Genocide, 214, 254. *See also* Holocausts

Geometry, 112, 280, 311

Geschlecht, 14–15, 78, 149–50, 200–201, 308, 318. *See also* Gender, Kinds, Sexual difference

Gibt, 14, 21, 231, 244, 262. *See also* Being, Gift

Gifts, 1–5, 7–21, 23–29, 33–34, 37–39, 41–46, 49–51, 58, 68–79, 93–96, 99–105, 112–27, 130–31, 148–54, 157, 159, 161, 165–66, 172, 175–77, 185, 187, 196, 199–204, 209, 212–15, 218–19, 221–22, 231, 235, 239, 241, 244, 247–50, 261–69, 271–72, 274–75, 279–95, 297, 299–302, 305, 310, 316, 318, 323, 327

Giving, 2–3, 11, 13, 16–22, 40, 100, 107, 116–18, 122–23, 127, 147, 159, 169–72, 177, 179, 185, 191, 196, 202–203, 206, 212–13, 217, 224–25, 231–32, 235, 238–41, 244–45, 248, 251, 256, 261–62, 265, 268–69, 274, 280, 291, 296, 299, 304, 308. *See also* Gifts

Glory, 3, 21, 24, 30, 86, 104, 109, 117, 128, 142, 166, 291–92. *See also* Levinas

God, 1–3, 10, 20, 32–33, 38, 44, 61, 65, 74, 79, 81, 106, 110, 117–18, 125–28, 134, 137, 139, 143, 145, 155–56, 159, 161, 165–66, 173–74, 176–78, 180–82, 185, 187–88, 191, 198–200, 214–15, 219, 236–37, 240, 244–45, 264–65, 284, 307–309, 312, 315, 317, 322, 325, 328. *See also* Goddesses, Gods, Sacred

Goddesses, 58, 90, 177

Gods, 3, 20, 23–25, 27, 29–34, 37–38, 40–41, 43–45, 51–59, 61, 64–68, 90, 96, 98–100, 103–104, 111–13, 115–16, 118–22, 125, 130, 143, 153, 161, 175–78, 181, 185, 196, 203, 216, 256, 279, 283, 297, 301–304. *See also* Goddesses, Sacred

Gogh, van, P., 195, 205–209, 211–13, 216

Goodman, N., 92–93, 320

Good, the. Everywhere.

Goodness, 8, 20, 26, 29, 31, 33, 36, 39, 48, 51, 54, 59, 96, 110, 114, 121, 219, 302, 328. *See also* The Good, Goods

Goods, 1–3, 5, 8, 19, 24, 72, 79, 94, 99, 115, 117, 133, 196, 215, 218, 239, 243–47, 251, 254, 261, 263, 265, 273, 276, 281, 286, 291, 297, 299. *See also* Economy, Exchange

Greatness, 11, 21, 25, 36, 48, 54, 57–59, 61, 66, 80, 89, 93, 103, 107, 111, 119, 122, 125, 127–29, 146, 148–54, 161, 167, 173, 178, 182, 185, 195–96, 200, 203, 206–207, 217, 225, 227–28, 231–32, 234, 279, 289, 294, 301, 305, 310, 312

Greece, 4, 31, 41, 52–53, 55–56, 58, 65, 99, 102, 160, 163, 168, 170, 181, 183, 190, 200, 202, 206, 208, 212, 216–17, 223, 280, 285, 288, 300, 303, 316, 319, 321, 328–29, 331

Griffin, S., 234, 313, 321, 332

Ground, 1, 58, 89, 131, 133, 138, 144, 162, 173, 212, 217, 220, 230, 287, 309–10

Guernica, 70

Guidieri, R., 173, 321

Guilt, 3, 53, 59, 66, 291, 303, 317. *See also* Curse, Sacrifice

Habit, 44, 100–101

Habitation, 87, 136, 156. *See also* Building

Hand, 14–18, 30–32, 35, 76–77, 96–97, 101, 112, 122, 134, 147, 156, 178, 184–85, 195, 199, 201, 204, 207, 209, 212, 216, 229–30, 247–48, 262, 272, 303–304, 318, 323, 326. *See also Geschlecht*, Heidegger

Happiness, 57, 98–100, 119, 139, 276

Harmony, 131, 142–43, 146, 175, 192, 218. *See also* Cacophony, Music

Heaven, 24–25, 32, 41, 44, 51, 53, 55, 66, 113, 117, 121, 127, 132, 136–37, 301. *See also* God, Sacred

Hegel, G. W. F., 76–77, 81–83, 85–86, 135, 149, 152, 154–55, 159, 161–69, 172, 174, 176, 183, 187, 197, 200, 223, 230, 254, 275–76, 309, 321

Hegemony, 89, 169–71, 227, 240. *See also* Domination